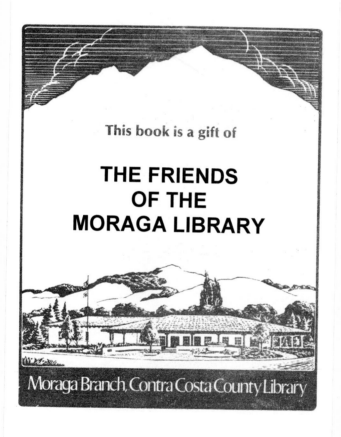

THE NEW MIDDLE EAST

THE NEW MIDDLE EAST

The World After the Arab Spring

PAUL DANAHAR

BLOOMSBURY PRESS

NEW YORK · LONDON · NEW DELHI · SYDNEY

Published by Bloomsbury Press, New York

All papers used by Bloomsbury Press are natural, recyclable products made from
wood grown in well-managed forests. The manufacturing processes conform
to the environmental regulations of the country of origin.

LIBRARY OF CONGRESS CATALOGING-IN-PUBLICATION DATA HAS BEEN APPLIED FOR

ISBN: 978-1-62040-253-5

First U.S. Edition 2013

1 3 5 7 9 10 8 6 4 2

Typeset by Hewer Text UK Ltd, Edinburgh
Printed and bound in the U.S.A. by Thomson-Shore Inc., Dexter, Michigan

For Bhavna

Optimus est post malum principem dies primus.
The best day after a bad emperor is the first one.

TACITUS

Contents

THE MIDDLE EAST AND NORTH AFRICA

Atlantic
Ocean

FRANCE

SWITZ.

AUSTRIA

HUNGARY

ITALY

SLOV.

CROATIA

BOS. &
HERZ.

SERBIA

AN.

SPAIN

MONT.

KOS

MACE.

ALBANIA

GREE

PORTUGAL

Mediterranean Sea

Algiers

Tunis

Sidi Bouzid

Rabat

TUNISIA

Tripoli

MOROCCO

ALGERIA

LIBYA

S A H A R A   D E S E

MAURITANIA

NIGER

CHAD

MALI

BURKINA

GUINEA

IVORY
COAST

GHANA

TOGO

BENIN

NIGERIA

CAMEROON

CENTR
AFRICA
REPUBL

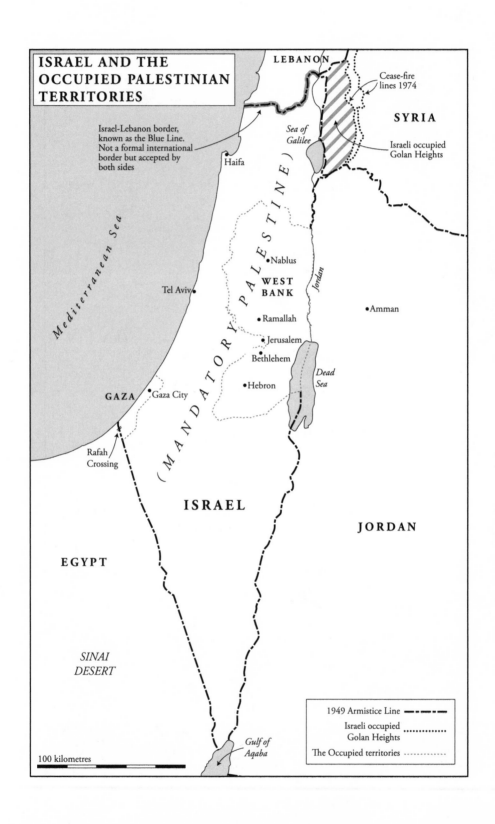

ISRAEL AND THE OCCUPIED PALESTINIAN TERRITORIES

LEBANON

Cease-fire lines 1974

SYRIA

Israel-Lebanon border, known as the Blue Line. Not a formal international border but accepted by both sides

Sea of Galilee

Israeli occupied Golan Heights

Haifa

Mediterranean Sea

(M A N D A T O R Y   P A L E S T I N E)

•Nablus

WEST BANK

Jordan

Tel Aviv•

•Amman

•Ramallah

•Jerusalem

Bethlehem

Dead Sea

•Hebron

GAZA •Gaza City

Rafah Crossing

ISRAEL

JORDAN

EGYPT

SINAI DESERT

1949 Armistice Line ▬ ▬ ▬

Israeli occupied Golan Heights ·········

The Occupied territories ··········

100 kilometres

Gulf of Aqaba

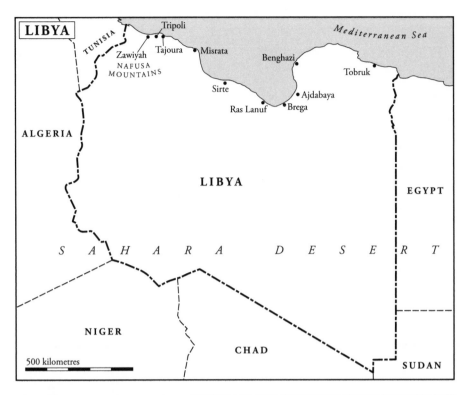

LIBYA

Mediterranean Sea

TUNISIA

Tripoli
Tajoura
Zawiyah
Misrata
NAFUSA
MOUNTAINS

Benghazi

Tobruk

Sirte
Ras Lanuf
Brega
Ajdabaya

ALGERIA

LIBYA

EGYPT

S A H A R A   D E S E R T

NIGER

CHAD

SUDAN

500 kilometres

SYRIA

TURKEY

Aleppo

CYPRUS

Latakia

Qubair
Houla
Tartus

Hama

Orontes

SYRIA

Homs

Mediterranean Sea

Beirut

LEBANON

Bekaa Valley

SYRIAN DESERT

IRAQ

Damascus

1949
armistice
line

Post 1967 occupied
Golan Heights

ISRAEL

Dera'a

JORDAN

200 kilometres

Introduction

'Even if you win, it is difficult to rule an angry people,' he told me. The world was glued to the crisis in Syria, but as we sat sipping coffee in the Foreign Ministry in Damascus in June of 2012, Jihad Makdissi had an old Jackie Chan film playing on the TV. In the movie the bad guys were getting a beating for troubling one of the nice families in the neighbourhood. In the real world it was the nice families who were getting the beating at the interrogation centres set up by Makdissi's colleagues. His country, the crossroads of the region, the 'beating heart' of the Arab world, was sliding into civil war. Makdissi was the very public face of the regime, answering its critics on TV screens across the world. But he and the other civilian members of the regime were not only scared of the opposition groups creeping closer to the capital. They feared the scrutiny of their own increasingly predatory security services.

The certainties of the old Middle East, the world Jihad Makdissi had always belonged to, were crumbling around him.

Just down the road the men in blue helmets were watching their mission spiral away from them. 'This is a YouTube war,' said the diplomat from the United Nations, leaning towards me, his voice low and throttled with anger. He pulled on his cigarette and sat back in his chair. We were in the bubble of their headquarters. This man *was* watching the news, constantly. It was dominated by images uploaded by tech-savvy teenagers armed with a video camera and a broadband line. His boss, the man leading the United Nations' peacekeeping mission in Syria, Major General Robert Mood, told me at the time that these images had driven much of the reaction in the West to the crisis. But as the war entered its third year he remembered the moment he told the youngsters it wouldn't be enough. ' "We saw Libya, when do you think they are coming?" they asked me. You could see the disappointment in their eyes when I said: "Honestly I don't think you can expect that in Syria." '

The UN was there to be a neutral pair of eyes, but the nature of the war meant it was often impossible to determine the truth. The previous day I had gone out with their 'ceasefire' monitors and ended up standing on a roof alongside them watching the Syrian army lob mortar rounds into a residential district of the city of Homs. The Syrian government had welcomed the UN into the country but now wouldn't let them into the area to see whom their army was bombarding. It was the last time the observers would try to enter, because five days later the worsening violence forced the UN to suspend all its patrols. The following month the number of killings in Syria began to soar.[1]

'This is a fight between Russia on one side with the Iranians, and the whole Western world. The Americans are now on the same side as al-Qaeda!' said the exasperated diplomat. Neither of us knew it then, but the man first charged with finding a peaceful solution to the conflict had also reached the end of his tether. Kofi Annan, the joint United Nations and Arab League envoy, would soon be resigning from his 'Mission Impossible' with a scathing attack on the 'finger-pointing and name-calling' between the members of the Security Council.[2] By the time I returned to Damascus in February 2013 the UN had said almost seventy thousand people had died in the conflict.[3] Jihad Makdissi had fled the country. As the year wore on the death toll kept climbing.

Nothing expressed the profound shock caused by the collapse of the old order in the Middle East more clearly than the confused and dithering reaction of the outside world to the war in Syria. It simply did not know what to do. The only Great Power, America, used to have a simple solution for problems in the region: ring the Israelis or ring the Egyptians or ring the Saudis. Or ring all three and let them get on with it. That easy set of instructions has been consumed by the political inferno that has raged through the region in the wake of the first Arab uprising in Tunisia. The telephone numbers may have stayed the same but the people at the other end, and their priorities, have not. Newly influential players have emerged. Writing the next rulebook has barely begun. Barbara Bodine, the former US ambassador to Yemen, told me: 'I really don't know anybody who liked dealing with dictators, but there is a perverse simplicity to it.' The world after the Arab Spring is now much more complex.

The old Middle East stopped making sense years ago. The Soviet Union had been dead for decades. One by one, around the world, in Africa, South America and in Eastern Europe, brutal regimes had fallen, or been abandoned by their foreign sponsors. Elsewhere, for better or worse, the world had moved on – but not here. In the old Middle East the unholy alliance between 'the Land of the Free' and the world of dictatorship limped on because no one knew what else to do. It took schoolteachers, farmers and accountants to achieve what generations of diplomats and world leaders failed to do. The creation of a New Middle East. But revolution is only the journey; it does not bring you to a destination. It is a process, not a result. We can see now that this journey is leaving behind the old socialist ideologies of Ba'athism and Pan-Arabism, and those carried by the founders of Zionism. There is a stronger Sunni, and a weaker Shia, Islam. There is a growing religious divide in Israel. The regional powers are now more strongly divided along sectarian lines. Christians and other minorities wonder if they still have a safe place in the new societies being formed. Religion, not nationalism or Arabism, is now the dominant force.

God has returned to the Middle East.

*   *   *

Yet the uprisings were not Islamic revolutions. The call did not come from the mosques. Even so, religion is going to play a much greater role in the politics of the New Middle East. Its level of influence will depend on the make-up of each society. The rise of political Islam will create a discussion about the role of religion in the post-Arab Spring era. It may lose sway in countries where Sunni Islam forms almost the entire religious spectrum. Even in places where political choices will be tied to individual faiths, being pious will not be enough. Voters want answers to problems like unemployment, an inadequate education system and poor health care. The young revolutionaries did not fight to overthrow dictators just to have their freedoms curbed by religious edicts. Political Islam will have to adapt to reflect a more personal approach to religion. Islamic, or Sharia, law is not wanted in these new democracies even if faith is their reference point.

In Europe there will be concerns about the mix of religion and politics. Many in America will fear the rise of political Islam, because the legacy of 9/11 has left much of the nation believing that Islam often leads to extremism. The bomb attacks by two newly radicalised young men, one of whom had been granted American citizenship, on the Boston Marathon in April 2013 can only have strengthened that conviction. It is likely that the next few years will further reinforce some of these stereotypes, because extremism feeds on chaos, and chaos is likely to be a strong force as the New Middle East emerges from the ashes of the old.

The Arab dictators ruled their countries by dividing their people. They did that by stirring suspicion and mistrust among communities and religions. Now the Arab Spring revolts have also breathed new life into the schism within Islam itself. Sunni and Shia Muslims are facing off against each other in some of the region's most volatile areas. Iran had a burst of influence after the US toppled regimes in two of the nations that had been boxing it in, Iraq and Afghanistan. The Sunni powers have used the Arab Spring to put that firmly in reverse. But even they are divided. The revolts reignited old rivalries between competing ideologies among the Sunni Islamists too.

The board on which all these new power games are being played stretches across the Middle East. The rules came from scripture and each player interprets them according to their faith. America not only does not understand the rules of the game, it can't work out what winning might look like. So it is roaming around the table looking at everyone else's hand, offering advice on which card to play, but because it has no stake in the game nobody is really listening.

Syria was where the last act of the old Middle East would be played out. The finale would drip with blood. It would hark back to the region's darkest days, to the decades when its societies were opaque, when 'the Arab street' couldn't raise its voice without getting its fingernails pulled out. Back then the world heard only the narrow view of a handful of dictators who ruled with an iron fist over hundreds of millions. Saddam Hussein, Assad, Ben Ali, Muammar Gaddafi and Hosni Mubarak all lived lives of cartoonish excess. States were fashioned that mirrored their paranoia. Their people were surrounded by symbols of their masters' omnipotence.

That narrative of the old Middle East lasted longer than the Cold War in Europe. It lasted as long as the Arab dictators did. The West propped up these men because, so the story went, the alternative was states falling first under the influence of the communist block and later into the arms of radical Islam. In Syria President Bashar al-Assad believed he could stem the tide of history by playing by the rules created by his father's generation. He helped rekindle Cold War rivalries between Russia and America to stymie international intervention. His army tugged at the fragile mosaic of sects and religions that made up Syria's complex society. It started a sectarian civil war that would bleed into the countries around it. I saw the regime's warning to the world scrawled across the walls of the Damascus suburbs that dared to show dissent: 'Assad or we'll burn the country'.

The rise of the Arab people against their tormentors took even the protesters who manned the barricades by surprise. These revolutions took place in societies locked down by a security apparatus that had had decades to hone its skills. Generations of men from

North Africa to the Levant had been trained in the craft of suppression. They had stalked their own people, snatched them from their beds, strapped them into seats and beaten them to pulp. These acts were not justified by religion or ideology. They were not necessary evils inflicted to further a cause or liberate a people. It was not done for God. It was done for a man and his regime. Now most of those men are gone. Locked up, exiled or buried in unmarked graves. They leave behind countries in transformation. The statues and posters of those dictators have been torn down and trampled underfoot. The people have been led blinking out of the dark days of oppression by their children, a generation of youngsters force-fed for their entire lives on the lie that nothing could or would ever change. Until it did.

'The Arab world was considered a stagnant pond of retardation and tyranny, inhabited by what appeared to be a complacent populace toiling fatalistically under the yoke of their dictators,' wrote the blogger Iyad el-Baghdadi, in the introduction to his satirical 'Arab Tyrant's Manual'.[4] 'It really felt like this state of stagnation was permanent,' he told me. 'A lot of us thought that something has got to give at some point, but we didn't really think it was going to happen for another twenty years. We thought it was not going to be our generation but the next generation that would be doing it.'

The ingredients that sparked the uprisings existed throughout the region. Nearly every country has a massive 'youth bulge', with half its population under the age of twenty-five.[5] That made the competition even tougher for the meagre opportunities available to young people. The aspirations of the youth across the Middle East and North Africa were the same. Everywhere I went I would hear identical demands from the young protesters on the streets. They wanted their rulers to allow them some dignity. They wanted to work. They wanted some hope for a life at least as good as their parents'. The 'youth bulge' didn't need to be a problem; it could have been an opportunity if the old Middle East had not been so dysfunctional. In East Asia I saw for myself that because the economies worked and made things people wanted, they were able to absorb and benefit from the suddenly larger workforce. In the Middle East the state knew how to turn out graduates, but not how to create an economy to usefully employ them. Even worse, the graduates it did produce didn't have the right skills to fit the few opportunities there were in the market.[6] The state had solved this problem with the parents of the revolutionaries by buying them off with 'jobs for life' in the government.

Professor Ragui Assaad studies labour markets in developing countries at the Humphrey School of Public Affairs. He told me the old regimes eventually no longer had the resources to do the same thing for the next generation:

> The only thing young people found themselves able to do was work in the informal economy, and that creates a lot of anger and frustration, so in a sense it's the unravelling of that social contract, with much of that unravelling being imposed on the youth. The adults kept their government jobs, they kept their benefits, they kept their subsidised housing, but all the adjustment was imposed on the young people.

During the revolutions the West realised for the first time that Arabs were people just like us. They weren't all brooding jihadis who needed to be kept in check by a reign of terror.

'We have been here for seven thousand years, but people in Europe, you think that I have the camel in front of my house and I'm living beside the pyramid.' I met Youssef, a 42-year-old engineer, at the height of the Egyptian revolution in Cairo's Tahrir Square. Before the uprising, Youssef kept his thoughts and feelings to himself. Now, in slightly broken English, and just yards from where pitched battles were still taking place, he was relishing the chance to talk freely for the first time in his life without having to look over his shoulder for a secret policeman. 'We live like Third World people but we are First World people. We want to be able to show that we have all the capabilities to be First World people. Even the poor people here are civilised.' If Youssef can now speak openly for the first time, then this is also our first chance to listen, to find out what people like him want from the post-Arab Spring era. We can ask what kind of societies they are going to build and learn how their decisions will change our lives.

The only people of the old Middle East that the Western world thought it understood were the Israelis. The West knew much of their lore because their histories were intertwined. The Israelis were still seen as the homogeneous group of Europeans, surrounded by a sea of troubles, that built the Jewish homeland. But as the West enjoyed the celebrations of democracy emerging from the revolutions in the Arab world, it discovered that Israel did not. Why does the country that likes to boast it is the 'only democracy in the Middle East' think the Arab Spring was a catastrophe? Why has the bit of the region we thought was the most like us stopped thinking like us? The Arab world may have been going through a very noisy transition, but a quiet revolution is taking place in Israel too. It has rarely been more politically isolated than it is today. Its neighbourhood has radically changed but it has belligerently refused to adapt to that reality. 'Israel doesn't know what its best interests are,' said President Obama privately after he won his second term.[7]

The Arab uprisings have presented Israel with its greatest political challenge for a generation, just as its society seems at its most fragile. The rise of political Islam in the Middle East has ended for Israel the era of the cosy deal stitched up in smoky rooms with generals from Arab dictatorships. Mike Herzog has spent the last decade at the centre of Israeli decision-making on all key strategic, defence and political issues. To a greater extent than in other democracies in the world the Israeli military plays a central role in the country's society and politics and its views have a huge impact on policy. Herzog is a former brigadier general and the son of an Israeli president. I asked him whether an Arab dictatorship was better for Israel than an Islamic democracy.

It's a very good question, and people in Israel don't usually think about it in that way. Over the long run an Islamic democracy is better than a dictatorship, over the short run not necessarily, because when it comes to Israeli interests I think [issues like] the security situation, the peace agreement, don't promise good news. The problem is that Israel is highly unpopular on the Arab street, there's a lot of hatred, resentment and so on. These people were educated that way for generations. So there's a lot of hatred when the street speaks now. It's clearly an anti-Israel voice and we don't know how to communicate with these people.

In fact the street that worries many Israelis is much closer to home. It has posters telling women not to enter their area without covering their arms, legs and heads. It has banners describing Israel as a 'Nazi state' and blaming Zionism for the Holocaust. On these streets, just a few kilometres from where Mike and I were sitting, are people who want an end to the state of Israel. And these people are not Arabs, they are Jews.

As far as Yoel Weber is concerned Mike Herzog is not a Jew. We met in his small apartment, which is on the outskirts of the old city of Jerusalem. Yoel told me that the country's ultra-Orthodox Jews believe that 70–80 per cent of Israeli Jews have no right to call themselves Jews at all. 'They were lost to Judaism,' he said. 'We believe if any Jew behaves non-religiously, even if he was born a Jew then he has nothing to do with Judaism. He's cut off his pipeline to Judaism.' What's more, Yoel said most of his community have no time for people like Mike who fought in the 1973 war to protect the state of Israel against its Arab neighbours. 'The Haredi or ultra-Orthodox community don't believe in the state of Israel. They don't believe the state has done any good for Judaism or the Jews. [They think] that the state of Israel is not a blessing, rather it is a curse for the Jewish people.'

Ultra-Orthodox Jews were a tiny proportion of the Israeli state when it was created. Today they still make up only 10 per cent of the population, but the fractured nature of Israeli politics has often given them disproportionate influence.[8] That is only going to grow, because one third of all the Jewish children in kindergarten today come from their community.[9] The ongoing battle for Israel's future is between the secular and the religious. Its outcome will have just as much influence on the Middle East of tomorrow as the consequences of the revolts that are still searing through the Arab world today. The old narrative forgot to tell us that Israel has changed too. Israelis no longer all think the same, talk the same or worship the same. Their society is split along ultra-Orthodox, religious Zionist (also known in Israel as religious nationalists) and secular lines.

Eight-year-old girls dressed in long skirts and coats have been spat at by Haredi men who called them 'whores' as they walked to school. Hard-line settlers are demanding Israel's democracy be replaced by Jewish religious law. Secular Jews are fighting attempts to segregate their buses along gender lines and want protection from the spectre of 'Jewish terrorism'.[10] Jewish religious extremists who reject the existence of the state of Israel have sprayed pro-Hitler graffiti on the walls of Yad Vashem, the nation's monument to the victims of the Holocaust. At the other end of this society are the Arab communities living within the recognised boundaries of Israel. The demographics show that the country will soon be dominated by the two extremes of its social spectrum.[11] The state of Israel's response to this, according to one of its leading newspapers, *Ha'aretz*, is to 'thrust Israel down the slope of apartheid'.[12]

The American people have failed to grasp the scale of the change going on in their most important ally in the Middle East. And that is also true of the American government. When Barack Obama gave his 'historic' speech at Cairo University in 2009 he was presenting himself as an honest broker to all sides in the region. Instead he alienated almost everyone. The Israelis couldn't believe their ears and the Arab people couldn't believe their luck, but later ended up feeling utterly betrayed by what they saw as empty words. In 2013 he tried again with another address to the Middle East, this time from Jerusalem. He launched a charm offensive, pouring his love on the Israeli nation, which made them mistrust him less though not like him more.[13] 'There were too many "buts",' said Elior, a young Israeli student in the audience. His trip left the Palestinians feeling they had been given the cold shoulder.

Barack Obama's symbolic 'first telephone call' as president on his first full day in the White House was claimed by the Palestinian president Mahmoud Abbas, who was 'president' in name only. The call to him and other Middle Eastern leaders was meant to show just how engaged the new American president would be in the region.[14] As he picked up the handset Barack Obama had no idea that during his first term he would see decades of US foreign policy collapse in front of him.

Back then it was so much easier. America could divide the Arab world into two camps. There were those it could largely trust: Egypt, Jordan, Saudi Arabia and the rest of the Gulf states. And those it could not: Iran, Syria, Hezbollah, Hamas and Libya. It's not that simple now. Despite US reservations it must engage with Egypt's Muslim Brotherhood after its democratically elected President was ousted in the July 2013 popular coup so the Brotherhood's wider membership does not turn inward and increasingly violent in response. After the coup how much effort is made to show Islamists that democracy still has a place for them will be crucial. It will decide how both moderate Islamists and Western governments deal with the rise in influence of the Salafists.

Salafists are ultra-conservative puritanical Sunni Muslims who model themselves on a form of Islam dating to the first followers of the Prophet Muhammad. Salafism is very close to the Wahhabism that is the dominant form of Islam in Saudi Arabia. That is why wealthy Saudis are so willing to support Salafists in places like Syria. But Salafist groups are quite disparate. They are not disciplined single units like the Muslim Brotherhood. In Egypt, where the Salafists have deep roots, they are largely peaceful, previously apolitical, advocates for greater implementation of Islamic Law. Because they did not get involved in politics they were largely left alone under Mubarak. But in North Africa, where they were brutally suppressed by the old regimes, they have been responsible for some of the worst violence since the revolts took place.

The rise in influence of the proponents of political Islam, or Islamism as it is also called, has reshaped the Arab world after the revolutions and it will redefine Western diplomacy. Political Islam is essentially the opposite of what the West would call the division of Church and State. Broadly speaking, at the core of Islamism lies the belief that the basic original principles of the Muslim faith still have a fundamental role to play in the effective governing of modern societies and should go beyond just the issues of personal law.

The rise in influence of the adherents of political Islam has already began to flow into the conflict that has fractured the entire region and confounded the peacemakers for decades: the struggle between the Palestinians and Israel. 'This victory will change the political map in the Middle East,' said Ghazi Hamad, a senior member of the militant group Hamas. He was speaking as tens of thousands of Muslim Brotherhood supporters were still on the streets of Cairo celebrating the election of their candidate to the presidency. 'Israel should understand that they've lost their friends and allies in the Middle East. The political game will be changed now. Israel will not find an umbrella, it will not find silence for its crimes against the Palestinian people.'[15] The following day Israel's best-selling newspaper, *Yedioth Ahronoth*, drew its inspiration from the language used in the First Testament to describe the biblical plagues. 'Darkness in Egypt' was the translation from Hebrew of its headline.

The Arab Spring brought Hamas very publicly back into the Sunni Muslim Arab fold. Along with Syria, Iran and Lebanon's Hezbollah it had been an integral part of the so-called 'Axis of Resistance' against Israel. Before the uprisings of 2011 its base was in Damascus, under the guardianship of the heterodox Shia Alawite sect of President Bashar al-Assad. Its funding had come largely from Shia Iran. It had coordinated its attacks on Israel with the Shia group Hezbollah. And yet Hamas was an offshoot of the Sunni Muslim Brotherhood. The 'Axis of Resistance' had always been a marriage of inconvenience essentially imposed on it by the old Egyptian leadership who feared the Islamist Brotherhood at home and so rejected its siblings abroad. Now the Islamists were in power in Egypt, and their natural inclination would be to support Hamas over the more secular Palestinian groups supported by the West. Hamas was back where it belonged. This was important for the group because the Arab Spring would heighten the schism within Sunni and Shia, the two biggest branches of Islam.

Jews, Christians and Muslims all worship the same God. What they disagree about is which prophet carried the final version of His message to mankind. In simple terms the First Testament, also called the Hebrew Bible, is the key text on moral life for the Jewish people. They do not accept Jesus as a prophet so they do not recognise the Second Testament, which is the Christian Bible. Muslims consider their Holy Book, the Koran, to be the final version of God's message to mankind. They recognise Adam, Noah, Abraham, Moses, Solomon and Jesus as all being prophets, but they consider Muhammad, who was born just under 1,500 years ago in Mecca, in what is now Saudi Arabia, to be the final prophet and therefore the most important one.

Muhammad had two sons and four daughters. His sons died young. The youngest of his four daughters, Fatimah, married Ali. Ali was the son of Muhammad's uncle, who had cared for Muhammad when he was left an orphan.

When Muhammad died there was no heir. A disagreement began from that moment about who should succeed him as the civil and religious leader of the Muslim faithful, the Caliph. The majority of his followers recognised the first four caliphs as the Prophet's successors, the fourth of whom was Ali. They are called Sunni Muslims. A minority thought God had chosen that role for Ali and his descendants alone. They became the Shia. The killing of the Prophet's grandson Hussein and his supporters by the Sunni Caliph Yazid in the year 680 at Karbala in what is now Iraq was a defining moment in the split. Hussein was killed for refusing to recognise the authority of the caliph. His death created a strong theme of martyrdom within the Shia faith.[16]

This rift between the majority Sunni and the minority Shia, like the one in Europe between Catholic and Protestant Christians, has been the cause of much bloodshed and persecution over the centuries.

It is the cause of some of the blood being shed in Syria today. It is at the heart of the struggle between the Sunni leadership in the Gulf and Shia Iran.

The countries engulfed by the Arab Spring are on the road from dictatorship to democracy. Together they will shape the New Middle East.

But why did some uprisings lead to the overthrow of regimes while others did not? Why did some revolutions take weeks while others took many months? Why in some of the most undemocratic countries in the Arab region did widespread protests not take place at all? Where revolutions did happen, why did some countries then vote for Islamist parties while other equally pious nations rejected them? Why was there international agreement to send NATO planes into the skies over Libya to pre-empt a *possible* massacre, whereas little was done in Syria when the bullet-riddled corpses of small children stared out at us from the front pages of our newspapers over morning coffee? Where and why did Western realism trump Western idealism?

To answer these questions properly it helps to have seen the transformation of the region from the beginning, when American troops drove into Baghdad a decade ago to impose a democratic 'Freedom Agenda' on the Arab world. My work as the BBC's Middle East bureau chief also took me to the front lines in Libya and the protesters' barricades in Egypt. In the pages that follow you'll find debates with ultra-Orthodox Jews about the merits of Madonna and theological rows with West Bank settlers over their self-declared right to kill Arab children. You'll meet Colonel Gaddafi at the beginning of the Libyan revolution, and stand before his bloodied and beaten body at the end. You'll witness the civil war that soaked Syrian villages in blood and divided the country, the region and the world.

We in the West need to understand this region, because the Vegas rules don't apply here. What happens in the Middle East does *not* stay in the Middle East.

We have no choice but to try to make sense of the changing dynamics in the Middle East because, as President Obama has acknowledged, 'whether we like it or not . . . when conflicts break out, one way or another we get pulled into them. And that ends up costing us significantly in terms of both blood and treasure.'[17] The new governments emerging from the revolutions will no longer act as client states doing Washington's bidding, so 'leading from behind' will not be enough.[18] 'We are in the middle of this struggle, it is going to take a generation, it is going to be very arduous and difficult,' said the former British prime minister Tony Blair in February 2013 as he looked back at events in the Middle East since he sent troops into Iraq to bring about the region's first regime change. 'But I think we are making a mistake, a profound error, if we think we can stay out of that struggle, because we are going to be affected by it whether we like it or not.'[19]

The decade since the first Middle Eastern dictator was toppled has seen fundamental change in the Arab world. It has forced people to re-examine their identities and decide what role their faith will play in their lives and their politics. It has made the West look at its conscience as it rebuilds its foreign policies for the region.

The Arab Spring has been tidying up a lot of other people's history. The toppling of the dictators provided the missing nail in the coffin of the Cold War era. The revolts also began to undermine the legacy of the Great War that came before that. After the First World War the Europeans conjured up plans for a whole raft of new countries, including Syria, Lebanon, Iraq, Jordan, Palestine and Israel. In many of these places the Europeans' actions left the minority communities in charge, thus building sectarian strife into them at birth. They in turn were only a little older than the 'Middle East' itself. That was a concept that had not existed before an American admiral, Alfred Thayer Mahan, referred in a 1902 edition of London's *National Review* to 'The Middle East, if I may adopt the term which I have not seen . . .'[20] It was soon also adopted by the European powers, which shifted the boundaries of this construct as they constantly redefined their interests in this new region.

Those interests have now been dramatically changed again, and some of those countries in the Middle East run the risk of falling apart.

If the West stays engaged, then over the longer term there is much to be optimistic about. When opposition movements, violent or otherwise, have come to government, whether it is in South Africa or Northern Ireland, they have become more moderate. When you are running a country, reality kicks down the door, parks itself in the centre of the room and demands answers that ideology alone cannot provide. Governments, which reflect the views of their people, are also better at tackling extreme versions of themselves. It was the culture shock of imported Western modernity and Soviet-style dictatorship that gave birth to much of the region's religious extremism. Diplomacy with the old Middle East was based on a lie. Earlier negotiations and peace treaties were not agreed with countries, they were signed off with the ruling family business. In the New Middle East the world's leaders will be talking with people who probably won't look, talk or think like them. But what both sides will share is the knowledge that each is speaking on behalf of their people. The men and women of the Middle East finally have a voice. When you think someone is listening to you, you are much less likely to feel you need to punch them on the nose.

The results of the elections which have taken place since the revolts have already revealed a political sophistication that belies the decades when people were denied the vote. Where Islamists were given a chance to govern it was largely because they suffered the most under the old regimes. But pity will only get them so far. If they don't deliver they will be kicked out. That reality is likely to change the Islamists more than they will change the democratic process. The overthrow in Egypt of the region's first elected Islamist president should not be seen as the beginning of the end for political Islam. As we shall see the Brotherhood has survived worse. But ejecting even an unpopular, incompetent government with military force has damaged Egypt's fledgling democracy. It was though a reminder to any new government or army that fails to listen to the public. The people of the Arab world have lost their fear. There is no going back to dictatorship, even if the future course still looks unclear.

The confusion about what will now follow is reflected by

disagreement even over what this dramatic change should be called. It has been argued that the phrase 'Arab Spring' is yet another inappropriate Western import into the region, drawn as it was from events in Prague during 1968 at the height of the Cold War. Some people, like US Secretary of State John Kerry, refuse to use it, preferring the term 'Arab Awakening'. 'Spring' does suggests something quick and pleasant. That may have broadly been the case in Tunisia and Egypt; it certainly wasn't in Libya and Syria. It was also clear by the summer of 2011 that these events would take many seasons to play out. However 'Arab Awakening' has been used before, to describe the surge of Arab nationalism in the 1950s, so reviving it now is also confusing. The Israeli government and its supporters first called these events 'the Islamic Spring' and then later 'the Islamic winter'. In the years that followed the start of these events some were calling it the 'Sunni Spring'. It is a testament to how much these revolts have changed the region that they mean so much to so many people in so many different ways. If I have tended to use 'Arab Spring' in this book, it is because it is the phrase most commonly used on the international stage. Every country, including Syria, is in the post-Arab Spring era, because they are having to deal with the consequences of the initial revolts.

Whatever people choose to call the uprisings, the challenge for the rest of the world is to embrace the changes in the Middle East, engage with its new leaders and form a partnership with these emerging forces to make sure democracy in the region survives its infancy. The road to democracy for the Arab world has been harder and longer than for almost any other region on the planet. It took so long that a casual assumption was made in parts of the West that it simply couldn't work there. That conclusion propped up dictators for decades. The key test for the revolutionaries of the New Middle East, now that they have fought and won their new states, is this: Can they accept democracy's fundamental characteristic? It expresses the will of the *majority* of the people. So many of them may not like what they are going to get.

Jerusalem/al-Quds, 4 July 2013

I

The Collapse of the Old Middle East

'Take a sheep and give me your vote,' said the placard in Arabic. It was held above the heads of two young Tunisian women standing in a crowd of a thousand people outside the results centre for the Constituent Assembly elections in the capital Tunis. They were waiting for the announcement of the final tally but they already knew who had won. Unusually for a protest in the Arab world, more than half the demonstrators were women. They suddenly felt they had the most to lose from the outcome of the first democratic process born of the Arab Spring.

After the revolts the rich educated urban youth, many of whom had propagated the uprising through their Facebook pages and with rocks and stones on the streets of Tunis, had woken up to the reality of their country. They were not the real Tunisia. Like many wealthy people living in the developing world, the poor were to them the men and women who served, cleaned and did jobs they did not want to do. And they did it quietly. The people eking out an existence just above the poverty line weren't necessarily thought of badly. They simply weren't thought of at all, except as an intellectual concept to be debated in coffee shops or over dinner.

The poor did not have a voice during the years of President Zine al-Abidine Ben Ali's dictatorship in Tunisia. Now they not only had a voice, they had a vote. And in October 2011 they used it to make the moderate Islamist party Ennahda the largest in the Constituent Assembly. This crowd of the liberal elite simply couldn't believe anyone would pick Ennahda unless their vote had been bought. They assumed the poor were gullible enough to swap their votes for livestock.

Standing among the placards was Manal Labidi, who taught accountancy at a college in Tunis. She was in her twenties, very fashionably dressed, with a pair of designer sunglasses pushed up onto her head. And she was angry. 'They stole the revolution,' she told me. The most remarkable thing about Manal Labidi's protest was not what she said, it was the fact that after she said it she wasn't dragged by her hair down to the local police station. Before the revolution her entire generation had been constantly warned by their parents to keep quiet, keep their heads down and avoid eye contact with the police.

In Tunisia you had only to compare the size of the force assigned to protect the country with that assigned to protect the regime to see what kept President Ben Ali awake at night. The internal security services were at least five times larger than the army.[1] Like all the Arab dictators, Ben Ali was much more afraid of his own people than he was of foreign invaders. And what scared him most about them was that one day they might get the vote. In a fair fight at the ballot box the Arab leaders all knew they'd be kicked out on to the streets. Fortunately for them, democracy in the Middle East did not suit their friends in the West either. The end of the Cold War in Europe in 1989 saw a wave of democracy wash around the globe, but it hit a wall in the Middle East. The academics of the day even had a phrase for it: it was called 'Arab Exceptionalism', and people studied it as if it was a supernatural phenomenon. It was not. It was man-made. Many in government in the West believed that letting the people of the Middle East make their own minds up only produced what became known as the 'Algerian problem', which 'crystallised as the nightmare vision for American policymakers of what democracy might bring to the Arab world: legitimately elected Islamist governments that are anti-American, and ultimately anti-democratic, in orientation'.[2] Dr Osman Hassan, from Warwick University, who has studied the attempts to bring democracy to the region, described the ideas of 'Arab Exceptionalism' to me in much clearer terms: 'It's inherently racist, there are no two ways about it. It becomes a really benign way of saying: "We don't need to do anything because Arabs can't have democracy because they don't want it because there is something fundamentally wrong with them."'

For much of the last sixty years the West didn't understand the region because the story we heard from the Middle East was simple. The news focused largely on the violence. The victims and perpetrators ebbed and flowed but the plot did not. At worst the Arabs were treated as an amorphous mass of people who were constantly trying to kill each other or the Israelis. At first glance even the revolutions fitted an easy narrative. There was a dictator against the people. Simplicity once again hid the subtleties. But there is nothing simple about the New Middle East.

We need to understand why the Arab people's fight for democracy was so long and lonely. There were broad forces that made the old Middle East collapse, but there were also distinct differences between each revolution because of the distinct differences between each nation.

'The Arabs' have never been thought of or portrayed as a collection of individuals. The world focused only on the things that made them the same. We need to focus on the things that make them different. We must dispel even those myths about the Middle East that were created with good intentions. By examining what made each uprising distinct, and how the societies differed in their religious and political make-up, we can see why each country has since taken a different path after the Big Bang of the revolt. That will help us work out where each country is going. It will also help us understand why the fire-storm of revolution was sparked in what had always been the least exciting corner of the region.

Democracy has finally arrived in the Middle East, but it has quite literally had a torturous journey. Many of the leaders of these new democracies were subjected to sadistic brutality by the old regimes simply because of their religious beliefs. Successive Western governments turned a blind eye to this abuse for the same reason. Now that these Islamists are being lectured by Western politicians about freedom and human rights, they wonder why the same people were silent when they were in jail. Understanding this legacy will help us understand those tensions. If the Western governments are suspicious of the Islamist politicians, then the Islamist politicians have plenty of personal reasons to mistrust Western governments.

The uprisings were described around the world as the 'Facebook' revolutions.[3] The West looked for labels it could understand to describe a region it did not. Across the Middle East and North Africa the nature of the demonstrations confused the state security apparatus. It was not designed to deal with this. The organisation through social media created a disorganised pattern of protest. Young revolutionaries would later recall coming across other protest marches entirely by accident, assuming at first that the crowd on the horizon was riot police ready to confront them.[4] The confusing nature of the rebellion was so effective at undermining the security forces that it led to the belief among the regimes that there must be some hidden hand or dark force at work.[5] But then these were old men who probably needed help from their grandchildren to operate the DVD player.

The essence of dictatorship is control of the public arena. It is done through stories shown on the state television, the editorials in the newspapers, the omnipresent image of the 'Father of the Nation' on posters or statues. Social media took that power away. The Grandads were too blind to see that their political class didn't control the message any more. By the time they tried to turn the Internet off it was too late. As the revolutions moved from country to country the role of the World Wide Web in getting an alternative message out became more and more important.

Yet many of those who emerged as the voices of the regional protest movements say that social media was merely an instrument of the uprisings, it should not have been used to define them. They argue that the West projected its own wishful thinking onto the revolutions, hoping that a third force of young liberals was emerging as an alternative to the old dictators and the resurgent Islamists. Their desire was that this group, which was unsurprisingly a reflection of the West's own image, would then determine the fate of the New Middle East. But the West got it wrong, the Egyptian–American writer and activist Mona Eltahawy told me:

> When you look at Facebook and Twitter, how many people do they reach? When we had the [constitutional] referendum in Egypt [in March 2011], if you followed the Egyptian Twitterverse the majority of the people were going to say 'no' and then seventy-five per cent of Egyptians said 'yes'. That shows you where Twitter is and where the rest of Egypt is. Social media was a tool in the way cassette tapes were a tool for Ayatollah Khomeini in the run-up to the Iranian Revolution, in the way the fax machine was a tool in the run-up to Tiananmen Square, the printing press in the run-up to Martin Luther, pamphlets for the Soviets. It's just a tool and it helped to connect people that couldn't find each other in an atmosphere where civil society was being decimated by the regime.

The dictators first began to lose control of the public sphere with the rise of the Arabic satellite news channels, the most important of which was Al Jazeera. It was where the Arab people found a common narrative, because Al Jazeera in its heyday, in the first decade of the new century, was reporting on causes that united the Arab people. There was the second much more violent uprising by the Palestinians against the Israeli occupation in 2000, and then came the partial and then total Western occupation of Muslim lands in Afghanistan and Iraq. Al Jazeera was also a catalyst for the Tunisian revolution. It picked up early and stayed with the protests as they gathered pace, and because of its constant coverage it increased the momentum. By the time of Egypt's revolution the channel was perceived by many in the Arab world as not just reporting but cheering on the uprisings, but as those who saw it that way were on the same side it upset no one.

Which is why Al Jazeera came in for so much criticism when it seemed to do its utmost to ignore the uprising in the Gulf state of Bahrain.[6] That was the moment it and Al Arabiya really began to be perceived by parts of their audiences as softer arms of their host states Qatar and Saudi Arabia. During the Libyan conflict, even though it was staunchly on the side of the opposition, revolutionaries became distrustful of the channel's motives. The rising tide of revolution took the viewing figures of every Arab news network with it, but the Arab-language Al Jazeera news channel saw its credibility damaged as staff members resigned, accusing the channel of allowing interference by the Qatari government.[7]

Unlike earlier revolutionary movements in the world's history, social media in the twenty-first century provided the capability to organise without central control. The revolution in Tunisia, like the ones that followed, was leaderless, so the usual government tactics didn't work. There was no one to buy off, lock up or scare away. It was the great strength of the Arab Spring when it began, but for the secular middle class it also proved to be its greatest weakness. They had formed the vanguard of the uprisings but they had no one to represent them when the dictators fell. As events wore on young democrats were sometimes campaigning to stop free and fair elections from quickly taking place because they knew they weren't ready to compete.[8] The spoils went to the groups who were the most organised. In Tunisia and then Egypt this meant that the first waves of democracy produced a surge in influence for the Islamists, not for the secular revolutionaries.

It is important here to explain the use of the word 'secular' in this book and throughout the Middle East. The words 'secular' and 'liberal' are used to describe people in the Arab world and Israel whose religion is part of their lives, but who don't define much of their identity by religion. When people in the Middle East talk about the 'seculars' it does not mean atheists or non-believers; they are talking about people less religious than they are. It is very hard to find people in the Middle East who have no faith in God at all. They exist, and are often described as radical seculars, but they are such a tiny minority they have very little impact on their wider societies. As in the US, religious people do not make up part of the political spectrum, they are almost the entire political spectrum. What varies along that spectrum is the degree to which religion impacts on their political thinking.

The cry that was born in Tunisia but went echoing across the Arab world was: 'The people want the overthrow of the regime.' It was not only a challenge to the dictators, it was a challenge to the army: 'Whose side are you on?' The answer to that question defines the nature of an authoritarian state. If the army sees itself as an instrument of the state it will ditch the regime to protect the People. This is what we saw in Egypt and Tunisia. If the army has no investment in either the state or the regime, then the military will crumble, which is what happened in Libya. If the army is not only an instrument of the regime, but helped build the state, it will kill the People to protect it. Then, the People must not only overthrow the regime, they must fight to overthrow the state, because they are one and the same. That is what happened in Syria.

Lisa Anderson is the head of the American University in Cairo and a professor of International Relations. Her office sits on Tahrir Square, and that gave her a ringside seat to indulge in the area of specialism for which she is world-renowned, namely regime change and the formation of states. 'The Tunisian military and the Egyptian military were prepared to sacrifice the regime because they were ultimately the protectors of the country,' she told me.

> So even though they were both very wrapped up in relations with the regime, particularly in Egypt, they could walk away. The Libyan military establishment was completely confused, just like the entire country, and it wasn't clear whom they worked for but they certainly didn't work for Libya. Whether they were the vanguard of [Gaddafi's Green] revolution, which is the way they had been represented for a long time, or whether they were a praetorian guard for

Gaddafi, they certainly were not Libya's military establishment in their own self-image. So as soon as things began to come apart . . . it's like you pull the string and the whole thing begins to unravel completely, and they had nothing that held them together. Being the vanguard of the revolution was something that very few people took seriously, and being his praetorian guard, unless you were one of the Gaddafi tribe, then you weren't part of that.

It wasn't hard to persuade the world to actively support the cry for freedom and democracy in Libya and thus help overthrow the regime. Within weeks of the start of the revolution the UN had agreed on a no-fly zone and NATO planes were attacking Gaddafi's army, turning the tide of the war. By diplomatic standards the intervention in Libya took place at lightning speed, and it was down to how the world felt about one man.

Colonel Muammar Gaddafi, more than any other Arab dictator, brought the fear and violence of life lived under a despot to the people of suburban Europe and America. He was, US President Ronald Reagan famously declared, 'The Mad Dog of the Middle East'.[9] The only other man from the Arab-speaking world to have impacted on the lives of Westerners in such a violent, direct and personal way was the al-Qaeda leader Osama bin Laden. It used to infuriate Libyans that the only thing people identified their country with was their quixotic leader, yet it was only because of Gaddafi's antics that Libya had a place in the international spotlight at all. The last time I saw him alive he was driving past me in a golf buggy through a scrum of loyalists and security men, waving at the crowd and heading straight for a lamppost. Gaddafi didn't care whether the outside world loved him or hated him. He just didn't want to be ignored.

A few weeks before the NATO jets began to rev up their engines to drop their first payloads on the regime of the world's most famous dictator, the man who would soon soar up the charts to grab that title from him was still pretty confident that he faced no serious trouble at home. Bashar al-Assad had hailed the uprisings in Tunisia and Egypt as a 'new era' in the Arab world, but he said of his country: 'We are outside of this; at the end we are not Tunisians and we are not Egyptians.'[10] Gaddafi said something similar, and he was wrong too. But Assad was right about one thing. Syria was not Tunisia and it was not Egypt, because when it came to the crunch in those two countries the dictators had not built regimes willing or able to butcher their own populations.

'Syria is stable. Why?' asked Assad. 'Because you have to be very closely linked to the beliefs of the people.'[11] He didn't say it then but he added later through deeds not words, that if being 'closely linked . . . to the people' doesn't work then you could just try killing as many of them as possible.

If, before the Arab revolts, the Western world was largely ignorant of the brutality of Bashar al-Assad's regime, it certainly wasn't afterwards. If ever there was a case for intervention to protect civilians, then Bashar al-Assad had made it. But the regime was allowed to take its society beyond the point of reconciliation. Then some Gulf states started to directly undermine efforts at a peaceful outcome, but still the West was reluctant to step up and play a greater role. Syria's geographic position and its kaleidoscope of religions and sects meant the Western world baulked at pulling at and unravelling the regime because it had no idea what would emerge from beneath.

The Assad family built the Syrian state by stitching together a patchwork of communities over which one of its minorities, the Alawites (also known as Alawis), presided. In Egypt and Tunisia the army was feted for staying loyal to the state and protecting the revolution. In Libya individual loyalties to family and region trumped loyalty to the military and the state, so the military establishment collapsed. In Syria loyalty to the state, to the regime, to the army and to family often all meant the same thing if you were part of the establishment and an Alawite.

The nature of the state that Bashar al-Assad's father Hafez built, Lisa Anderson told me, meant that Syria was always going to be more resistant to change than Libya ever was, with or without outside intervention from NATO or anywhere else.

[In Syria] the regime's project was to build the state out of what were fairly autonomous identities. [There] you do get the solidarity of the praetorian guard, which is ethnic, so all the Alawis have to rally around. But – and this is why things have been so horrid in Syria – you have a lot of people that bought this state-building project. You don't have to be Alawis to say: 'Syria is an important thing and this military represents Syria,' whereas nobody thought the military in Libya represented Libya. There was hardly even any sense of 'Libya'. Syria has enough national identity and enough conviction that the military's function is to build out that national identity, that a lot of people have bought that and will support that and will say that: 'Yes, the people that are trying to undermine this are bad guys and are just trying to create chaos.' So the opposition has much less legitimacy in the view of substantial numbers of Syrians. So it becomes much more like a real civil war.

This is why some revolutions took weeks and others took months and years. Some of the regimes built by the dictatorships had been hollowed out with age. The socialist ideologies that created them were long gone. The regimes had died inside but the façade was still standing. It still looked menacing, but when the young people pushed against it, it collapsed.

The regimes that still had a purpose – in Syria's case to protect a particular sect, the Alawites – were more resilient. Egyptians and Tunisians felt a little sheepish after the revolt that it had taken them so long to stand up to their bully. By the time the Syrian conflict entered its third year, those people who by now were living in shattered cities, scavenging for firewood and selling their possessions to buy food, wondered if it would ever end and whether the revolt had been worth it.

While there were many differences in these uprisings, there was one thing that united them. 'The five countries where you have had revolutions, Egypt, Tunisia, Libya, Syria and Yemen, all shared one thing,' Shadi Hamid from the Brookings Center for Middle East Policy in Doha told me.

There was a very unpopular repressive leader and that figure was able to unite the opposition because, as fractious as these oppositions were, the one thing they could agree on was: 'We don't like him and we want to get rid of him' and they couldn't agree on nearly anything else. Having that kind of personalised figure was a critical part of why these revolutions were able to occur.

But these weren't the only Arab countries where demonstrations took place. In Bahrain, Jordan and Morocco protests were successfully and quickly either put down or defused.[12] And these countries too had something in common. They were Arab kingdoms. 'No monarchies have fallen, no monarchies have even come close to falling, and that's not by mistake,' says Shadi Hamid.

Monarchies are a fundamentally different form of governmental structure. They tend to have more legitimacy, more popular support [and] it's also more difficult for the opposition to come and say: 'We want the fall of the leader' because they don't want that. They want, maybe, constitutional reform, but because the monarchy has this elevated status [the protesters] have to have a different call to arms. And saying: 'We want constitutional monarchy' on a bumper sticker, that's not very catchy, it's not able to unify the opposition and give them a clear sense of purpose.

And if someone does have to go, an Arab monarch always has the option of blaming the mere mortals in his kingdom's largely useless and ineffective parliament. King Abdullah of Jordan, where street protests started in the first month of the Arab Spring, has only been on the throne since 1999. The Jordanian branch of the Muslim Brotherhood, which the King described as a 'Masonic cult', dominates the opposition.[13] The Arab kingdoms without oil or gas had to try to slowly reform their way out of trouble. By the time of the general elections, which had little credibility because the Brotherhood boycotted them, had been held in January 2013,

King Abdullah had already worked his way through ten prime ministers during his reign.

Many people in the Arab world who followed the progress of the uprising in Tunisia on Twitter, Facebook or on Arab satellite TV channels saw the potential for change in their own lands too, and took to the streets. At first glance neighbouring Algeria also looked ripe for revolution. It had a patriarchal leader in President Abdelaziz Bouteflika, who had been in power for more than a decade. Like Egypt it was at the time being governed under emergency rule, though that was quickly lifted. The economy was in trouble and it had the same demographic 'youth bulge'. But Algeria had already had its landmark 'free and fair' elections in 1992, and as in the elections that took place in the Arab world twenty years later, Islamists had won. Back then the Algerian military were not ready to hand the country over to the winners, the Islamic Salvation Front (FIS). The elections were annulled, a civil war ensued, and more than 150,000 people died in the violence.[14] The people of Algeria were still exhausted when their next-door neighbour began its struggle against dictatorship. In Algeria most people who watched the Arab uprisings unfold on their TV screens saw in them the potential for another round of appalling bloodshed, so they mostly stayed at home and locked their doors.

In most of the Arab world countries the dictatorships had pretended to keep up with the times by putting up a little democratic tinsel to catch the eye of the Western world. In the Gulf states they hardly bothered. The reason why revolution was not sparked there was less complicated than in the other nations. In the Gulf, oil money is sloshed around society at the slightest hint of dissent to try to co-opt the vast majority of the people into a docile acceptance of the status quo. The few who won't settle for a pay rise are easily picked off by the well-funded internal security services. But the Gulf countries will not be able to buy their way out of trouble for ever, says the labour market specialist Professor Assaad:

> It is absolutely not sustainable. It's basically a perpetuation of the authoritarian contract where we'll throw money at you and give you a whole bunch of giveaways but you don't question the

authority of the state and you don't demand democracy. That is the model that was operating in most of the region, but it became unsustainable in places like Egypt and Tunisia. The oil economies are still able to afford that model for the time being, but I don't see with the increasing number of young people, with the increasing education levels, that that sort of social contract can be sustainable.

It may not be affordable for the Gulf states soon either.

New technology in the form of the Internet played an important role in bringing down the regimes that have no oil. New technology may eventually do the same to the regimes that have it. 'Fracking', or more accurately hydraulic fracturing, is opening up huge deposits of shale gas and increasingly what is called 'tight oil' across North America. As that technology spreads around the world, so will these alternative energy sources, and that may fundamentally change the world's relationship with the present energy-exporting nations. 'We are talking about a massive reduction in demand for Middle East energy, and in the case of Middle Eastern countries that live off exported energy they really have nothing else,' Dr Aviezer Tucker, the assistant director of the Energy Institute of the University of Texas, told me. 'So it could seriously destabilise regimes that have got used to using this income from the export of energy to subsidise the stability of the regime. Saudi Arabia and Kuwait have nothing, absolutely nothing else. They don't have an educated population, they don't have the engineers, there's nothing.'

For now the numbers of protesters in the Gulf states have been small enough for the security forces to crack down. They got away with it because in the oil-rich and therefore strategically important Gulf states Western values come a poor second to Western interests. Nowhere was this more publicly displayed than in the barely audible US reaction to Saudi Arabia sending troops and armoured vehicles across the causeway to help violently suppress the largely peaceful demonstrations for political reform staged by the Shia majority that had been taking place in the neighbouring Sunni kingdom of Bahrain.[15]

And it soon became clear that Bahrain was just a prelude to the main sectarian event. The Western world's willingness to take a back seat as protesters were chased around Manama's Pearl Roundabout was a hint of the almost free hand they would give the Gulf states to meddle in Syria too. The US will compromise over its values as long as it needs the Gulf's energy exports. But if over the coming decades the Western nations can adapt their transport systems and infrastructure to these new forms of energy then they will not need the Saudis to sustain the world economy. Their relationship will then end in a quick divorce.

History has given us some unbelievably evil rulers, men who have tortured and murdered with their own hands. Many of the worst were in the Arab world. But history has in return nearly always rewarded us for the excesses of a great dictator with a demise as dramatic and theatrical as the life that preceded it. History had stood still in the Arab world for thirty years. When it came back to life with the collapse of the old Middle East the fate of the Arab dictators did not disappoint. What went through their minds as they absorbed the truth, as they finally understood it was time to scurry down into the network of tunnels like a rat in a pipe to try to make their escape? What went through the minds of these men, as the Arab Spring drove them from their seats of absolute power? What were the words used by the trusted aides of Tunisia's Ben Ali, Egypt's Mubarak or Libya's Gaddafi to convey the news? How do you tell someone who believes his people will willingly sacrifice their lives to protect his own that they are massing outside right now to rip his throat out? Did all those loyal lieutenants pause at the door, hand poised over the handle, still formulating the words to convey to their lord that it was over? And what happened next? Were there tantrums? Was there a stony silence? Were there exhortations to their God to help them, despite their many Godless acts of cruelty?

However they met their ends, their lives were big enough to create enduring iconic imagery: Saddam firing off a rifle from his balcony; Gaddafi raging against America from the rubble of his Bab al-Aziziya compound; a fallen Mubarak being wheeled into court wearing sunglasses and a scowl. They were the 'Strong Men' of the Middle East, but one of them, the black sheep of the family, knew history would not stand still for ever.

More than any other Arab leader, Gaddafi understood just how dispensable the old order was to the Western powers when its Strongmen stopped being useful. He warned them all during a scathing speech at the Arab League summit in Damascus in 2008 as he addressed the fall of Saddam Hussein. The camera operated by Syrian state TV was fixed on him as he railed against the Arab League's inaction over the invasion of Iraq by the American-led coalition. Suddenly he stopped and looked around the room, realising that his words were eliciting only condescending smiles. Then he heaved a deep and exasperated sigh. 'A foreign force occupies an Arab country and hangs its leader while we are looking and laughing,' he said. Clearly frustrated by the reaction in the room, again he asked: 'How is a ruler and head of an Arab League member state hanged? I am not talking about Saddam Hussein's policies or our falling out with him. We all had our disagreements with him; we all disagree with each other. Nothing holds us together except this hall!'

This remark produced knowing laughter from the assembled Arab League leaders, but the camera stayed on Gaddafi's face, which broke into a smile. He took a long pause and looked around the room, and then Syrian TV cut to its own leader, Bashar al-Assad, who was himself laughing at Gaddafi's remarks. 'An entire Arab leadership is killed and hanged on the gallows. Why?' Gaddafi raised his hand and waved it towards the leaders of the Arab world states. 'In the future, it is going to be your turn too!' he said. The whole room broke into loud laughter. 'Indeed!' he said as the laughter continued. 'America fought alongside Saddam against Khomeini. He was their friend! . . . In the end they sold him. They hanged him. Even you, the friends of America, no, I will say we, we, the friends of America. America may approve of our hanging one day.' Again loud laughter ran through the room. He was of course absolutely right.

The revolutions were the breaking of a contract between these Strongmen and the secular middle classes. The people had traded democracy for stability. The dictators made the same pact with the Western governments. The deal was made in the wake of the Iranian revolution in 1979. That too had been a popular uprising, against the autocratic rule of the Iranian Shah. But his overthrow eventually led to an equally repressive regime. That one, because of its religious nature, started to reach into the homes of the urban middle classes and try to tell them how to think, how to live and how to dress. So the message for decades from the Arab dictators was 'Islamist extremists or me'.[16]

Over time the people stopped believing this, but the outside world did not. The people in the Arab nations were ready for democracy but the Western world was convinced otherwise. The Iranian uprising not only created the first militant Shia state, thus upsetting the balance of power in the region, it also produced a theocracy that wanted to export its revolutionary fervour. In Shia Islam the powerful position of its religious leaders means they can easily become the ultimate political authority too, as happened in Iran. That is not usually the case in Sunni Muslim societies, where religious figures are generally expected to advise, not rule. But when the West saw the Shah being overthrown by what were quickly labelled at the time the 'mad mullahs' it was thoroughly rattled. The Sunni-led authoritarian states played on those fears. Sometimes the Strongman claimed he was holding back Islamic fundamentalists, sometimes he said he was all that stood in the way of wild sectarian violence.

The Western governments not only bought this line, in the twilight years of the old Middle East they were quietly acquiescing in the extension of dynastic rule across the Arab world. It had already happened in Syria, though not quite as the father Hafez al-Assad had planned. His favoured son Bassel, whom he had been grooming for power, was killed in a car crash in 1994, so Bashar became the accidental dictator. In Libya the struggle for succession was between the second son, Saif al-Islam, and the fourth, Mutassim,[17] though with most of his siblings dishing 'enough dirt for a Libyan soap opera' many Libyans, according to the US embassy in Tripoli's secret diplomatic cables, saw Saif as their 'knight in shining armor'.[18] In Syria and Libya, though, the public had no say about who would come next, and the instruments of the state were either sidelined or signed up to the plan. In Egypt it was different.

Hosni Mubarak had not built the regime he led, he was a product of it. The military built the state, and it was from there that the leadership had been drawn since the country had overthrown the monarchy in 1952. And so it was the grooming of Mubarak's younger son, Gamal, that helped seal Hosni Mubarak's fate. Gamal was a corrupt businessman, not a soldier. The military saw a dynastic succession as a betrayal of the 1952 revolt – something Mubarak failed to grasp right up to the end.

If the Middle East had not had oil it would have been allowed to make its own mistakes and get on with building democratic states. But it did have oil, and the West wanted oil more than anything else. Easy access to oil required stability across the region, and that gave the Cold War era regimes of the Middle East a shelf-life well beyond the expiry date of the geopolitical circumstances that had nurtured them. Everyone, but most importantly successive American administrations, believed that democracy in the Middle East would simply cause them too much trouble. The dictators argued that their people were not ready for it. Many of the kings in the Gulf states said the whole idea was un-Islamic. Then along came a man carried by events beyond his own making who tried to forge a philosophy from the wreckage of the 9/11 attacks to make his country feel safe again. The cause of democratising the Arab world suddenly had a new and powerful champion.

George W. Bush announced the tenets of the big idea of his presidency, the 'Freedom Agenda', in his second inaugural address in January 2005. 'The survival of liberty in our lands increasingly depends on the success of liberty in other lands,' he said. 'The best hope for peace in our world is the expansion of freedom in all the world . . . So it is the policy of the United States to seek and support the growth of democratic movements and institutions in every nation and culture, with the ultimate goal of ending tyranny in our world.'[19]

God was returning to shape the region again and George W. Bush was the first person to realise that. He told a senior Palestinian leader: 'I am driven with a mission from God . . . God would tell me "George, go and end the tyranny in Iraq." And I did . . . And now, again, I feel God's words coming to me: "Go get the Palestinians their state and get the Israelis their security, and get peace in the Middle East." And, by God, I'm gonna do it.'[20] But he didn't.

He pushed for elections in the region, but then Arabs started voting for the wrong people, Islamists. That wasn't the plan. So Western governments supported economic reform instead, but that only helped the dictators steal even more money. So Western aid started going back into civil society projects that seemed like a nice safe way of being seen to do something while, critics said, not doing very much at all. The 'mission from God' became rather less driven. Instead it sort of ambled about a bit, took in the view and told the Arab people to be patient. The 'Freedom Agenda' in the Middle East was put on the back burner. Meanwhile its consequences quietly bubbled on.

The branches that form from big policy initiatives often live long after the roots have been dug up and thrown on the compost heap. And so the American embassy in Tunisia, during the last years of the Bush administration, was still cheerfully cabling back to base about their attempts to spread the word. 'Advancing the President's Free-dom Agenda is Post's number one Mission Strategic Plan goal,' Washington was earnestly informed. 'Some of our outreach efforts involved musical performances that also served as useful vehicles for promoting the Freedom Agenda's underlying values.' One of which was an 'extraordinary fusion of Arab and Appalachian music'.[21]

Democracy was coming to the region, though nobody knew that yet. There was a Freedom Agenda for the Middle East, but its programme would be written by people ashamed of their past and desperate for a future. The era of the Strongman was about to end.

The vanity of the dictators had blinded them to the infirmity of age and the fact that their regimes were well past retirement. The old Middle East was finally ready to collapse under the weight of its contradictions. It just had to start somewhere.

Tunisia was not a place from which the world, or the region, expected great drama. The young revolutionaries in neighbouring Egypt were genuinely embarrassed that it was not they, but the Tunisians, who had started the Arab Spring. Even the few Western academics who studied the country before the uprisings felt duty-bound to explain why 'anyone should bother to write or read a book about Tunisia's modern economic and political development'.[22] There was certainly nothing to indicate what was to come, because 'Revolutionary change [has] never been part of the country's history.'[23]

So what led the Tunisians to kick-start a global event as significant as the revolutions of 1989 that brought to an end the Soviet Union and the Cold War in Europe?

Despite the best efforts of the culture club at the US embassy, it wasn't fiddlers from the Appalachian mountains who finally brought real democracy to the Middle East, though the leaking a few years later of many of the embassy's more candid cables would help to poison the well for the regime. It was actually a couple of home-grown fiddlers performing in the Tunisian capital Tunis who created the mood music for the revolutions of 2011.

Middle-class people don't riot, or at least they didn't before the Arab revolts. Middle-class people, by definition, have something invested in the system. It might not be much but it is theirs. So when trouble breaks out their instincts are normally to moan, not to march. But nothing upsets the middle classes like a show-off. And if the flashy neighbours are showing off with your money, the gardening gloves come off. Tunisia's urban population prided themselves on their worldly sophistication, but when the social contract broke down the country had been reduced to a Mafia state. Sitting at the top, running the show, was a lower-class, badly educated former ladies' hairdresser who had connived her way into everyone else's pockets.

It was 'easy to hate' Leila Ben Ali, agreed the American ambassador to Tunis between 2006 and 2009, Robert F. Godec.[24] Mrs Ben Ali, or Leila Trabelsi, to use her maiden name, was indisputably the most loathed of the regional First Ladies Club. It had been that way for years. The crown was only snatched from her by Asma al-Assad when it was revealed, as Syria began its descent into chaos, that she had spent the early days of the crisis shopping online for Ming vases and luxury goods at Harrods.[25] Until then though, Leila Trabelsi was in a class all of her own. She had married President Ben Ali in 1992, five years after he ousted the Republic's first president, 84-year-old Habib Bourguiba, by announcing his medical 'incompetence' on national radio.[26]

When it was widely reported that Mrs Ben Ali's last act before leaving Tunisia and going into exile had been to fill her private jet with one and a half tonnes of the central bank's gold in handbag-size ingots, worth almost sixty million dollars, it was readily believed by everyone even after the bank swore its assets were still intact.[27] It wasn't that she and her extended family took the occasional backhander. It was that they had had their snouts in every trough in town. This was all catalogued in some wonderfully undiplomatic cables from Ambassador Godec in which he excoriated 'The Family' as he called them. The cables were released by the WikiLeaks site from 28 November 2010. Less than two months later Mr and Mrs Ben Ali were gone.

Ambassador Godec described how:

President Ben Ali's extended family is regularly cited as the nexus of Tunisian corruption. Often referred to as a quasi-mafia, an oblique mention of 'the Family' is enough to indicate which family you mean. Ben Ali's wife, Leila Ben Ali, and her extended family – the Trabelsis – provoke the greatest ire from Tunisians. Along with the numerous allegations of Trabelsi corruption are often barbs about their lack of education, low social status, and conspicuous consumption.[28]

In another cable he described having dinner with the Ben Alis' son-in-law Mohamed Sakher El Materi, who served him 'ice cream and frozen yoghurt he brought in by plane from Saint Tropez' and who 'has a large tiger ("Pasha") on his compound, living in a cage [which] consumes four chickens a day'.[29]

Perhaps if 'The Family' had spent less time feeding the tiger and more throwing a few scraps to its loyalists within the ruling Democratic Constitutional Rally (RCD) its world would not have collapsed so quickly. Instead the party at the centre of what was still effectively a one-party state found it was no longer being invited to sit at the top table. And not only did Ben Ali and his wife suck all the graft out of the system, leaving very little for those lower down the food chain, they also divested the party of any real political power. 'It was not only the Tunisian political space that had been clamped down on all of these years, it was the RCD, and the apparatus of the state,' said Kamal Morjane, a few weeks after his old boss had fled the country. Mr Morjane was once part of the inner circle and served as defence and foreign minister, posts which he said over time became irrelevant. 'Leila Trabelsi controlled everything, the media publicising his foreign and interior policy positions, everything. The ministers were completely stripped of their powers. Even access to the president was totally controlled.'[30] The Americans even had her down as a 'dark horse candidate' to take over formally when her already ailing husband finally died.[31]

All the regimes that fell during the Arab Spring, and all of those that didn't, attempted the same ruse when they thought the street protests were sapping their power. They organised 'spontaneous' rallies of support for the leader. I was present at many of these in various countries. The most amusing one was in Tripoli, when our official driver accidentally took a short cut and we arrived to find the protesters idling around a housing estate, leaning up against their cars, chatting and smoking. Only when we got off the minibuses did they realise that we were early and they were late. They hurriedly pulled their posters off the back seats and started the usual performance, but we both knew this one had not gone well for them, so our minders quickly ushered us back on the bus and drove off.

This sort of thing didn't happen in Tunisia, because the RCD couldn't find enough supporters willing to go through with the panto-mime. The party's last effort to mount a show of support was held on 14 January, just hours before Ben Ali and his clan began making their way to the airport. Some RCD supporters did turn up in 7 November Square, named for the day of Ben Ali's coup, but at the same time there was also an anti-government rally. The pro-government protest-ers promptly swapped sides.[32] The RCD claimed one million members, but it could not organise a single decent demonstration in its support when the country rose up against it.[33] Everyone, it seemed, had had enough of 'The Family' and its culture of corruption, which had permeated deep down into Tunisian society. As the ambassador said:

> Whether it's cash, services, land, property, or yes, even your yacht, President Ben Ali's family is rumored to covet it and reportedly gets what it wants. Beyond the stories of the First Family's shady deal-ings, Tunisians report encountering low-level corruption as well in interactions with the police, customs, and a variety of government ministries.[34]

Despite the stupendous wealth 'The Family' flaunted around the Tuni-sian capital, it would eventually be the ubiquitous low-level corruption which spewed from the regime that would bring them down.

Being young in the Arab world was often an emotionally crippling experience. It was hard for women, who played just as big a role as men in the revolutions; but in societies as patriarchal as those in the Arab world young men saw no opportunity to step up to the role of breadwinner, that helped define their manhood. And just in case they were in any doubt about how bad their lot was, they were reminded every time they interacted with the state. That might be having to find money to pay bribes to venal officials, or random and often violent harassment by the equally corrupt police force. 'Wasta' was the only hope young men had that they might get on in life. 'Wasta' is the Arabic word for what in the West is called 'clout': getting something not because you deserve it or are entitled to it or have earned it, but because you have connections.[35] *Wasta* though is something you acquire over time; you have to be somebody to have *wasta*. So again, young men fast approaching their late twenties would find themselves going to their fathers for help instead of being able to strike out on their own. No job meant no dignity. But according to Professor Assaad:

> It's not just dignity, you cannot become an adult unless you have a job and you cannot marry unless you have a job and so there is this whole issue of transition to adulthood that is associated with having a job and being able to care for a family etc, and they considered the informal jobs that they have to do as a temporary thing that is not satisfactory in its own right and will eventually, hopefully, lead to a permanent job that they can be proud of. Even if that job doesn't pay very much. The fact that they have it, that it's a permanent job, that it's a formal job, has a lot of value, so dignity is part of it, but it's more than dignity, it's essentially being a full member of the society, an adult, a citizen etc.

Nor, for most people, were there many diversions from these woes, because these are socially conservative Muslim societies. They could not drown their sorrows in drink. Not being able to marry often meant not being able to have sex. Using drugs was a world of trouble if you were caught. They did not even have the chance to complain. Democracy is a safety valve. The ability to get together with a bunch of like-minded people and wander down the street hurling abuse at your leaders is a good thing for society. Without it the pressure just grows.

It was the uncontrollable rage of a generation over the prospect of a wasted life that devoured Ben Ali and the other Middle Eastern dictators. It had been bottling up for years. It took a single life to release it. That was given by a young man called Mohamed Bouazizi. Mohamed was twenty-six years old and a street vendor. He sold fruit and vegetables from a wheelbarrow that he pushed along the dusty streets of the small, poor provincial Tunisian town of Sidi Bouzid. He had left school at seventeen to become the sole provider for his widowed mother and his six siblings. He had light brown skin, drawn over high cheekbones that were framed by a thin face. His hair was short, gelled and jet-black. At least, that's how he looked in his second-from-last photograph.

Around midday on Friday 17 December 2010 Mohamed walked to the regional council offices. He stood in front of the high gate, doused himself in gasoline and set himself alight. 'On that day Mohamed left home to go and sell his goods as usual,' said his sister Samya. 'But when he put them on sale, three inspectors from the council asked him for bribes. Mohamed refused to pay. They seized his goods and put them in their car. They tried to grab his scales but Mohamed refused to give them up, so they beat him.'[36]

Bouazizi did not have a licence to sell fruit because getting any kind of official documentation in the Arab world is impossible unless you pay a bribe. It was the state's insidious way of criminalising the entire population and leaving them vulnerable to harassment and prosecution. Bouazizi couldn't get a licence to sell fruit because he could not afford a bribe. He could not afford a bribe because without a licence he wasn't allowed to sell fruit. It was his individual hopeless reaction on that day to just one of the thousands of petty indignities Tunisians had all been forced to swallow their whole lives that set in motion the region's most tumultuous change for more than half a century.

Bouazizi's story resonated with everyone. The poor immediately saw themselves in him. And the rumour mill repackaged him to the educated middle classes as an unemployed university graduate forced into eking out an existence in a menial job. The idea of Bouazizi as 'no ordinary street pedlar' even gained currency in reports by international human rights groups.[37] This version was key to the resonance of his case among the wider population, because while almost 90 per cent of the country was defined as 'middle-class', half that number were categorised as 'living with the ever-present danger of falling into poverty'.[38] The prospect of dropping off the edge had been made worse by a spike in world food prices since 2007. The Arab countries still import up to 80 per cent of their foodstuffs, and so their people are always hit hard.[39] The cost of living was also a key factor in the demonstrations that followed in Egypt, while the situation in Syria was made worse by a five-year drought that destroyed local farming.[40] In Tunisia the two versions of the Bouazizi myth bridged the class divide and united the people.

In his final photo, taken as a publicity shot during a hospital visit by the now increasingly beleaguered President Ben Ali, Mohamed Bouazizi was propped up in a hospital bed with his entire body swathed in bandages. This was all held together with surgical tape. All that was visible of what was left of his face were his charred lips where a gap had been left in the dressings to put the ventilator into his mouth. Ninety per cent of the surface area of his body had been melted away. He existed like this for three weeks and then he died on 4 January 2011. The old Middle East died with him.

Tunisia may not have had a history of revolution until this point, but it had been quietly radical. In 1860 it became the first country in the Arab world to promulgate a constitution.[41] A few years earlier, though under much pressure from the European powers, it had drawn up a civil rights charter known as the Fundamental Pact, which gave Muslims, Christians and Jews equal rights under the law.[42] Just under a hundred years later the region was throwing off the shackles of colonialism. After winning independence President Habib Bourguiba decided his calling was to modernise Tunisia. He used his initial popularity as 'the Father of the Nation' to push through a programme of social engineering that made Tunisia one of the most socially liberal and well-educated countries in the region.

Bourguiba was a masterful schemer and raised political opportunism to an art form. This played a key role in the country's relatively peaceful transition from a French protectorate to an independent state, and would define his leadership afterwards. Tunisia was less important to France than neighbouring Algeria was, and so the

French had no stomach to fight for it as they did next door. Things were settled largely through negotiation and brinkmanship, which played entirely to Bourguiba's strengths. He also bucked the trend towards Pan-Arabism that swept the region as colonisation receded, though this was largely because he had just as big an ego as President Nasser in Cairo and he wasn't ready to play second fiddle to anyone.[43]

He saw Islamic traditions as the biggest obstacle to change, and described the veil as that 'odious rag'. 'It is unthinkable,' he said, 'that half the population be cut off from life and hidden like a disgraceful thing.'[44] His most fundamental reform was the Code of Personal Status introduced in 1956, which 'attacked Tunisia's social structure at its very roots, the family, by abolishing polygamy and making marriage a voluntary contract'.[45] The following year women were given the right to vote. He overhauled and expanded the education system, stripping it of almost all religious instruction.[46] 'We are obliged to throw out the worst customs,' he said.[47] He even attacked the fast during the holy month of Ramadan because he thought it wasted economic effort.[48]

Bourguiba was determined to drag the Tunisians with him along the road to modernisation whether they liked it or not. He was no liberal democrat. When he was asked during the early years of independence about the country's political system, he replied: 'The system? What system? I am the system!'[49] He ran a one-party state and used patronage and the threat of its withdrawal to keep his opponents in check.

'Habib Bourguiba was famous – or perhaps infamous – for his liberal interpretations of the Quran and other Islamic texts. In fact, Bourguiba famously drank juice in Ramadan . . . and [his] views and policies framed the social progress that defines Tunisia today.'[50] That is how the American government still saw his legacy decades after his death.

Bourguiba got himself made president for life in 1974, but the job didn't last that long. As he got older and slid into senility his cronies started thinking about their future after he was gone. The more adventurous saw his growing weakness as an opportunity. Despite his ailing health, Bourguiba lost none of his passion for scheming, but it became more and more irrational. His government first took on and broke the country's powerful labour union. Then in the early 1980s it turned its sights onto an increasingly popular Islamist group, the Islamic Tendency Movement or MIT, led by Rashid Ghannoushi. Ghannoushi's organisation initially trod a moderate path and was committed to non-violent democratic change. The prime minister, Mohamed Mazali, who hoped to replace Bourguiba, waxed and waned over whether it was best to woo or attack the MIT as it grew in size and influence. Despite his illness the president was still lucid enough to spot when his prime minister was running amok, so he sacked him, though the attack on the Islamists continued. That was being led by a former military policeman who had risen in 1986 to become interior minister, Zine al-Abidine Ben Ali.[51] Ben Ali built up the internal security services and went after all comers: union leaders, journalists, human rights groups and, of course, the Islamists. The following October the now quite decrepit Bourguiba declared Ben Ali prime minister, and in November his new prime minister got seven doctors to declare Bourguiba unfit to govern. Ben Ali took his place.

When he took power the conflict with the Islamists had dragged the country to the brink of civil war. Ben Ali was smart enough to recognise just how much of a mess the country had been left in by Bourguiba's increasingly demented machinations and so he sought to defuse the fight with the Islamists. He announced a raft of amnesties, including one for the jailed MIT leader Ghannoushi, and began to make noises about real democracy. What he was actually building though was a walled garden. It gave the illusion that liberalism was blooming, but Tunisian politics remained well sheltered from the winds of change.

For a while the MIT looked for its place in the sun within the new set-up. It changed its name to the 'Renaissance Party', or 'Ennahda', to abide by a rule that banned religious references. Despite all the obstacles placed in its path, including one that stopped its members standing for election under the party banner, Ennahda supporters did well in legislative elections in April 1989.[52] A little too well for Ben Ali and his ruling RCD. Realising where this was likely to head, the Ennahda leader Rashid Ghannoushi left the country, as a campaign of intimidation grew eventually into a full-scale onslaught. He would not return for twenty-two years, until the 2011 revolution was complete. However, in exile: 'Ghannouchi, now trying to direct the movement from abroad, felt compelled to toughen his own rhetoric in order to maintain his base inside Tunisia. By the summer of 1990 he had begun calling for veiling women, suppressing foreign tourism, applying Islamic law more strictly, and a popular uprising against the government.'[53]

This kind of hard-line Islamic rhetoric would come back to haunt Ghannoushi and his party. It was what provoked the suspicions of the crowd with Manal Labidi after the Constituent Assembly results. Many women feared that the religious groups would try to steal both the spoils of their revolution and what little they had gained during the bad old days. They were worried that the Islamists would try to turn back the clock on social reforms.

The secular dictatorships' championing of women's rights gave them a popular stick with which to beat the Islamists. The regimes presented their First Ladies as the symbol of these policies, so the Islamists after the revolutions in both Tunisia and Egypt tried to discredit feminist ideals by associating them with the hated wives of the hated dictators. Women's rights would prove to be one of the biggest areas of dispute in the years that followed the 2011 revolutions. Conservative Islam would constantly seek to redefine the role of women in the new nations that surfaced once the smothering hand of the dictatorships had been removed.

And, for the first time, the rights of religious minorities and the balance between religious and civil law were also up for grabs. Under the old regimes the function of religion in society had been pushed out of what little debate there was. Islam was feared by all the dictatorships because they did not want the people listening to a higher authority than their own. In the urban centres Islam receded from many people's lives and hid quietly in the mosque. When its most fervent supporters occasionally dared to use their voices, the strong arm of the state took them by the throat. In the big cities the state had encouraged material concerns to replace spiritual ones, but in the countryside the state hadn't even tried to buy the people off with the Faustian contract of government subsidies in return for political silence. The rural poor had been given nothing by the state, and so the only thing they had of any value was their faith. The only people who had stood by them were the local imams. After years of being suppressed by the regimes, grass-roots support translated into significant political power for the Islamists after the revolts.

Ben Ali was as ruthless as Bourguiba, but he was even more careful. He did not use the army to do his dirty work, in fact he didn't seem to want anything to do with it at all. Instead he quadrupled the size of the internal security services.[54] The new president cranked up the machinery of state to lay waste to Ennahda.

Under both presidents the army was kept deliberately weak so that it would not emerge as a threat. It had only 35,000 men and had never fought a war. Tunisia spent just 1.4 per cent of its GDP on the military, less than half that of neighbouring Algeria and Libya.[55] It was made up of the rural poor, largely because the middle classes could often bribe their way out of national service.[56] Because the army was marginalised and unloved by the regime it remained apolitical. It didn't have to choose a side when the revolution happened. Ben Ali had made it clear from the start that they weren't on his team. Therefore when the time came it was an easy decision for the army to protect the people from the police and thus secure the revolution.

Over the years Ben Ali built a monster of an internal security force that was at least 150,000 strong.[57] But even then he didn't feel safe, so he built yet another force, the Presidential Guard, to protect him in case his first creation turned against him. The 5,000 members of the Guard were the best paid, the most arrogant and the least liked, even by the other security services.[58] With all that in place, Ben Ali must have felt that he had the country sewn up. He never got less than 89 per cent of the vote in every 'election' that took place. So, having destroyed any opposition, strangled freedom of expression and scared the middle classes into becoming 'grudgingly complicit in Ben Ali's authoritarianism [by] skillfully exploiting their fear of the Islamists', Ben Ali and his wife settled down to doing what they did best.[59] They robbed the country blind.

Ben Ali's was one of the most oppressive and quietly brutal dictatorships in the Middle East. The eyes and ears of the state security apparatus were everywhere. The regime used to claim it had no political prisoners, only criminals, but it defined a criminal as anyone who might present a challenge to the state over just about anything. It used a corrupt justice system to lock them up, and inflicted what Juan Méndez, the UN Special Rapporteur, called the 'notorious and endemic practice of torture' to deter them from doing it again. The revolution itself was broadly portrayed at the time as a relatively smooth transition. In fact the UN said the regime killed around 300 people and 700 more were injured as it fought for its survival during the month-long revolt. The protests may have begun as a small-town affair, but social media and Al Jazeera made sure the word spread quickly. It took just days for the troubles to reach the capital and not much longer before the Ben Alis were heading into exile.

After they had fled in January 2011 with as much of their ill-gotten gains as they could carry, the people they had spent a lifetime mugging started trying to refashion the kleptocracy that had been left behind. The Tunisians quickly put 'The Family' on trial, convicted them in absentia and sentenced them to several decades in jail for theft. A subsequent trial sentenced Ben Ali to life for the killing of protesters during the revolt. Saudi Arabia, where he had flown to exile, refused to extradite him. His countrymen eased their frustrations with a bit of retail therapy and celebrated the second anniversary of the uprising with a month-long public auction of everything the Ben Alis didn't have the time or space to stuff into the private jet. Among the things they left behind was $42 million in cash in a variety of denominations which they had stored in a walk-in closet of their bedroom, which a Tunisian official told me he saw with his own eyes. I asked him where Mrs Ben Ali put her shoes. 'Oh, she had a pavilion for those,' he said with a laugh. But once the January 2013 sale was out of the way, attention shifted back to the real world.

Revolution, once its makers pluck up the courage, is the easy part. It is what follows that is so hard. Every nation that rose up has found this. There is a real 'now what?' moment that hits people once the dictator has gone. Suddenly right and wrong are less obvious. Overnight, people who weren't allowed to decide anything their whole lives have to decide everything. It is not a learning curve, it is a sheer cliff.

In Tunisia the politicians continued their work on the new constitution and preparations for more elections. The young revolutionaries who swept them into power weren't working at all. In the years that followed the revolt unemployment went up, and so did prices. Life got no better for the vast majority of Tunisians. How could it? The country had been left in a financial mess. Foreign investors were waiting to see what happened next before they spent their money.

Tunisia's coalition government was led by Ennahda. It and its partners were still feeling their way on a whole range of issues from the role of Islam to the rights of women. The most pressing issue remains the economy, and it is likely to be several years before it can be turned around.

All the while, tensions simmer and suspicions linger between the secular people and the Islamists. It may not have been hugely popular in the years following the overthrow of the Ben Ali regime, but because it had gone into exile Ennahda was not tainted by it. Unlike the Muslim Brotherhood in Egypt, from which it was spawned, it had not constantly capitulated to the dictatorship. Many Tunisians may not have liked it, but they could not accuse it of years of collusion. But in the view of Olivier Roy, professor of social and political theory at the European University Institute in Florence, this means that its leaders don't yet understand the country they have returned to, and that may be their undoing: 'Ennahda's problem is that it is far less rooted in Tunisian society than the Muslim Brotherhood is in Egypt. The Ennahda people were either in jail or in London, and so they don't know their own society, which is very diverse. They are just far more isolated.' They did not know what to do in a crisis, and a violent minority among Salafist groups exploited that ignorance to push their own agenda. They have smashed up hotels and bars selling alcohol, disrupted art exhibitions and attacked the US embassy. Many believed that they might have been linked to the assassination of the secular opposition leader Chokri Belaid in February 2013 which provoked a crisis in the government and led to the eventual resignation of the prime minister. The political turmoil and violence undermined what had started to look like a slow recovery in the economy.

Tunisia is now a democracy. The trade unions, which played a key role in the uprising, remain extremely powerful. Its society is not afraid to stand up to tyranny. The fact that around a million people took to the streets of the capital Tunis to express their fury at the murder of Mr Belaid says more about the country's future than the handful of violent Salafists trying to drag it into the past. There will inevitably be more acts of violence by these fringe groups. There will also be regular protests against the government by secular demonstrators, and some of those will turn violent too. But Tunisia still promises to be a success story. History has rarely revolved around Tunisia, because outsiders didn't want to fight too hard over it. It has no oil and no strategic importance. It will drop back out of the headlines and it will be the better for it. Tunisia gave the region a new start. Most importantly it was the first Arab state to make the transition to democracy by choice. The afterglow of being the first people to rise up may have worn off, but these are remarkable achievements.

The spontaneous overthrow of authoritarian rulers by the people of overwhelmingly Muslim nations gave the democracies that followed Arab, not American, roots. It undercuts the argument made by the kingdoms in the Gulf that democracy is un-Islamic and unwanted. There may be an argument over where the seed came from, but there is no real debate about who nurtured it and brought it to fruition. That surely makes the democratisation process irreversible in the countries where it has started, and possible where it has not.

'Those who spread the myth that democracy is against Islam are the oppressive regimes and monarchies [in the Gulf] who sell their wealth cheaply to the Americans. Therefore, democracy is a threat to them and they tried to export the idea that democracy is against Islam.' So said Abdul-Moneim Aboul-Fotouh as we sat in his party office in Cairo. For decades he was one of the most influential figures in Egypt's Muslim Brotherhood, which inspired the creation of Ennahda. He left the organisation in 2011 to run for the presidency. 'All the basic principles of democracy are in harmony with Islam. If the people [in the Gulf] are allowed to rule themselves, they will not leave in place oppressive rulers or corrupt princes who steal the country's resources for themselves.'

'Islamists coming to power in places like Tunisia and Egypt is very important,' Princeton's Professor of Near Eastern Studies, Bernard Haykel, told me in late 2012.

Islamists feel for the first time that the West is not going to stop them from coming to power, that's an important thing. If Islamists get their act together, if they manage to run the country properly, then I think there is a very serious challenge to the Saudis. The Saudis and the Muslim Brotherhood compete ideologically on more or less the same terrain, which is Islam and its representation. So the Muslim Brotherhood represents a threat if they get their house in order. I think Egypt in particular is a very important country. If the Egyptians manage to create an order that is transparent, accountable, economically successful, if they reproduce Turkey in Egypt or something even approximating Turkey, then I think that could have a tremendous effect on the whole region. Because people will want that.

As they surfaced from the chaos of the revolutions, many countries began to look at Turkey as a potential model for their societies. It was once under military rule but is now governed by moderate Islamists. After the revolution Egypt's Muslim Brotherhood consulted Turkish officials over the best way to move the generals out of politics. President

Obama has invested heavily in his country's relationship with Turkey, an experience that made him less anxious when Islamists finally came to power in the Arab world. At one stage Ankara had achieved its stated foreign policy aim of 'zero problems with neighbours'. Then things began to unravel with Israel and the Arab Spring created big problems with Syria. Ankara seemed to be ready to play a key role in the early months of the crisis on its southern border, and then seemed to lose its nerve as Syria descended into chaos. Suddenly some of the shine faded from the great Turkish success story. Its aspirations to be the regional leader took a knock. They were further damaged by the anti-government protests in Istanbul and beyond in June 2013.

The dictators were right when they said: 'It's the Islamists or me'; they were wrong when they implied that democracy was not suited to either one of them. America was traumatised by 9/11. Many Muslims around the world were traumatised by its aftermath. The religion of hundreds of millions of people around the globe was and continues to be vilified because of the atrocities carried out in the West by a tiny minority of Global Jihadists. It is hard to find a Muslim in the Middle East who did not feel viscerally distressed by that period.

Now the people of the Arab world have spilt their blood in revolutions to overthrow their dictators and speak for themselves. They used the Arab Spring to try to reclaim their identities from al-Qaeda and Hollywood's central casting. The vast majority of those revolutionaries are religious. The vast majority of them are Muslims. They are Muslims who have fought harder and suffered more for democracy and human rights than most Westerners alive today.

The Arab people finally have the chance to embrace Western-style democracy, but there shouldn't be disappointment when they don't embrace Western-style everything else. Voting like Europeans is not going to make people think like Europeans. The West itself has not reached a shared definition of democracy, so there will be debate on its form in the New Middle East too. Democracy absorbs the flavour of the culture and society it is mixed with. Democracy in the Arab world will have its own flavour too.

It was the people of the Arab world, not the schemes of the Western world, that finally brought democracy to the more despairing corners of the region. Their uprisings wiped away the last vestiges of the Cold War. But there was one more war they brought to a close. This one too had been going on for decades. Men from within the ranks of these two foes had plotted against, schemed with and assassinated the leaderships of the other. They had been revolutionary comrades and implacable foes. They had fought together in desert wars and then tortured their old allies in prison cells. Their arena was what was left of one of the world's great civilisations: Egypt.

The present-day tensions between the secularists and the Islamists in Tunisia are dwarfed in scale by the epic battle that has taken place in Egypt, the dominant Arab state. There, the mother ship of all the region's Islamists groups, the Muslim Brotherhood, has been in a long war with the Grandaddy of secular Arab nationalism, the Egyptian army. It has been a clash of the regional Titans. Because the outcome of this conflict will shape the future of Egypt, that means it will also shape the New Middle East.

Egypt's Long War

I: THE BATTLE BEGINS

'I can't believe we've won, I can't believe we've won!' shouted a man to me over the noise of the chants and firecrackers as Cairo's Tahrir Square exploded into an ecstatic mix of joy and relief. The people had ousted 'the Last Pharaoh', the Egyptian president Hosni Mubarak. They had ended three decades of his dictatorial rule in the most populous and important Arab country. It was a seminal moment in the Middle East. It would begin to redefine the entire region.

The heroes of the hour were the army. I watched the crowds lifting the soldiers onto their shoulders. The uniformed young men sat grinning above a sea of flags, their faces framed by fireworks that were exploding overhead. 'The people and the army are one hand,' the crowd chanted. State TV had just broadcast the announcement by the recently appointed vice-president and former intelligence chief Omar Suleiman that Mubarak's rule was over. On the streets outside their studios I watched toddlers being handed up to soldiers still sitting in their tanks as proud parents captured the moment on their camera-phones.

It was the night of Friday, 11 February 2011, and it seemed the army had chosen the people over the dictator. Its standing had never been higher. It would require a remarkable amount of incompetence to squander that much good will, but over the coming months the old generals proved they were more than up to the task as they mismanaged their way from public adoration to public enemy number one. If the tens of thousands of people with me at that moment had known what was to follow, they would not have left the square and headed home that night. They would have realised that their revolution was not yet over. They would have understood that while the man had gone, the regime he helped to create was still alive, and would soon be kicking against the freedoms the revolutionaries in Tahrir Square thought they had just won.

The army leadership had removed Mubarak, not to protect the people but to safeguard itself. Nothing more typifies the shamelessness of the old order in Egypt than the whereabouts of the man whom Mubarak apparently chose as his confidant and confessor as he felt his power slipping away. Every night of his last five days in power, Hosni Mubarak, hero of the 1973 war against Israel and former air chief marshal, revealed his innermost feelings to a retired army general at the other end of a phone line in the land of his old enemy, Israel.

Binyamin Ben-Eliezer was born in Basra in Iraq. When he moved to Israel at the age of thirteen, he changed his name from Fouad, but that was the name Mubarak called him by throughout their long friendship. The walls of Ben-Eliezer's cramped little office in the Israeli parliament, the Knesset, are plastered with photographs of him meeting Arab and world leaders. Most are rather formal-looking, but the one in the centre of the wall shows two old men caught in a roar of laughter. 'I had the feeling that with me, he felt like he was speaking with his brother,' Ben-Eliezer told me. 'Our relationship became very deep from the time I was appointed Israel's minister for defence in 2001.' They had known each other for twenty years. Ben-Eliezer has denied claims that he was so close to Mubarak he was even on the government payroll.[1]

In the first night he said: 'Fouad, Cairo is not Tunis,' but by the second night he said: 'Yes, there is a revolution.' The third, fourth and fifth night was all criticisms of the Americans. He was very angry, very sad, he couldn't understand why after he served the

West for thirty years they came with the great idea of democracy, he said: 'Tell me how I can implement democracy to sharia law, how I can implement democracy when the majority of the women are wearing [the veil].'

Ben-Eliezer described the moment Mubarak told him he was step-ping down. It would be a full twenty-four hours before the people in Tahrir Square and the entire Egyptian nation would learn of the deci-sion. It was also the final time the two men would speak. 'The last night before he shifted to Sharm el-Sheikh, I said: "What's happened to you?" and he told me: "Listen, [Field Marshal Mohamed] Tantawi advised me to go to Sharm el-Sheikh. Don't worry, he's guaranteed my security and my honour."'

I asked Ben-Eliezer what made Mubarak realise his time was over.

No one told him to go, but once he felt the Americans are pushing him to go away then I think he lost confidence, then he was listening to Omar Suleiman, because he was very close to him, and I under-stand Omar Suleiman slowly, slowly, told him there is no chance. I know one thing, this I know from him, he said: 'Tantawi told me everything will be alright,' that's what I know.

It was not all right. Mubarak was sacrificed because the army was less worried about losing him than losing to the organisation they had been fighting for decades, the Muslim Brotherhood. The army and the Brotherhood, then still a banned organisation, were the two most powerful forces in the land. They had been slugging it out for years, but now they both knew the final round was coming. The only ques-tion for the army the night it toppled Mubarak was which one of them would eventually emerge from the revolution as the victor.

The generals had reasons to worry. Since 1979 the United States had given Egypt an average of US$2 billion a year, of which by far the most was military aid. The combined total made Egypt the second-largest recipient of US aid money after Israel.[2] A Western diplomat told me his country believed millions of dollars of that military aid was siphoned off to plough into the army's business ventures. No one knew for sure how much of the country's economy it controlled. Estimates varied wildly from 5 to 30 per cent. Whatever the figure, everyone agreed that in a sea change the Egyptian army had much at stake. A new vindictive government would have a lot to get its teeth into.

Exactly 500 days after the army announced that Mubarak was stepping down, Egypt was about to be told who its new head of state was. There were once again tens of thousands of people packed into Tahrir Square. Yet in stark contrast to the crowds that waited for the announcement of the end of the Mubarak era, their chants rising up into the night air, the gathering on Sunday 24 June 2012 was disciplined and silent. This was the same square, but not the same sector of society that had basked in the earlier moment of triumph. The night Mubarak fell, Tahrir was packed with men, women and children. I met Muslims and Christians. There was the secular youth who started the revolution and the Islamists who helped finish it. There were the dirt-poor and the very rich. Throughout the protests I had always found the full spectrum of the country's often chaotic society standing alongside me. On that cold February night Tahrir Square had belonged to all of Egypt. But on this hot summer's afternoon a year and a half later it belonged to the Muslim Brotherhood.

In the end, after a tortuously self-indulgent preamble by Farouq Sultan, the head of the Presidential Election Commission and chairman of the Supreme Constitutional Court, the results were read out.

The Muslim Brotherhood was not a revolutionary organisation either by deed or design, but the voice droning over the loudspeaker system told its supporters that they had taken what spoils remained from an uprising they had not started. They erupted in jubilation. By nightfall what had begun as an almost exclusively Brotherhood party was again like the one that had celebrated the downfall of Mubarak. A broader mix of Egypt was now on the streets. But the new arrivals were not there because of the victory of the Brotherhood's Mohamed Morsi. They had come to celebrate the failure of one of the *'feloul'* (the Arabic word for remnants) of the regime. In the final round of voting Morsi had been up against Mubarak's last prime minister, Ahmed Shafiq. Shafiq was seen as the army's preferred candidate.

'We always have Tahrir' was the reaction to every setback the revolution faced. The Square had taken on a mythical role in the democratic process. So, late into the night, the crowd allowed themselves the luxury of forgetting that their voyage from dictatorship to democracy had won them a president elected to a post which a few days earlier had been stripped almost bare of its powers by the generals running the Supreme Council of the Armed Forces, SCAF.

Egypt had staged the first free and fair elections for a head of state in its five thousand years of history. And yet, after the people had spent their lives, the country had a seemingly impotent presidency, no parliament, no sign of the long-promised constitution, and a military junta still in charge as it had been since the republic was created almost sixty years before.

The history of the long war between the generals and the Muslim Brotherhood is important because it has shaped modern Egypt and has often set the parameters for its engagement with the outside world. Egypt's Muslim Brotherhood is the most important non-state actor in the region. Its offshoots have fought battles against or formed alliances with every player in the Arab world. It introduced political Islam to the region, and it is this force that will fashion the New Middle East.

Until the revolution of 2011 the Muslim Brotherhood had survived for over eighty years by working within the boundaries set by the system. It had managed to navigate its way through the ocean of bureaucracy and oppression with which the state had surrounded it. It had emerged intact after the revolt, but its years of flexibility had also given it a reputation for slipperiness. This willingness to compromise on almost every issue, its trademark 'pragmatism', is a legacy of its founding father, Hasan al-Banna. What was beyond reproach though was the integrity and dedication to the cause of many of its ordinary members, including much of the leadership. Unlike the leaders of Ennahda in Tunisia, the vast majority had not escaped into exile. Over

the years ten of thousands of its members had endured torture, imprisonment and persecution. None of the Brotherhood's leadership in
Egypt escaped prison. Most of the leadership were tortured. Until after
the fall of Mubarak it had been an illegal organisation. Its presence in
the lives of millions of people, either because of direct membership or
through its social welfare programmes, was the worst-kept secret in
Egypt. It was everywhere; it just wasn't everywhere officially.

Despite being one of the most important movements of the last
century, the Muslim Brotherhood is not very well understood outside
the region. A poll carried out in 2013 found that the first word Americans thought of when asked about the Muslim Brotherhood was
'terrorists'.[3] Successive Egyptian governments cultivated the idea that
it had a secret, dark agenda for world and local domination, a plan to
restore an Islamic caliphate. That scare tactic played well both at home
and abroad. It gained currency partly because the Brotherhood was
forced by the regime to spend much of its existence in the shadows of
Egyptian society, and partly because when it did pop its head up it
rarely seemed able to provide a straight answer to a straight question.

Then the rise of al-Qaeda and 9/11 seemed to provide the elusive
smoking gun, because, the wider world learned, the Brotherhood had
links to some of modern history's most notorious Islamist extremists.
The inspiration for the ideology of al-Qaeda came from one of its
members, Sayyid Qutb. Ayman al-Zawahiri, the man who took over
from Osama bin Laden had also once belonged to the movement.
The fact that the Brotherhood had decades earlier rejected the ideals
of these figures was lost in the swirl of the post-9/11 era. Even so, the
Brotherhood had not renounced offshoots like the militant group
Hamas in Gaza, which though seen by the Arab world as participat-
ing in legitimate armed resistance to Israeli occupation, was seen by
Western governments as a terrorist group. Tying the Brotherhood to
the wrong side of the 'War on Terror' was not hard for those inclined
towards that narrative, even if the world jihadi community actually
mocked the Brotherhood, and Hamas, for conducting jihad 'for the
sake of territory' rather than for the sake of Allah.[4]

But the rank and file of the Brotherhood today, as they were before 9/11, are no more inclined towards blowing up themselves, or anyone else, than Christian conservatives in the United States. In fact when it comes to social issues like the sanctity of marriage, alcohol, pornography, etc., these two groups largely share the same set of values, though they reached them via very different paths. The Brotherhood too draws much of its membership from the educated middle class.

I met Somaya Hamdy in Tahrir Square on the first anniversary of the revolution. She was trying to steer a large pram and two small children, Memma who was six and Sohail who was three, through a swarm of people. She was in her twenties and wore jeans, a tight white top, and had a fashionable denim handbag slung over her shoulder. Over her head she wore a long aquamarine-coloured scarf, which framed a pretty face devoid of make-up. She had come with the kids to celebrate the day. '[The Brotherhood] are not radicals as some people are saying about them,' she told me. 'This is all propaganda from the last government, they used to arrest them all the time and paint a bad picture of them but they are not like that.' That may be largely true now, but it had not always been. The Brotherhood's founder had set up a big tent in Egypt, and though the likes of Somaya had always been welcome inside it, so were those who wanted to return Egyptian society to the time of the Prophet and a form of Islam they saw as superior to that which had been polluted by modernity. That was an aim some members of the Brotherhood were once willing to kill and die for.

The generals and the Brotherhood had been battling it out for generations, long before Somaya was born. Not once during that time had the people who paid the price been asked what they wanted. In 2011 they had risen up against the old order and the people had decided that, for now, the Muslim Brotherhood was the lesser of two evils. A movement steeped in a ritual of compromise had finally abandoned its political traditions and sought to lead. It had gambled that now, finally, was its moment of triumph, but in an echo of past betrayals the generals had once again snatched it from their grasp. In the summer of 2012, by stripping all the newly elected institutions of their powers, a Western diplomat in Cairo told me, the Egyptian army had reached 'the zenith of their powers' and the Brotherhood seemed to have lost again.

Hasan al-Banna founded the Society of the Muslim Brothers, al-Ikhwan al-Muslimun, in 1928. At the time he was a primary school teacher in the city of Isma'iliyah. It was there al-Banna saw the humiliation heaped on Egyptians living under British colonial rule.[5] Within twenty years his movement had become the biggest Islamic organisation in the country, with around half a million members.[6] Much like the young Internet activists of the twenty-first century, al-Banna used the social networks of the day to spread his message and gather new recruits. Instead of the Internet he used grassroots activism and word of mouth in mosques, welfare associations and neighbourhood groups. The substance of their message was simple – 'Islam is the solution' – though it was never as clearly and publicly articulated as that until the Brother-hood coined the phrase for its 1987 parliamentary election campaign.

Al-Banna's philosophy was aimed at turning Egypt, eventually, into a state governed by the teachings and values of Sunni Islam. Like the more radical Islamists who would follow, his movement was provoked by the culture shock of having Western values and ideas imposed on society, in Egypt's case through the British occupation and their co-opted lackeys in the ruling class. Al-Banna wanted to change Egyptian society through teaching and persuasion, not force, though he was willing to bend his own rules under the weight of the Brotherhood's more radical members.

Al-Banna was one of the greatest CEOs of his time. He created a fabulously successful brand, he was a brilliant organiser, and he was ready to adapt his product to suit the changing market. But just like many other CEOs, he found as his organisation grew that he needed help to run it, and then the 'help' began to have ideas of their own. Eventually the schoolteacher found he wasn't radical enough for some of his pupils.

Militarism being the mood of the movement, it was inevitable that al-Banna would create a paramilitary wing. If he wanted to be relevant to young people he had to give them a sense that they were going to participate in the nationalist struggle for the liberation of Egypt and also the 'liberation' of Palestine, which became the cause of all causes in the Arab world in the late 1930s.[7]

Al-Banna created the Al-Nizam al-Khas, or Special Apparatus. It began carrying out violent attacks against the occupying British forces and assassinations of members of the Egyptian elite whom it saw as collaborating with the colonial power. The West would soon start making its mind up over what it thought the Brotherhood was. 'El Banna . . . put together the tightest-disciplined assortment of cutthroats and idealists in the country, half a million fanatics . . . reaching into every wadi in Egypt,' reported *Time* magazine in January 1954. 'Objective of the Ihkwan el Muslimin: expel the foreigners, return Egypt to the simple brotherhood of primitive, eighth-century Islam. The Ihkwan battle-cry: "We will knock at the doors of heaven with the heads of the British." '[8] A version of that view of the Brotherhood still exists around the world today.

By the late 1940s the Brotherhood was a formidable political power in the country. In 1948 members of the Ikhwan joined the five Arab armies that attacked the new state of Israel which had been declared on 14 May that year. The Brotherhood's men took up arms hoping to find glory in the first Arab–Israeli war, but like the other Arab armies they were left reeling after being thoroughly beaten by the tiny nation they had assumed would be a pushover. The creation of the state of Israel and its subsequent hammering of the invading armies disgraced the leaders of the Arab world in the eyes of their people. It also left hundreds of thousands of Palestinians as refugees. The collective shock at the time led to a group of young Egyptian officers, including a man called Gamal Abdel Nasser, setting a course that would eventually topple the country's monarchy.

The first warning that King Farouk's days on the throne were numbered came with the return of the Brotherhood's fighters, who like the regular army placed the blame for their defeat on the battle-field at the door of the Palace and its government.[9]

The Brotherhood led waves of riots and protests that culminated with the prime minister Mahmoud Fahmi al-Nuqrashi approving a decree dissolving the movement on 8 December 1948.[10] Twenty days later that act cost him his life. The decree and the arrests that followed sent al-Banna's carefully structured hierarchy into convulsions. He lost control of the organisation, and the organisation lost control of its senses. As al-Nuqrashi walked into the interior ministry on 28 December he was shot first in the back and then, as he turned, in the front by a 23-year-old member of the Brotherhood who had dressed himself as an officer. Al-Banna tried to negotiate with the new prime minister, but then another member of the Brotherhood tried to bomb a courthouse the following January. Although al-Banna condemned the men who carried out the violence, saying: 'They are neither brothers, nor are they Muslims,' the government was done talking.[11] At the same time al-Banna's words infuriated many of his followers.

Isolated from the fractured remains of his life's work, al-Banna wrote his final pamphlet. In it he laid the blame for the bloodshed at the door of the authorities for dissolving the movement and locking up the moderating hand of the Brotherhood's leadership. He said the British and the Zionists were the hidden hand behind the ban. He also disassociated the movement from the violent actions of its members, saying they had operated alone.[12]

The only anomaly in the authorities' actions at that time was that they had not jailed al-Banna himself. He interpreted the 'failure of the government to arrest him [as] his official death warrant'.[13] It was served as the evening drew down on 12 February 1949. As he climbed into a taxi outside the Young Men's Muslim Association building in Cairo he was shot; he died shortly afterwards in a hospital.[14]

The king's men didn't know it then, but their regime, which probably had al-Banna killed, was also about to reach the end of its life.

'Within the Arab circle there is a role wandering aimlessly in search of a hero,' wrote Gamal Abdel Nasser in his book *Egypt's Liberation*, published in 1955:

For some reason it seems to me that this role is beckoning to us to move, to take up its lines, put on its costumes and give it life. Indeed, we are the only ones who can play it. The role is to spark the tremendous latent strengths in the region surrounding us to create a great power, which will then rise up to a level of dignity and undertake a positive part in building the future of mankind.[15]

Nasser was consumed by a sense of purpose for himself and the Arab people. When he and his Free Officers toppled King Farouq in July 1952, ushering in the end of British domination, they began the rule of Egypt by Egyptians for the first time in two and a half thousand years. Two years later he celebrated his revolution by officially renaming Cairo's central square as 'Tahrir' or Liberation Square. Nasser would go on to become one of the most influential people on the planet.

Many in the Brotherhood assumed that, having fought alongside the army and shared its aims for national self-determination, this would be a new era for them too. Around a third of the officers in the army during the king's time were said to be part of the organisation.[16] It has been claimed that Nasser too was once a member. The army and the Ikhwan were co-conspirators in Egypt's first revolution, but just as in the uprising that followed nearly sixty years later, the Brotherhood stayed out of the limelight, and for similar reasons. '[There was] agreement among all concerned that open participation of the Society would assure automatic Western intervention in the revolution and its destruction.'[17] The Ikhwan hoped that in return for their support the army would introduce Islamic rule.

This was a key moment. The two sides had to choose between working together and attempting to destroy each other. It would be the latter. This was when the long war began.

It was largely al-Banna's charisma that enabled him to build the Brotherhood into such a large movement. He was able to attract support from many tiers of Egyptian society. The Brotherhood still tried to use that 'everyman' appeal after his death, but the 'man of the people' role was something Nasser wanted for himself, and that would require the removal of any alternative offering. He took on and decimated the Brotherhood, and then began to project his own vision for the future. He rallied the region with the same call that sixty years later would be used against the military regime he created: dignity for the Arab people. While the remnants of the Brotherhood languished in jail, Nasser would attempt to fill the vacuum they left behind with his own movement, Pan-Arabism.

The Brotherhood was being run during Nasser's heyday by al-Banna's replacement, Hasan al-Hodeibi, a compromise candidate who suited nobody in the movement. He was told soon after taking up his position by members of the Special Apparatus that: 'We want nothing from you; you need not even come to the headquarters . . . We will bring the papers for you to sign or reject as you will . . . We only want a leader who will be a symbol of cleanliness.'[18]

At this crucial moment in its history al-Hodeibi would prove to be a disaster for the Ikhwan. His refusal to even attempt to live up to the standards set by his predecessor and his constant bungling of the relationship with the army's Revolutionary Command Council, RCC, eventually led to paralysis in the organisation's leadership. After the revolution the junta needed the credibility of the Brotherhood while it found its feet. It made the right noises and gestures – the leadership, including Nasser, even joined the annual pilgrimage to al-Banna's tomb.[19] In January 1953 the Brotherhood's pragmatism hit new heights when it connived in the abolition of all parties and groups while it was given an exemption.[20] But the RCC was just biding its time. The Ikhwan stood by as the army picked off its enemies one by one until their own turn finally came.

First the RCC tried to wreck the Brotherhood from within by promoting an internal leadership coup. When that failed they used the Brotherhood's own complicity against it. In January 1954 the movement was declared a political party and banned under the same law it had supported the year before. Then Nasser showed he would be ruthless with all his challengers.

When the coup against the king was announced on national radio by one of the Free Officers group, Anwar Sadat, it was done in the name of the new commander-in-chief of the armed forces, General

Muhammad Naguib.[21] When the institution of the monarchy was abolished in June 1953 and Egypt was declared a republic, Naguib became its first president. But, like al-Hodeibi's in the Ikhwan, his position was also largely symbolic: the power rested with Nasser.

Naguib tried to rein in Nasser and briefly got the ban on the Brotherhood and other political parties lifted, but his days in power were numbered. The Ikhwan was still bordering on dysfunctional. Once again its members would try to take the movement's destiny into their own hands; once more that would be disastrous.

Nineteen fifty-four would prove to be a tumultuous year, and decisive for Egypt. It turned around the evening of 26 October, when as Nasser was giving a speech before a crowd in Alexandria, a member of the Ikhwan stood up and 'fired eight wild shots' at a distance of forty feet.[22] The closest shattered a lamp above his head, but Nasser stood firm.[23] His coolness under fire, and the inability of his would-be assassin to shoot straight, turned him into a living legend. It also gave him the ammunition he needed to see off all his rivals.

'To be shot at and missed is a happy state of affairs for a Middle Eastern leader,' reported the *Economist* magazine at the time. 'Multitudes deduce that Allah did not will his end and so the crowds applauded Colonel Nasser after his escape from assassination.'[24] Another reporter in Cairo reflected that the incident was 'the moment of truth for Gamal Nasser; it gave him the inspiration and the chance to step from the background and assume open command'.[25] Six members of the Brotherhood were tried and hanged; thousands more were arrested; the organisation was almost destroyed.

The attempted assassination also gave Nasser the opportunity to deal with the irritant of a president who thought he was there to preside. During the trial Naguib was improbably implicated in the plot. Nasser had him dismissed. It was improbable because even the Ikhwan leadership were ignorant about the plan. The hopeless assassin was selected for his task by the entirely unconstrained Special Apparatus unit. Despite being tagged as fanatical by the Western media, the Special Apparatus knew its limits. One early incarnation of the plot to kill Nasser involved a suicide bombing. Someone was supposed to wear a belt of dynamite, get close to Nasser and blow them both up. 'There were no volunteers,'[26] so they found a 'round-faced shock-haired man' called Mahmoud Abdul Latif, a tinsmith from Cairo, to shoot him.[27] Latif, a member of the Brotherhood since 1938, had been selected for his task two months earlier.[28] He sobbed his way through the court formalities that would condemn him to death, accusing the Brotherhood of duping him into his crime.[29]

The entire process of trying the Brotherhood members was a farce. One of the three judges, who was himself from the military, spent the proceedings abusing and heckling the witnesses, declaring at one stage: 'See, people! There is the Brotherhood. They're all liars.'[30] The defendants all turned on each other, abandoning any loyalty to the movement. 'Egyptians openly laughed at the Brotherhood as, one by one, its high dignitaries, shorn of their imposing beards, shambled forward to stammer confessions and recriminations like so many cringing schoolboys,' wrote a reporter in the court.[31]

The conspiracy was likely confined to just a handful of the Cairo branch of the Special Apparatus, but it is impossible to know for sure because the 'confessions', which were largely obtained by or through the threat of torture, implicated almost everyone.[32] The courts and the media produced an array of 'evidence' that proved that 'the Brothers were the agents and lackeys of the monarchy, the ruling classes, the British, the French, the Zionists, Western Imperialism, communism, and capitalism'.[33] The leadership was accused of everything from homosexuality to serial adultery and theft. It was, in short, not a fair trial.

On 5 December 1954 seven death sentences were announced for those found directly implicated in the plot. But al-Hodeibi had his sentence commuted to life with hard labour, because the government said 'he was an old and sick man who was under the influence of terrorists'.[34] Other leaders were also given long prison terms. Hours before the verdicts were read out, Nasser announced the RCC was once again dissolving the Muslim Brotherhood, and this time it would stick.[35]

This was the Brotherhood's lowest point in its struggle with the army. It would face other crises and brutal crackdowns, but none of the severity of this one. The ban on the organisation would only be lifted after the membership's great-grandchildren had taken to the streets in January 2011. Having beaten all his opponents, Nasser could now concentrate on reshaping the Middle East in his image.

I've often heard Egyptians being mocked by other Arabs for taking themselves too seriously. Many nations in the Middle East owe their creation to a small bunch of meddling Europeans drawing lines on maps over a cup of tea. In those countries a sense of nationhood was often tempered by clan or sectarian loyalties. Egypt, though, was created by the Egyptians, and the pride they have in their identity runs deeper than in most parts of the Arab world. Because that was lacking among other peoples in the region Nasser offered to fill the gap for them: pride in their identity as Arabs instead.

Nasser began his reign by playing the two Cold War rivals, America and the Soviet Union, off against each other to build up his military might. By 1956 he had consolidated his grip on power and settled on the Soviets. 'I know everything that goes on in this country,' he told a reporter. 'I run everything myself.'[36] He was ready for his first big play on the global stage.

Nasser had already managed to humiliate the old colonial master, Britain. A deal done in 1954 meant the last British troops left Egypt after seventy-four years on 13 June 1956. A month later Nasser added insult to British injuries after he had been left 'mad as hell' by a decision by the Eisenhower administration to withdraw its financial support for the huge Aswan dam project that Nasser saw as totemic of his vision for the Arab world.[37] A week after his ambassador was told that the US didn't think Egypt could afford it, Nasser came up with a way that they could. He seized control of the Suez Canal, the most important stretch of water in the world and a lifeline for the economies of the European powers. The nationalisation of the Suez Canal infuriated the British and the French, who already loathed Nasser. World opinion at the time was largely divided on Cold War lines: 'London's Tory Daily Mail calls him "Hitler on the Nile." The Peking press coos: "Egyptian brother."

France's Premier Guy Mollet has called him "a megalomaniac" dictator . . . The Cairo press calls him "savior of the people," the Israelis say
"highway robber," "treacherous wolf." '38

It was in concert with the Israelis that France and Britain planned their
riposte. They persuaded the Israelis to attack Egypt so that they could
then pretend to step in as a peacekeeping force and secure the water-
way. All three parties conspired to deceive the Americans with their
ruse, leaving President Eisenhower, who was a week away from elections for his second term, furious with them all. 'Nothing justifies
double-crossing us,' he complained.39 The French and British invaded
the Canal Zone region on 31 October 1956 and were then forced into
a humiliating withdrawal just weeks later after immense pressure from
Washington. During the Suez Crisis Israel captured Egypt's Sinai
Peninsula. When they eventually pulled out they were replaced with a
United Nations force that acted as a buffer between the two sides.

The Suez Crisis signalled a key shift in geopolitics and it forced
America to rethink its policy in the Middle East. The Americans
believed the Suez fiasco proved the Arab world couldn't be left to the
Europeans to manage any more. From that moment on the European
powers lost much of their influence in the region. The Middle East
became America's backyard. Suez is seen by many as the full stop at
the end of Britain's time as a Great Power.

Nasser emerged triumphant. Despite his military losses he had seen
off the two most meddling European powers, Great Britain and France.
Almost every person in the Arab world would have had first-hand experience of the insult of being second-class citizens to these two nations,
of being just 'wogs', as the British used to call the Egyptians. Now the
town bullies had been given a good hiding. The diplomatic intrigue
surrounding the incident did not even register. As far as the Arab people
were concerned, Nasser had thrown the decisive punch, and they rallied
to him as to no other Arab leader before or since.

The first consequence of the Suez Crisis was that in the Arab world
Nasser was now 'The Boss'. He used his charisma and stature to

launch his project in earnest. He embraced the new technology of the day to spread his message using his 'Voice of the Arabs' Cairo radio station to broadcast a call for Pan-Arab unity. The voice of Nasser floating across the airwaves inspired another young officer, Muammar Gaddafi, to launch his own revolt. 'Tell President Nasser we made this revolution for him,' Gaddafi told one of Nasser's ministers after he had overthrown his own monarchy.[40] Shortly before his death Nasser would repay the compliment. 'You know, I rather like Gaddafi,' he said. 'He reminds me of myself when I was that age.'[41]

At home Nasser's socialism built a new middle class in Egypt on the back of a hugely expanded social welfare programme and an enormous government bureaucracy that gave millions of people jobs for life. In the decades that followed it outlived its usefulness, but none of his successors found a way to reform it, leaving the state today saddled with a bloated, creaking system that rewards sloth and corruption.

Abroad, Nasser sent his spies throughout the Middle East to ferment dissent:

> During a 1966 visit, former [US] Treasury Secretary Robert Anderson told him: 'Mr. President, the U.S. Government has received complaints from every Arab government of subversive activity by your people.' Nasser, feebly professing surprise, said that surely there were at least one or two states where nothing had ever been attempted. 'Mr. President,' Anderson said, 'there are no exceptions.'[42]

But Pan-Arabism was never achieved. The only thing the Arab leaders shared was a sense of self-importance and desire to put their own interests first. The Arab people may have yearned for unity, but the various attempts to forge permanent alliances between states during and after Nasser's reign all failed. North Yemen joined them to create the United Arab States, but Egypt's dominance and the geographical separation between them doomed the project. Egypt's union with Syria, the United Arab Republic, lasted only three years before collapsing in 1961. The Arab Federation of Iraq and Jordan collapsed in six months. Nasser's young disciple Colonel Gaddafi tried the project again by forming the Federation of Arab Republics, which lasted for five years, but existed in name only. His later effort to create an Arab Islamic Republic between Libya and Tunisia was stillborn.

The Brotherhood would not begin its recovery until after Nasser's death, which was hastened by the hammering his army took when it fought and lost to Israel in the 1967 'Six Day War'. Like his army, Nasser was crushed by the defeat. He resigned and then allowed himself to be called back by popular demand, but he was a shadow of the man he had been. He had blamed the outcome of the 1948 war on the Egyptian leadership he had overthrown. This catastrophic defeat of the Arab armies was largely of his own making. Nasser found enough energy, just before his death, to interfere in the Jordanian civil war of 1970 between the monarchy and Palestinian militants, but these were Pan-Arabism's death throes. The war in 1967 killed it off and the same war still physically shapes much of the struggle for land between the Israelis and Palestinians today.

It also began to shape the Arab view of America. Nasser's actions had finally united the Arab world, but only in a shared sense of humiliation. The anger that flowed from that was channelled by the Arab states back towards Israel and increasingly towards the US. The Arab nations believed that Washington had given Israel the green light to stage its attack.

The new president, Anwar Sadat, tried to present himself as a more pious figure than his predecessor, but this was largely just a way to assert his leadership against the Nasserists. In doing so he slowly brought the Muslim Brotherhood back to life. But those men who began to be released from jail were less influenced by the teachings of al-Banna than by a man who was little known at the time by the outside world but whose philosophy would arguably lead to some of the most traumatic incidents of the century that would follow.

The story published in the *New York Times* of the execution of Sayyid Qutb in Cairo on 29 August 1966, along with two other members of the Muslim Brotherhood, was only four sentences long. Just over thirty-five years later reams of column inches would be taken up around the world describing his life and ideology after 'a consensus [emerged] that the "road to 9/11" traces back to him'.[43] Qutb was described as the 'intellectual grandfather to Osama bin Laden and his fellow terrorists'.[44]

Sayyid Qutb was one of the few really influential voices to emerge from the Ikhwan, but he wasn't of its making. He joined the group in 1953, by which time he was already in his late forties and a recognised Islamic scholar. He entered the fold only because he decided he had to pick a side as the relationship between the army and the Brotherhood slid into open warfare.[45]

It has been argued that his loathing of Western society was driven by the two years he had previously spent in the United States on a scholarship sponsored by the Egyptian Ministry of Education, where he worked. In his own writings he detailed his disgust with Western morality, which was undoubtedly shaped by incidents such as a 'beautiful, tall, semi-naked' woman trying to get into bed with him on the boat going over.[46] Matters weren't helped by the fact that she was drunk and collapsed on the floor outside when he kicked her out of his cabin. What he found when he got off the boat also greatly offended his sensibilities.

But what really radicalised Qutb was not the thought of being confined in a small space with a beautiful woman but actually being confined in a small space with a bunch of sadistic Egyptian prison guards. He was arrested four years after his return from the US during the crackdown on the Ikhwan after the failed assassination attempt on Nasser in 1954.

The world wasn't changed by what Sayyid Qutb said, it was changed by what the people who listened to him did. Some scholars have reacted to his demonisation by asserting that the 'ambiguity in his thought was partly to blame'[47] and that 'it is unwise to assume a direct link between Sayyid Qutb and Usama bin Laden'.[48] There is some evidence for that argument in the sense that his insistence that modern Muslim societies had been polluted by Western thought and needed to return to the pure model of the Prophet's era resonated with an entire generation of young Egyptian Islamists who did not turn to violence. Qutb's thoughts also inspired the thinking of men like the Tunisian Rashid Ghannoushi and many of the modern and moderate leaders of Egypt's Muslim Brotherhood.

But while the argument can be made that Qutb would not have approved of the mass murder of civilians, it is clear that his ideas were both the loaded gun and the justification for pulling the trigger of those that did. While he was locked up and being tortured he rewrote and expanded much of his earlier more moderate thinking to produce his seminal work *Milestones*, which reflected his new radicalised outlook. His were the words of an angry, tortured man. These words would inspire the men who brought down the Twin Towers of the World Trade Center in New York and the man who sent them and hundreds of other Islamic extremists around the world to carry out other appalling acts of violence.

'Qutb's writings represented an exceptional state of mind because it represents the suffering of torture and abuse in prison. There is no doubt that I respect Qutb's bravery, although I disagree with his thoughts, which never represented the mainstream Muslim Brotherhood's way of thinking,' said Abdul-Moneim Aboul-Fotouh, who was a member of the Brotherhood's highest governing body, the Guidance Bureau, for more than twenty years. He was also imprisoned for long periods by the Egyptian military. The shared experience of jail and, for many in the leadership, torture bound the group together throughout the years of the dictatorship. It only began to unravel after the revolution. Aboul-Fotouh told me he was also once a 'fundamentalist' in his youth, but over time he helped shape and rebuild the Ikhwan into a more moderate organisation after the Nasser years. 'I consider Qutb's ideas a danger to the Islamic movement worldwide much more than it is for the Muslim Brotherhood. The latter by nature not only read Qutb, they also read al-Banna and others. The other foreign Islamic movements were negatively affected by Qutb's thought because he is all they read.'

Sayyid Qutb's critique of Islamic societies and what he saw as their failure to follow the true path of Islam went well beyond the teachings of al-Banna or any other Islamic scholar of his era. Al-Banna wanted Egyptian society to be run according to traditional Islam. He thought some Muslims were bad Muslims and he sought to persuade them to move back to the core values of the faith.

Qutb concluded that you were either his kind of Muslim or you weren't a Muslim at all. *Milestones*, which was smuggled piecemeal out of jail,[49] was his manifesto for political Islam, and in it he declared that 'all the existing so-called "Muslim" societies are *jahili* societies.'[50] *Jahili* means ignorant or backward. This was the word used to describe the state of the pre-Islamic Arab world before God revealed the tenets of the Islamic faith to the Prophet Muhammad. According to Qutb:

> The position of Islam in relation to all these *jahili* societies can be described in one sentence: it considers all these societies un-Islamic and illegal. Islam does not look at the labels or titles which these societies have adopted; they all have one thing in common, and that is that their way of life is not based on complete submission to God alone.[51]

He lumped together every nation and everyone living in them as being in a state of ignorance. 'Such a society is to be counted among *jahili* societies, although it may proclaim belief in God and permit people to observe their devotion in mosques, churches and synagogues.' And what should be done about these ignorant 'backward societies'? '[P]hysical power and jihad' should be used 'for abolishing the organisation and authorities of the *jahili* system'.[52]

Qutb had stepped over the line that few Muslims care to cross. He had got into the business of 'Takfir'. That is the word used when one Muslim accuses another of apostasy. Qutb gave future generations of violent extremist Sunni Muslim groups like al-Qaeda the right, in their own minds at least, to decide who was or was not a good Muslim, and the permission to wage war against the Muslims who failed to meet the extremists' criteria. By definition these fringe fanatics were few and far between, and in the years that followed the publication of *Milestones* had very little impact on the world. But the war against the Soviets in Afghanistan drew them all together in one place where they formed alliances, then the Internet enabled them to stay in touch, find more recruits and spread their message of intolerance and hate.

Sayyid Qutb was silenced on the gallows in the early hours of the morning on 29 August 1966, though his words still resonate among extremist jihadi groups today. He had been briefly released from prison and then rearrested for being involved in another plot to kill Nasser. His final words, spoken through the hood placed over his head, were the Islamic Profession of Faith: 'There is no god but God, and Muhammad is His Messenger.'[53]

His death under Nasser's rule was to change the life of one fifteen-year-old boy who in turn would take the lives of many others. Al-Qaeda's Ayman al-Zawahiri was living in one of Cairo's then leafy southern suburbs.[54] He too would join the Brotherhood. Then, inspired by Qutb and by his anger over the execution, he helped form the militant Al-Jihad Group. 'Sayyid Qutb's call for loyalty to God's oneness and to acknowledge God's sole authority and sovereignty was the spark that ignited the Islamic revolution against the enemies of Islam at home and abroad. The bloody chapters of this revolution continue to unfold day after day,' wrote al-Zawahiri while he was the deputy leader of al-Qaeda and presumed to be hiding in a cave complex in Afghanistan following the 9/11 attacks.[55]

Nasser was the greatest foe the Muslim Brotherhood would face, because he had a vision for Arab society that competed with theirs. But when he suffered a heart attack in September 1970 that vision died with him. There would never be another Arab leader to match him, though the likes of Gaddafi and Saddam Hussein would try. The importance of his passing was acknowledged even by some of the men who hated him most. 'The myth of the Leader of Arab national-ism who would throw Israel into the sea was destroyed,' wrote Ayman al-Zawahiri. 'The death of [Nasser] was not the death of one person but the death of his principles . . . and the death of a popular myth that was broken on the sands of Sinai.'[56]

From here the Brotherhood began to slowly rebuild and rejuvenate. It needed to adapt to survive. There were many peaks and troughs in the coming decades, but the curve was upward. The army by contrast was beginning its gradual decline. It was still incredibly powerful, however, said a secret US embassy cable, 'following the military's poor performance in the 1967 war . . . officers began a descent out of the upper ranks of society'.[57]

But, says the former Muslim Brotherhood youth leader Muhammad al-Qassas, the crushing by Nasser left its mark on the Ikhwan leadership, and it is a legacy they still struggle with today.

> They learnt a painful lesson under Nasser. They thought they were very strong and had lots of followers, but when the regime came to crush them the Egyptian people did not support them. The Muslim Brotherhood leadership were jailed at a young age and Qutb was hanged. Therefore the leadership today doesn't trust the people. Most of them still live in fear from the experience of this era, although some now don't. However, the latter don't have the upper hand in the group now.

'We're suffering two plagues at one time. First Nasser dies. Then we get Sadat,' was the joke doing the rounds in Cairo when Anwar Sadat assumed the presidency after Nasser's death.[58] Nasser was a tough act to follow, and in the beginning nobody thought Anwar Sadat was up to the task. He'd always been regarded in military circles 'as Nasser's "poodle" or "Colonel Yes"'.[59] He was described as 'shattered by Nasser's death', so much so that he fainted during the funeral.[60]

Eight months later, though, he had turned the tables on all his detractors. On 15 May 1971 Sadat carried out what became known as his 'Corrective Revolution'. He locked up all his Nasserite opponents in the government and finally had the confidence to start having pictures of the great man replaced in the government offices with ones of himself.[61] 'There was nothing in President Sadat's long career as a Nasser loyal lieutenant to suggest that he was the man who would take Nasser's Egypt to bits,' wrote the Economist in May 1971 under the headline 'The Man Least Likely'.[62] Sadat's actions seemed so 'blatantly pro-American' that leftist groups were 'naturally convinced that the whole affair is a Central Intelligence Agency plot'.[63]

His philosophy, such as it was, was neatly summed up by another jibe doing the rounds at Sadat's expense. 'When Sadat's car came to a fork in the road, his chauffeur asked him which way to turn, left or right? He asked the chauffeur which direction Nasser would take, and was told he would turn to the left. Sadat thought, then told the driver: "Okay, then signal left and turn to the right." '[64]

Because he was held in such low esteem by the Nasserists, Sadat tried to use the Islamists as a counterweight. Just a few months into his presidency he started releasing some of the Brotherhood members from prison. Many were part of the Special Apparatus, and they came out of prison a much tougher bunch than when they went in. They had no time for al-Hodeibi and they prised what was left of the movement away from him.[65]

One of the first things Sadat did was try to win back some of Egypt's lost pride. After two years lobbing artillery rounds at one another, on 6 October 1973 Egypt launched an attack on the Israeli forces that were still holding the Sinai since the 1967 war. The attack took place on the holiest day of the Jewish year, Yom Kippur, the Day of Atonement. The Israelis were caught completely by surprise, and though they eventually won the war there was fury in the country that it had been so ill prepared. Although in their hour of need the US had come to the Israelis' rescue with arms and ammunition, Sadat could still present the war as a victory of the Egyptian forces thwarted only by an unfair intervention by the United States.

But by the time this war was fought the Arab states had a new weapon, which may not have frightened Israel, but scared the pants off its closest ally America. Oil.

On the eve of the 1973 'Yom Kippur War' there was very little slack between oil production and demand in the world economy. The Arab world's reaction to the American rescue was to hit them back where it hurt, in their gas tanks. The Arab states now knew just how much political power oil had given them. The 'Oil Shock' would bring the world's economy to its knees and profoundly change the power dynamics in the region.

The 1973 war began to level the playing field in the Middle East.

As the largest oil producer, Saudi Arabia emerged as a key player. The US now saw that it had to be actively and constantly involved to make sure that those with the most influence in the region understood where America considered its interests lay. But insuring those interests now also meant managing the Arab world's concerns too, not just Israel's. From this point until the uprisings of 2011, Israel, Egypt and Saudi Arabia were the three immediate go-to countries for every American president who dealt with the region's problems.

Like all the Arab dictators before and since, Anwar Sadat believed his own hype. If the 1973 war hadn't worked to get back the Sinai from Israel, then he was going to try peace. He first hinted that he was ready to do the unthinkable in a speech on 9 November 1977. He told the Egyptian People's Assembly: 'I am ready to go to their country, even to the Knesset itself, and talk with them.' Ten days later that is exactly what he did.

Sadat is remembered around the world for being the first Arab leader to sign a peace treaty with Israel. The deal agreed with Israel's Prime Minister Menachem Begin and overseen by President Jimmy Carter eventually won them all a Nobel Peace Prize.[66] This award is often given to an individual who symbolises a broader peace movement. Anwar Sadat's prize was an exception. His actions symbolised absolutely nothing about the wider Arab world, because hardly anyone agreed with his overtures to Israel. By going to Jerusalem to speak before the parliament he was recognising the state's right to exist. It is hard now to appreciate just how ground-breaking his move was. Equally staggering is the way in which he totally ignored the wishes of most of his people and the wider Arab world. It was a trait that would persist with his successor.

The Egyptian president had already signalled which side of the Cold War he wanted to be on. He had kicked out 5,000 Soviet advisers the year before, after his pleas to them for more weapons fell on deaf ears. It was a chance for America to make friends with Egypt again.

In April 1974 Kissinger told President Nixon: 'Egypt has made an enormous turn in its foreign policy – from war to peace. Sadat is the first leader to commit his country to peace on terms other than the extermination of Israel . . . He has also broken the Soviet link . . . Sadat has to demonstrate to his people that the new policy has benefits and that he has ties to the United States.'[67] But the closer Sadat moved towards Washington, the further it took him from the people he ruled.

The maxim 'Possession is nine-tenths of the law' could have been designed for the Middle East. And when Sadat came to power Israel was still in possession of the Sinai Peninsula. Sadat believed the longer that lasted, the harder it would be to retrieve it.[68] The peace treaty that Sadat eventually signed with Israel returned the Sinai Peninsula to Egypt.

If the peace deal won Sadat international acclaim, he drew his sense of worth in Egypt from the war of 1973, and in particular the first act of that conflict known as 'The Crossing', when Egyptian soldiers managed to seize the east bank of the Suez Canal from the Israelis after they launched their surprise attack. As this is still the closest any Arab state has ever come to winning a war with Israel, the bold move is still celebrated in Egypt today. In terms of establishing his authority in the country it was as important a moment for Sadat as nationalising the Canal had been for Nasser. Each year on that day the 'Hero of the Crossing' Anwar Sadat bathed in the glory of his shining hour with a national holiday and a military parade. It provided a little light relief for a nation that, after the peace deal, was totally isolated from its Arab neighbours. Egypt was not allowed back into the Arab League until 1989.

At the parade held on the morning of 6 October 1981 Sadat was sitting to the left of his vice-president Hosni Mubarak, who had won fame in the same conflict as an air force pilot. The men were in the front row of the podium as their soldiers drove by. Both were in full military regalia and they had just watched five fighter planes spewing coloured jet streams fly by when the first grenade was thrown. Seconds later gunmen leaped from one of the army trucks and started shooting into the stand. Sadat was shot several times and declared dead a few hours later after being airlifted to hospital. His assassination was caught on video camera and immediately broadcast around the world. Hosni Mubarak can be seen being whisked away by security men while Sadat lies dying on the floor. A few hours later he announced to the nation that Sadat was dead.[69]

There was gunfire that day in Lebanon too, but it was part of the public jubilation that erupted across the Arab world as they celebrated Sadat's demise.[70]

The Americans sent three former presidents to join a host of international mourners. All but one of the Middle East's Arab states, tiny Oman, boycotted the funeral.[71]

'I am Khalid al-Islambuli, I have killed Pharaoh, and I do not fear death,' said the man who led the gunmen as they rampaged around the stand.[72] At his trial the following year al-Islambuli yelled to the gallery that he had killed Sadat because he did not rule in accordance with Sharia and because of the treaty he signed with Israel. He was one of five men executed for the attack. The men were all part of the Islamist group Al-Jihad which the young Ayman al-Zawahiri had helped set up shortly after Sayyib Qutb's death.

Sadat believed he could get away with defying almost the entire Arab world because he thought he had neutralised opposition at home and was winning new friends in the West. That mistake cost him his life. '[Anwar Sadat] took the fundamentalists out of the bottle,' wrote al-Zawahiri. '[His] assumption of power marked the beginning of a new political transformation in Egypt represented by the end of the Russian era and the start of the American era.'[73]

'Sadat was personally attuned to an Islamist idea of life,' Ambassador Daniel Kurtzer told me as we sat in his study in Princeton University. During his twenty-nine-year career in the United States Foreign Service he acted as his country's ambassador to both Egypt and Israel.

[Sadat] saw the repression of the Muslim Brotherhood under Nasser as a negative, and right after he came to power after 1970 there was the attempted coup by the Left. So everything would have led him to turn to the right as an internal stabiliser, and in that respect I think Zawahiri is right, there was a sense of opening that door or letting it out of the bottle a little. He tried in 1981 to stuff it back in but by then it was much too late.

By the late Seventies, the Brotherhood had been brought back to life by a huge transfusion of young blood. It came by absorbing new Islamist movements that began to flourish on the university campuses in the decade that followed the defeat in 1967. The most important figure in this trend was Abdul-Moneim Aboul-Fotouh, who in 1975 would become the president of Cairo University's Student Union.

> Nasser, his regime and his oppression, were broken, which allowed us to openly express our religious belief once more. Therefore, as university students we succeeded in creating an Islamic wave which was not affiliated to any trends, neither Muslim Brotherhood nor anything else. But our movement belonged to the Islamic identity in its simplest and shallowest forms. It had no depth. This continued until 1974 or 1975 when the Muslim Brotherhood leaders started to get out of prisons. For us the Ikhwan were the heroes of Islam, they were executed, thrown in prisons, etc. We embraced them and because they were older, it was natural for us to put them at the top of the movement, the popular Islamic trend.

The Brotherhood leadership walked out of jail to find themselves able to take over, shape and absorb a newly rejuvenated Islamic movement into the Ikhwan fold.

The moment that best reflected this new-found confidence of the young Islamist movements was a live debate between Student Union president Aboul-Fotouh and Egyptian president Anwar Sadat. It is still talked about in Egypt today, because during it Aboul-Fotouh publicly mocked Sadat, while Sadat angrily demanded the young Islamist show him some respect. 'It was really not planned, it just happened,' Aboul-Fotouh told me with a wide smile.

> I honestly did not expect Sadat to be that angry because I did not mean to offend him. After the event my colleagues came over and started bidding me farewell, but luckily the meeting was on air, so I

was saved. But Sadat made sure I was never appointed in any university, although I was top of my class at medical school. My father was really horrified, because rumours spread that Sadat ordered his guards to kill the student who had talked and to run him over with a car on the spot. For months later, my father, the poor man, would suddenly be frantically running around campus looking for me after hearing new rumours of my death, to make sure I was still alive!

Over time with the new members came new ways of working, less secrecy and less blind obedience. During this period the Brotherhood publicly renounced violence. As it evolved it also moved decisively into tackling people's physical, not just spiritual, health. Its new leadership, some of whom are still influential figures today, spoke out about the poverty and corruption that were gnawing at the country. The Brotherhood began to fill the gap left by the failures of the state. Its legendary pragmatism was now used to find practical solutions for ordinary people rather than just self-preservation for the movement. This approach brought them new members, many of whom came from the middle classes. The Brotherhood also by now had a new leader, Omar al-Tilimsani. When he took over in 1973 he was supposed to be another façade for the Special Apparatus, but he was cannier than al-Hodeibi.

Early on in his leadership many members were still heavily influenced by the radical thinking of the men from the Special Apparatus, which was still in thrall to the ideas of Qutb. He balanced out the influence of the radicals by introducing more moderates to the leadership group. He then managed the two sides until Sadat's assassination led to the more extremist elements all being locked up again.

In 1981 Ambassador Kurtzer was doing his first tour in Cairo as a young political officer at the US embassy in Cairo:

Six to eight months before the assassination the ambassador pulled us together and said: 'There's something wrong here. I don't want to see anyone in the embassy, you've got to be out knocking on doors.' So we were reporting for six to eight months the stench of

a society that had gone wrong. Shortly after we started that Sadat
began his crackdown. It was an undifferentiated crackdown because
he was arresting everybody, left, right, centre, it didn't matter. So
the actual assassination of course shocked everybody because you
never expect it to happen, it's the 'black swan', but you're not
surprised that that situation produced something dramatic.

For a week afterwards the only concern we had was that this was
something larger than a one-off killing. Islamists were attacking
police stations and so forth. When the government reasserted control
in a sense everyone got comfortable again. We knew Mubarak, he'd
been the vice-president for years. I don't think anyone thought he
would be a short-term leader, but nobody knew how long he would
last. But the key in everybody's mind was restoring stability, and once
that happened the comfort groove just took over.

The comfort groove stretched on for thirty years. The assassination of
Anwar Sadat by an extremist Islamist group with links to the Brotherhood provided a good reason for a whole new generation of American
foreign policy makers to fear them, so they began building their policy
instead around Hosni Mubarak and what he represented, which was
no big ideas and no big surprises. He remained true to form until the
end. He was not a great man, he was not an inspiring man, and he did
not achieve great things.

During Mubarak's rule the cycle of accommodation and confrontation between the army and the Brotherhood would go on. In that
time the army's position in Egyptian society sank further, as did the
calibre of its leadership. Its dependence on American aid grew, and so
it started to lose its capacity for independent thought. While the
Ikhwan adjusted to the changing world, the last Egyptian dictator
would spend his rule trying to hold together the system he inherited
as it crumbled around him. And he would fail.

II: REVOLUTION

'We are turning into Afghanistan,' said Ahmed. 'It's an uncompleted revolution, and if you are asking me which direction we are going in, then honestly I don't know.' Ahmed ran a travel agency. It was an industry hammered by the violence and uncertainty of the first year after the revolution took place. I met him walking with his two teen-age daughters in January 2012 a few blocks from the People's Assembly building in Cairo just after it had started its first session of the post-Mubarak era.

'Last January I was very proud, very proud, now I'm disappointed. Did you see the parliament, how they were looking? I mean, first time in my life to see in the Egyptian parliament, gallabiyas [traditional long Arab robes] with jackets over it!'

The new parliamentarians, most of them Islamists, wore Western suit jackets over their traditional long shapeless robes. Not only did they not look like modern democrats, they did not act like them either.

'For me parliament is a circus, it's big beard versus small beard, who can be more right-wing than the other, who can be more obsessed with sex and moral values than the other, and who can waste all this time talking about Internet porn and not teaching English in school, whereas the majority of Egyptians' concerns are unemployment, poverty and security on the streets,' said the writer and activist Mona Eltahawy, who was still recovering from being attacked and sexually assaulted three months earlier in protests against the ruling SCAF. 'The Muslim Brotherhood have been utterly ineffective in delivering any of that, so I think for the average Egyptian who thought: "OK, you know what, they seemed like good people, they helped me when the regime didn't and they talk about God," they look at them now and say: "They are crap at politics, they can go back to the mosque."'

But they did not. This was not what the young people who led the Egyptian revolution wanted, but it was what they had feared they might get. It was not what the most powerful man on earth had been hoping for from the start either. 'What I want is for the kids on the street to win and for the Google guy to become president. What I think is that this is going to be long and hard,' said President Obama to an aide at the time of the uprising.[1] He was referring to Wa'el Ghonim, a Google executive and Internet activist who was held by the police for eleven days during the protest. President Obama did not get his wish, and it was longer and harder than anyone imagined.

The second year after the revolt was full of anger and protest too. The army and the Brotherhood were still dancing around each other looking for weaknesses. Each knew a decisive moment would come. As they did so they trampled over the rights and ambitions of the Egyptian people who had led the revolt. The decline in quality of the officer corps had been hidden under Mubarak, but now it was there for everyone to see as the army bungled its way through a period of direct rule. For years promotion in the military was about stepping into dead men's shoes, but the top generals had just lived on and on. They were totally out of touch with the generation that had taken to the streets. These old men were publicly abused from the outside and privately cursed from within.

The Brotherhood's leaders were no spring chickens either, and their power structures were almost as top-down as the military's. But they adjusted quicker to the new political landscape, because that was something they had been learning to do for decades just to survive. They would claim victory in a major battle of their long war with the army, though not without suggestions of a bit of match fixing. Flush from that, they would immediately square up against a new opponent: the People. In July 2013 that was a battle the Ikhwan would lose.

As the second anniversary of the Egyptian uprising drew near, the title of 'Pharaoh' long associated with Hosni Mubarak had been resurrected to describe President Morsi. He had launched a power grab by issuing a decree that put himself and his office above the courts. He claimed he did it because the legal system was still stuffed with Mubarak regime counter-revolutionaries. Everyone else saw it for what it was, an attempt to force through the completion of the new

constitution being written by the Islamist-dominated assembly before
the courts could stop it, and driven by the Muslim Brotherhood's not
entirely unjustified and by now institutionalised paranoia that everyone was out to get them. Then Morsi rushed through a referendum
on the hastily completed constitution, which as expected was approved
because of the Brotherhood's ability to mobilise its huge membership.
Two years after Egyptians had got rid of Mubarak, the man in the
Presidential Palace once again seemed to think that he and his party
were bigger than the nation they presided over.

'New pharaoh?' Morsi laughed. 'Can I be? I've been suffering. I've
been suffering, personally.'[2] He was referring to his imprisonment by
the old regime. Now he had swapped places with the man who originally put him there. Hosni Mubarak was at this stage sitting in jail,
because of the life sentence he had been given in June 2012 for
complicity in the killing of more than 800 protesters in the uprising
against him. As the newly elected Muslim Brotherhood presidency
started revealing some rather undemocratic tendencies, Mubarak
must have been shouting: 'I told you so!' to anyone who would listen.
He was right, he had, from the very moment his best friends in Washington presented him with the novel idea that he might allow his
people the chance to choose their leaders for themselves.

If President George W. Bush's 'Freedom Agenda' had a high-water
mark, then it was in the city of Cairo in June 2005. That was when he
sent his new secretary of state, Condoleezza Rice, to what she described
as the 'cultural and political heart of the Middle East'.[3] Ms Rice
believed: 'A democratic Egypt would change the region like nothing
else. It was in that spirit I went to the American University in Cairo
to deliver a speech on democracy in the Middle East.'[4]

Her boss wrote later: 'I was hopeful that Egypt would be a leader
for freedom and reform in the Arab world.'[5] Ms Rice said she intended
to deliver a speech that was 'bold', but before she did she went to see
Hosni Mubarak at his seaside home in the resort city of Sharm
el-Sheikh.[6] By this stage Mubarak was partially deaf, and so the

secretary of state 'talked loudly and looked directly at him, hoping the elderly leader could hear me or, if necessary, read my lips'. Either way he got the message and replied: 'I know my people. The Egyptians need a strong hand, and they don't like foreign interference. We are proud people.'⁷ He was probably talking about himself.

Ms Rice's speech was remarkable because it publicly articulated, at a venue in the heart of the Arab world, what everybody knew was wrong with the Middle East. Just as importantly, it was being said by the diplomat-in-chief of the country that had been propping up the whole rotten system.

'For sixty years, my country, the United States, pursued stability at the expense of democracy in this region here in the Middle East – and we achieved neither. Now, we are taking a different course. We are supporting the democratic aspirations of all people,' she told her audience.⁸ 'President Mubarak's decision to amend the country's constitution and hold multiparty elections is encouraging,' she said; he had 'unlocked the door for change'.⁹ Which was exactly what Mubarak was worried about. Mubarak was furious about the whole idea, but he could draw comfort from the fact that there was still one issue over which he and the US could agree. In a question-and-answer session just after her speech Ms Rice made a point of reiterating who was not invited to the democratic party. 'We have not had contacts with the Muslim Brotherhood . . . we have not engaged the Muslim Brotherhood and we don't – we won't.'¹⁰ In addition the Bush team followed successive US administrations in turning a blind eye to the way the Mubarak regime persecuted the Ikhwan even after it had clearly steered a path away from violence. Only when non-Islamist politicians were harassed and jailed were they willing to speak out.

Throughout Mubarak's rule, after the crackdown in the wake of the assassination of Sadat, the Brotherhood evolved towards a more moderate position that inevitably led it into the political arena.

The Brotherhood took its first steps into parliamentary politics in 1984 in an alliance with the more liberal Wafd Party. Mubarak eased restrictions on moderate Islamists to counter the radicals he had been fighting earlier on in his presidency. In the years that followed the Brotherhood candidates took part in a series of clearly rigged parliamentary elections, standing as 'independents' because the organisation was still banned. It reassured the regime that it would not directly challenge its authority with another Orwellian expression of its pragmatism: 'participation not domination'. This meant that until Mubarak was overthrown the Ikhwan never fielded enough candidates to actually win power.

Under pressure from Washington, even before Rice's Cairo speech, Mubarak announced in February 2005 that Egypt would, for the first time, hold presidential elections in which candidates other than him would be able to run. Parliamentary elections were also being held later that year in which Muslim Brotherhood members would again stand as individuals.

In those parliamentary elections the Brotherhood did much better than Mubarak had expected. The mood of his regime was conveyed in a confidential briefing to the then FBI director Robert S. Mueller ahead of his visit to Cairo in 2006. The memo from the US embassy in Cairo informed him:

> The Egyptians have a long history of threatening us with the MB bogeyman. Your counterparts may try to suggest that the President's insistence on greater democracy in Egypt is somehow responsible for the MB's electoral success. You should push back that, on the contrary, the MB's rise signals the need for greater democracy and transparency in government. The images of intimidation and fraud that have emerged from the recent elections favor the extremists both we and the Egyptian government oppose. The best way to counter narrow-minded Islamist politics is to open the system.[11]

George W. Bush's 'Freedom agenda' may have broadly failed in the region, but it did expose just how undemocratic Egypt was. Mubarak ran again as president in 2005 and 'won' and then locked up his only serious challenger on trumped-up forgery charges for three years.

*   *   *

But by the time the next parliamentary elections were held in the winter of 2010 George Bush had retired to his ranch, and promoting democracy in the Middle East seemed to be less of a priority for his successor Barack Obama. After three decades of untrammelled corruption Mubarak's people considered themselves pretty good at cooking the books. Unfortunately for the regime its last act of political fraud was shameless even by its usual spectacularly crooked standards, and it took place just weeks before Mohamed Bouaziz, in Tunisia, lost patience and hope with his own venal leadership.

'Tunisia coincided with a particular time in Egyptian history,' said Shadi Hamid of the Brookings Doha Center.

> It came right after the most rigged parliamentary elections in history. I was there for the 2010 elections, it was so blatant, it was embarrassingly blatant, and I think people learned after that that 'there's no hope within the system, we have to work outside the system, we have to find alternatives, civil disobedience, mass protests,' so I think Tunisia happened at a time when Egyptians were ready for that sort of message.

In the first round of the winter poll held on 28 November 2010, the Brotherhood, which had a fifth of the seats in the previous parliament, was reduced to none. The second-largest opposition party in the previous parliament, the Wafd, got just two seats.[12] They both pulled out of the second round, by which time the government was trying to rig things the other way so that at least a token opposition was elected. Mubarak's ruling National Democratic Party (NDP) had proved beyond doubt that it was not democratic at all. It ended the year 2010 with 83 per cent of the seats in parliament and zero credibility.

The following month, on 25 January 2011, groups of young people began to gather around the country to mark national 'Police Day' by protesting against police brutality. 'Police Day' commemorated the refusal by Egyptian officers in 1952 to obey an order by the occupying British forces to withdraw from the city of Isma'iliyah, near the Suez

Canal, and surrender their guns. The British government issued a statement back then saying: 'The Egyptian police casualties were 41 killed, 73 wounded, and 886 surrendered.'[13] The event provoked anti-British riots across the country and placed policemen in the vanguard of resistance to the colonial power. It was an event Egyptians were genuinely proud of.

However, by the time President Hosni Mubarak declared in 2009 that the event would be marked by a national public holiday it symbolised much more just how far the nation and its police force had fallen in the public estimation. As in Tunisia, in modern Egypt policemen were people you avoided at all costs. Your treatment at their hands was not decided by your guilt or innocence but by the mood of the officer whose attention you had been unlucky enough to attract. Often it was small bribes to escape trumped-up offences, or youngsters getting slapped around for being youngsters. The really awful beatings, torture and murders tended to happen to the poor, to members of the Muslim Brotherhood or to political activists – anyone who lacked the *wasta* to save themselves. After 2011, 25 January would for ever be remembered not for the bravery of the police, but for that of the Egyptians who fought against them.

During Mubarak's rule the country was still being run under an uninterrupted state of emergency introduced since the assassination of Sadat three decades earlier. One former police brigadier said that the police 'don't have enough resources, so they use other techniques that save time and money. Usually they cuff your hands and put a bar under your knees and beat your feet. In state security departments, they might bring someone's wife, sister or daughter and rape her to make him confess.'[14] The worst abuses would provoke some outrage from human rights groups and journalists, but then it would die down. That was apart from the rare occasions when the police were stupid enough to film themselves carrying out the abuse on their mobile phones and it made its way onto the Internet.

Normally though the outrage didn't gain traction, because the authorities controlled the media. If the victim was poor the authorities wove a web of lies about them. If the victim was a member of the

Brotherhood the fear of Islamic extremism meant that sympathy among liberals was often in short supply. In each case the victim came from a different world to much of the liberal middle classes, so they could say: 'Well, maybe he did have it coming.' They kept telling themselves that until one day it happened to one of them, and that suddenly made a whole new class of people feel more vulnerable.

Late on the evening of 6 June 2010 two policemen beat to death a young man called Khaled Said, whom they had just dragged out of an Internet café in the port city of Alexandria. Why they picked on him has never been ascertained, though the usual swirl of government-inspired rumours soon emerged to paint him as a petty criminal. What they couldn't cover up was his middle-class credentials. And what they couldn't explain away was how a man the police medical examiner claimed had died of asphyxiation after trying to swallow his drugs stash ended up with what Human Rights Watch described as a 'mangled face'. This time Egyptians could judge the truth for themselves, because Khaled's brother Ahmed managed to take photographs on a mobile phone of the corpse. Human Rights Watch documented the injuries on 'Said's battered and deformed face' as a 'fractured skull, dislocated jaw, broken nose and numerous other signs of trauma'.[15] The pictures, juxtaposed with an earlier image of Khaled's fresh smiling face, went viral on Egyptian social media. A few days after Said was killed, Wa'el Ghonim, the Egyptian marketing executive working for Google in Dubai, set up a Facebook page called 'We Are All Khaled Said'. It went well beyond his expectations.

As the following year began, Ghonim's Facebook page had five hundred thousand supporters and was being commented on in the mainstream Egyptian media.[16] The middle classes had always known there was a risk of falling prey to the savage internal security system. Khaled Said became the physical embodiment of that fear. Suddenly it was something they could no longer live with or ignore.

The year 2011 may have been when the wider world woke up to the use of social media for political change, but it was not a new phenomenon in the Middle East and certainly not in Egypt. The 'April 6th Youth Movement' had used Facebook to support a planned nationwide strike on that day in 2008. As National Police Day approached, Ghonim, the 'April 6th Youth' and other Internet activists combined their efforts to encourage support for the planned demonstration. Because social media had been used to organise protest in Egypt before, the authorities were not unaware of it. But they were dismissive of the young people, their message and their medium. 'I tell the public that this Facebook call comes from the youth,' declared the much-loathed interior minister Habib el-Adly through the pages of the state-owned newspaper *Al-Ahram* on the eve of the revolution. 'Youth street action has no impact and security is capable of deterring any acts outside the law.'[17] El-Adly would soon be granted a long period of reflection to ponder the wisdom of his predictions. His removal and the end of police brutality were among the initial demands of the protesters. He was sacrificed by Mubarak during the height of the protest and the following year he found himself sitting next to his old boss as they were both sentenced for complicity in the killings of the young people he had so casually scorned.

All of which must have seemed an impossible outcome for the youngsters busy swapping encouraging messages in the last few hours before they began their historic protest. What el-Adly didn't realise was that long before Tunisia showed that a successful rebellion was possible, people in Egypt had started to lose their fear.

Hosni Mubarak had always been a bit of a joke. He was disparagingly known as the 'Laughing Cow', after the picture on the front of the popular French soft cheese spread. He got that name because Sadat made sure his deputy kept his mouth shut, so Mubarak was always seen just standing next to him grinning. Most jokes about Mubarak though nearly always focused on his mental ability or supposed lack of it. It is a tribute to the ingenuity of the Egyptian people that despite having to make the same joke for thirty years they still found new ways to make it funny.

One began doing the rounds when Bill Clinton was president and a referendum was being held to grant Mubarak a third presidential term. The story went that Clinton presented Mubarak with a monkey, saying: 'I'll double your aid programme if you make this monkey laugh and cry.' Soon after, the monkey laughs and cries. 'How on earth did you do this?' Clinton asks. 'I told him that I am president,' Mubarak says. 'He laughed. Then I told him that I am trying for a third term. And he cried.'[18]

By the end of the first month of 2011, Khaled Said's death, high food prices and low wages had dragged the Egyptian public to the edge of rebellion. If the 2010 elections had shown them there was no other alternative to revolt, then the uprising in Tunisia had given them the courage to consider the leap. Their fear of the regime was waning. Only a last little nudge was needed. El-Adly's men in the police force were, as ever, ready to oblige.

On the morning of 25 January 2011, despite all that had just gone on in Tunisia, the state still thought it had the people beaten. Egypt was not Tunisia, the government said confidently. The remarkable arrogance of the regime was revealed by the reaction of the police force to a protest against police brutality. They tried to beat everyone up. They believed they could get away with it because they always had. But the protest's organisation through social media meant that for the first time the security forces found themselves facing huge crowds in Cairo and in other cities too. The usual strategy of riot police, tear gas and water cannon didn't scare the crowd off. That failure changed the rules. 'It feels like a revolution,' said Abd-Allah, one of the protesters on that day. 'I see people who are determined, people who have nothing to lose, people who want a better future.'[19] By evening the police did have the city under control, but it would not last.

Three days after the police attempted to put the first demonstration down, the people hit back. The 28th of January was declared by the young protesters to be the people's 'Day of Rage'. It was to be a turning point for both Egypt and the Arab world, because it was the moment when people around the region realised they too stood a chance of winning. Tiny Tunisia was one thing, but if it could be done in enormous Egypt it could be done anywhere. By now the government had switched the Internet off and largely disabled the mobile phone network, but it was too late. The demonstrations had taken on a life of their own, because for the first time it was not just young activists. Despite the police opening fire with live ammunition, a swathe of Egyptian society joined in the revolt.

More than 200 people were killed during the uprisings in Cairo, many of them during the 'Day of Rage' protests.[20] The demonstrators around the city couldn't communicate with one another, but they all knew where they wanted to be, Tahrir Square. Everything else just happened. The only element of organisation I saw that day was an old man sitting on a street just off the Nile with a bag of onions, which he was breaking into pieces to give to those of us retching from the effects of tear gas. The vapour released by raw onions counteracts the effects of the gas, but by nightfall even that wasn't needed. After a series of running battles the people owned the streets, their tormentors were on the run, and I was being jostled and pushed by streams of young men running in and out of the symbol of the ruling National Democratic Party, its enormous headquarters, which sat on the banks of the Nile a few hundred metres from Tahrir Square. By day it was a towering reminder of the power of the party. By that night it was a towering inferno symbolising its end. As its upper levels were being gutted by fire, its lower levels were being looted. The men pushed through the open gates, their arms filled with tables, cabinets and obscure bits of office equipment, in fact anything they could grab before the flames got to it first.

The uniformed police had melted into the night, but most of them hadn't just given up on their own. They were sent home by the government. I was told this by a Western diplomat in Cairo. 'We *know* that's what happened,' he said. The NDP hoped that their absence would provoke chaos on the streets and within forty-eight hours the population would be begging them to come back and restore order. Egyptian society thrives on rumours, so it went straight into a frenzy at reports of criminal gangs preying on the middle-class suburbs. But instead of terrifying Cairo's society it unified opposition to President Mubarak. Everyone suddenly felt vulnerable, and so everyone got together and began to organise with neighbours they'd often barely troubled to acknowledge. Suddenly people who had never had a conversation with each other before were swapping telephone numbers, and rotas were created to allow people to go to Tahrir Square to protest while others guarded their homes.

As I walked back to my bed each night I had to stroll through a parade of vigilante checkpoints. I'd be stopped by nice polite middle-class people, who would then ask for my ID, smile, and let me through. Fifty paces later I'd do it again. A community spirit that had always been missing from this dirty sprawling city had been born. This went on night after night. On one chilly evening I saw that a checkpoint of decent law-abiding citizens had chopped up and were burning their local police post to keep warm. One of my Egyptian friends, Angy, who was spending her nights in the street outside her home armed with her best kitchen knife, told me: 'Someone who if you see in the street you wouldn't know, now you are trusting him to secure your family while you are protesting. This is amazing.'

Sending away the police rebounded spectacularly on the Mubarak regime, but its longer-term effects on society were profound and went on to undermine the process of creating a new democratic state. The police left work that night and they didn't come back. 'On January 28 my brother went home and stayed at home. He lost interest,' said Nihad, whom I met by accident in a coffee shop in Cairo.[21]

Sure there was a lot of corruption, but everywhere, not only in the police, everywhere. My brother takes two thousand Egyptian pounds [US$330] after twenty years in the police. With two thousand how can you feed and educate your children? They work away from Tahrir now, away from any demonstration. They don't want to mingle with anybody belonging to the revolution because in the end they don't respect their orders, they don't respect them, so what is the point?

In the first days after the 'Day of Rage' the prospect that Mubarak might end up behind bars still seemed preposterous. It was at this time that Tahrir Square firmly became and stayed the bastion of the revolution, and its battleground. But the humiliation of the police force generally and the cleansing of their presence from Tahrir Square in particular would have far-reaching consequences for Egypt. It caused huge problems for the Morsi-led government, because Tahrir Square and the streets around it, which contain key ministries and foreign embassies, remain even now Egypt's wild frontier where the law has lost its writ. A broad section of the Egyptian people had defied authority to win their freedom in this arena. A much narrower group of them would return again and again to pick new fights on what had become almost hallowed ground. Not all these gatherings though were noble in cause. This little piece of Egypt is still often owned by the mob. After the revolution, along with the persistent harassment of women Tahrir was the scene of some savage sexual assaults by gangs of young men. This eventually prompted vigilante groups to form to fill the vacuum left by the state.

During the uprising though, the mob represented all the people. On the front lines defending the square were the 'Ultras'. They were fanatical football fans who supported Cairo's premier league football club, Al-Ahly. The hooligans among them were the one section of Egyptian society that had had the chance to perfect the art of street battles with the police. Most of the fighting during the revolt involved lobbing rocks and stones at the plain-clothes thugs from the internal security services trying to fight their way into the square. Occasionally though the Ultras would run through the barricades and the battle would take place out in the open just in front of the Egyptian Museum that holds the treasures of Tutankhamen. I watched all this in a riot hat, but the rest of the men around me had to make do with motorcycle helmets, kitchen pots or wads of cardboard wrapped together with tape. One man was photographed with bread rolls sell-otaped to his head. The sky rained stones, which bounced and clattered around me. Men were holding their bleeding heads or dragging unconscious colleagues back behind the barricades. It went on like this for days. The most notorious moment was the 'Battle of the Camels', when Mubarak loyalists rode into the square on camels and horses to charge at the protesters.

Slowly though the protesters wore down the internal security services, which realised that the army were not going to let them draw arms. Many people believe that the police ultimately took their revenge on the Al-Ahly fans the following February when seventy-four of them died in the country's worst-ever football violence after a match in Port Said.[22] The trial that followed and the verdicts in January 2013 would present the new Egypt with one of its darkest moments.

While the Ultras made up much of the front line during the revolution, it was the thousands of people behind them who added real legitimacy to the protests. It was their numbers that convinced the world it was a popular uprising. Among them was Sondos Asem, a Muslim Brotherhood activist in her early twenties who took part in the revolution from the first day, even though the leadership had specifically told their supporters not to. The Ikhwan did not believe at the start that the uprising would be successful.

Like her forefathers in 1952, Sondos wasn't ready to admit her membership of the Brotherhood at the time to the crowd around her. 'No, no, no, of course not,' she told me when we met later during the campaign period for the 2011 parliamentary elections. 'We were there as Egyptians, not as members of any political party. We were not there to make any propaganda for ourselves.' Sondos had helped set up, and was now running, the Brotherhood's English-language Twitter feed. She estimated that on the first day of the revolution only around 10 per cent of the demonstrators were active members of the Brotherhood. But though their numbers grew in the following days, she said they still all kept a low profile.

The revolution, it would have failed [if we had been open] because
the security crackdown would have been more fierce. They could
have stopped the protests very violently and the international
community support would not have been that strong and also the
liberals here in Egypt and many of those who don't know the
Brotherhood very well might have changed their decisions to
participate. It was important to keep it a popular uprising and it
was a popular uprising.

Their numbers were not overwhelming at the beginning. Only on the
28th, on the 'Day of Rage', did the Brotherhood firmly take sides.

Muhammad al-Qassas led the Muslim Brotherhood youth wing
into the demonstrations on 25 January. He told me that while the
Ikhwan's participation ultimately secured the revolution, taking part
went against all their instincts:

Basically, the Muslim Brotherhood in their core principles do not
believe in the idea of revolutions in general. On the contrary, lots
of the Ikhwan's literature and sayings affiliated to Hassan al-Banna
and other leaders reject the notion of popular revolutions and
uprisings as chaotic and unproductive acts. There were also internal
differences among the Brotherhood about the ideas of civil disobedience and strikes, because they do not understand these notions
and they don't understand their nature. They were satisfied with
the reality on the ground, which was that they were the strongest
opposition in a cat-and-mouse battle with the regime and would
take whatever the regime allowed them to have.

The morning after Mubarak formally stood down, the angry young
men who had led the revolution had been replaced in the square by
their mothers, who were now cleaning up the mess. After weeks of
reeking of tear gas it now stank of disinfectant. The pavement where
I had stood with the revolutionaries as they had exchanged rocks and
stones with the government yobs was being busily rebuilt by dozens

of schoolgirls and young women. What they didn't know was that they were actually just putting them back for next time, because before the year was out these stones would be whistling through the air again. If the mums of the revolution had taken over the square, the grandads in the army had taken over power.

'The last ten years, President Mubarak was not ruling, it was President Mubarak's family who was ruling, namely his son, wife, [Mubarak's chief of staff] Zakaria Azmi and the interior minister [Habib el-Adly]. They were in control over everything.' I met General Abdel Moneim Kato at his home in Cairo. Though retired from the Egyptian army he still acts as an adviser to them and is close to the leadership. 'The armed forces had long ago decided that they would not allow the rule of Egypt to be inherited under any circumstances. It had made its mind up that Gamal will not be the next president after Mubarak.'

So the octogenarian Mubarak was replaced by his equally 'aged and change-resistant' commander-in-chief, Field Marshal Mohamed Tantawi, who as chairman of the SCAF was now the de facto head of state. Though 'charming and courtly', the US had always seen him as someone still living in the past. Like the man he replaced, he 'simply [did] not have the energy, inclination or world view to do anything differently'.[23]

The demonstrators in the square would soon be demanding his dismissal, which was something many in his own ranks had also been wanting for years. The US embassy wrote to Washington in September 2008 to report that a source described 'the mid-level officer corps as generally disgruntled and ... openly expressing disdain for Tantawi'. 'These officers refer to Tantawi as "Mubarak's poodle",' the cable said, in an echo of the slights against Sadat. It noted the officers' complaint that 'this incompetent Defense Minister', who reached his position only because of unwavering loyalty to Mubarak, was 'running the military into the ground'.[24]

In Tunisia when Ben Ali went, the regime went with him. The army had been so sidelined that it had no vested interest in maintaining the status quo. In Tunisia after more than fifty years of dictatorship things could only get better for the army. In Egypt after more than fifty years of dictatorship the old generals knew things could only get worse. In Tunisia the army was poor, apolitical and had no friends in high places. In Egypt the army had provided every leader since Independence and had vast wealth. Nobody knew exactly how much, because the army's worth was a state secret. It was against the law to ask in the media why the army runs thirty-five businesses producing chemicals, cement and consumer goods.[25] Egyptians couldn't enquire why the army was raising chickens, making pasta, baking bread, bottling mineral water and producing olive oil. It was certainly not so that it could invite the people around for lunch, because the army's businesses are not there to serve the people who live outside the confines of the barracks.

Political power after the revolution was enjoyed by a select few in the army. The vast majority of the officer class had nothing to gain from the army being in charge, but they had quite a bit to lose. The longer the army was in the spotlight the more questions were being asked about its role in Egyptian society and, more importantly for the generals, its role in the Egyptian economy. Stepping away from the public gaze put the focus back on the government, but eventually the function of the army will have to be tackled. 'No ministry should have its private economy,' the economist Ahmed el-Sayed el-Naggar from Cairo's al-Ahram Center told me. He believes the size of the army's grip on the economy has been vastly overstated by Western observers and is probably closer to 5 per cent of GDP. However, even that damages the country:

> Such logic of having its own economy leads to the dismantling of the state, because the Ministry of Agriculture could do the same and take lands to give it to its own people, and eventually things will look as if each ministry is a state within the state. The army's present position has been legalised by creating laws to support it. In addition, all of the army's companies dealing with civil services don't pay tax. When their contracting company competes with

other private and public companies, they can present better bids because they are exempted from taxes. From the very start, they have an advantage. So it is unfair competition.

Diplomats believed that the army had vast assets across Europe in places like Luxembourg, Switzerland and the United Kingdom, along with lots of cash washing around bank accounts in the United States and the Cayman Islands. What the diplomats did not know was how it was all controlled, and by whom. What they did know was that American military aid, and the threat of its reduction, was what gave the Obama administration its most direct leverage on the country's transition in the post-Mubarak era.

The revolutionaries who overthrew Mubarak had not had a chance to think much beyond the act of getting rid of the man. It was clear almost from the moment Mubarak stepped down that the secular middle-class youth who led the uprising were the least equipped to convert their achievements into political capital. During the revolution there seemed for the first time to be the chance of a third force emerging to provide an alternative to the old choice of army or Ikhwan. It didn't happen. Some of the social media activists who helped spark the protests leveraged their newly found fame into books and speaking appearances. Others like the football fans on the front lines went back to their daily lives. None of the new players in the game managed to build political parties to challenge the established order, because none of them had an infrastructure to build on.

Some of the wealthier Westernised protesters I met in Cairo sulkily refused to take part in any political process at all, including voting in the elections, because they failed to meet their lofty expectations. These hardliners protested in the square for months after the revolution. They were joined by a motley band of street vendors, hawkers, petty thieves and vagabonds. Tahrir grew as dirty and dishevelled as most of the people in it. Many in the capital wearied of the permanent occupation of the people's space by these people who did not reflect the broad view of the nation.

During this period the SCAF seemed intent on going out of its way to undermine any faith the young revolutionaries might have had in them. After the country had voted to amend nine articles of Egypt's 1971 constitution in March 2011 it turned out that the SCAF had quietly added a few of its own amendments, suggesting, as it later turned out, their reluctance to hand power back as quickly as the public wanted.

In the months that followed the SCAF was constantly issuing decrees and government drafts that sucked power back into their hands. There were regular protests and the army regularly gave more reasons to mistrust them. One of the worst incidents, which scandalised what is still a conservative society, was the army's doctors performing 'virginity tests' on young women activists who were arrested during protests. The SCAF's youngest member, General Abdel Fattah al-Sisi, told the human rights group Amnesty International that it was done to protect the army against claims the women had been raped in custody.[26] The police were also accused of deliberately firing rubber bullets at the demonstrators' eyes. One officer was nicknamed the 'eye sniper' and his image was spray-painted by protesters on Mohammed Mahmoud Street off Tahrir Square under a sign saying 'Wanted'. Military not civilian courts were still used to try thousands of people, just as they had been before the revolution.

The sense of anger, frustration and the lack of a clear timetable for a transition to civilian rule built up throughout the year and reached its peak in November 2011 with massive demonstrations once again by a broad sweep of Cairo's society. This followed a surge in sectarian tensions, because the security forces in Cairo had the previous month killed twenty-four Coptic Christians who were protesting against an attack on a church. The army claimed the protesters had attacked them and killed a number of soldiers.

To try to end November's stand-off in Tahrir Square the SCAF sent in the army and the riot police. Amnesty International said 'the security forces used tear gas and fired shotgun pellets and live rounds against protesters in five days of clashes . . . Some 51 people died and more than 3,000 were injured.'[27] It was a huge miscalculation of the public mood. The capital began to feel as if it was getting ready for a second revolution. The generals blinked first and handed the protesters a significant concession. Tantawi announced that presidential elections and the return of power to civilians would take place by 1 July 2012. This replaced its earlier vague promise of it happening sometime in 2013 or 2014.

That suited the Muslim Brotherhood, who withdrew from the continuing protests, fearing they might jeopardise the timetable for the imminent parliamentary elections – the first round of three was due on 28 November. This act once again led to accusations that the Ikhwan was willing to sell out the revolution and do secret deals with the SCAF if it suited their own political ambitions.

Then in the middle of December 2011, when large crowds rallied in Tahrir to demand a faster transfer of power, the army's fall from grace was captured in what became an iconic image of the chaotic post-revolution period. Soldiers were photographed dragging along the ground a half-naked woman who had been wearing a niqab, a full-face veil. As she was pulled through the square the picture showed one of the soldiers stamping on her bare stomach. That was catastrophic for an army that had presented itself as a protector of minorities and women against the growing influence of the Islamists.

The Muslim Brotherhood used the period of military rule to build up its political apparatus. Its new political wing, the Freedom and Justice Party (FJP), was functioning by the end of April 2011, just two weeks after Mubarak's National Democratic Party had been dissolved by the courts. The FJP was a legal party by 6 June. At its head was Mohamed Morsi, who was transferred from the Muslim Brotherhood's Guidance Bureau to run things.

The Supreme Guide of the Bureau is Muhammad Badie. However those who have studied the group believe the real power lies with his deputies, including people like Khairat al-Shater, who was the

Brotherhood's first choice as presidential candidate, and Mahmoud Ghozlan, its official spokesman.[28]

The Brotherhood's shift into the political mainstream began with a lie, descended into farce, and, exactly a year after the president's inauguration, it led to huge protests that drove Morsi from office. In the December 2011 parliamentary elections there had been an enthusiastic turnout for the Islamists. By the June 2012 presidential elections the mood had soured and voters merely considered the Brotherhood's to be the least worst candidate. By the following summer many were much less sure even about that. After he was elected Morsi resigned from the Brotherhood and the FJP to try to present himself as president of all the people. The people were not convinced. They believed they had been duped by the Ikhwan. It was a sense they were starting to get used to.

Even before the debris from the January 2011 revolution had been cleaned from the streets, the Brotherhood tried to win over the secular youth and an equally suspicious outside world with a promise. The Ikhwan issued a statement that read: 'The Muslim Brotherhood . . . are not seeking personal gains, so they announce they will not run for the presidency and will not seek to get a majority in the parliament and that they consider themselves servants of these decent people.' It added that they were not 'seekers of power'.[29]

They soon broke that promise, and fielded enough candidates in the December 2011 People's Assembly elections, as did the hardline Salafist groups, to crowd the parliament with Islamists.

'The Muslim Brotherhood and its political wing, the Freedom and Justice Party, does not really grasp the idea of democracy and freedoms,' said Abdul-Moneim Aboul-Fotouh. 'You can't expect people who don't practise democracy in a truthful way within their own organisation to practise it within the society. Like anything else, if you don't have something you cannot give it to somebody else.'

'This is a big fat lie that democracy is not applied in the Muslim Brotherhood,' Mahmoud Ghozlan told me when we met at his office in Cairo two years after the revolt. He is a key member of the Muslim Brotherhood's Guidance Bureau.

> This is absolutely false. All our affairs have two sides, the first of which is what we call 'Shura', which is democracy. The other side is 'listening and obedience'. There is not a single decision taken at any levels within the Ikhwan, whether the Guidance Bureau, the Shura council or the local offices, without democratic discussion. Here at the Guidance Bureau, we sit and discuss and differ until we see what the majority vote for, even if this majority does not include the General Guide. However, once the majority decides, everyone must obey and abide by this decision whether they were with or against it. You have to respect the rule of the majority.

After the revolution, and for the first time in over eighty years, the Brotherhood was forced out into the open. Political Islam for the first time had government within its grasp. But that meant the Ikhwan were no longer able to hide in the shadows, play the victim, hedge their bets and fudge on every issue.

'It's a paradigm shift for us,' said the Muslim Brotherhood's Amr Darrag, who was also the secretary general of the Egyptian Constituent Assembly:

> All of a sudden we find ourselves under the spotlight, everybody is talking to us as if we are in charge rather than as the banned group we were before the revolution. The Brotherhood has been there for more than eighty years, and we have a lot of experience and we can adapt quite well, but on some levels sometimes this change is not very easy. The mentality that sometimes people behave with is as if we are still this banned group, and what is strengthening this feeling is that almost everybody is attacking us. The media, the remnants of the old regime, the so-called opposition.

The Brotherhood was the best placed, most organised, least loathed of the two old conservative institutions vying for power, but it failed completely to translate that into broader support. The Ikhwan's highly evolved sense of internal discipline, which had helped it survive the Mubarak years, seemed in the eyes of the wider population more like the actions of a creepy cult that punished its members for uttering a single word out of line. This was illustrated by the way it treated those younger members who had first dragged the leadership into grudgingly supporting a revolution from which the Ikhwan eventually gained so much.

The Brotherhood claims that the FJP is independent from the Ikhwan. But when Muhammad al-Qassas and other members of the Brotherhood youth wing created a party to unite all young activists, they were immediately thrown out of the movement. 'The problem with the group that leads the Muslim Brotherhood is that it does not trust the people or the other political forces, they only ever trust their own organisation,' Muhammad al-Qassas told me in early 2013 as the country descended into legal wrangles over the timing of the second post-Mubarak parliamentary elections due later that year.

> This mentality and spirit is making them always in a hurry to win something and then pause to look around. We had several meetings and dialogues with Morsi [in 2011] and our hope was that he would expand the circle around him to include other political forces. But Morsi, because of the way the Muslim Brotherhood thinks, trusted no one but the small group he had around him. Even now it's the Muslim Brotherhood's Guidance Bureau that really calls the shots.

The Muslim Brotherhood's first foray into governance was a disaster. After years of suffering at the hands of the regime it attracted a huge sympathy vote, even from those not naturally inclined to support it. That though was soon squandered. The 2012 parliament was televised, allowing the middle classes to watch their new democracy in action. It started going wrong from day one, when many of the new

MPs dismissed the sanctity of the oath of office and decided instead to add their own caveats about what they were or were not willing to uphold. That produced a long row between the MPs over whether or not it was illegal to tamper with the oath, and things went generally downhill from there. Any goodwill the electorate might have been ready to show the fledgling institution evaporated almost overnight. The intellectual elite who should have been defending democracy went on a verbal rampage, telling diplomats, journalists and anyone else who would listen that it was a joke.

Things did not go any better in the first parliament for the Salafists either. They were a loose collection of grass-roots puritanical Sunni Muslims whose priority was a greater role for Sharia law in society. In Egypt they are a more conservative version of the Muslim Brotherhood. 'They are a bit like the Tea Party was in the United States in regard to the Republicans,' says Princeton's Professor Haykel. 'They are the ones who will ideologically pull the Muslim Brotherhood to the right.'

Before the revolution the Salafists had always rejected politics as un-Islamic, so they were not expected to figure at all in the political make-up of the new Egypt. Then at the last minute they flip-flopped and stood in the polls as the Al-Nour Party, the 'Party of The Light', and won 25 per cent of the seats in the parliament compared with the Brotherhood's 47 per cent. They had never figured prominently in mainstream society before, so the Salafists were a fascination for urban Egyptians when they started turning up on their TV screens. The Salafists quickly proved themselves susceptible to the narcissism of public life. One of their supposedly pious MPs had to resign for making up a story about a carjacking to hide the fact he'd just had a nose job, something strictly forbidden by the movement.[30] Another was caught having sex with a veiled teenager in a car park. The MP said it was all a big misunderstanding and that the young woman was just feeling a little sick, so he had been helping her wash her face.[31] Egyptians began mocking them as the Al-Nose Party.

The Brotherhood though had to take them very seriously, because they were eating into their power base. 'I was surprised, although the explanation was right there in front of me. I don't know why I did not see it happening,' said the Brotherhood's Mahmoud Ghozlan.

For thirty years the Ikhwan faced a hostile state which hunted, persecuted and tried to isolate the Brotherhood from society. At the same time, the Salafists were allowed to work in mosques, and because they were not involved in politics, they were not harmed in any way. Therefore they were able to grow in popularity, and when the election happened it was normal that the poor people, who used to listen to the Salafists in mosques, supported them.

'Our ideas are the same as the Brotherhood, we both want an Islamic society which is pure without any additions, myths and innovations. It's the practical implementation on the ground where the differences appear,' Mohamed Nour of the Al-Watan Salafist party told me. 'The difference between the Muslim Brotherhood and us is that they want to change things from the top down. The Salafist school of thought is to start at the bottom and work up.' That wasn't the biggest difference. Salafism is a principle, not a disciplined unit like the Brotherhood. Mohamed Nour's party was a breakaway group from the Al-Nour party. The Salafists had barely cut their teeth in politics and they had already begun to split.

The Egyptian People's Assembly is the lower house of parliament, and as in the UK it is the most powerful chamber. The upper house is called the Shura Council, and like the UK's House of Lords, its powers are limited. After the elections members of the Muslim Brotherhood dominated both. The main function of the first parliament was to pick a 100-member Constituent Assembly made up of two halves: MPs and individuals from outside the chamber. Together they would draw up a new constitution to define the balance of power between the parliament and president, the role of Sharia law in society and the role of the army. The Brotherhood packed it with Islamists. In response, the handful of liberals, Christians and women's rights supporters walked out, allowing the SCAF to rightly claim that it wasn't representative of the nation.

The Brotherhood's complete mismanagement of the process of drawing up this new constitution would dog it through the 2012 presidential campaign, into the Presidential Palace and beyond. It would give the army the chance to try to reassert its authority and usurp the democratic process.

In April 2012 the courts disbanded the first version of the Constituent Assembly. MPs then elected a second Constituent Assembly, which was also dominated by Islamists, in June 2012. A few days later the Supreme Court dissolved the People's Assembly, ruling that some of its members had been improperly elected. The Supreme Court then pondered dissolving the second version of the Constituent Assembly because it was elected by a body the court had just ruled was unconstitutional. If all that seems confusing that is because it was. For months on end everyone in Egypt was confused too. Each party blamed every other, and no one knew what was going on or how the impasse would end. The SCAF were accused of running the courts behind the scenes, the judges of being Mubarak-era stooges, the Islamists of trying to stamp their interpretation of Sharia all over the country's institutions and laws. The people wondered what was happening to their revolution.

Now that they were fully immersed in the country's politics the Brotherhood had to balance appealing to the moderate centre without alienating its religious base. It naively tried to do this by constantly selling two very different messages, one to its core supporters and another to the broader Egyptian public. Somehow it convinced itself that nobody would notice. It even tried that tactic when tackling issues relating to foreign policy. After violent demonstrations in Egypt over the deliberately insulting film *Innocence of Muslims*, made by a US-based film-maker, the Brotherhood tried to spin two different responses. One was moderate for external consumption, the other raged for internal consumption. That prompted the American embassy in Cairo, whose walls had been breached by protesters, to tweet back to the Brotherhood's English Twitter feed: '.@ikhwanweb Thanks. By the way, have you checked out your own Arabic feeds? I hope you know we read those too.'

If foreign bureaucrats were cynical about the Brotherhood, that was doubly the case for many of the locals. Every time the Brotherhood did something that raised the suspicions of the general public in Egypt it pleaded for their trust. Yet little in their history or their actions after the revolt suggested that that trust was deserved.

By the time the country and the Brotherhood were preparing for the presidential elections in the summer of 2012 the country was awash with guns. Many had been 'liberated' from post-Gaddafi Libya and then driven across the border and sold on the Egyptian black market. Everyone, including my most mild-mannered friends, seemed to have bought a weapon and a huge steel front door. The sense of civic pride and unity created by the revolution was gone. People were fearful and scared. They were desperate for a restoration of law and order, though they still didn't trust the police. Their withdrawal by the NDP backfired over the eighteen days of the uprising, but over eighteen months it worked out quite spectacularly for the army, because they were the only institution people trusted to provide security. Conspicuously little effort had been expended to rejuvenate the damaged institution that was the police force, despite, as one diplomat told me, many offers of help from Western governments. Perhaps it was not surprising that Ahmed Shafiq, a man from the past who campaigned on a ticket promising a return to order and stability, would turn out to be the most formidable challenge to the Brotherhood in the presidential polls.

The men and women formed different queues that circled in opposite directions around the Al-Bahiya Girls Middle School on Port Said Street in the Sayeda Zeinab district of Cairo. The city is notorious for its chaos and confusion, but on polling day there was order and calm despite the summer heat, which left people leaning into the walls to escape the burning sun. The men looked largely the same in loose shirts and wide trousers. It was on the women's side that I could

clearly see that all of Egypt's various layers of society had turned out
to do something unprecedented. The Egyptian nation was going to
freely elect their leader. The women's line was a rainbow of colour,
punctuated with pockets of black. It was impossible not to be infected
by the enthusiasm of the people waiting patiently to play their small
part in history. Many had gone through this process before under
Mubarak. What was different now was that as they stood in line to
put their mark next to one of the twelve men seeking their vote,
nobody knew who was going to win. The ballot boxes were all arriving empty. And for the first time anywhere in the Arab world the
Muslim Brotherhood was openly contesting for the presidency and
was seriously trying to win.

These were the first elections for a head of state after the Arab uprisings, and they were taking place in the most influential country.
Egypt's problems of poverty, sectarian tensions and poor infrastructure are much closer to those of the rest of the region than rich,
well-educated, homogeneous Tunisia's are. All these things made this
event remarkable not just for Egypt but for the whole Middle East
and North Africa region. Here was the proof that it could be done.

The choice people were making that day had already proved controversial because ten of the men the country thought they would
probably have to choose between had already been disqualified from
standing. Among those was the Muslim Brotherhood's first choice for
president, Khairat al-Shater. He was barred because of a rule stating
that no one could run within six years of having been released from
jail. Al-Shater had been jailed by the old regime in 2007 and was only
released by the SCAF after Mubarak fell.

The Brotherhood announced in March 2012 that it was going back
on its pledge not to field a presidential candidate so that it could
oppose the candidacy of the man who had put Mr Shater in jail,
Omar Suleiman. In the end Suleiman couldn't run because the old
spy's new team of political agents couldn't add up. His team failed to
submit the 30,000 signatures required by law to contest the poll, so
he was disqualified. He would die just months after the polling ended.

There were two more factors in the Brotherhood's U-turn. They feared that if they did not try for the presidency and the parliament was undermined they would end up with nothing. Just as important was the risk of the presidency going to the former Brotherhood leader Abdul-Moneim Aboul-Fotouh. He had backed the uprising from the start, and went to Tahrir Square. He decided to seek the presidency at a time when the Ikhwan's position was that it would not run a candidate in the poll. He was still very popular within the Brotherhood. In the President's Palace he would be a serious threat to its unity.

I wandered along the queue on the first voting day with a female colleague who politely asked the women if they would be willing to talk to me as they waited for their turn to come. Not a single woman declined, though not all wanted to give their full names. The first we spoke to was wearing a niqab. The black cloth covered her entire body. All I could see was her eyes. I could tell she was old because the bags beneath them pressed gently down on the black veil that lay across the bridge of her nose. Her voice was a whisper that my translator struggled to hear against the noise of the bustling traffic. I asked how long she had been waiting to vote. 'Today,' she said in Arabic, 'I have been waiting for one hour, but before I have been waiting my whole life.'

Standing a few places in front of her was Manal al-Subair. She was twenty-eight years old and wore a bright purple headscarf wrapped around her neck and tucked into a long black shalwar kameez embroidered with matching purple flowers. 'Does the revolution end today?' I asked. 'Inshallah' – 'God willing' – she replied. It did not.

The run-off vote was held on 16 and 17 June 2012. The two men left were the Brotherhood's last-minute replacement for al-Shater, Mohamed Morsi, and Hosni Mubarak's last prime minister, Ahmed Shafiq, who was widely seen as the army's man.

Once again the two most powerful organisations in the country were squaring up, but for the first time it was in a free and fair fight at the ballot box. Neither man was wildly popular with the electorate and neither got more than 25 per cent of the votes in the first round. The results revealed a sharp drop in support for the Brotherhood compared with their performance in the parliamentary elections. This may have been partly due to the late substitution of the uncharismatic Morsi, which left him derided as the 'spare tyre' before the poll and as the 'accidental president' afterwards.

But the excitement caused by polling day was nothing compared with the drama staged by the SCAF. This was the moment when the SCAF conspired with the courts to dissolve the People's Assembly just as the people were preparing for the presidential poll. Then two hours after the people finished voting for their new president the SCAF took back more power. It nullified the first thing the people had voted for after Mubarak fell, the new freedoms that were enshrined in the 30 March 2011 constitutional declaration.

In the space of four days, and with the help of a compliant Supreme Court, the generals had wiped out all the democratic gains of the post-revolutionary period. The army's new amendments to the constitution announced on 17 June 2012 meant, a diplomat told me, that whomever the people put in the driving seat, the SCAF controlled the handbrake, and it was now full on.

And just in case people weren't edgy enough, the announcement of the results was delayed by several days, and everyone I met thought the SCAF were trying to mess around with them too. The country believed it was on the brink of another upheaval. So severe was the tension that the Brotherhood tried to calm things down. 'What happened in Algeria cannot be repeated in Egypt,' promised the former speaker of the dissolved parliament, Saad al-Katatni. 'We are fighting a legal struggle via the establishment and a popular struggle in the streets. This is the ceiling. I see the continuation of the struggle in this way.'[32]

The Brotherhood saw it was walking into a replay of the last Egyptian revolution in 1952, when the Ikhwan again was seen to have capitulated to the army only to have the Generals turn on them later. This time they began their 'popular struggle' by sending their supporters back into the square.

It may have been a new government in a new era, but these were not new faces and it was not a new struggle. The old political elite of the Mubarak regime had been replaced by the old political elite of the Brotherhood. The Brotherhood won the presidency not because of its Islamist agenda, but because it was not the army. And it didn't win by much. Morsi got 51.7 per cent of the vote, Shafiq 48.3 per cent. The minority groups like the Christians voted overwhelmingly for Shafiq because they feared for their future under Islamists. Secular women had a tough choice because they had been beaten up and subjected to 'virginity' tests by the army but weren't sure they'd be much better off under the Brotherhood. Shafiq's first act after the poll was to flee the country to avoid an arrest warrant for corruption. He denied the charges, describing them as the 'settling of scores'.[33]

When President Mohamed Morsi finally took his oath of office it would turn out to be the Brotherhood's last act of public subservience to the men in green. The newly anointed fifth president of the Egyptian Republic received many rapturous standing ovations throughout his speech. It seemed that the generals clapping enthusiastically in the front row were actually congratulating themselves. They thought they had won again, and so did much of Egypt.

But if the new president felt angry or humiliated he didn't show it. The Muslim Brotherhood had survived battles with smarter, more ruthless soldiers than Tantawi. So Mohamed Morsi fell back on the instincts of his movement. He compromised and he waited.

Once again the Sinai Peninsula would settle the fate of an Egyptian leader. When Egypt signed its peace treaty with Israel in 1979 it got the Peninsula back, but there were strings attached. Its military presence on the border was strictly limited. This probably went some way to explaining why on 5 August 2012 a group of Islamist militants were able to storm an Egyptian border post, killing sixteen guards. It was the deadliest attack on Egyptian troops in the Sinai for decades, and it infuriated the nation. The army under Tantawi immediately launched a counter-offensive against the militants, though many probably escaped back through the illegal underground tunnels into Gaza, while others fled to hideouts in the Sinai mountains.

Israel made a point of saying it had shared intelligence with Egypt that an attack was imminent. Tantawi and his generals had either been incompetent or had hoped that an attack by Islamists might weaken Morsi. Nothing represented the change that had taken place in the Arab world more than the announcement at the time by Egypt's new Islamist president that he had approved airstrikes on other Islamists in Sinai.

A week later Mohamed Morsi made another announcement, and this one was even more remarkable than the first. On 12 August he sacked Tantawi. He sacked the chief of staff, Sami Annan. And he cancelled the constitutional declaration made just days before he won his post that had stripped it of all its powers.

When the news was announced the whole nation took a huge breath and waited to see what would happen next. The answer was nothing. For the first time in Egyptian history a civilian had taken on the heads of the military and won, though the generation of soldiers who had ridiculed Tantawi were clearly complicit in the move. Altogether seven of the military's top brass lost their jobs. As a parting gift the 'Poodle' got a new choker, though to be fair it was a rather nice one. The 'Nile Collar' is Egypt's highest state honour and is awarded for exceptional public service. The irony of that, after his eighteen months of mismanagement, was probably lost only on the field marshal himself. Morsi was also clever enough to keep both Tantawi and Annan on as presidential advisers, which gave them a fig leaf of respectability and avoided the old soldier's total humiliation.

Tantawi was replaced by General Abdel Fattah al-Sisi, who was thirty years his junior and had defended the virginity tests. General al-Sisi became both the commander-in-chief of the armed forces and the defence minister. No one expected that the following year al-Sisi would oust Morsi.

'We went through this battle representing the Egyptian people, it was not just our battle,' said the Amr Darrag in February 2013.

Ironically it was somebody who belonged to the Muslim Brotherhood who really finished the control of the military over political life with what Morsi did in August 2012. That was really, in my opinion and the opinion of many, the day when the revolution achieved a big part of what it aspired to. Getting rid of Mubarak was one thing, but for the military rule to have continued it would have been like we had never had a revolution.

'I've been dealing with Egypt for a long time. Morsi has proven to be smarter than most of us thought,' said one of Israel's top Defence Ministry officials while the Ikhwan were in power. I asked him if Israel thought the Brotherhood had finally tamed the Egypt army. 'Yes, he has Sisi and the Supreme Council of the Armed Forces under his foot. What [Turkey's] Erdogan only dared after five years, he has done it in six weeks. He deserves a medal.' His last remark was dripping with sarcasm.

I put the same question to General Abdel Moneim Kato. 'Absolutely not,' he said indignantly.

On the contrary, Sisi's loyalty is to Egypt and its army. In all his statements he always declares that the armed forces side with no one but the army. Therefore, all of the ongoing attempts by the Muslim Brotherhood to infiltrate the army will not succeed. Tantawi took a decision for the sake of Egypt. He could have said you do not have this authority and then a coup d'état would have taken place.

Professor Olivier Roy told me in early 2013:

The Muslim Brotherhood is not a revolutionary movement, it is not an ideological movement. And the army is not ideologically minded, the army is not secularised and it is not democratic. The army, at least the new generation of its officers, know it is in their best interests to stay in the background. Then they can keep their economic power, they can keep their autonomy and they are in a position to negotiate with all the other political forces if they have

a problem with the Brotherhood. I don't see the army at all resent-
ing the Brotherhood coming into power because Morsi, at least,
has given to the army a lot of assurances and guarantees. So the
attempts by the Saudis and the people in the Gulf to get rid of the
Brotherhood by supporting the army are doomed to fail.

The long war between the Brotherhood and the army is over. It is over
because a much more powerful foe has finally set foot in the arena, in
the shape of the Egyptian people. These two old institutions will no
longer be able to fight between themselves over the destiny of Egypt,
because the Egyptians now have the deciding say in the matter.

'No one can now oppress the Egyptian people any more.' That,
says Abdul-Moneim Aboul-Fotouh, is the greatest legacy of the revolution. 'They have taken back their country and broken the barrier of
fear. Egyptians are now free, and when angry they can take to the
streets to express themselves. I believe the Egyptian people will never
go back to their couches to watch from a distance.'

The Muslim Brotherhood expected to be able to run the country
the way it ran the Ikhwan; it wasn't used to having to justify its decisions to anyone. Its imperious style, once it held the levers of power,
began to infuriate people. As the second anniversary of the uprising
approached, Egypt's President Morsi tried to explain all the missteps
by saying of the new democratic process: 'It's a first experiment, it's a
first experience for us in our history. So what do you expect? Things
to go very smooth? No. It has to be rough, at least. Not violent, but
rough. So, we have enough patience.'[34] That patience had begun to
run out for everyone else as soon as the Brotherhood's new MPs
started taking their oaths of office.

The question everyone in Egypt was asking, even though Morsi
officially resigned from the movement when he was elected, was, did
the new president govern for the benefit of the Brotherhood or the
country? I asked the senior Brotherhood leader Mahmoud Ghozlan,
in February 2013, how the relationship between the president and his
old comrades in the Ikhwan was working. He told me:

The ideas and principles of the Muslim Brotherhood are part of who he is, but from the organisational point of view he has nothing to do with the Ikhwan, or the Freedom and Justice Party. However, I can say a person can leave his position but can never leave his beliefs and principles. But the moment he became a head of state he became president of all Egyptians, which include the Muslim Brotherhood. He looks at the Muslim Brotherhood just like he looks at all Egyptians, but his principles remain to apply the parts of Islam which are not applied in the society in a gradual way.

And was President Morsi getting instructions from the Ikhwan leadership?

No, no, no! He now has his own group of advisers. But the Muslim Brotherhood are still Egyptians, and if they have an idea or suggestion they should be able to share it with the president just like Al-Wafd Party and other parties. The [Brotherhood's] Supreme Guide looks up to Morsi as his president. Morsi has left the Ikhwan and he has no relation with our notion of listen and obey. This is for us only.

The Brotherhood was in power not because it landed a knockout blow, but because the military conceded defeat. The army realised it no longer wanted, or had the capacity, to rule. The army watched from the sidelines as the Brotherhood wrestled with the problems of governance. These are issues the military men are glad they have now left behind. The Brotherhood was in charge, but it did not have the full obedience of the institutions of the state. It has started to stuff government bodies with its own people, but it will take many years to take charge of Egypt's vast bureaucracy, most of it appointed through 'wasta' with the old regime. But key to running the new Egypt is the consent of the people. Both the old foes now know that. This was illustrated by the mayhem that resulted from the death sentences imposed on twenty-one football fans for their role in the Port Said football riots.

Tensions were already high after protests on the second anniversary of the revolution, 25 January 2013, against the Muslim Brotherhood and President Morsi. Fighting took place between demonstrators and the security services in Tahrir Square, in Suez, Alexandria, and Isma'iliyah, where the Ikhwan headquarters was set ablaze. Hundreds of people were injured and five died.

But it was on the following day, when the football riots verdicts were read out, that the country descended into a political crisis, provoking Tantawi's replacement General al-Sisi to warn: 'The continuing conflict between political forces and their differences concerning the management of the country could lead to a collapse of the state and threaten future generations.'[35] That is the sort of thing that generals like to say just before they embark on a coup. That did not happen. The protesters claimed that the football fans who had been sentenced to death were made scapegoats to protect the police and security officials, who they say should have been held accountable for failing to take action to stop the riots taking place. Their fury was only quelled after the army was deployed along the Suez Canal Zone where the violence was at its worst. More than fifty people died, hundreds were injured and the Muslim Brotherhood learned its most important lesson since it took power. It might be hard to live with the army, but it is impossible to govern without them.

The challenges facing the new Muslim Brotherhood-led government in Egypt were huge. Most of the big ones – unemployment, corruption, bad infrastructure, poor education – they inherited from the old regime. Three-quarters of Egyptians under thirty years old are jobless and increasingly frustrated with the lack of change in their lives after the revolution.[36] The regular violent protests have damaged its crucial tourism industry, leaving Egypt in 2013 at the bottom of the rankings for safe and secure places to go on holiday, below even Pakistan.[37] The new government shied away from making politically painful economic reforms in an election year. Instead, by the spring of that year, public sector salaries had gone up 80 per cent since the revolution.[38] That all led to protracted discussions with the IMF over the conditions for a US$4.4 billion loan, when what was needed was immediate action. Until Egypt could show it was sorting out its finances investors withheld their cash. Egypt is the world's largest importer of wheat, and so as the currency slid, finances became even tighter. The country had to keep going cap in hand to more Arab states for more loans. So while they inherited a mess, the new government made matters worse. Egypt tottered on the verge of bankruptcy.

The economist Ahmed el-Sayed el-Naggar warned that Morsi was making getting agreement on reforms harder because he had already made some of the same mistakes as the old regime:

> Morsi has surrounded himself with the same business entourage as Mubarak had, and they all have the same ideas, the same interests, and they are stopping him from reforming the economy because it is not in their direct interests. So the environment and the people that surround the Presidency haven't changed. All that's different is that in the middle of this is Morsi, not Mubarak.

These challenges would be a tall order for even the most adored of revolutionary parties or leaders. The Muslim Brotherhood is not adored by most of the Egyptian people. It is not even liked by very many of them, because it is barely trusted. The rushing through of the foundation of the new Egypt, its constitution, only made that worse. It set up a struggle over the role of women in society, which has begun in all the new democracies that have seen Islamists come to power. Now that women have a real vote they will help decide the fate of the new Islamist governments.

I asked Egypt's leading women's rights campaigner, Nehad Abul Komsan, if the new constitution there was good or bad for women.

> It is a disaster. 'Bad' is a very nice word. It's a disaster for women and human rights in general. It is very vague and open to interpretation. We could end up with women leaving their homes only

twice. Once to move from their father's house to their new husband's house, and once to be carried to their graves. There is no guarantee that there will be a liberal interpretation of the constitution. There are no guarantees the situation for women won't be worse than Saudi Arabia.

Was she more worried by the Salafists or the Brotherhood?

Both, but sometimes we think the Salafists are much better than the Muslim Brotherhood. Both of them believe in the same thing but the difference is the Salafists are very honest about how they see the role of women. That means you can have a proper discussion with them and sometimes you can change their views. If you don't, then they will say honestly: 'We are not convinced.' The Muslim Brotherhood is completely different. They have the same beliefs, they have very conservative views, but they talk nicely about how they believe in women's rights. But their double, or triple, standards mean you cannot trust them. The last two years have shown they lie about everything. They just want to build a new dictatorship around religion.

Nehad was speaking as a woman who also took her faith seriously. When we met she was wearing a headscarf that entirely covered her hair. But her identity as a Muslim did not make her any less feisty about her rights as a woman in an Islamic society.

The Brotherhood entered the third year of the post-revolution era with not many friends at home and even fewer abroad. It struggled to find answers to Egypt's many problems simply because there are so many. For now the more elections it fights the more it is likely to lose support from the wider population. The sympathy it once had is long gone. The clean image it was so proud of has been sullied by the dirty business of politics. In power the Brotherhood was accused of using the same instruments of state security that oppressed its membership for so long to now try to silence its detractors. Its instincts were to try to impose obedience, but it failed. The people of Egypt had found their voice.

The Ikhwan had a mandate, but not an overwhelming one. They were reminded of that reality every time their own authoritarian streak got the better of them in the period that followed. 'The Muslim Brotherhood has not done very well because it is not a party of power, so now that they are in power they are a bit lost and they have been quite clumsy on many issues,' observed Professor Roy in the spring of 2013. 'They don't have a proper programme, so they have fallen back on the traditional tools of power: trying to control the press, trying to control the religious sphere and working with the security forces. But I think this is more about being a bit lost than having a hidden agenda.'

'Egypt is a place that needs the rest of the world,' one of Israel's senior military strategists warned me in April 2013, correctly predicting the coming chaos:

> It's got ninety million people and huge problems with water, food and the economy. I believe that more than likely Morsi, eventually, will fail, but not because Morsi will fail but because anyone would fail. Whoever comes first it is almost impossible to succeed there. I look at Egypt both as a potential threat but also as an opportunity. If there is an engagement between political Islam and the region and the rest of the world which works, well then the opportunities will grow. If not it will turn to radicalism.

A failure of the Muslim Brotherhood does not mean a failure of political Islam. It is perhaps the only thing the senior echelons of the Israeli military and one of the Brotherhood's most important figures of the last forty years, Abdul-Moneim Aboul-Fotouh, can agree on: 'I believe that Islam as a culture and its principles must be respected because whoever wants to represent the people of this region must understand that he can't rule without respecting the foundations of Islam's beliefs and principles.'

You cannot take God out of the politics of the Middle East any more than you can take God out of the politics of middle America. Both groups care deeply about their religion. Egyptians will happily sit around for hours, even with foreigners present, and savagely deconstruct the failings of their society. But even the educated Westernised elite, post-9/11, feel protective towards their faith. Many of these people took part in the uprisings and are still trying to work out what they want from the brave new world they helped create. Many will lean towards a moderate Sharia model for social issues in the public space but a secular model to guide their personal freedoms.

Islam is a religion that has a lot to say about politics. It offers guidance not only about individual morality but about wider society and governance. The more vocal minority of the urban elite might disagree, but the vast majority of Egyptian Muslims are quite comfortable about having aspects of Islamic law and tradition as a cornerstone of their new society. Political Islam is a reality that America and the wider West need to build into the foundations of their new foreign policies for the region. It is not going to wane in influence, even if, eventually, the Brotherhood does.

Egypt failed its first democratic test. Morsi's leadership was incompetent, divisive and hugely unpopular but he was fairly elected. A way should have been found to vote him out. It was the People who demanded his removal but by approving the short cut of a military intervention they may have damaged Egypt in the long run. Many Egyptians think toppling Morsi and having new elections gave them a clean slate. In fact it has permanently stained their democratic enterprise. The People may have now taken on and won their battles against both the army and the Ikhwan but they've also set a dangerous precedent. And they did it without building a viable political alternative. The Brotherhood may be down but they are not out.

After years of fighting, the Muslim Brotherhood and the army briefly realised they have more in common with each other than they do with the people who launched the revolution. These two organisations have grown old together. They began as a totally mismatched couple whose union was forged in the passion of Egypt's first revolution in 1952. They fought with, cheated on and betrayed one another. But through that process the institutions, if not always the individuals inside them, learned about, understood, and in their old age began to accept if not entirely trust each other. This was the realisation they reached soon after the 2011 revolution. But the popular coup in 2013 may get up a new generational struggle.

They both took a beating, quite literally, when they tried to shove the newly emboldened Egyptian people around during the periods when the generals and then the Ikhwan each got their chance to run the country. But the fact that the Muslim Brotherhood was in power at all in Egypt is as revolutionary an outcome for the region as the uprisings themselves. And when it comes to its role in the New Middle East, the Brotherhood has much more right to say it represents democratic values than many of the other regional Arab players. The Muslim Brotherhood has much less money, but it does have much more credibility, because it was democratically elected, however grudgingly and briefly. That is something the Gulf rulers cannot claim. The struggle will continue between the Muslim Brotherhood and the Saudis, as they compete for influence within Sunni societies. It is likely to be an important one, which is why the Gulf states were the first to congratulate the Egyptians on their 2013 popular coup.

If at home there is much that divides the three new forces in Egypt – the people, the Brotherhood and the army – abroad there is one issue that unites them. The cause of Palestine was the first thing that brought them together, and they all still think about it the same way. The ascension to power of the Islamists in the region has already begun to change the struggle for the creation of a Palestinian state. The new power wielded by Islamist parties has strengthened the Islamist movements in the Palestinian conflict too, at the expense of the more secular ones that have their roots in Nasser's socialist Arab nationalism.

The Brotherhood, in power, held off pushing hard on the Palestinian cause because it hoped for a successful first term in the Presidential Palace. The Ikhwan did not have a free hand in regional affairs because it needed Western help to sort out the economy. Domestic policy and the state of the economy will still, for now, consume the Brotherhood in whatever political role it plays in Egypt. But it will return to the issues it cares deeply about, and it cares deeply about the Palestinian issue. If there is one lesson to be learned from the Brotherhood's fight with the army, it is that this is an organisation with incredible patience. It will wait for its moment because it believes that, God willing, its moment will come.

3

The Problem

Sana Kadir was scurrying around her home in the Gaza Strip collecting her daughter's dolls, dusting them off and placing them in a small pile. Her husband and the neighbours were busy loading their possessions onto the back of a flatbed truck. The Kadir family was moving house. That had not been their intention the night before, but now they had a large hole in their living-room wall from which they could see the pancaked remains of the house of the man who had lived next door. His name was Ibrahim Saleh, and he was a senior member of Hamas's internal security forces. Mr Saleh still held his job that chilly winter morning because the Israeli airstrike had missed him. He wasn't at home. The same could not be said of his relatives, over a dozen of whom were now in hospital, having been dug out of the rubble.

The Salehs' house, in the Jabalia Palestinian refugee camp, had probably been hit by one of the Israeli drones that were still whirring above me. They drifted lazily across a brilliant blue sky that was etched with the swirling jet streams of outgoing Hamas rockets. Thumps and drones were the accompanying sound to the eight-day war fought between Israel and Hamas in November 2012. The Gazans called the drones the 'Zenana' because of the noise their engines make. Zenana is Arabic for 'whining child'.

When Sana had tidied up she was going to see her five children – three girls and two boys – who were in Gaza's Shifa hospital. 'I've become a refugee again,' she said as we stood in the wreckage of her home. 'I don't know where to go, perhaps to my father's house. We want to find a safe location, but only God knows where is safe or not. Perhaps nowhere is safe.' Gaza is just forty kilometres long, between six and twelve kilometres wide, and is home to more than 1.5 million people. With so many civilians in such a small space it is not the best place to have a war. For now though Sana's children were safe. They were not badly injured and they would soon be back with their parents once they'd been patched up. Omar Misharawi would not.

'Every day he would play here and watch his brother go around with his bicycle,' said Jehad Misharawi. We were standing in the hallway of the small single-storey breezeblock living area of his family home in Gaza. Omar was a beautiful eleven-month-old boy. In the picture Jehad showed me on his mobile phone Omar was wearing dungarees, a blue top and a wide, chubby, toothless smile. He had light almond-coloured skin and wispy brown hair which, because it was a little too long, had been brushed across his forehead away from his big brown eyes. 'He only knew how to smile,' said his father lovingly.

In the next picture Jehad scrolled to, Omar didn't even have a face. It had been burned off along with all his clothes and most of his skin by a missile that had burst through the roof of his house the day before. 'Look what they did to my Omar,' Jehad said quietly.

In war, seconds and inches are the difference between life and death. Omar was one step behind his mother, who was carrying his four-year-old brother Ali. Omar was in the arms of his uncle Ahmad. The missile crashed through the corrugated iron hallway roof and hit the wall above the outside door. Omar's mother Ahlam had just walked out over the threshold. Ahmad Misharawi, a step behind her, carrying Omar, had not. They were both engulfed in flames. The front door was reduced to charcoal. The neat rows of family shoes opposite were melted onto the rack they had been placed on.

This was 14 November, the first day of the war. Israel had just killed Hamas's military commander, Ahmed Jabari, and now it was bombing what it believed were missile sites and warehouses and Hamas was firing back. A missile went astray and hit the Misharawi home. The family and human rights groups said it was an Israeli airstrike. Privately, at the time, so too did Israeli officials. Publically, for months afterwards, the Israeli Defence Force, IDF, said it could not confirm or deny whether it had hit the house.[1] Then in March 2013 the UN Human Rights Council said that it was probably a Palestinian rocket falling short. The next month an investigation by the Israeli Military Advocate General reached the same conclusion.[2] Jehad dismissed the UN claims as 'rubbish', as did Hamas. Like much else in this corner of the Middle East the cause of the fireball that ripped through the family home was fodder for the competing lobby groups and they argued viciously over it. But the effect of the missile was indisputable.

Omar lived just an hour before his tiny body gave in to the terrible injuries it had sustained. His uncle Ahmad lived a few days beyond the announcement of a ceasefire before he too succumbed to the burns that covered him. His aunt who was also in the house was killed too. Jehad was a colleague of mine at the BBC. He was doing his job as a picture editor in our Gaza office when the rocket struck. We hugged outside the wreckage of his charred home just after Omar's funeral. 'God will look after your little boy,' I whispered to him. 'I should have been there to protect him,' he wept.

The Gaza war of 2012 was the first test of how the New Middle East would tackle the problems of the old. It also revealed for the first time how the Arab Spring had changed the balance of power on the ground. Before the uprisings the Islamists in the Gaza Strip were politically marginalised and confined by a blockade imposed on all sides by Israel and, against the wishes of his people, Mubarak's Egypt. The peace process between Israel and the moderate Palestinian leadership on the West Bank had been going nowhere for years, but security was under control, and that was what mattered to the Israelis and their friends in America. But once the Brotherhood was in power in Egypt, Hamas's isolation came to an end. During the November conflict a parade of Arab League ministers visited the besieged Strip offering their support for the Palestinian people. They stood side by side with the Islamist leadership of Hamas and condemned Israel as the aggressor. 'Egypt will not leave Gaza alone,' said President Mohamed Morsi to a crowd in Cairo during the conflict. 'I speak on behalf of all of the Egyptian people in saying that Egypt today is different from Egypt yesterday, and the Arabs today are different from the Arabs of yesterday.'[3]

'Hamas' is the acronym of 'Harakat al-Muqawamah al-Islamiyyah', which means 'the Islamic Resistance Movement'. It began life in 1987 as a wing of the Palestinian branch of the Muslim Brotherhood, which was founded in the territories in the 1930s. It was essentially a Palestinian version of the Special Apparatus wing of the Muslim Brotherhood in Egypt.

In Egypt the Brotherhood leadership eventually won back control of the wider movement from its militant wing. In the Palestinian territories the opposite happened. Hamas, which soon had an armed wing, replaced the Muslim Brotherhood, subsuming its identity and all its functions within it. The Hamas leadership runs everything from the military campaign against Israel to the social welfare programmes. In effect Hamas is what the Egyptian Muslim Brotherhood would have looked like if the Special Apparatus had won that fight. In Egypt the moderates eventually triumphed because their circumstances began to change after the death of Nasser. Hamas has not given up its armed struggle because as far as it is concerned the situation in the Palestinian territories has not changed. Hamas refuses to recognise Israel's right to exist and it pours scorn on the idea that negotiations alone with Israel will ever win concessions.

Mahmoud al-Zahar is one of the most powerful men in Gaza. He is a co-founder of Hamas and one of its hardliners. He is officially only Hamas's foreign minister, but that belies his real influence. As far as Israel is concerned al-Zahar is a high-ranking terrorist.

When I met al-Zahar on a chilly spring morning in 2013 he was sitting in the only sunny corner of his sandy courtyard. Outside the house the main street was blocked off and armed guards stood on each corner. They checked my bags on the way in, though the real threat to al-Zahar is always going to come from the air. In 2003 the Israelis tried to kill him by dropping a huge bomb on the compound we were now sitting in. He was slightly injured but his eldest son Khaled was killed and al-Zahar's wife was left paralysed. His youngest son Hussam was killed in an Israeli airstrike in 2008 during an operation to fire rockets into Israel. Al-Zahar, who is now in his seventies, told me he thought in contrast to the present Palestinian leadership in the West Bank: 'The crucial point about the people in the Hamas leadership is they have been seen to make sacrifices just like the ordinary people.' I asked him what Hamas's relationship with the Brotherhood in Egypt was, now that the Ikhwan were in control there.

'We are not taking our orders from anyone outside Palestine. Don't believe that,' he told me.

> The Muslim Brotherhood left each region to deal with their internal and external affairs according to their situation. So ideologically we are the Muslim Brotherhood, but we are not taking our orders from the Muslim Brotherhood in Egypt or Syria or elsewhere. Here we are running a policy against the [Israeli] occupation. In Egypt they did not consider the [Mubarak regime] to be occupiers, so they challenged them by peaceful protest. But we were forced to deal with the occupation, once the peaceful method failed, by resorting to an armed struggle.

Which is why the West has tried to marginalise his group. However, the Arab Spring began to overturn decades of Western mediation by weakening the Palestine Liberation Organization, the PLO, that the West had made so much effort to control, and strengthening an Islamist group that it could not. Hamas was a terrorist group in the eyes of most Western governments, whose diplomats were forbidden to officially meet with them. That meant the US and Europe, like Israel, had to deal through third parties. Which meant working through then Muslim Brotherhood-led Egypt and Qatar, both of whom sympathised with Hamas much more than they did with the

PLO, which is dominated by Abbas' Fatah movement. In 1974 the Arab League recognised the PLO as 'the sole legitimate representative of the Palestinian people'. Now that the Arab Spring has brought Islamist governments to power, it is quite clearly not seen that way by Egypt, the Arab League or even Israel any more.

The Arab Spring had forced Hamas to take a gamble. As it became increasingly clear that most of the victims of the Syrian government's violence were Sunni Muslims, Hamas began to lose credibility by sitting quietly in Damascus. The shift out of Syria, followed by a public declaration of support for the uprisings, brought them under the more moderate influence of Turkey and Qatar, which became their primary funders. Politically they moved closer to the new Egyptian government led by the Muslim Brotherhood.

The rise of political Islam meant Hamas once again had friends among the Sunni Muslim Arab states. This clearly infuriated the man in charge of Israel's 'Egypt file', Amos Gilad, a former major general and seasoned intelligence officer who now advises the minister of defence on policy towards Egypt. 'There is no dialogue between Egyptian president Mohamed Morsi and Israel's political echelon and there won't be. He won't talk to us,' he complained just before the Gaza war. 'Out of the desire for democracy, an appalling dictatorship has emerged in Egypt.'4

'This cycle of violence has definitely strengthened the political legitimacy of Hamas in the Gaza Strip and in the Palestinian territories in general,' Professor Mokhaimer Abu Sada from Gaza's Al Azhar University told me while the Israeli airstrikes could still be heard rumbling around us. 'President Mahmoud Abbas and Fatah are irrelevant. No one is talking to them.' That wasn't quite true: America was. The then secretary of state, Hillary Clinton, had gone that week to the city of Ramallah in the West Bank to consult with the leader of the Palestinian Authority, Mahmoud Abbas. It was a desperate attempt to make the Obama administration's only Palestinian 'partner for peace' look as if it was still a player.

*   *   *

President Mahmoud Abbas runs the Palestinian Authority. He is the chairman of the Palestine Liberation Organization, the PLO, and he heads the most important Palestinian faction in the PLO, and Hamas's arch-rival, Fatah. But he is ultimately in control of nothing. He ended up with all these titles because George W. Bush hated his predecessor, Yasser Arafat, and would only deal with the Palestinians after they elected someone else. Abbas was, wrote President Bush, 'a friendly man who seemed to genuinely want peace'.[5] Mahmoud Abbas, or Abu Mazen, as he is also known from his Arab world honorific, which means literally father of Mazen, his son, was promised that if he led these various institutions away from violence, and suppressed the Islamists, he would eventually be remembered as the man who got the Palestinians an internationally recognised state. Instead he has been humiliated by Israel, often abandoned by the US, and sidelined by events. Now, despite the odd dramatic flourish at the UN, he and the institutions he created to provide for the longed-for state have lost the faith of his people.

'Shame, shame, we can't live like this' had been the chant from the crowd of Palestinians in Ramallah on a bright autumn morning a few weeks before the Gaza war broke out. For more than a generation these streets have echoed with indignation and defiance against the Israeli occupation and expansion of Jewish settlements – homes built by Jews on occupied Palestinian territory. The West Bank has been the scene of an epic battle between two peoples over the ownership of land, with claims that go back to the time of the First Testament.

The problem for the Palestinians in general and Abu Mazen in particular is that it is a struggle with which the Western world is now largely bored.

'The international community is tired of an endless process that never produces an outcome.' On 19 May 2011 President Barack Obama delivered these words during his first speech on the Arab Spring revolutions. His address was 'to mark a new chapter in American diplomacy'. His speech was full of hope and tales of courage and freedom until he came to the old chapters of American diplomacy:

'The world looks at a conflict that has grinded on and on and on, and sees nothing but stalemate.'[6]

That stalemate was over long before the missile crashed into the roof above little Omar. During his short life the aftermath of the Arab Spring accelerated – something that before had been too incremental to see. The peace process is dying. That is because the premise behind it, the 'two-state solution', may already be dead.

The Palestinians insist that the bare minimum they will settle for from the 'two-state solution' is 'the independence of the state of Palestine, with east Jerusalem as its capital, on all the Palestinian territory occupied in 1967, to live in peace and security alongside the State of Israel, and a solution for the refugee issue on the basis of [UN] Resolution 194'.[7] Resolution 194 relates to the Palestinian refugees who fled or were expelled from their homes in the 1948 war. It says: 'Refugees wishing to return to their homes and live at peace with their neighbours should be permitted to do so at the earliest practical date.'[8]

The Israeli prime minister Binyamin Netanyahu had reluctantly accepted the idea of the two-state solution for the first time in 2009, but he had added: 'the Palestinian area must be demilitarised. No army, no control of air space. Real effective measures to prevent arms coming in, not what's going on now in Gaza.' The Palestinians must 'truly recognise Israel as the state of the Jewish people . . . with Jerusalem remaining the united capital of Israel' and 'the problem of the Palestinian refugees must be solved outside the borders of the State of Israel'.[9]

Four years on, the Israeli right had moved further to the right and Prime Minister Netanyahu was uncompromising. He made a new campaign pledge ahead of the January 2013 elections for the Israeli parliament, the Knesset. The growing political strength of the hardline religious Zionist settler movement means he is probably going to keep it. He was asked in an interview with the Israeli newspaper *Maariv*: 'Can you promise that during the next four years, no settlement will be dismantled?'

'Yes,' Netanyahu replied. 'The days when bulldozers uprooted Jews are behind us, not in front of us. Our record proves it . . . We haven't uprooted any settlements, we have expanded them,' and he added in a swipe at the newly resurgent pro-settler party Jewish Home: 'Nobody has any lessons to give me about love for the Land of Israel or commitment to Zionism and the settlements.'

The Israeli general election turned out to be the first for many years where the issue of the stalled peace process wasn't much of one in the campaign at all. The election saw two parties become serious players in the Israeli political scene for the first time, one from the centre and one from the hard right, but neither made the peace process easier.

The surprise on the night was Yesh Atid (There is a Future), the party of former journalist and TV personality Yair Lapid, which won nineteen seats. But the Israeli public voted for his centrist social policies, not for a peace deal. Lapid had said he favoured resuming talks, but was equally clear that he wasn't ready to compromise over Jerusalem or the major Israeli settlements. He used his Facebook page to say: 'I do not think that the Arabs want peace . . . What I want is not a "New Middle East", but to be rid of them and put a tall fence between us and them.'

Many Israeli politicians did better on polling day if they entirely rejected the idea of a Palestinian state. A key policy of the religious Zionist 'Jewish Home' Party, which more than doubled its number of seats in the parliament to twelve, was for Israel to annex 60 per cent of the West Bank. The party was led by the former software multi-millionaire Naftali Bennett. His supporters, many drawn from the settler community, had already managed to push Netanyahu's Likud Party to the right by ousting its more moderate MPs in the party's primaries and then voting instead for Jewish Home at the general election that followed. After a month of wrangling, and just days before Obama's state visit in March 2013, a new Netanyahu-led government was formed. The hard-line Jewish Home Party became part of the new coalition and Bennett joined the cabinet as economics and trade minister. He also became the first senior minister of the new government to publicly reject President Obama's appeal for compromise made during his rousing speech in Jerusalem. 'Giving territory to our enemies is not the answer,' he said.[10]

The only party that did want to talk about a peace process was the former foreign minister Tzipi Livni's. But at a polling station in an affluent area of West Jerusalem I watched two of her supporters try and fail for more than an hour to hand out her election material. Livni's campaigners had blue T-shirts sporting a big picture of her with an unsmiling, grumpy-looking face. The party activists were smiling though at the parade of middle-class voters in their slumber suits and just-rolled-out-of-bed hair. The voters smiled back, but they shook their heads at the offer of a pamphlet. And the outcome of the poll showed that the nation had largely shaken its head too at the prospect of making concessions to get a deal with the Palestinians. The tight nature of the race meant her party's six seats in the Israeli parliament were enough to get Livni a post in Netanyahu's coalition cabinet and the position of exclusive negotiator with the Palestinians, which was unlikely to win her any plaudits from the Israeli public. She had once said privately: 'I would join the cabinet even if it's only to hold his shaking hand while he signs the peace deal.' Her challenge now was trying to get Netanyahu to pick up the pen.

The reason why many Israelis do not care much about the peace process with the Palestinians on the West Bank is that they do not have as much to fear from those Palestinians any more. They have reacted to the cataclysmic unravelling of years of laborious peace negotiations by sitting on the beach in Tel Aviv, looking across the Mediterranean and pretending they are in Europe. They have the American-funded 'Iron Dome' anti-missile system to defend them in the skies. On the ground they have built a physical barrier to keep the Palestinians away. The Israeli government thinks it has the situation in the West Bank under control. It knows that is not true in Gaza.

Some Israelis are conflicted by the barrier because intellectually it repulses them. These people see it as a cruel collective punishment of hundreds of thousands of largely peaceful men, women and children. But they hold a guilty secret. In their hearts and in their homes, in private, they are grateful it is there. They don't eat in restaurants any more with one eye on the door in case a suicide bomber walks in.

Using public transport no longer feels like a life-or-death decision. Left-wing Israelis sometimes loudly condemn their government's refusal to move towards a just peace with the Palestinian people, but on the barrier their voices sink to a whisper. 'There is some kind of cognitive dissonance,' said an Israeli woman in her thirties to me privately at a dinner in Tel Aviv, attended by a mix of journalists and diplomats.

> Emotionally I think the Wall is completely wrong, and whenever I see it it moves something in me. But growing up in Israel I do remember [that period] as being horrible, frightening, going on a bus was terrible. I grew up in Jerusalem and I knew that you couldn't go on a number 18 bus and in Tel Aviv you couldn't go on a number 5 bus because those were subjected to [suicide] bombings. So there is the rational and the emotional and there is a huge conflict. I find myself thinking about it quite often, but the bottom line is that that sort of violence has stopped.

And what of those Palestinians in the West Bank stuck behind the barrier? Nazar was part of that noisy crowd standing in the streets of Ramallah shouting 'Shame, shame' and demanding their rights. Like the lady in Tel Aviv she too was in her early thirties. She was employed in the Consumer Protection department of the Palestinian Authority. What made Nazar's protest unusual was not her anger, but whom she was angry with. She was not denouncing the Israelis with her chants, though she believed they were behind many of her woes. Nazar and the rest of the protesters were in a stand-off against other Palestinians. These men were in uniform and they were protecting the offices of the Palestinian prime minister, Salam Fayyad, a former economist at the IMF, whom Nazar ultimately worked for. She and the people around her were demonstrating about the cost of living in the West Bank. 'Everything is very expensive, we cannot live like this, we need a solution for our problems,' she shouted to me over the noise of the loudspeaker.

'Hunger is disloyal,' Salam Fayyad's boss, Mahmoud Abbas, said of the protests. He was quoting from a Palestinian proverb about hungry people thinking only about food. But, he said, the protest meant that a Palestinian Spring had begun, 'and we are in line with what the people say and what they want'.[11] In one sense he was right, because the issues the protesters were shouting about were very similar to those of 'Bread, dignity and social justice' that I heard during the uprisings in Egypt. Where he was wrong was in thinking that his administration was on the same side as those people. And the International Monetary Fund told him these were scenes he might as well get used to. It warned that the situation in the coming years was likely to get worse: 'Looking ahead, with persisting restrictions, financing difficulties with aid shortfalls, and a stalemate in the peace process, there is a high risk of a continued economic slowdown, a rise in unemployment, and social upheaval.'[12]

'I can't imagine what will happen to my children,' Nazar told me. 'They will finish their education and they will not be able to live here, they may have to emigrate to another country. There are no jobs for the new generation. They just get their degree from the university and stay at home. This is a big problem.' It is exactly the problem that led to the Arab revolts. The Palestinian youths in the West Bank are also highly educated young people with very few opportunities to reach their full potential. But the fear of the generation of Palestinians who came before them, which fought in the two uprisings or 'intifadas' against the Israeli occupation in 1987 and again in 2000, is that their children are going to vote with their feet. What really worries them is the direction they'll take. They believe it will not be towards the Israeli checkpoints and military bases that dot the West Bank, but to the border with Jordan and beyond. The people who exhausted themselves against the army of Israel are worried that the next generation in the West Bank will give up on the state of Palestine without a fight.

Dr Khaleel Rashmawy was the manager of the bus company in the southern West Bank town of Beit Sahour. His business had been hit hard by a surge in fuel prices. His buses run on the roads around where the Second Testament says an angel told shepherds about the birth of Christ. The area is close to Bethlehem, and like Bethlehem is largely made up of Palestinian Christians. It is also a community from which an exodus is taking place away from the Holy Land. 'The big problem is emigration. Families are leaving the country,' Dr Rash-mawy told me. 'If this situation continues there will be a collapse, the [Palestinian] government will be demolished. Now the question is not how to fight the occupation, now the question is how to stay in the country.' That increasingly means that the people who are identi-fied as fighting the occupation are not the secular moderate Palestinian Authority but the Islamist militant groups in Gaza, the largest of which is Hamas.

'We ask ourselves, where is the Arab Spring in the West Bank?' This question did not come from a Palestinian, it came from a man sitting with me on the other side of the Green Line, or Armistice Line, which marks the ceasefire position from the 1948 war between Israel and the Arab nations. He was a senior commander in the country's army, the Israeli Defence Force, IDF, and he was paid to care what happens in the West Bank so that the people on the beach just down the road from his headquarters in Tel Aviv didn't have to. The commander told me:

> We ask ourselves what are the differences between Tahrir and Manara Square in Ramallah. And there are a lot of differences, but this might be a strategic shift in the West Bank. Our interest from the military point of view is to secure relative stability in order to give the political echelons on both sides the freedom to decide whether they want to go forward with some [peace] treaty.

That is a question that has been hanging in the air for decades. The conversation has only been held with the Palestinian groups who have renounced violence. They had been persuaded that if they gave up their arms then the world would work to give them a state. But they have seen the land upon which it was supposed to be built riddled with illegal Israeli settlements. They were promised a middle-class dream they suddenly could no longer afford. Meanwhile most Israelis, most of the time, felt they were already at peace without having to negotiate anything with the PLO.

It was an irony not lost on the region that during the first term of the Obama presidency the Israelis, even if by remote control, indulged in more successful negotiations with the 'bad' Islamist Palestinians running Gaza than they did with the 'good' moderate Palestinians running the West Bank. The PLO had given up their guns, recognised the state of Israel, swapped their fatigues for suits and ended up shuffled into irrelevance. Hamas in Gaza had done none of the above. It regularly fired rockets into Israel. It allowed violent hardline Salafist groups to operate on its turf, though it also used an equal level of violence to control them. And after the Arab revolts Hamas garnered more and more political support from Sunni Islamists outside. They were by far the greater threat to Israel and thus could not be ignored. The wider changes in the Middle East undermined the long campaign by the West and Israel to isolate and physically contain Hamas. The political influence within the Palestinian resistance against the Israeli occupation shifted away from the West Bank and towards Gaza.

President Obama began his first term seemingly determined to make Israel deal seriously with the moderate Palestinian leadership. Instead he allowed short-term domestic political opportunism in Israel to undercut America's long-term regional interests. The reputation of Mahmoud Abbas, the man whose credentials he had sought to embellish with that first phone call during his first full day in the White House, was in tatters by the time President Obama took the oath for the second time. The Palestinian groups on the West Bank, who had forsaken violence, were eclipsed by those in Gaza who had not. The Palestinian people were still not much closer to a proper state of their own than they had been when the conflict over the land began in earnest in 1936.

The state of Israel came into existence when the British Mandate for Palestine, which covered the areas of present-day Israel, Jordan, the West Bank and Gaza, ended on 14 May 1948. The British Mandate was part of the European powers' broader administration over areas of the old Ottoman Empire that had ruled the Middle East since the sixteenth century but then collapsed as a consequence of the First World War. The Transjordan part of the British Mandate, which is now just called the Kingdom of Jordan, was granted limited autonomy in 1923.

'Under the stress of the World War', the British made two offers as they struggled to defeat Germany. 'In order to obtain Arab support in the War, the British Government promised . . . the greater part of the Arab provinces of the Turkish Empire would become independent. The Arabs understood that Palestine would be included in the sphere of independence.' And 'In order to obtain the support of World Jewry, the British Government in 1917 issued the Balfour Declaration. The Jews understood that, if the experiment of establishing a Jewish National Home succeeded and a sufficient number of Jews went to Palestine, the National Home might develop in course of time into a Jewish State.'[13] That is how in 1937 the UK's Palestine Royal Commission, also known as the Peel Report, summed up what it called 'THE PROBLEM'. It was appointed in August 1936 'To ascertain the underlying causes of the disturbances which broke out in Palestine in the middle of April'.[14] If that summary sounds as if the British promised two peoples the same land, that is because they did.

This contradiction was supposed to be glossed over because of 'the belief that Arab hostility . . . would presently be overcome, owing to the economic advantages which Jewish immigration was expected to bring to Palestine as a whole'. The Commission concluded that the Arab people were financially better off, though 'not unnaturally they deny it'. However, 'Their feeling in the matter has been put in some such figurative language as this. "You say we are better off: you say my house has been enriched by the strangers who have entered it. But it is *my* house, and I did not invite the strangers in, or ask them to enrich it, and I do not care how poor or bare it is if only I am master in it." '[15] Even back in 1937 the authors believed that the two sides were as 'incompatible as their national aspirations'.[16] Those aspirations spread to a broader mass of the Jewish people, becoming profound and urgent after six million of them were murdered by the Nazis during the Second World War.

The Arab–Israeli war of 1948 settled none of the underlying issues raised by the creation of the state of Israel. So successful was Israel in repelling the Arab armies in that war that it ended up with 78 per cent of the former Palestine rather than the 55 per cent allocated under the United Nations partition plan adopted by the General Assembly on 29 November 1947. The UN plan had been immediately rejected by the Arab states. The day after the state of Israel was established the Arab armies invaded and tried to destroy it. The 1948 war didn't actually come to an end. The Israelis managed to push most of the Arab forces to the edges of the former Palestine Mandate boundaries. The West Bank, the Gaza Strip and East Jerusalem were all areas bounded by what became the 1949 Armistice or Green Line. The Jordanians controlled the West Bank and the Egyptians controlled Gaza. West Jerusalem was controlled by Israel, but the eastern part was controlled by Jordan. This included the ancient walled city and its important Jewish, Muslim and Christian religious sites. The Green Line formed the boundaries of what the world recognises today as Israel.

The region continued to seethe with resentment. There was no talk of peace or reconciliation. The Arab nations refused to accept the reality of Israel. The Israelis believed their reality was that if they let their guard down they would be driven into the sea. What changed between the first and second Arab–Israeli wars was the entrance of a new and enduring player in the region, America.

When the Cold War marched into the Middle East, each nation had to pick a team. The Israelis chose the right side of history, those who bought into Nasser's Arab brand of socialism did not. In 1967 Nasser, ever the gambler, overplayed his hand by threatening Israel with a war he couldn't win. He set himself up and the Israelis knocked him down, shaping the contours of the struggle between the Israelis and Palestinians to this day.

In the spring of 1967 Israel was threatening action against Syria for the growing number of guerrilla raids across its border by Palestinian gunmen.[17] This escalated into a dogfight between their fighter planes, with Israel downing six Syrian MiGs. Then the Soviet Union upped the ante by sending Egypt a bogus piece of intelligence that Israel was massing troops on the Syrian border. Egypt and Syria had a mutual defence pact.[18] But the American embassy in Cairo wired back to the State Department that it didn't believe protecting Syria was driving Nasser's thinking: 'It . . . seems clear that Nasser has resolved to deal with this imagined threat thru massive power play which, if successful, will be his biggest political victory since Suez, even if no shot is fired.' The cable was sent on 21 May 1967.

> If Syrians continue Fedayiin incursions and Israelis retaliate, there will be serious hostilities and Arabs apparently confident they can win in long run. If Israelis do not retaliate, Nasser will have forced them to back down and will have won first Arab victory over Israelis, and incidentally will have won another victory over US in Arab eyes. He is playing for keeps and we should make no mistake in this regard.[19]

As part of his bluster, on 16 May Nasser moved his troops across the Suez Canal and into the Sinai so that they could travel up towards Israel with the intention of massing ominously near the border. Only they could not, because there was still a UN peacekeeping mission between them and the Israelis that was left over from the last conflict in 1956. Having the UN in the way meant Nasser's play was unlikely to be taken seriously, so Egypt asked the UN to pull out from the eastern frontiers between Israel and Egypt. The UN said it was either all or none of the four thousand five hundred troops in the Sinai. On 18 May Nasser chose none, and so by default the UN handed back to Egypt control of the Straits of Tiran, which were an important shipping route for Israel. Nasser then closed the Straits to them. By 31 May all the UN troops were gone.[20] Everyone, publicly, was ready to go to war.

'Our basic objective will be the destruction of Israel. The Arab people want to fight,' said Nasser on 27 May 1967.[21] But it was a huge bluff, because he knew the Arab armies were in a pitiful state. More importantly the White House knew it, and so did the Israeli military, though they tried to suggest they were less equipped to take them on than they really were. The CIA said of an assessment by Mossad, the Israeli intelligence service: 'We do not believe that . . . was a serious estimate of the sort they would submit to their own high officials.'[22] So, 'Informed by these [CIA] assessments, President Johnson declined to airlift special military supplies to Israel or even to publicly support it. He later recalled bluntly telling Israeli Foreign Minister Abba Eban, "All of our intelligence people are unanimous that if the UAR [Egypt and Syria] attacks, you will whip hell out of them." '[23] One of those CIA assessments said: 'Israel could almost certainly attain air supremacy over the Sinai Peninsula in less than 24 hours after taking the initiative.'[24] And that is exactly what they did. The Egyptians blustered and stumbled their way into a conflict they were bound to lose. The Israelis listened to the constant threats and assumed they would have to fight another war with the Arabs, and at this moment they knew they had the upper hand. Israel launched a pre-emptive strike on the morning of 5 June.

They drove the Arab forces from the divided city of Jerusalem, capturing the holy sites. By taking the entire Sinai Peninsula up to the Canal Zone, the West Bank, the Gaza Strip and the Golan Heights they also more than trebled the area of land under their control. The fate of the ancient city, perhaps more than anything, is still the main stumbling block for attempts to find a peaceful resolution to Israel's dispute with the Palestinians and the Arab world at large.

Contained within the old walled city is what the Jews call the Temple Mount and what the Muslims call Al-Haram Al-Sharif, the noble sanctuary. This is where the seventh-century Dome of the Rock was built over the spot where Jews believe Abraham was about to sacrifice his son to God. The golden dome is the iconic symbol of Jerusalem. This is also the location of the eighth-century Al-Aqsa mosque. Judaism's Western Wall, or Wailing Wall, which is believed to be a perimeter wall of the second biblical Temple, is below. It is an important Jewish prayer site. But the most sacred site for Judaism is the Temple Mount. The Jews believe the biblical King Solomon built the first temple there 3,000 years ago. Many Jews believe they are forbidden by ritual law from visiting the Temple Mount out of fear they might tread on sacred ground where the faithful believe the Holy of Holies, which enshrined the Ark of the Covenant, once stood. A second temple was razed by the Romans in AD 70. Christians believe Jesus taught at the Temple during the Roman period and this was where he drove out the money-changers.

Muslims see Al-Haram Al-Sharif as the third-holiest site after the cities of Mecca and Medina in modern Saudi Arabia. They believe that this is where Muhammad was transported by the archangel Gabriel on his way to ascend to the heavens. The Koran began to be revealed to Muhammad from the age of forty, and this went on for more than twenty years. It culminated in that journey to Jerusalem where he rose from the rock to be in God's presence and receive his final revelations. The passion felt for this small area of land by both Arabs and Israelis still fuels their unwillingness to compromise. The loss of Jerusalem and control over access to Al-Haram Al-Sharif became a rallying cry for the Islamists. They increasingly saw it as their role to fight against Israel and its Western allies after the failures of their national armies. Liberating Jerusalem and their holy sites became their new cause.

Unlike the war of 1948 and the war that would come in 1973, according to a future Israeli prime minister, Menachem Begin, the 1967 conflict could have been avoided:

In June 1967 we . . . had a choice. The Egyptian army concentra-
tions in the Sinai approaches do not prove that Nasser was really

about to attack us. We must be honest with ourselves. We decided to attack him. This was a war of self-defence in the noblest sense of the term. The government of national unity then established decided unanimously: We will take the initiative and attack the enemy, drive him back, and thus assure the security of Israel and the future of the nation.[25]

There are still arguments over who was to blame for the war, but there was no getting away from the fact that the Arab armies had been thumped again by a nation just a fraction of their size. It was partly that the Arab armies were just not good enough, partly that Israel had superior military hardware. But there is a more fundamental issue at the core of the outcome of the three Arab–Israel wars. The Arab states did not and do not, even today, properly understand the stakes. These were essentially wars of choice for the Arab armies, even if they didn't always fire the first shot. For Israelis in their own minds they were and always will be wars of survival. They have no other choice but to defend where they are because they have no alternative. Their military leaders believe that when it comes to fighting wars, lack of choice is Israel's biggest advantage. The present Israeli chief of staff, Benny Gantz, once showed me a photograph on the wall of his private office. It was of the main entrance of the Auschwitz-Birkenau concentration camp. This history reminds Israel's military leaders of the stakes they believe they are sometimes playing for.

The 1973 war with Egypt was the closest Israel had come to losing. The oil embargo or 'supply shock' imposed by the oil-producing Arab nations meant that the Americans were to remain fully engaged in the region from then on. When Sadat made it clear that he was serious about talking to Israel, it completely surprised Washington but also energised the then US president Jimmy Carter into working towards a grand plan to bring peace and stability to the region.

The 1979 peace deal with Egypt changed everything for Israel. It wasn't just about making peace with the largest Arab nation and the region's biggest standing army. The treaty fundamentally changed

Israel's ability to wage war against its other Arab neighbours and enabled it to keep a firm grip on the Palestinian territories it occupied in 1967 and still occupies today. 'From that moment Israel enjoyed dramatic changes,' Major General Giora Eiland told me. As an Israeli paratrooper he had fought in the 1973 war. He went on to serve as the country's national security adviser, and even in retirement still advises the Israeli government today.

> After we signed this peace agreement we could assume that whatever Israel does on other fronts it is not going to cause any security risk from the Egyptian side. So we could have the first war in Lebanon in 82, in which we sent most of our divisions to Lebanon and we did not have to be too concerned about the possibility that Egypt will take the opportunity to attack us from the south. We conducted the second war in Lebanon [in 2006]. We had a very wide large-scale ground operation in the West Bank in 2002, we attacked Gaza in 2008 and in all those years although we knew the Egyptians would criticise us at the political level we could be quite confident that Egypt would not take any real military measures. For many, many years we used to say almost as a mantra: 'Well we will continue to assume that Egypt is not going to be part of our enemies as long as the situation is intact.'

The rise of the Muslim Brotherhood in Egypt took Israel's old military certainties away.

That's not to say that without the Camp David Accords Israel would not have fought these conflicts. In each case the government said it was acting to protect the nation from external threats. But without the peace treaty the bar for military action would have been set much higher because the risks of a wider war would have been much greater.

Sadat believed that by doing the two Camp David deals with Israel he was not only ensuring peace for Egypt but would solve the 'Palestinian Problem' which had eluded Nasser. He was wrong. Not having had much luck with the Arab states that do exist around it, Israel has not been in much of a hurry to help create another one. President Jimmy Carter told me as we sat together in East Jerusalem:

> The Camp David Accords came about in 1978, and that was a commitment by the United States and by Egypt and by Israel to give the Palestinians full autonomy and to withdraw Israeli 'military and political forces' from the West Bank and Gaza and from East Jerusalem, from Palestine. Then six months later came the Peace Treaty which only involved Israel and Egypt and the United States.

But with a clear feeling of bitterness even now, Carter added that in the end Israel took what it wanted from the agreements and ignored the rest.

> The Peace Treaty [with Egypt] has never been violated. Not a single word has been violated. But from the very beginning, as soon as I left office as a matter of fact, Israel did not follow through with their commitment to give the Palestinians their rights. And so that was an unfortunate decision made by Israel to abandon that part [Palestinian autonomy] of the Camp David Accords which was ratified by the way by the Knesset and by the US Congress and also by the Egypt Parliament.

Peace with Egypt now gave Israel the opportunity to deal with the guerrilla movement, the Palestine Liberation Organization, which since 1969, under the leadership of Yasser Arafat, had launched thousands of attacks on Israeli targets. The PLO had been based in Jordan but was driven out in the so-called Black September of 1970 by King Hussein, who was trying to protect his kingdom and his rule from being overthrown by the Palestinian militants. The PLO, as was clear from its title, did not see itself as an Islamist project; it was a secular liberation organisation. The PLO moved to Beirut and continued its fight with the Israelis. In 1982 Israel invaded Lebanon to expel them from there too. This last conflict would end up putting US and European boots on the ground in an ill-fated peacekeeping mission. It also led to one of the most shameful episodes of Israel's brief life.

As the PLO leadership left Beirut for exile in Tunisia its forces were strewn across the Arab world. 'Their expulsion from Beirut marked the end of the PLO as a coherent fighting force.'[26] Left behind in the Palestinian refugee camps were the fighters' families. These camps were under the protection of the IDF when the Israeli defence minister Ariel Sharon allowed the deployment into the Sabra and Shatila camps of a Christian militia group that was already fired up after the assassination of its leader, which it blamed on Palestinian militants. On 16–18 September 1982 these militiamen carried out a frenzy of rape and murder, slaughtering at least eight hundred men, women and children anywhere they found them. Their bodies were left to rot in the alleyways in which they fell. Survivors reported hearing the militia groups tell each other to use axes so as not to alert other Palestinians to what was about to happen to them too. There was outrage across the world, including in Israel, where Sharon had to resign after a commission said he bore indirect responsibility for the deaths.

Ariel Sharon seemed to have a profound impact on everything he touched. Before he was the defence minister he was the agriculture minister. At that time he was helping Israeli Jews trying to settle in the occupied West Bank to get around international law by claiming that the land was actually needed for military not civilian use, which is allowed under international law. But the Israeli Supreme Court stopped him. Sharon immediately called a meeting of all his advisers in a big hall and asked them for ideas about what to do next. Among them was a West Bank military legal adviser called Alexander Ramati. 'I was sat somewhere in the middle. I raised my hand and said: "There's a concept called 'Mawat Land'." [Sharon] stood up and came around to me. He told the person sitting next to me to get up. The guy got up. Sharon pushed him aside, sat down and asked: "What did you say?"'

Ramati told him that under the laws of the old Ottoman Empire, land that had not been cultivated for three years was declared 'Mawat' or 'dead'. At this point it returned to the Empire. In light of this old law the courts revised the ruling to declare that Israel was at present the custodian of the land. That meant that until the land's status was resolved, it could be used for Jewish settlements as long as no Palestinian could prove that it was privately owned by them. The history of the beginning of the settler movement was told by Ramati, and other elderly judges and lawyers, in the 2011 Israeli documentary *The Law in These Parts*.

The definition of 'dead land' was that it had to be far enough away that when standing on it you couldn't hear the crow of a rooster on the edge of the nearest village. When Sharon heard of this loophole he told Ramati: ' "With or without your rooster, be at my office tomorrow at 8 o'clock." [Sharon] issued orders to look for uncultivated land with helicopters. Overnight we had a helicopter and a pilot. Someone from operations and myself sitting in a cockpit with the pilot searching for "Dead Land".'

The process that would create what became euphemistically known as 'facts on the ground' had begun. The first settlers, who began arriving after the 1967 war, were driven by a religious belief that the West Bank, or 'Judea and Samaria' as Israel calls it, was given to the Jews by the Almighty. The 1967 war was a watershed for Israel's religious Zionist movement. The victory against the Arab armies was seen by them then, and is still seen by many religious people today, as a modern miracle. It was a sign from God that He was protecting the land of Israel. The religious Zionists saw it as their duty in return to reclaim all the land of Israel that He had bestowed on the Jews. They are still trying to do that, and after the 2013 elections they have never had as much political power as they do today.

Over time though, after the 1967 war, many more secular or ultra-Orthodox people just moved in to the occupied territories in the West Bank and Gaza because the government provided them with cheap housing. The growth of the settlements, some of which have swelled into huge population centres, has become the biggest threat to the possibility of creating a viable Palestinian state. The 4th Geneva Convention prohibits the transfer of the occupying nation's civilians on to the land it has occupied. The United Nations' bodies regularly issue demands calling for the withdrawal of settlers from the territories based on article 49 of the convention.[27] But Israel claims historical and biblical links to the land and says the convention is not relevant to the territories because 'as there had been no internationally recognized legal sovereign in either the West Bank or Gaza prior to the 1967 Six Day War, they cannot be considered to have become "occupied territory" when control passed into the hands of Israel.'[28] But even its best friend, America, considers the land to be occupied. I was in the audience on 21 March 2013 when President Obama told a packed convention centre in Jerusalem of Israeli university students:

> It is not fair that a Palestinian child cannot grow up in a state of their own, living their entire lives with the presence of a foreign army that controls the movements, not just of those young people but their parents, their grandparents, every single day. It's not just when settler violence against Palestinians goes unpunished. It's not right to prevent Palestinians from farming their lands or restricting a student's ability to move around the West Bank or displace Palestinian families from their homes. Neither occupation nor expulsion is the answer. Just as Israelis built a state in their homeland, Palestinians have a right to be a free people in their own land.

Thirty years earlier, with the scattering of the armed wing of the Palestinian resistance and a growing number of Jewish settlers moving onto their land, life under the occupation of the Israeli security forces slowly began to push the Palestinian population to the brink of revolt. Their anger exploded in 1987 and led to six years of widespread rioting and the establishment of Hamas. Its charter,

produced in 1988, calls for Israel's destruction and in effect says it is
every Muslim's duty to 'liberate' Palestine. Its content has been used
by Hamas's opponents to accuse the group of anti-Semitism.
Mahmoud al-Zahar told me the charter is not a reflection of Hamas
thinking today:

> The charter was just an attempt to put the movement into an ideo-
> logical framework. It is not a covenant such that before anybody
> does anything they go and read it. You [the West] have abused the
> charter to give the impression that Hamas is fanatical and extremist
> and so forth. But I think the accusations against the charter are
> now finished with because the same [Islamist] character is now
> present [after the revolutions] in Egypt and Tunisia and Morocco
> and everywhere.

Hamas was born of the First Intifada, which was itself the response to
the coming of age of the first generation of Palestinians who had only
known life living under Israeli occupation. The images of young men
and boys in the West Bank and Gaza using rocks and stones against
heavily armed Israeli troops won the Palestinian cause much more
international sympathy than the militancy of the PLO. It also
re-established the boundaries they were fighting for. In 1979, a month
after he had concluded the signing of the Camp David Accords,
Prime Minister Menachem Begin had declared that 'the Green Line
no longer exists, it has vanished for ever . . . We want to coexist with
the Arabs in Eretz [the land of] Israel.'[29] The Intifada brought the
Green Line back into people's lives because most Israelis, apart from
settlers, were suddenly restricted from entering the West Bank and
Gaza for their own safety. That remains the case for most areas today.

The PLO's leadership had been physically and politically marginalised in Tunis, but Yasser Arafat used the momentum of the Intifada to
rethink his strategy. In 1988 the Palestinian leadership accepted the
idea of the two-state solution envisaged by UN Resolution 181 from
1947, and thus recognised for the first time Israel's right to exist. The

Palestinian government in exile also renounced terrorism. It was in stark contrast to Arafat's response to the peace process between Israel and Egypt ten years before, when he declared from Beirut: 'There will never be an alternative except the gun, the gun, the gun.'[30]

In 1991 the US, under President George Bush Sr, and the soon to be defunct Soviet Union co-sponsored the Madrid Convention. It was the first time in forty-three years that Israel sat down with all its Arab neighbours to discuss peace. The Palestinians were part of a joint delegation with Jordan. The PLO and Yasser Arafat were not invited. It led to Israel's 1994 peace treaty with Jordan, but more importantly to secret negotiations hosted by the Norwegians in Oslo which produced the first face-to-face agreement between the PLO and the Israeli government, the 1993 Oslo accords. Arafat though went into the negotiations with a weaker hand internationally because he had infuriated the West and the Gulf states by supporting Saddam Hussein in the First Gulf War in 1991. He had emerged from the crisis, after Saddam was kicked out of Kuwait, looking, to his financial and political backers, both treacherous and clueless.

Arafat had already shown by then that he was not very good at international diplomacy. He put himself on the wrong side of the Sunni–Shia divide by becoming the first foreign 'head of state' to visit the new Shia leadership in Tehran after the 1979 revolution. He eventually fell out with the Iranians too, and also for supporting Saddam in the eight-year Iran–Iraq war. The new Supreme Leader Ayatollah Ali Khamenei described Arafat as a 'traitor and an idiot'.[31] It was a sentiment many Arab heads of state could agree with.

There had been other peace processes in the past, but the 1993 Oslo agreement was the one that led to the creation of the Palestinian Interim Self-Government Authority. The negotiations planned under the Oslo accords were to lead 'to a permanent settlement based on Security Council resolutions 242 and 338'.

Security Council Resolution 242 was passed on 22 November 1967, after that year's war. It required:

the establishment of a just and lasting peace in the Middle East which should include the application of the following principles:
Withdrawal of Israeli armed forces from territories occupied in the recent conflict;
Termination of all claims or states of belligerency and respect for and acknowledgement of the sovereignty, territorial integrity and political independence of every State in the area and their right to live in peace within secure and recognised boundaries free from threats or acts of force.

The vagueness of its language, and in particular the phrase 'from territories', still has the two sides arguing whether it meant *all* territories or just *some* territories. Resolution 338 was drafted in 1973 after the Arab–Israeli war of that year and is essentially a reaffirmation of Resolution 242. Resolution 242 embodies the idea of an exchange of land for peace.

On 13 September 1993 there was, amid much fanfare, a signing ceremony in front of President Bill Clinton on the White House lawn. The agreement was between the state of Israel, represented by Prime Minister Yitzhak Rabin, and the chairman of the Palestine Liberation Organization, Yasser Arafat. The following year the two men, along with the Israeli Foreign Minister Shimon Peres, were awarded the Nobel Peace Price. The expectation was that the Palestinian Authority it created would last a maximum of five years, hence the word 'Interim' in its title. Implied in the agreement is the idea of two states. Fundamental to reaching it was the PLO recognising Israel's right to exist and Israel recognising that the PLO represented the Palestinian people. On that day

The Government of the State of Israel and the PLO . . . representing the Palestinian people, agree that it is time to put an end to decades of confrontation and conflict, recognise their mutual legitimate and political rights, and strive to live in peaceful coexistence and mutual dignity and security and achieve a just, lasting and comprehensive peace settlement and historic reconciliation through the agreed political process.

But they did not. Rabin was assassinated for his part in the deal by an Israeli ultra-nationalist religious Jew, Yigal Amir, in 1995. Arafat continued to wrangle with his successors.

Nearly twenty years later Nazar and her colleagues were still able to shout at the PA because the 'interim' Authority still existed. Temporary has a tendency to last in this corner of the Middle East. Mahmoud Abbas has occasionally threatened to dissolve the PA and leave the Israelis to pick up the pieces. Some Palestinians have urged him to do just that and put the dying Oslo process out of its misery. But he has never looked likely to follow through on the threat, and many people I've met on the West Bank believe that's because the Palestinian leadership in general has simply got too comfortable with the few trappings of power they do have to want to give them up. Of the three architects of the Oslo accords only Shimon Peres has lived long enough to see them widely reviled by both sides. Peres is now the President of Israel and when we met in April 2013 he had just become, at eighty-nine, the world's oldest head of state. We sat together in his private office at his official residence, and his Nobel Prize sat on the shelf behind him. I asked him whether he agreed that the Oslo Peace Process had run its course. 'I don't think so,' he said. 'The choice is clear. Either to have one state where two [peoples] are quarrelling endlessly or two states where the two of them have good relations.' So why, twenty years later, was there still no deal? 'To negotiate is not a simple matter. Many people think to negotiate is to convince the other party. No, it's a problem of convincing your own people and I'm speaking as a man who worked all his life for it. The people say "Yes we are for peace. Yes we are ready to pay the price of peace, but why do you pay so much? You don't know how to negotiate! Why do you trust them so much? You are naïve!" And I say there are two things that cannot be achieved in life unless you close your eyes a little bit. And that's love and peace. If you want perfection you won't obtain either of them.'

Oslo wasn't the last big deal; there were several other agreements and false dawns. All, like Oslo, were built around the idea of a state of

Israel living alongside a state of Palestine. The foundation for each was the formula of 'land for peace'.

In 2000, as President Bill Clinton's time in office drew to a close, he tried to speed up the full implementation of Oslo by tackling some of the so-called final status issues like defining borders, control of Jerusalem and the right of return of the hundreds of thousands of Palestinian refugees who had fled or been driven out of their homes in the 1948 war. He set out what became known as the 'Clinton Parameters'. The talks were between the then Israeli prime minister Ehud Barak and Yasser Arafat. They failed. Clinton blamed Arafat. Unfortunately they failed in the middle of an Israeli election campaign.

A political stunt by the man who was challenging Barak in the polls, Ariel Sharon, and Palestinian frustration at the failure of the peace process sparked the Second Intifada. On 28 September Sharon made a visit to the place in East Jerusalem known to Muslims as Al-Haram Al-Sharif. It is also the location of the Al-Aqsa mosque. The Jews call the area Temple Mount. It would have been hard to find a more sensitive place to make the political point that he would never concede any of Jerusalem in a peace deal. Fighting broke out at once between police and protesters. The following day there was rioting across Jerusalem and the West Bank. The unrest barely paused for the next five years.

The second Palestinian Intifada was well under way when Ariel Sharon won the premiership in February 2001. It was thoroughly brutal, with children and other civilians being killed by both sides. The Israeli military opened fire on the Palestinians as they tried to put down the unrest. Israeli civilians were blown to pieces in buses and bars by Palestinian suicide bombers. The Israeli human rights group B'tselem said around three thousand Palestinians and a thousand Israelis died during violence between 2000 and 2005.[32]

The Second Intifada was nothing like the first. It reduced parts of the occupied Palestinian territories to war zones. The memories of the horror and suffering they experienced in those years at the hands of the Israeli army are the main reason why the Palestinians in the West

Bank have not resorted to a third uprising despite the failures of the peace process. The Palestinian people cannot bring themselves to go through it again. The Second Intifada also marked the steady decline of the left and the peace movement in Israel. Many Israelis concluded that they couldn't live side by side with people who had blown up diners in restaurants. Many people on both sides lost all sympathy for the suffering of the other.

The years of the violence of the Second Intifada took place while the Western world's attention was firmly elsewhere in the wake of the 9/11 attacks, the invasion of Afghanistan and the war in Iraq. But by contrast it got a lot of attention in the Middle East, because the Arabic news network Al Jazeera was now broadcasting. People across the Arab world could watch an overwhelmingly sympathetic portrayal of the Palestinians' struggle against Israeli occupation around the clock and contrast that with the inaction of their own leaders.

The Second Intifada ended only after Arafat was dead.

The man who replaced him, Mahmoud Abbas, finally declared a ceasefire with Sharon in February 2005. Sharon did two things that have fundamentally changed the political and physical landscape in the conflict. In 2002 he began to build the barrier that snakes around and often encroaches into the Palestinian territories. In 2004 he announced a unilateral withdrawal from the Gaza Strip.

These were profound shifts in policy for the right-wing Sharon. They both struck at the core of the debate in Israel about what the priorities of the state of Israel are. What should come first, the land of Israel or the people of Israel? The hard-line religious Zionists consider the boundaries of Israel to have been set by God, and so for a politician to decide where Israel begins and ends is a blasphemy. The centre and what remains of the dwindling left thinks it is the people of Israel that matter most, so building the barrier and withdrawing from the occupied territories if peace can be assured becomes their priority.

The barrier is now a defining factor in the conflict, even though Sharon said: 'The fence is a security rather than political barrier, temporary rather than permanent.'[33] But even today, people can't agree what to call it. Journalists say simply the 'separation barrier', because that's what it does. The Israelis call it the 'security fence' because that's how it makes them feel and most of it is fence and barbed wire. The Palestinians call it the '*jidar al-fasl al-'unsun*', Racial Segregation Wall, because that's how it makes them feel.

Whatever people call it, the barrier more than anything else has changed the dynamic of the peace process. The International Court of Justice issued an advisory opinion in 2004 that said where it deviated into occupied West Bank territory it was illegal.[34] That's true for 85 per cent of the barrier. Israel said the court had no jurisdiction in the matter. The barrier had a calamitous effect on employment for Palestinian men because those who worked in the Israeli construction or agricultural industries lost their jobs. Israel ended up importing labourers all the way from Thailand to pick fruit and vegetables while thousands of Palestinians a kilometre away sat idle. The pull-out from Gaza also led to the slow ascent of Hamas over Fatah in the Strip. The rise of Islamist forces in Gaza who regularly fire rockets into Jewish communities living on the other side of barrier persuaded many Israelis that a similar pull-out from the West Bank would lead to the same result. This mistrust will only be further entrenched over time. Most Israelis now never set foot inside the West Bank and so have no idea how much it has changed since the years of the Second Intifada. Their children grew up amid the suicide bombings of that period and are generally more right-wing than their parents. Many Palestinians living on the West Bank or Gaza grew up mixing with ordinary Israelis on beaches or restaurants in Tel Aviv and Haifa. Their children have not had these experiences. They've rarely seen an Israeli who isn't carrying a gun.

Sharon was cursed by the right for his decision to pull out of Gaza. It was welcomed by President Bush, who wrote later that Sharon 'as the father of the settler movement' was making a 'bold move'. In April 2004 the two men swapped letters to put on record a quid pro quo. Sharon outlined his plan, and in return Bush wrote a letter to Sharon implying that he would support some of the larger Jewish settlements in the West Bank staying with Israel under any future deal. 'In light of new realities on the ground, including already existing major Israeli population centers, it is unrealistic to expect that the outcome of final status negotiations will be a full and complete return to the armistice lines of 1949,' he wrote.[35] The then United Nations Secretary General Kofi Annan thought the Gaza pull-out was 'the right thing, done the wrong way' and he wrote later: 'The barrier was built with both a security *and* a political purpose in mind. The same was true of Israel's disengagement from Gaza.'[36]

When Ariel Sharon suffered a serious stroke in 2006, which left him in a permanent coma, some Israeli religious extremists considered it divine intervention for his actions in Gaza. But during the final years of his active life, he was not the only player trying to shape events on the ground.

The Saudis came up with a plan in 2002 promising full Arab recognition for Israel if it went back to the 1967 borders. That got no further than 2003's 'roadmap' drawn up by the 'Quartet' made up of the United States, Russia, the European Union and the United Nations. The reality of the Quartet, a former member of the Envoy's team told me, was that 'We were in Disneyland and Tony Blair was Mickey Mouse.' The Quartet made no progress on a peace deal either. The Palestinian Authority leadership regarded Blair as biased towards Israel, and in private they constantly lobbied for his replacement.

The 'roadmap' was preceded by George W. Bush becoming the first US president to explicitly call for the creation of a Palestinian state in 24 June 2002. At the same time he called for the Palestinians to dump Yasser Arafat as their leader. That prompted George W. Bush's mother to call him disapprovingly 'the first Jewish President'.[37] This was because the son was more willing to take Israel's side than the father. George H. Bush had taken a much tougher line with Israel during his presidency, opposing loan guarantees to Israel because of its settlement building.

Bush Junior though always had Israel's interests at heart, a fact initially made easier by his loathing of Yasser Arafat. Arafat embodied in Bush's mind what the 'War on Terror' was being fought for, even though Arafat was fighting for turf, not for God. 'The President was disgusted with Yasir Arafat, whom he saw, accurately, as a terrorist and a crook,' wrote his secretary of state, Condoleezza Rice.[38] With Abbas at the helm, Bush later sponsored another round of talks in Annapolis, but they too came to nothing.

'Wouldn't it be amazing if democracy in the Middle East sprung first from the rocky soil of the West Bank?' asked George W. Bush of his staff in June 2002.[39] Instead his hopes floundered on the rocky soil of Gaza four years later because his push for elections produced a result he did not want and led to a fundamental split within the Palestinian opposition movement.

As George W. Bush had willed, the Palestinian people went to the polls to elect their legislative representatives. The expectation of almost everyone who didn't have to live in the occupied territories was that Abbas's party, Fatah, would win. They reached that conclusion exactly *because* they didn't live in the occupied territories, and so they didn't have to put up with the hopelessly inefficient and corrupt Fatah officials who were a legacy of Arafat's rule. Abbas himself was overwhelmingly elected as the president of the PA in January 2005 because he was considered to be an honest, decent man. The same could not be said for many of the people around him. They were thieves and the Palestinian people knew it.[40]

Hamas ran on a platform of clean and good governance which was backed up by its long history of social-support systems modelled on the Muslim Brotherhood. It won seventy-four of the 132 seats in the legislative council. Fatah won forty-five. The Bush democratic road-show had veered wildly off course.

The election of Hamas did three things. It marked the beginning of the end of the 'Freedom Agenda', it eventually led the people of Gaza into their present miserable existence, and it slowly elevated an Islamist group to the forefront of the resistance against the Israeli occupation of Palestinian land. Hamas though, unlike the other Islamist groups on Washington's list of terrorist groups, is not a Salafist jihadi organisation. Like the PLO it is primarily fighting for the sake of land, not God. Unlike the PLO or Hezbollah, it says it has never taken its war outside the boundaries of historic Palestine.

For eighteen months Hamas and Fatah shared power with Mahmoud Abbas as president and Hamas's Ismail Haniyeh as prime minister. It was a match made in hell, and no one expected it to last.

Months of sporadic violence between fighters from Fatah and Hamas culminated in what was effectively an all-out war in Gaza between the two sides in June 2007. It took a week for Hamas to rout the Fatah forces and secure their control of the Strip. They threw a number of the captured Fatah fighters off the roofs of tower blocks in the city. Hamas's Mahmoud al-Zahar told me he thought there could be no genuine reconciliation with Fatah while Mahmoud Abbas is in charge because he says Abbas is too weak to ever go against the wishes of the US and Israel. 'Why did Sharon leave Gaza?' he said. 'Because of our resistance. And who is delaying the withdrawal of the Israelis from the West Bank? It's the PLO, and Abu Mazen in particular. His security is "cooperating" with the Israelis. What is "cooperating"? They are spies. Abu Mazen and his group are spies.'

After Hamas took over, Israel immediately tightened its restrictions on what was allowed into Gaza, introducing a blockade, a variant of which still persists today.

In 2008, at the tail end of Ehud Olmert's time as Israeli prime minister, he and Abbas came close to a deal. By then, though Abbas was representing all Palestinians at the talks, he had no sway over Gaza. However the two men apparently came close to agreeing between themselves the borders of a Palestinian state. The Israelis say Abbas was given maps. His chief of staff, Mohammad Shtayyeh, told me Abbas was shown a map that he then had to scribble down on a napkin from memory and take back to his team for discussions. Olmert left office, because of a serious corruption allegation of which he was later partially cleared, before a deal could be ironed out. Netanyahu won the election and replaced him and is still there. Abbas said four years later that he and Olmert had been 'two months' away from a deal. For those four years there were no serious peace talks and no progress on the process at all.

Kofi Annan blames many of the failures of international diplomacy 'on the unhealthy possessiveness that Washington has over the Arab–Israeli peace process, and its reluctance to share it meaningfully with others, even those working towards the same ends'.[41] The truth is that Israel has very little time for the United Nations because it rightly considers the majority of its members to be hostile. 'You don't write in any applause lines when you're writing a speech for the UN,' joked Prime Minister Binyamin Netanyahu's speechwriter to a colleague.

While Abbas sat around waiting for peace talks to start up, the situation in Gaza for many people got harder and harder under the blockade. The public reason given for the restriction was to stop dual-use items that could be used to manufacture weapons. The private reason, articulated to me many times by senior Israel politicians and military men, was to make life unpleasant for the ordinary people of Gaza. The hope was that they would compare their lives with those of the Palestinians in the West Bank and, if they got the chance again, would vote Hamas out. A secret US diplomatic cable sent in late 2008 said:

> Israeli officials have confirmed to Embassy officials on multiple occasions that they intend to keep the Gazan economy functioning at the lowest level possible consistent with avoiding a humanitarian crisis . . . As part of their overall embargo plan against Gaza, Israeli officials have confirmed . . . on multiple occasions that they intend to keep the Gazan economy on the brink of collapse without quite pushing it over the edge.[42]

Included in the list of items refused entry at various times were light bulbs, candles, musical instruments, crayons, clothing, shoes, mattresses, sheets, blankets, pasta, tea, coffee, chocolate, nuts, shampoo and conditioner. Canned meat has been allowed in, but not canned fruit. Gazans could sip mineral water but not fruit juice.

In October 2012 the Israelis lost a long legal battle to keep secret an embarrassing document that showed they had meticulously calculated 'the point of intervention for prevention of malnutrition in the Gaza Strip'. In it they worked out the minimum daily calorie intake needed for the adults and children there.[43]

I used to have regular private conversations with Israeli officials in which they constantly complained about the way the media reported the restrictions. They were very defensive because even they thought some of the restrictions were indefensible. The conversation normally ended when I asked: 'So why do you ban coriander?' They never had an answer for that, something that was publicly acknowledged only after many of those restrictions were lifted. 'We never understood why the Ministry of Defence actually forbade coriander to enter Gaza,' said the Israeli Foreign Ministry spokesman Yigal Palmor. 'It did reflect some kind of petty interference with items that seemed of little note.'[44]

The restrictions were eased, though the blockade continues, after the Israelis in May 2010 bungled a raid on a Turkish boat, the *Mavi Marmara*. The boat was part of a flotilla trying to symbolically break the blockade. The vessel was intercepted by Israel's IDF. Instead of disabling the boat they tried to board it by abseiling from helicopters. This meant one by one their men dropped into an angry mob that began to beat them up as they landed on deck. In the chaos that followed the IDF shot nine of the activists dead. That refocused the world's attention on the situation in Gaza. A UN inquiry found that Israel's soldiers had faced 'significant, organised and violent resistance' but added that the decision to board the ship and the use of substantial force was 'excessive and unreasonable'.[45]

The flotilla was the latest in a series of campaigns by often European pro-Palestinian activists which had gained momentum after the Gaza war of 2008–9 when the IDF attacked the Strip because of rockets being fired into Israel. That conflict, like the one in 2012, was launched in the middle of an election campaign for the Israeli Knesset. However during that three-week war, in addition to airstrikes, Israel also launched a ground invasion. Human rights groups say that more than fourteen hundred Palestinians, including three hundred children, were killed. Thirteen Israelis were also killed in the conflict.[46]

Gaza in a material sense is not as bad as other parts of the Arab world I have seen. What makes Gaza one of the most depressing places to be on earth is its isolation from the real world. In July 2010 the British prime minister David Cameron said: 'Gaza cannot and must not be allowed to remain a prison camp.'[47] Under international law, Israel is still the occupying power in Gaza, although it no longer has a permanent military presence there.

But at that stage Israel held the keys to just three sides of this 'prison'. The full blockade could only be sustained because Egypt under Mubarak kept its border with Gaza locked too. He did not want to see a strong Islamist group like Hamas emerging on the Gaza side of the Rafah border crossing because he did not want them inspiring their co-Islamists on the Egyptian side. 'Who wants Gaza?' Israel's then chief of staff, Gabby Ashkenazi, asked me with a laugh in 2010 soon after the *Mavi Marmara* fiasco. 'We don't want Gaza. Mubarak doesn't want Gaza. No one wants Gaza!' At least he was honest; the so-called champions of the Palestinian cause were not.

'Huge hypocrites' was how someone in the United Nations described the Arab world's dealings with the Palestinians to me before the 2011 uprisings. The Arab states used the descendants of the 1948 refugees as a political stick to publicly beat Israel on the world stage. They used oil in 1973 when it was the Arab armies getting a pounding, but they didn't use it to pressure America to get a better deal for the Palestinians. At home they often treated their uninvited Palestinian guests with the kind of contempt Europeans reserve for the traveller or Gypsy communities. Entire generations of Palestinians have now grown up with refugee status. All were encouraged to keep their Palestinian identity by refusing them anything else, even though many refugees have never set foot in the land from which that identity derives. In Jordan they were given citizenship. In Syria they were given the chance to participate and work almost as citizens. In neighbouring Lebanon, with its even more fragile balance between religions and sects, they were not. It is a shock to walk around the slums the Palestinian refugees in Beirut are still forced to live in.

Even though their forefathers were farmers, the generation in exile are thoroughly urbanite. Barred from the safety net of government jobs, they had to make their way in the cut-throat world of the private or informal sector. Many flourished, and in places like Jordan the fact that they have been so successful and have become so wealthy has increased tensions with the state. In fact despite the best efforts of almost every actor in the region the Palestinian people have shown an ingenuity and creativity in business that has been sorely lacking in the people that have ended up representing them in politics.

'The Israel–Palestinian conflict is quite easy to understand,' a diplomat once told me as we stood looking over the Mount of Olives on a hot summer's day in Jerusalem. This was the place where Jesus once prophesied the end of days. On this day though we were discussing a phenomenon that seemed to have already outlived its usefulness: the peace process. 'It's a competition for victimhood,' spat the diplomat. He was referring to the perpetual struggle between Israel and the Palestinian Authority to win international opinion. And it is a game to which many of the players seem addicted.

From 1994 to 2011 the European Union donated around €5 billion in assistance to the Palestinians. Over the same period the US government has committed $4 billion to the Palestinian Authority.[48] This has paid, among other things, for the institutions of the state the PA is building and the people it employs to run everything from security to social welfare. But the Palestinian Authority is still often lurching from one funding crisis to the next. Things are made worse if it's had a recent spat with Israel. In a system worked out around the Oslo peace accords, Israel collects tax revenues on the PA's behalf, so it will sometimes withhold them to punish it for its political manoeuvring.[49]

In 2013 the online 'CIA World Fact Book' stated: 'Israeli closure policies continue to disrupt labour and trade flows, industrial capacity, and basic commerce, eroding the productive capacity of the West Bank economy.' Which partly explains the contrast in the 'Fact Book' between its being able to credit Israel, among a long list of industries, with 'aviation, communications, computer-aided design and manufactures, medical electronics, fiber optics', but listing the *entire* range of West Bank industries as 'small-scale manufacturing, quarrying, textiles, soap, olive-wood carvings, and mother-of-pearl souvenirs'.

The small amount of industry is supplemented by thousands of projects employing thousands of people supported by international NGOs on the ground and NGOs overseas. They range from 'Doctors without Borders', which says on its website that its 'teams provide medical care, short-term psychotherapy and social assistance and referral to people affected by violence and conflict in the West Bank', through to 'Clowns without Borders', who were presumably encouraging the locals to find the funny side of life on the West Bank at a circus school in Nablus.

The Oslo accords were supposed to lead to one Palestinian state. Events by now have conspired to create two very different Palestinian entities. The one in the West Bank offers the Palestinians a normal-ish life, though the Hamas leader Khaled Meshaal told me sarcastically in 2010 from his old headquarters in Damascus: 'Fayad is building up a better system for a people inside a prison.' But this was not the view shared by the wider international community. Instead they saw the West Bank as an opportunity for the Palestinians to show that they could build the institutions of a viable state, with law and order and good governance, and which, through negotiation, would lead to a state of Palestine.

As life got worse in Gaza under the blockade, life improved for the Palestinians in the West Bank, because millions of dollars of aid money created a false economy. It bought acquiescence from much of the population still worn out by the two Palestinian intifadas. Even Israel's most senior military figures doubt there will be a third one. The people on the West Bank were given cheap loans and they used them to buy new homes. These homes soared in price, and just like people in the West the people in the West Bank used that rise in value as an asset to get more loans, and then bought new things and fell deeper in debt. The story is familiar. It has been told in every Western economy over the last ten years, but the circumstances in the West Bank are very different. There houses prices went up because in most of the West Bank, Palestinians don't control where they can and can't build – the Israelis do.

Under the so-called Oslo 2 peace accords, signed between Israel and the Palestinians, the West Bank is divided into three areas: A, B and C. The Palestinians have almost total control over Area A, which includes their main urban centres, and partial control over Area B. But in the remaining 62 per cent of their land known as Area C Israel retains near-exclusive control, including over law enforcement, planning and construction. This is the area where the most rapid expansion of Jewish settlements has taken place. It was this area that the Jewish Home Party campaigned in the 2013 elections to annex. Around 325,000 Israeli settlers live in some 135 settlements and around 100 outposts in Area C.[50] There are also 150,000 Palestinians living there. The Israeli government dismisses the settler numbers by saying they occupy only a tiny proportion of the land. That is true, but to protect them and the roads they drive on Israel insists on controlling a much larger area. The United Nations states that:

> Most of Area C has been allocated for the benefit of Israeli settlements, which receive preferential treatment at the expense of Palestinian communities . . . Palestinian movement is controlled and restricted by a complex system of physical and administrative means. These include the Barrier, checkpoints, roadblocks, and a permit system, which undermine livelihoods and access to basic services, as well as the ability of humanitarian organisations to deliver assistance.[51]

The daily grind of dealing with the occupation leaves Palestinians on the West Bank with a perpetual sense of frustration and humiliation.

Seventy per cent of Area C is included within the boundaries of the regional councils of Israeli settlements and is therefore off limits for Palestinian use and development.[52] Most Palestinians can't get planning permission. If they do build homes without it these are regularly demolished and the families are forcibly evicted.[53] Because the amount of land available for Palestinian housing is restricted it artificially inflates prices.

Population pressure meant the same was true even in the Gaza Strip, where in some places a square metre of land just before the war in 2012 could cost up to twenty thousand dollars.[54] The most expensive bits of land are where the international organisations are based, because developers think those areas are less likely to be bombed. The few who could afford the prices had often made their money getting around the blockade by going under it. They built huge tunnels across the border into Egypt's Sinai through which they smuggled foodstuffs, fuel and livestock. If someone had the money they could get an entire car dragged through them too. The border with Egypt at Rafah was a mass of small tents. Under each one was a huge tunnel. They were a remarkable sight, and if you were good at digging the tunnels could make you a millionaire.

The tunnels were also the military lifeline for Hamas, which used them to bring in guns, ammunition and rockets to attack Israel. Before the Arab revolts they also brought in suitcases full of cash from Hamas's then financial backers in Syria and Iran. Without cash the organisation would grind to a halt, so Israel took a particular delight in hitting the moneymen. 'They are in a very bad economic situation. They need money,' a member of the Israeli cabinet told me a few months into the Arab Spring. 'Certain deliveries of money [to Hamas] were intercepted by us. One of them by targeted killing operations. The money was in a certain car and we exploded it.'

Hamas in the post-Arab Spring era doesn't have to play cat and mouse with the Israeli drones to get hold of cash any more. The month before the war, in October 2012, the Emir of Qatar, Sheikh Hamad bin Khalifa al-Thani, became the first head of state to visit the Strip since Hamas took power. He brought with him a pledge of $400 million for building projects. Gaza today looks like a huge building site. The Emir's visit was an acknowledgement of the new reality. The Islamist Hamas, which had much more in common with the policies of Qatar than Fatah did, was on the up. That was something that was not lost on Israel. 'It's odd that he interferes with the Palestinians' internal conflicts and chooses to offer his support to Hamas,' said an Israeli Foreign Ministry statement. 'With this visit, Qatar has thrown the chances for peace under the bus.'[55] If that was an accurate description of what dealing with Hamas meant for the prospects for peace, then Israel had certainly helped nudge them into the road.

The year before the Emir's visit the Israelis agreed to swap more than a thousand Palestinian prisoners in return for the release of one Israeli soldier, Gilad Shalit, who had been captured and held for five years by Hamas. The huge disproportion in the numbers was an illustration of how much the Israeli people wanted Shalit back. Most Jewish Israelis have to send their children to do military service, and so Shalit's capture resonated with parents across the land. The deal was a milestone because it proved that Israel could deal with Hamas when it thought it was in its interests. And in the zero-sum game of Palestinian politics the swap boosted Hamas and made the PA look impotent. Again Israel acted for short-term political gain. The Israelis wanted to punish Abbas for attempting an always jinxed bid for full state membership status for the Palestinians at the United Nations. A successful bid would have given Palestine all the rights and recognition of any other country at the United Nations, instead of being a territory. But creating a new country would have required Security Council approval, which the Palestinians would not have got.

Even though it was doomed to failure, Hamas wasn't happy either with the PA's bid, which held out the vague hope of progress through non-violent resistance. And Hamas needed something to stem the growing frustration with its rule. It was running out of money and started introducing unpopular taxes on cigarettes and other consumer goods that produced a general backlash. The people of Gaza were also weary of living under the constant threat of Israeli airstrikes just so that a few young extremists could show off their revolutionary credentials by firing rockets into Israel. Both the Israeli and the Hamas leadership had something to gain politically, and both wanted the PA to lose.

So Israel dealt with its devil. It negotiated via the Egyptians with Islamists bent on its destruction. The man Israel arranged Shalit's release with, and who walked the young soldier to the border crossing, was Ahmed Jabari. It was the assassination of Jabari on 14 November, as he was driven down Omar Muktar Street, Gaza's main thoroughfare, that led to the eight-day war in 2012.

The PA's weakened position after the kidnap deal and the Gaza conflict was acknowledged by its prime minister, Salam Fayyad: '[The] Palestinian Authority stands for a non-violent path to freedom – we have not been able to deliver, it was Hamas that was able to release over 1,000 prisoners, to get this much attention. I think it's absolutely important to recover from this – but we need to be honest with ourselves.'[56]

'The weakness of Abbas with his negotiations with Israel is that he is not backed by anyone. He is just waiting for [help from] the United States or the international community but he has no teeth,' Ghazi Hamad, who is Hamas's deputy foreign minister and one of its more moderate voices, told me just before President Obama made his 2013 trip to Israel and the West Bank.

> So Israel, they don't care about him, they say 'OK, we can negotiate for ever with him.' But Hamas, we have some cards in our hands, for example when you have the Shalit card you can get your prisoners from Israel, you can push them to give concessions. When you have rockets or missiles, even though they are primitive, sometimes you can exert pressure on Israel.

The reality the PLO found itself in led to promises at the end of 2012 that the international community 'will work urgently . . . to restart the peace process before the window for a two-state solution closes'.[57] But 'urgently', like 'temporary', is a word that has also lost its meaning here. And the voices of moderation are being drowned out by a cacophony of those on the two extremes. It is their voices that have become the engine of this conflict. Words have become more dangerous than the rockets and missiles. They are used by each side, but perhaps most viciously and irresponsibly by their unaccountable supporters and lobby groups worldwide to dehumanise the other. Over time the words used to justify violence seem to have corroded the sense in both peoples of right and wrong when it comes to the way they wage war.

During the last war I heard the news of a bomb attack on a civilian bus in Tel Aviv, which badly injured several people, being greeted by celebratory gunfire in Gaza city. Then over the loudspeakers in the mosques it was described as a 'victory from God'.

On the other side, despite the already disproportionate loss of life among the Palestinians, Israel's right wing was not satisfied. Ariel Sharon's son Gilad, who is a major in the IDF, wrote during the conflict: 'We need to flatten entire neighborhoods in Gaza. Flatten all of Gaza. The Americans didn't stop with Hiroshima – the Japanese weren't surrendering fast enough, so they hit Nagasaki, too.'[58] The then interior minister in Israel's ruling coalition, Eli Yishai, said: 'The goal of the operation is to send Gaza back to the Middle Ages. Only then will Israel be calm for forty years.'[59]

Many Israelis would distance themselves from this kind of jingoism, but the state also works hard to persuade the Israeli public of the justification of its actions. 'Unbelievable but true: 111 Israelis wounded today,' wrote the IDF spokeswoman Avital Leibovich on her official Twitter account during the height of the war. 'Unbelievable' was a fair assessment: the Israeli ambulance service's own figures on that day reported that eighty-two of those 'wounded' were suffering from what they called 'anxiety'. On another day sixteen casualties were reported. The ambulance service said nine were 'anxiety' and six had 'bruises'.

The IDF also took great pains to find good reasons why so many civilians had died in the conflict. The UN's Office for the Coordination of Humanitarian Affairs (OCHA) said on 22 November that two-thirds of the by then 158 people killed by Israel were civilians. Leibovich tweeted that only a third of the dead were 'uninvolved' in terror. Six Israelis died during the conflict, four of them civilians.

The worst single incident of the conflict was the bombing of the home in central Gaza's Nasser district where a mid-ranking Hamas policeman called Mohammed Dalou lived with his extended family. He was an unlikely target for such a massive airstrike. Mohammed and the nine other members of his family in the house died. So did two neighbours. Among those killed were five women and four children. The dead spanned three generations; the youngest was one-year-old Ibrahim Dalou. At the time of the strike I was reporting from Gaza's Shifa hospital when it suddenly burst into chaos as bloodied and screaming children began to arrive. Minutes later I was on the street they had just come from, watching a desperate and ultimately futile attempt to dig more survivors out of the rubble. Much of the Dalous' home had been flattened into a deep crater. Around the section that wasn't, rescuers were trying to use a crane to lift up the top floor to get to the collapsed rooms underneath. There was a brief moment of hope when seven-year-old Sarah Dalou, dressed in a pink top and grey track pants, was pulled out from beneath. But it quickly grew clear, from the way her small body hung limp in the arms of the man who held her, that she was dead.

The Dalou house was where the visiting Arab ministers went to express their fury against Israel over the loss of civilian life. It became in the Arab world a symbol of what it saw as Israeli aggression. The bombing was a PR disaster for Israel, made worse by the fact that the IDF for days could not get its story straight. Human Rights Watch said the strike on the family was unlawful.[60] In private Israeli government officials admitted to me from the start that the bombing of the Dalou home was a mistake. Six months later that was confirmed by the Israeli Military Advocate General who said the deaths of the family were 'regrettable' but that there was 'no basis to open a criminal investigation or to take any additional measures' against the IDF personnel involved in the air strike.[61]

The Israeli government and the IDF considered the reporting of much of the conflict by the Western media unfair because it focused so much on the civilian deaths in Gaza. Israel rightly pointed out, as I reported at the time, that Hamas was firing rockets from central residential areas and that those rockets were being deliberately fired at Israeli civilians. Human Rights Watch called that a violation of the laws of war.[62]

The problem for Israel is that it's not a level playing field when it comes to civilian deaths. Most Western governments consider Hamas to be a terrorist organisation exactly because it kills civilians. Israel is a democratic state, and when it ends up killing, as it did in Gaza, lots of children, it is held to a very different standard. The UN Human Rights Council report that said the IDF was not responsible for killing Omar Misharawi went on to say of the final death toll of 168 Palestinians 'killed by Israeli military action ... 101 are believed to be civilians, including 33 children and 13 women.'[63]

The way the war is reported also plays into the regional dynamic and the sense among people from the Arab world of a Western double standard towards the conflict. There is a disconnect between how the West and the Arab world view the same events. Arab audiences on their TV screens during the Gaza war saw in all their gruesome detail the images of every child killed by Israeli bombs. They cannot understand how Westerners can look at those images and not be moved. What they do not understand is that different cultural sensitivities mean Western audiences do not look at those images, because they are considered too gory for broadcast. The news bulletins about the same stories may contain similar facts in the Arab and Western world, but they carry entirely different images. In the West the belief is that if viewers are confronted with graphic scenes of violence they will literally switch off and so will not learn about what has happened at all. So in the Gaza war and also in other conflicts like Syria and previously in Iraq, the true horror of what has just happened to civilians on the ground is rarely explicitly conveyed to audiences in the Western world. To audiences in the Arab world it always is.

Instead, the blame game in the West is often played around the level of violence as described by the statistics. So the numbers and the words to describe them become key. Lobby groups on both sides focus on things like whether reports say people 'died' or were 'killed', whether 'people were bombed' or 'targets hit'.

The last Gaza war was an important milestone in the conflict, and not just because it was the first battle fought after the sea change in the Arab world. During the war Hamas proved for the first time that it had rockets that could hit Israel's biggest cities like Jerusalem and Tel Aviv. Suddenly more than half the country's population had cause to feel vulnerable to attack again. Among the Arab public the scale of civilian deaths caused outrage. Unlike the previous conflicts, this time their opinions actually mattered to their leadership, because they had been elected by them.

The two main campaign issues of recent years regarding the Palestinian cause have been the illegal Jewish settlements and the situation in Gaza. The first made the secular Fatah look ineffectual. The second made Hamas in Gaza look like the only serious players in the struggle with the Israelis.

The last war again increased the strength of Hamas and so weakened the Palestinian Authority's leaders. That produced a sense of panic in the international community, because it coincided with a very public shift to the right in Israeli politics after the ruling Likud dumped many of its liberals. The Europeans were suddenly alarmed by polls that said Israel was likely to vote in a more right-wing government than it actually did – one that didn't want to talk to the Palestinians no matter how moderate they were. It raised the prospect of Mahmoud Abbas and his Palestinian Authority being consigned to the scrapyard as a legitimate vehicle for the aspirations of their people.

Something had to be done, and this time something was, by the European states at least.

On 29 November 2012, exactly sixty-five years to the day after the United Nations decided to divide British Mandate Palestine into a Jewish and a Palestinian state, another landmark event took place at the UN. The member countries voted overwhelmingly to upgrade the Palestinians' status from an observer entity, represented by the PLO after the 1993 Oslo accords, to a 'non-member observer state' like the Vatican. Only one European nation, the Czechs, opposed it. The word 'state' had moved into the international lexicon, though it still did not mean that a Palestinian state had been internationally recognised. But it was a word that mattered. Israel was isolated during the vote from all but its allies in North America. As important as the vote was the fact that it showed that the Obama regime could now not bend either the Israelis or the Palestinians to its will.

Two months after the vote the Palestinian leadership decided to celebrate with some new stationery bearing the legend 'State of Palestine'. They also had a new placard made up saying the same thing for their first appearance of the New Year 2013 at the United Nations. The US's UN ambassador, Susan Rice, immediately objected to it. The PA left important documents like ID cards alone. 'At the end of the day, the Palestinian Authority won't cause trouble for its people,' said one of President Abbas's spokesmen, which underlined the point made by the US State Department, which declared dismissively: 'You can't create a state by rhetoric and with labels and names.'[64]

No one is bothering to dress up the battered remains of the two-state solution, which seems more and more likely to dissolve into a one-state reality. That suits the Jewish right, which wants to formally annex the whole of the West Bank. That would leave the state of Israel with a choice. It cannot be Jewish, control all that land and be democratic. The demographics of absorbing that many Palestinians mean that a greater Israel can only have two out of those three things, though the Israeli right has some vague notion that it could keep the

Palestinian land but not the 2.65 million Palestinian people who live on it.[65] The 'One-state' solution also increasingly suits the Palestinian left, who view it as an opportunity to launch a version of the Anti-Apartheid campaign that worked so successfully against South Africa.

But the man who first coined the phrase 'land for peace' for a speech he wrote in the 1980s for the then secretary of state George Shultz told me there just cannot be any alternative to the two-state solution. 'For seventy-five years since the Peel commission everybody knows that there has got to be partition,' said Ambassador Daniel Kurtzer.

> The only people that seem to believe there is an alternative are nut cases like Dani Dayan [the former leader of Israel's Settler movement], who writes in the *New York Times* that everything's fine, everything's just dandy, but it's not, and there is no right-minded Israeli who would agree with a one-state solution even if they didn't know that the Palestinian intention is to do an apartheid campaign. The alternative of trying to swallow the Palestinian population just doesn't work, so if you want to plan for a short lifespan for the state of Israel you can try to live that way and at some point the thing just implodes. And if the right wing thinks it can rely upon the Haredi multiplication table [the high birthrate among ultra-Orthodox Jews], well, this is a large segment of that society that doesn't support the state anyway. So you know it's a fool's paradise to think otherwise.

The growing shift in Europe, as illustrated by the UN vote, was not something that the Israeli leadership had been blind to. It just didn't care very much. Israeli officials told me privately that those around Binyamin Netanyahu recognised this change but that it was impossible to persuade Netanyahu that it mattered. He'd put all his eggs in the American basket because he believed he could contrive the support of the American public, even if it meant going over the head of the American president. This view was shared by the right-wingers in his cabinet. A minister in the present Israeli cabinet put it to me once like this: 'I know the American people support us but I'm not sure about the White House. In Europe I know the leaders support us, I'm not sure about the people.'

During the Gaza conflict both the American people and the American government did support Israel. It worked to get a ceasefire between the two sides, but made it clear it fully supported Israel's actions during the fighting. The go-to man for President Obama to get that ceasefire was President Mohamed Morsi, who was reluctantly praised even by the Israelis. The agreement was described to me by a senior Israeli military figure as 'a strategic compromise we can live with'. That deal entailed the Israelis promising not to assassinate Hamas leaders and having to further relax their blockade. Most of Gaza's population is crammed into the urban strip, but there are larger open areas around it. Under the deal, land closer to the separation barrier was allowed to be farmed. Gazans also got more fishing rights, and more construction material was allowed in. Once again the violent resistance from Islamist groups in Gaza won new concessions from the Israelis while the attempts to negotiate by the moderate Palestinians in the West Bank did not.

In 1997 Binyamin Netanyahu sent Mossad agents to try to assassinate the Hamas leader Khaled Meshaal in neighbouring Jordan with a complex plot involving a rare poison. Meshaal then had to spend the years that followed hiding in Syria. But after the 2012 Gaza war Netanyahu had to sit back and watch Meshaal end his decades in exile with a very public and triumphant visit to the Strip for the first time ever. A few months later Meshaal, who is now based in Qatar, was re-elected by the leadership for another four-year term.

President Morsi, like the broad mass of the Muslim Brotherhood, was not willing to accept the status quo. He made that clear during the 2012 Gaza conflict and he has done so since, but when he spoke about the ceasefire negotiations he revealed that the Brotherhood's pragmatism at home will also be applied to its dealings abroad. 'President Obama has been very helpful, very helpful,' he declared. 'We are not against individuals or countries or states, we want to live in peace with others, but real peace, comprehensive peace.'[66]

But Morsi's unvarnished views were uncovered by a pro-Israeli

press-monitoring group the following year when it released comments
the president made about the previous Gaza conflict, before the Arab
Spring catapulted the Muslim Brotherhood into power. In an excerpt
from an interview given in 2010 he described Zionists as 'these blood-
suckers who attack the Palestinians, these warmongers, the descendants
of apes and pigs'.[67]

The Axis of Resistance, the previous champion of armed Palestinian groups, which contained Syria, Hezbollah, Iran and Hamas, is in
the process of being smashed. The Assad regime will not be around to
support the cause, and the mask slipped anyway with the bombing of
the Palestinian refugee camp in Yarmouk on the outskirts of Damascus in December 2012. That left dozens of Palestinians killed or
injured. When I tried to visit the camp two months later it was still
sealed off by Syrian security forces.

Hezbollah, by sticking with Syria, has undermined its credentials
with huge swathes of the Arab world. Hezbollah is a creation of Iran,
so while Tehran supports Syria it will too. But Iran, the fulcrum of it
all, is in economic meltdown because it is under a form of international siege. It is also facing a resurgence of Sunni forces in the region
and the threat of a military attack from the strongest nation on earth.

Hamas is now much more beholden to Egypt, Turkey and Qatar,
but its leadership believes the Arab Spring has permanently shifted
regional support in its favour, because it, not the PLO, shares the
same broad ideology as these regional powers. 'These have not been
revolutions, they have been an Islamic awakening,' Mahmoud
al-Zahar told me. 'Look who took power after elections in Egypt, in
Tunisia, in Libya and even in Morocco, without a revolution. It will
take a decade, but then you will see a very big change in the geopolitical status. The Islamic countries will unite and will cooperate and
will not be tools for the West or the East, they are going to represent
themselves.'

The Israelis and the Egyptian leadership may hate each other, but that
does not mean they cannot find ways to work together. This will

continue to take place through military channels with the private acquiescence of the politicians on each side, who will continue to snipe at each other in public.

Israel is more worried about militancy in the Sinai than it is about militancy in Gaza. Hamas now has the responsibilities of government. It is not single-mindedly preoccupied with attacking Israel any more. But Sinai does concern Israel, and it needs Egyptian cooperation to deal with the growing militancy there. Egypt is worried about losing control of Sinai too. The Sinai has always been the transit point for Iranian weapons to Gaza, which were flown to Sudan then smuggled up through Sinai to the Strip. The revolt in Libya has produced a flood of weapons, looted from Gaddafi's military, onto the black market. Many of those weapons ended up in Syria and North Africa but Israel knows a lot also ended up in the hands of militants in the Sinai who live in an area that is mountainous and difficult to control. A consequence of the peace treaty between Egypt and Israel was that the Sinai was largely demilitarised. During Mubarak's rule nothing was done to build up the peninsula's infrastructure and economy, so drugs and gunrunning became the most lucrative enterprise. Egypt too does not want Gaza becoming a safe haven for Sinai militants. It does not want the tunnels being used as their conduit. It warned Hamas of that when in February 2013, even after the Muslim Brotherhood came to power, the Egyptians flooded some of the tunnels with sewage.

Israel's shared boundary with Gaza is tiny. Its border with the Sinai is huge. Strategically speaking everything has now changed for Israel after the Arab Spring. Over the last forty years, since the 1973 war, the Egyptian and Syrian borders were quiet. Israel was fighting against either armed Palestinian militants in the West Bank and Gaza, or the militant group Hezbollah on its northern border with Lebanon. All these battles were over turf. All these groups were created as resistance movements against Israeli occupation: Hamas and the PLO for the Palestinian groups; Hezbollah was created and funded by Iran after Israel invaded Lebanon in 1982.

The PLO has renounced violence. The Israeli military sees the security threat from the West Bank as merely 'an area of inconvenience'. Hamas and Hezbollah are still militarily strong but they both now have some statehood responsibilities. When battles take place between Israel and these groups it is more likely to be a short brutal fight stemming from a gradual escalation than a sustained, preplanned event. After years of conflict each side now understands the other, and that brings an element of stability to the hostilities. The US-funded 'Iron Dome' anti-missile system that Israel now possesses has neutralised much of the offensive capabilities of these groups.

The previously quiet borders of Sinai and Syria are where Israel feels the greatest threat. For the first time it is not from militant resistance groups fighting against an Israeli occupation but from jihadists fighting about religion. The battle over land is being replaced by a battle over God. This is a fundamental change for Israel. Unlike America and Europe it has never faced a serious threat from violent Salafists before. By definition there is no reaching a compromise with those people. 'We know we are the next target for the jihadists in Syria. First they want to take care of Assad, then they want to use this huge place against us,' the senior Israeli military strategist told me.

The Palestinians are hoping, now that the leaders of the new Arab democracies have to listen to their voters, that their cause will move up the agenda. The Gaza conflict of 2012 did present the Brotherhood with a choice. It could assume the mantle from Syria of the activist champion of the Palestinian cause, and thus alienate the US. Or it could show that on issues Washington cares about it could be hard-headed and sophisticated. It chose the latter, and for the time being will continue to do so.

This suggests that while Palestine will remain an emotional draw for the people of the Arab world, until they have got their own house in order it is not a cause they are able to make great sacrifices for. If Israel has never been more isolated, then also for the time being the issue of Palestine has rarely been less important to the lives of its core supporters in the region.

That doesn't mean the cause is lost. Once the Arab world surfaces from the turmoil of the next few years it will come back to the issue. And when it does it may find that some of the Western nations that once stood firmly on the opposing side have changed too. The sense of self-assuredness felt by much of the Israeli political establishment, the belief that it doesn't need to worry that much about 'The Problem', will be short-lived. When Israel is forced to seriously confront 'The Problem' again it may find that the Islamist militants in Gaza are even stronger. Hamas's will then be the voice Egypt listens to most.

But by then the Palestinian leadership in the West Bank is likely to have grown more politically militant too. Once the ageing and ailing Mahmoud Abbas finally departs the scene, chances are that he will not be replaced with a similar moderate figure, ready to wait for an elusive breakthrough in the peace talks. The leadership will pass to someone like the Fatah commander Marwan Barghouti, who is serving several life sentences in an Israeli jail. Mahmoud Abbas is probably as good as it is going to get for Israel when it comes to finding a partner for peace negotiations. If they do not do a deal with him soon, they may end up dealing with two much more hostile and more politically united Palestinian movements in the West Bank and Gaza. Mahmoud Abbas may turn out to be Israel's missed opportunity. The Palestinians want a state. The countries transformed by the Arab Spring want that too. 'The Problem' is not going away.

A few weeks before the 2012 Gaza war started, a European diplomat who considers himself a friend of Israel told me privately that he feared Israel was increasingly losing the sympathy of the outside world:

> I genuinely believe the opinion polls, the opinions in parliament, the opinion in the media is perceptibly, incrementally, becoming less warm to Israel. With foreign policy there is often a lag [but] when public opinion begins to move in a direction, policy normally follows . . . [and the public is] less tolerant of the status quo and increasingly see this as David and Goliath, where Israel is no longer David.

The Palestinians today trace their problem back to the creation of the state of Israel on 14 May 1948. Since 1988 every 15 May is marked by Palestinians and Arabs as al-Nakba, 'the Day marking the Catastrophe'. The defeat of the huge Arab armies by the tiny Israeli one, which led to the first Egyptian revolution and then to Nasser's Pan-Arabism, took place in a seminal period for the region matched in significance only by the Arab Spring. It was an incredible period for the Jewish people too. After centuries of persecution, followed by the horror of the Holocaust, they finally had a home. They had a place on earth where they could feel safe, where they trusted the strangers living in the house next door not to turn on them. But in order to get that homeland, the secular Zionists, the people who pushed, cajoled and lobbied the world for the state of Israel, had to make some compromises that in the following century would begin to tug at the complex fabric of Israeli society.

Egypt had a fast and noisy revolution in 2011 that has left it wrestling with issues concerning religion and the state. Israel has been involved in a much longer, quieter revolution, but it centres on the same issues. The advance of political Islam has been felt in the Palestinian territories and changed the balance of power. The rise of religious Zionism has done the same, as Jewish settlements are built in the belief that they are an expression of God's will. Egyptians are trying to work out now where the writ of religious law should begin and end. The expansion of the ultra-Orthodox Jewish community has left Israel with the same question. After the Arab uprisings very little unites Israel with the Arab states, but there is one thing they share. They are both struggling within their societies to reach agreement over the role and reach of religion in their lives.

4

Israel: It's Complicated

It was a bright spring morning and thousands of Israelis were wandering through the fern and pine-tree forest on Mount Herzl. Today was a national holiday and many of the men, women and children were dressed casually, in T-shirts, jeans and skirts, even though they were about to observe one of the most important occasions on their calendar. Israel is a country steeped in traditions, but for most of the population that rarely extends to their clothing. So relaxed are Israelis about their appearance that friends of mine who were married in Israel – one an Israeli Jew, the other a British Christian – printed two versions of the invitation to their wedding ceremony. One was in English. The other was in Hebrew and included the additional line 'No shorts and flip-flops'. But the relaxed dress code does not mean that Israeli traditions are taken less seriously, and on this day, for the people slowly walking up the gentle rocky slopes of one of Jerusalem's most famous landmarks, it did not make the moment they were about to mark any less solemn. Mount Herzl is dedicated to the founder of Zionism, Theodor Herzl, who is considered to have fathered the modern Israeli state. It is the most iconic of the nation's war cemeteries. Every spring, on the fourth day of the month of Iyyar in the Jewish calendar, the families of the fallen make their way to the graves of their relatives who are among the thousands of military servicemen and women killed trying to create or fighting to defend the state of Israel.

I was invited to the Remembrance Day ceremony by two Israeli friends. One of them, Avi, was himself a reservist combatant in the Israeli military. Several of his army colleagues were buried in the military cemetery and he was there to honour their memory. As the top of the hour approached the crowds began to settle, huddling around the neatly arranged graves, which rose knee-high and were bounded by flagstones. They were, like most Jewish graves in Israel, simple and sparse. Even the inscriptions held just the barest information. I stood slightly away from the grieving families on a ridge above a section of the cemetery. Below me, an elderly woman, surrounded by younger members of her family, wept into her handkerchief. The gravestone in front of her gave simply the name of the young man who lay beneath it, and that he had died at the age of twenty-two in Lebanon. It did not say how much he was loved or missed, though that was obvious. And it did say not say how exactly he had died in one of the regular conflicts Israel has faced with its Arab neighbours.

At eleven o'clock exactly a siren began to wail and the people in the cemetery, and Jewish people across the nation, stopped everything for two minutes of silence. Cars on highways were parked in the middle of the road as their occupants stood by, their heads bowed. Shopping malls were hushed and schools were silent. After the siren ended and prayers were said, the voice of the Israeli prime minister, Binyamin Netanyahu, crackled over the speakers in the cemetery. He was there as the nation's leader, but also to mark the death of his older brother Yoni, who was killed leading the 1976 rescue of Israeli hostages at Entebbe in Uganda. Yoni Netanyahu is one of those buried on Mount Herzl. Mr Netanyahu delivered a very personal message to the nation in which he talked first about his own loss and then about the nation's. He told his countrymen:

I know they say that time heals everything. That is not true. The years go by and the pain remains, but over the years that moment of sharp pain is mixed with other moments, with memories of the good times we have known with the people we love the most. Dear families, this is the pain we feel daily, but on this day, on Memorial Day, our private pain turns into national grief.

Avi had invited me, a non-Jew and non-Israeli, to attend this memorial because he wanted me to see 'a moment when all the Jewish people are united'. But what this ceremony displayed to me was not the unity of the nation but the deepening divide within it. Because among the thousands of people marking the sacrifice made for their country I saw just one member of the ultra-Orthodox Jewish community in the entire cemetery. The vast majority of them had no need to make the slow walk up the hill to pay tribute to friends and family who had died in defence of the nation, because they had no war dead. Ultra-Orthodox Jews describe themselves as 'Haredim', which means 'those who tremble in awe of God'. They were almost entirely exempt from the compulsory military service enforced on most other Jewish families in the country. And on this day few of them would even pause at the sound of the siren, because they consider Memorial Day to be an adopted Gentile tradition and they want no part of it. Binyamin Netanyahu described it as a moment of 'national grief'. It was not.

'If Israel has any holiday or mourning day it means nothing to a religious Jew, because a religious Jew thinks that anything that is made by the state of Israel was not made for the benefit of the Jewish people,' Yoel Weber told me. His ultra-Orthodox neighbourhood of Me'a She'arim is the largest and most conservative in the country. It was created in 1874 and was built just outside the walls of the old city of Jerusalem. Its narrow alleyways and cobbled streets have barely changed since the time they were built, and that is not by accident or neglect. This is a community that reveres the past. And it despises much of the present because it considers the state of Israel to be an insult to God. The divine redemption of Israel was to be brought about by the Almighty, not by men. For men to have pre-empted God's will by creating the state of Israel is for them the ultimate blasphemy.

Yoel was a bear of a man. He rattled through his words with a strong New York accent. He had long curled 'peots' or sidelocks, which hung down from his temples framing a wide bearded face. At his most animated he leant forward on his thick arms, and where his square glasses trapped his peots they waved gently up and down to the rhythm of his voice. We had met in the street on a hot summer's day and he walked me up a flight of stairs to his very modest apartment. He offered me a glass of water and apologised for being a few minutes late, which had kept me waiting in the heat. He took off his black wide-rimmed hat and his long heavy black coat. Underneath he was wearing a waistcoat, his prayer shawl and a white shirt. It was 28C outside, but regardless of the weather the Haredim continue to wear the clothing of their forefathers, designed for the weather of nine-teenth-century Europe. Every Sabbath I would see, near my home on the outskirts of Jerusalem, Haredi men struggling up and down the hill through the stifling heat to the synagogue in their formal clothing of knickerbockers, a long cloak and an enormous fur hat. All this clothing is cultural not religious attire, but the ultra-Orthodox consider it an important part of sustaining their beliefs. The fur hat is said to have been originally forced on Jews as an act of anti-Semitism in Europe. It was later adopted as a defiant statement of their faith.

Continuing to wear clothes so completely at odds with the environment around them is both an internal and external expression of their deliberate separation from the less religiously observant Jews around them – people they do not consider to be Jews at all.

To get to Yoel's apartment I had to park my car a short distance away and walk down the narrow cluttered streets. Slapped across every wall, layer over layer, were Haredi 'Pashkevilim' or wall posters. The tradition dates back to sixteenth-century Rome, where they orig-inated as a form of protest before the creation of the newspaper industry.[1] The world may have moved on but this remains, for the Haredim, the most important source of local news, rabbinical decrees or information on planned protests. It allows them to keep in touch with their wider community without being polluted by the influence of the mainstream media. They speak the once thriving but now almost dead European language of Yiddish. They avoid everyday use of the national language, Hebrew, because they believe it should only be used in religious ceremonies. The language of the words of the Pashkevilim was biblical in its forceful condemnation of the state of Israel, Zionism and its 'Nazi-like' oppression of the 'Jewish people', by which they meant the Haredi community.

There was only one poster that was both moderate in tone and printed in English, and that was because it was meant for outsiders who strayed into their community. It was addressed 'To women and girls' and it said in large black capital letters: 'WE BEG YOU WITH ALL OUR HEARTS PLEASE DO NOT PASS THROUGH OUR NEIGHBORHOOD IN IMMODEST CLOTHES'. It then helpfully pointed out that: 'Modest clothes include: closed blouse with long sleeves, long skirts, no tight-fitting clothes'.

When Yoel had heard the siren's call to honour the nation's military dead he was sitting at his computer. He just carried on typing. 'Zionism and the state of Israel is what brought this dangerous, dire situation in this place,' he told me. 'All these slurs on Jews and these terrorism attacks were never a factor here before. Basically we think that the state of Israel is part of the problem, not part of the solution.'

The real problem is that Israelis cannot agree collectively what the problem is, so they cannot agree on the solution. The yawning gap that exists between the religious and secular is the biggest issue facing the Jewish communities of Israel today. There is no other country in the world where the citizens of a shared history, shared religion and shared ethnicity argue among themselves whether the state they live in should exist or not.

The broader issues confronting Israel today are about the essence and identity of the state: what it means to *all* its people, whether they are religious nationalists, Modern Orthodox, ultra-Orthodox, Arab Muslims or secular. Israel is debating many of the same issues as post-revolution Egypt, and like Egypt they revolve around religion. The government in Israel sees no contradiction between declaring itself a Jewish state and protecting the rights of its non-Jewish minorities. The new Egyptian government sees no contradiction between Egypt being an Islamic state and protecting its minorities. In both cases the minorities disagree. There is a similar debate in both countries as to how far religious law should take precedence in the public sphere. In Egypt the Salafists are the ones pushing for a greater role for religion in a society that they believe should draw more of its identity from the origins of its faith. The ultra-Orthodox in Israel believe exactly the same. They want Jews to emulate the founding principles of their religion, unpolluted by modernity.

In both countries, though much more recently in the case of the Salafists, both religious communities have realised that they need to play a role in politics if their spiritual aims are to be met. Both have almost identical views on many social issues, particularly concerning the role of women in society. The difference is that in the Arab world the people now have the confidence to openly and loudly disagree with each other. It's different among Jews in Israel, because they don't want to wash their dirty linen in public. They don't want the outside world to see them as divided, because divided means weak, and the outside world has exploited their past weaknesses to try to obliterate them. The country's culture minister, Limor Livnat, reacted to the Oscar nomination in 2013 of two Israeli films, which she said 'slander the state of Israel before the whole world', by urging Israeli film-makers in future to exercise 'self-censorship'.[2] This kind of attitude means that much of the debate there is in Israel, and there is lots of it, is often lost to outsiders because it largely takes place in a language few non-Jewish people learn, Hebrew.

The ultra-Orthodox care less about the democratic nature of the state of Israel and more about its Jewishness.[3] They believe, like the Salafists in Egypt, that religious law should take precedence over the laws made by men. Their problem with the rest of Israel is that they believe most of the people in it do not revere God or his laws as they should, and so no longer act in accordance with the Jewish faith.

The ultra-Orthodox do not care about many of the battles the state of Israel feels it must fight to ensure its survival, because many of the Haredim do not care whether it survives or not. The ultra-Orthodox want the state of Israel to leave them alone. They do not want to take part.

The ultra-Orthodox don't care about boundary and border disputes because they don't recognise the state. On the margins of their community are people that champion the Palestinian cause. They don't care about the bile coming out of Iran towards Israel because they agree with it. These are the reasons why secular and Orthodox Jews want to change the Haredim before the Haredim change Israel. They fear that the growth in the ultra-Orthodox community is undermining the economy, the security, even the very idea of the state. And because of the demographics of Israel they want to change things fast before, for them at least, it is too late.

But the Haredim are not the only ones who regard many of the actions of the state of Israel with scorn. On windswept hilltops in small flimsy structures are religious ultra-nationalist Jews who believe that the destiny of their people is to take back the West Bank, or what they call Judea and Samaria. They will fight the state of Israel for the right to hold on to and expand their present outposts, which even Israel has declared illegal. When the state acts against what they see as their interests, they make sure that the actions of the state carry what they call a 'price tag'. These 'price-tag' attacks have been formally declared as acts of terrorism by the US, and include burning mosques and desecrating Arab graves.

The majority in Israel sees them as terrorists too. One senior government official described the attacks as 'meant to drag Israel into a religious, national Armageddon'.⁴ These men, while still tiny in number, have caused outrage in the country. They have attacked Israeli soldiers, thrown firebombs at cars holding Palestinian families and vandalised Christian holy places, once scrawling the words 'Jesus is a Monkey' on the walls of a monastery.⁵ Yet some highly charged political acts of 'price-tagging' – for instance uprooting Palestinian olive trees which have been nurtured for centuries – are not dealt with seriously at all, because the Jewish settlers are bound by different laws than the Palestinians in the land they occupy. The Palestinians fall largely under military law, the Jewish settlers under Israeli law. Attacking olive trees often ends up being dealt with in a Tel Aviv court like a row between two neighbours over a hedge. It means there is a growing sense of impunity among these extremist communities for many of their crimes.

The spectrum of Israeli society is enormously wide and in constant churn. It struggles to accommodate people drawn from every corner of the globe and also communities that have lived on these lands before the modern state of Israel was born. It has some of the brightest software engineers and most creative hi-tech industries in the world. It also has people who think using the Internet is a sin.

Israel is complicated.

The results of the Israeli elections in 2013 were a signal that the secular majority wants to deal with many of the country's divisive issues now. Israel has a thriving economy, and yet, because of its Haredi and Arab populations, the level of poverty is one of the worst among the world's leading industrialised nations. Sixty per cent of both communities are simply broke. Low employment in the Israeli Arab community happens because the women are not working. By contrast, in the Haredi community it happens because the men are not working.

Arab women are unemployed because there are fewer job opportunities within their local communities, their levels of education are much lower than those for Jewish women and, as an International Monetary Fund report said in 2012: 'Arab females face double discrimination problems, one for being women and the other for being Arabs.'[6]

Haredi men are unemployed because they do not want a job. They spend all day studying the Torah: Jewish law and tradition. If both the Arab and Haredi communities worked at the same level as everyone else it would add 5 per cent to the country's GDP.[7]

At present, 40 per cent of six-year-olds in Israeli primary schools come from either the Haredi or the Arab communities. Both communities have large families, typically six or seven children for the Haredim and three or four for Arabs.[8] That demographic means that the two communities least connected to the state are going to have a huge impact on a society they at present do not feel part of.

'Ten years from now we are going to see something completely different demographically in Israel,' the justice minister Tzipi Livni once told me in conversation while she was still leader of the opposition. 'It's not only about the state of Israel as a democratic and Jewish state but also the substance of the nature of the Israeli Jewish state. What does it mean from a religious perspective, from a national perspective . . . the Jewish-ness of the state?'

The country has many different splinters of Judaism, but its society can be broken down in religious terms into three main strands. The largest group, by far, are secular Jews. They are Zionist, which means they believe in the creation of the state of Israel for the Jewish people and they believe it is the right of all Jews anywhere in the world to come and live there. They are often only mildly religious, and pick and choose to what extent their faith constrains their lifestyle. In and around Tel Aviv, which is Israel's biggest population centre, even on Shabbat, religion barely impinges on people's lifestyles. However elsewhere in the country a whole industry has bloomed to cater for the desire of those secular Jews who want to adhere in principle to the key tenets of the faith, like not doing work on Shabbat, the Jewish Sabbath, but to go about their business as if it were largely an ordinary day.

Among those work activities forbidden under Jewish religious law is making fire. Electricity falls into this classification, so pressing buttons to turn on the TV or the cooker or to start the car are all forbidden. Modern technology helps them work around it. People set their electrical goods on timers to come on and go off by themselves between sundown Friday and sundown Saturday, which is the period of Shabbat. Shabbat lifts stop at every floor, so you can ride them without pressing a button. Touch-screen technology is also starting to stretch what is technically allowed.

These workarounds though are not used by most Modern Orthodox Jews, who in modern Israel are normally just called Orthodox Jews. They tend to be religious Zionists or 'Dati Leumi', which means National Religious. They believe in the state of Israel, over time their families or they as individuals have become more religious, and they follow much of the religious life of the ultra-Orthodox. The women will cover their heads, though that often doesn't stop them being fashionable about it. The men will wear Western clothes, but there will be tassels hanging from under their shirts. These tassels are called tzitzit, and they are attached to the four corners of the prayer shawl they are wearing underneath. The display of the tzitzit shows that the wearer is religiously observant. Orthodox Jewish men also often shave their beards and wear a kippa, a small skullcap, which symbolises their deference to God. But like secular Jews, both sexes will work, receive a mix of religious and secular education and serve in the Israeli army or do other national service. In terms of nationalism, the spectrum of this community is very broad. It ranges from those who are willing to accept the present boundaries of Israel, to those who want to hold on to the West Bank, right through to the small minority which claims a Greater Israel that would include Jordan and the Sinai.

The style of kippa chosen tells you a lot about the politics of the wearer. The Haredim, like Yoel Weber, wear a black one under their hats, so their head is still covered when the hat comes off. Knitted kippas tend to be worn by National Religious Jews. Large knitted kippas are often worn by the religious, ultra-nationalist settlers. Therefore a gun and large knitted kippa are not an usual combination. Other styles of kippa, in suede, satin and cloth, are worn more broadly by Modern Orthodox Jews who, while Zionist, are less stridently nationalist than the knitted kippa wearers. The mildly religious liberal Jews will sometimes wear kippas with, perhaps, their football team's logo on, which is heavily frowned upon by more religious people.

*   *   *

The ultra-Orthodox, as is their intention, stick out like a sore thumb from the rest of Israeli society. They are lumped together by the rest as one big mass of scrounging layabouts. The only workaround they regularly use is chemical hair remover, which the men dab on the ends of their beards to keep them in check without actually cutting them. And the women will often wear cheap, and therefore ill-fitting, wigs to cover their own hair for the sake of modesty. The uniformity with which the Haredim dress tends to be seen by the majority as a symbol of the uniform uselessness of the Haredim to the wider society. But like everything in modern Israel, even that is not as simple as it seems.

Yeruham Klausner was holding two identical wide-brimmed black hats. 'Now these,' he said to me, 'are two very different hats.' At first and even second glance, to the non-ultra-Orthodox eye, the men of the Haredi community often dress exactly the same. In fact they look just like Yoel Weber and Mr Klausner – long beard, black suit, white shirt and big black hat. But the similarities mask the differences. Yeruham Klausner was in his sixties and sold hats for the famous Ferster Hat Company. Their motto is 'We don't sell hats; we live hats.' He could spot one of his from across the street and he could also tell which sect the wearer belonged to.

This is a community where high fashion is seen as a pointless indulgence that distracts from devotion to the Almighty. But it does not deny individuality, so trends within hat wearing are constantly changing, though they border on the microscopic. Lately the fashions have drifted towards the hats getting higher, millimetre by millimetre. There has been more movement on the rim, which has jumped by two centimetres in recent years. The width of the almost indistinguishable black ribbon is another magnet for change.

While I was in Mr Klausner's shop in Jerusalem his mobile phone rang. It wasn't a particularly fancy one, but like all phones these days it could do the basics: Internet, texting, take pictures and make calls. At least it could when it left the factory. Mr Klausner's phone was now kosher, and it had a little rabbinical stamp on it to prove it. This meant it had been stripped of all its functions apart from being able to make phone calls.

Mr Klausner did not strike me as the kind of man who might form illicit relationships via SMS, take photographs of women who were not his wife, or spend hours surfing the murkier corners of the Internet. Regardless of that, the temptation had been removed. However, having a kosher phone is more about being *seen* not to want to have access to these things. It is another mark of religious observance.

Everyone else on the globe, eventually, ends up being influenced by fashions championed by pop stars and models that are transmitted around the planet by the mass media. This is a community that shuns that. So I asked Mr Klausner: who sets the trends among the Haredi hat buyers? 'Often it's a particular rabbi,' he told me.

> He may wear his hat in a certain way and then it'll be copied by his followers. Or sometimes a man will walk in and say: 'I've had the same style for ten years, I want something different. Perhaps a pinch or a little more height,' and then, after there's a big Jewish holiday where his hat has been seen, there will be a rush of requests for a similar look. Sometimes it's the young people wanting more width so they can turn down and style the brim.

I asked him how long the men took to choose their hats. 'Around an hour,' he said. 'They'll be wearing the same hat every day for two years, so they want to be sure. But if anyone spends more time than that, then his thoughts are clearly too much with himself and not enough with God, so I throw him out of the shop.'

The way the Haredim dress is a deliberate and a very important part of their attempt to isolate themselves from a world they hold in contempt. But within their own community the differences in clothing, like the differences in their lifestyles and their relationship with the state of Israel, are very important and can be very divisive.

It was a long narrow stone corridor and she knew we were waiting at the end of it to put faces to the disgust felt across the country. She began to walk as casually as she could, but the more doors she failed to enter along the way the more she piqued the interest of the photographers. She was a fragile little woman in her fifties, but the scarf that covered her head, and her clothing, which was black and shapeless, undermined her attempt at studied nonchalance.

The instinct to hide must have been bubbling up inside her. Suddenly she gave in to it. Two doors up from the one I was standing at her pace quickened sharply and she brought her hand to cover her face. The camera shutters went off and the pushing and shoving, the unedifying trademark of my profession, began in earnest. As she reached the courtroom door her left hand pushed it open as her right reached up to touch the small thin metal cylinder found on the door frame of every Jewish home and building. It is called a mezuzah. It can come in other shapes, but what is important is that it contains passages of a particular prayer written by a specially trained observant Jew in a tradition that dates back to the instruction from God that Jews must mark their dwellings to protect their first-born sons from the tenth plague visited on the Egyptians in the First Testament.

Mrs Ostrowitz's first-born son was about to become notorious, and he needed all the help he could get.

The courtroom was tiny, and looked more like a cluttered office than legal chambers. It was presided over by Judge Simon Fienberg, who decided he didn't have the space to accommodate the day's larger-than-usual collection of reporters and photographers, so he left us clogging up the corridor outside. Technically Judge Fienberg was dealing with a pretty straightforward case of vandalism. Two men and one teenager had been arrested the night before and had quickly confessed to the crime. What made this case unusual was what they had written and where they had written it.

They were all members of the extreme Neturei Karta sect of the Haredi community. Two weeks earlier they had crept to the front of Yad Vashem, the nation's memorial to the six million Jews murdered by the Nazis during the Second World War, and in the early morning light had scrawled across its walls in Hebrew using black spray paint the words: 'Thanks Hitler for the wonderful Holocaust you organised for us'.

They were caught after they exchanged text messages by mobile phone congratulating each other on their actions. Of the three suspects, a man called Avraham Ben Yosef was released under bail conditions. The unidentified minor was spared the parade before the press. Elhanan Ostrowitz was not. He arrived in a crisp white shirt that he wore beneath his thin prayer shawl. He was in his mid-twenties with a short ragged brown beard and ringlets hanging from his temples. He wore a kippa, handcuffs, and a vacuous expression that he maintained as he walked towards the courtroom chaperoned on either side by a plain-clothes policeman. He seemed utterly indifferent to the circumstances in which he found himself.

He was, as requested, remanded in custody for five days. As we milled around before the hearing we found the lawyer for the youngest of the three accused. He was dressed in cargo pants and training shoes. His one concession to the usual formality of the justice system was a black tie, though it was strung around his neck by a piece of elastic, so it was at best a half-hearted effort. He was cagey about whether his client had been in trouble for this kind of thing before. However the court heard that the vandalism at Yad Vashem was the culmination of several months of attacks on a range of national monuments including those commemorating soldiers killed in action. These young men had been brought up by their families to believe that the Holocaust was the collective divine punishment of the Jews for the sins of the secular and the Zionists.[9] Mrs Ostrowitz was hiding her face, but she wasn't hiding it in shame.

If the vast majority of Israelis simply don't get the ultra-Orthodox, then the vast majority of the ultra-Orthodox simply don't get the Neturei Karta and other fringe groups like them. The Neturei Karta made headlines in Israel for sending a delegation in 2005 to meet with the Iranian president Mahmoud Ahmadinejad at his 'World without Zionism' conference in Tehran. They then issued a statement saying: 'It is a dangerous distortion, to see the President's words, as indicative of anti-Jewish sentiments.' They were, they said, 'saddened by the hysteria'. They are used to it by now though.

More recently their members laid a wreath in Lebanon at the tomb of a Hezbollah leader, and the sect regularly takes part in pro-Palestinian protests, burning the Israeli flag. But they are not even the outer edge of the fringe. Members of their sect denounced what has been described in Israel as the 'Jewish Taliban' cult, a small group of newly religious ultra-Orthodox women who cover themselves entirely in thick black cloaks so nothing at all of them can be seen.

Stories about the utterly obscure elements of the ultra-Orthodox are combined in the Israeli mainstream media with a constant diet of items that reinforce the message that the Haredim are all mad or bad for Israel. Headlines scream: 'Rampant child abuse in ultra-Orthodox families',[10] or 'Modesty Patrol lynched me'.[11] This invective has been around for years, and grew out of the clash of ideas between Zionism and the teachings of Orthodox Judaism.

Back at the creation of the state, while the numbers and influence of the Haredim remained small and insignificant, they were tolerated because they could be ignored. But the growth in their population combined with the country's political system, which produces huge fractious coalition governments, has given the Haredim much more political power. Or, as the country's most liberal newspaper, the English-language *Ha'aretz*, headlined in an op-ed by one of its leading commentators, Amir Oren: 'Israel's Haredi minority is ruining the majority's life'.[12]

The Babylonian exile in 586 BC saw the beginning of the move-ment of Jewish people out of the Middle East to form new communities in Europe and North Africa.[13] Israel's Jewish population is broken down into three main strands based on the geographical origin of their ancestors who branched out from the original commu-nity. The Ashkenazim came from central Europe. The Sephardim are the descendants of those Jews expelled from Portugal and Spain in the fifteenth century during the Inquisitions established by the Catholic Church. The Mizrahim are Jews originally from the Middle East and

North Africa. These were also areas to which many Sephardi Jews had fled, so these two groups have a shared modern history and are politically closer today than they are to the Ashkenazim. The Ashkenazim are often seen by the rest of society as the core of the self-serving establishment. Men from Ashkenazi backgrounds earn a third more than the average monthly salary.[14]

'But the most basic thing to understand about this country is that this is not a country of European Jews,' says Professor Alexander Yakobson from the Hebrew University of Jerusalem's Department of History.

> Whether one thinks it was a wonderful thing or one thinks it was a colonial enterprise, it is always those poor German Jews or those sinister Zionists, but they are all Europeans and they are Westerners and they came to Palestine and they established a Western colonial outpost. It is true the pioneering labour Zionist elite that led the creation of the state were largely homogeneous. But within this salad which is called the Jewish Israeli society, roughly half of it originates from the Middle East. With a Libyan component and Moroccan, Egyptian, Syrian, Iraqi, Yemenite and so on.

The complications of managing this society, which is so mixed and so divided between the secular and the religious, go back to the creation of the state.

The Zionists who led the struggle to create a homeland for the Jews were driven by political not religious zeal. Zionism emerged from nineteenth-century central and Eastern Europe. It offered a modern alternative to traditionalism, but one that still claimed to be no less legitimately Jewish. The Haredi way of life started then, as a reaction to this modernity. The Zionist leadership could see the conflict that would exist within the new Jewish society because the same tensions existed within the diaspora as Zionism grew in strength. David Ben-Gurion led the struggle for the creation of Israel and became its first prime minister. In the year before the nation was born he sought to settle where the boundaries between religion and state would fall. On 19 June

1947 he wrote a letter to the World Agudat Israel Federation, which was the political arm of Orthodox Judaism, in which he said: 'we have no intention of establishing a theocratic state.' But he was striving for unity among the diaspora and so set out 'The Structural Foundation for Religio-Political Accommodation' in the new state of Israel.

This was based on four points. The first and second were that the legal day of rest would be Saturday, the Jewish Sabbath, and that state kitchens would serve kosher foods. The third was a promise regarding marital affairs: to 'do all that can be done to satisfy the needs of the religiously observant in this matter and to prevent a rift in the Jewish People'. This led to the Orthodox Chief Rabbinate having jurisdiction over all personal status issues, not just marriage, without a civil alternative being available. Finally, and as it turned out even more importantly for the modern state, they would 'accord full freedom to each stream to conduct education according to its conscience and will avoid any adverse effects on religious conscience'.[15] The details set out by Ben-Gurion's points were not legally binding, but they became known as the 'Status Quo Agreement'. It has been the basis for managing the communal relations between the secular and religious. Or rather it was the basis for all the squabbling and shady backroom deals through the years, particularly once the Haredim started to wield political power.

The teachings of individual rabbis, who interpret and apply religious law in society, can be extremely influential, and their personal piety and way of living is often a great influence on their followers. They are at the heart of the long, and for those subjected to them tortuous, debates about who is or is not a Jew. And that is important, because all Jews anywhere in the world have the right to make 'aliyah', literally 'ascent' – to return to the Land of Israel. It is one of the basic tenets of Zionism. So someone has to decide what constitutes being a Jew.

The Haredim can be divided between those who refuse to recognise the state of Israel and those who have decided to work within it to claim as much of the public space for the religiously observant as they can. The latter, who have entered politics, are largely uninterested in issues of foreign policy for example, but they will agree or oppose policy depending on what they can get in return to further their aims.

There are two main political parties drawn from the Haredi community. The bigger is Shas, which was originally drawn from the Sephardi Haredi community but now gets much of its support from Mizrahi Jews. In 2010 it became the first ultra-Orthodox party to join the World Zionist Organization.[16] It has only been around for twenty years, but it has become incredibly influential in political life because it often acts as a kingmaker when it comes to building Israel's unwieldy coalition governments. Many of its supporters now are Orthodox Jews, and so too at present is the party leadership.

The other, smaller, Haredi political party is United Torah Judaism, or UTJ, which draws its support from Ashkenazi Jews. They end up with fewer seats in the Knesset, largely because much more of their community chooses not to vote and partly because the UTJ is itself an often unstable coalition prone to infighting. However they often combined forces with Shas within Israeli coalition governments to push through their joint religious agenda.

In the 2013 Israeli elections, of the 120 seats up for grabs, Shas got eleven and the UTJ got seven seats. But this time it wasn't enough. 'Coalition math: Settlers in, ultra-Orthodox Jews out' trumpeted the liberal *Ha'aretz* newspaper.[17] The ultra-Orthodox had joined almost every Likud coalition government since it first came to power in 1977.[18] During that time they had managed to antagonise large sections of Israeli society all of whom *were* represented in the new government. The Haredi community were not very hopeful about their prospects under the new coalition. One of its newspapers summed up the mood with the front-page headline 'Government of Evil'.[19]

During Binyamin Netanyahu's previous governing coalition, the Shas Party was given control of the Ministry of the Interior. The ministry was then accused of allowing the Chief Rabbinate to decide who was a Jew, rather than the government's Jewish Agency, which is actually responsible for the immigration and absorption of Jews. But even if you were lucky enough to get in, despite the interior minister, and then lucky enough to fall in love, when you wanted to get married you might not be able to find a rabbi who would marry you, because they might not consider you a Jew. And there was no second option, because there is no civil marriage in Israel, in accordance with the 'Status Quo Agreement'.

The Halakha, or religious law, as interpreted by Orthodox Judaism says that to be a Jew by birth the mother at least must be Jewish. Reform Judaism, which is found mainly in Jewish communities outside Israel, says you can be Jewish by birth if either parent is Jewish. It sees the Halakha as a set of guidelines rather than as rules. Israel's 'Law of Return', which gives Jews anywhere in the world the right to citizenship in the country, was modified in 1970 to enable people with a Jewish grandparent to make aliyah even if they themselves are not Jewish according to the Halakha. This led to the very rare but bizarre and deeply troubling situation for the country, of an Israeli man being arrested in 2011 for leading a neo-Nazi gang that assaulted foreign workers, drug addicts and religious Jews. These Israeli citizens filmed themselves giving a Nazi salute.[20]

But this case was an anomaly. The biggest clash between what the state accepted as Jewish and what Israel's religious establishment accepted as Jewish came when the Soviet Union began to collapse and Jews there finally got a chance to escape their long history of persecution. Their problem stemmed from the fact that they often had to hide their faith to avoid abuse by the communist state. They found when they immigrated with the blessing of the state of Israel that they couldn't get the blessing of their local rabbi. So though they lived as Jews and considered themselves Jews they were not Jews according to religious law. To get married they were first forced to go through a full, very long Jewish conversion process as if they were not Jewish at all.

The issue became the focus of a controversial party-political TV advertisement in the 2013 election campaign by Shas which mocked the piety of the Russian-speaking Jewish community and the party they largely vote for, Yisrael Beiteinu. It featured a tall beautiful blonde bride with a crudely exaggerated Russia accent standing next

to her rather dumpy-looking kippa-wearing groom. They were standing under the chuppah, the wedding canopy. Between them was a fax
machine.

'Marina, what's the fax for?' says the groom.

'Beiteinu sent it, it's a wedding present,' she replies.

'How nice. But what the hell, why a fax?'

'To receive permission.'

'Permission for what?' he asks, looking confused.

'From 1-800-convert.'

'1-800-convert?'

'Da,' she replies. 'You call 1-800-convert and receive permission.'

'Wait,' he says in shock. 'You aren't Jewish?'

At that moment the fax whirrs into life and a certificate of conversion spews out.

'I am now!' she says, brandishing the document, and her family
break into celebration as the groom looks on in disgust. He pulls
away as she tries to kiss him.

The Shas Party pulled the ad before the National Election Committee could get to them, but it served its purpose and got the party and
its point wide coverage in the Israeli media.

This issue of where the authority of the state and religion begin and
end is the crux of most of the tensions within Israeli society today.
Should religious Jews only be able to expect the strict observance of
the tenets of their faith in their homes, or should the secular only be
able to ignore those religious requirements in the privacy of theirs?
Key to the issue is where the writ of religious law runs and whose
interpretation of religious law takes precedence. The question that
plagues Israeli society is the same one now being debated in the new
democracies of the Arab world: who owns the public space?

Every little girl gets a bit nervous during her first few days at a new
school. There is the new teacher, new schoolmates and a new class-
room. And for Na'ama Margolis there were also the dozen or so grown
men who made her walk the gauntlet along her short journey to the
school gate, spitting on her and shouting 'Whore'. Na'ama was eight

years old. She and her mother Hadassa belong to the Orthodox Jewish community. That means they are religiously observant Jews and therefore cover their arms and legs, and the women will wear a headscarf. But that wasn't good enough for the men of the Beit Shemesh ultra-Orthodox community who made their way down the hill each morning and afternoon to stand outside the girls' school to abuse the children and their mothers as they walked by.

'It began on the second day of school. When I picked Na'ama up they were waiting outside,' Hadassa Margolis told me.

> They started to spit at us and they were yelling and cursing us shouting 'Prostitutes' and 'Whores', 'Immodest' and 'Non-Jews get out!' and spitting all the while. We managed to push past them and there were other men still yelling on the other side of the street. And I thought to myself there's no way this is going to happen again tomorrow. The police will come and do something. This can't happen, this can't go on. But it continued, on and off, for four months.

The definition of 'immodest' is lacking humility or decency, being immoral, brazen, wanton or loose. It means to be overtly and deliberately sexually provocative. In most parts of the world, standing in the street and shouting at the top of your voice that you find an eight-year-old girl sexually provocative is enough to put you on a child sex offenders register. That did not happen to those men. In fact nothing at all happened to any of them. Every day for those four months Na'ama woke up wondering whether they were going to be at the bottom of the stairs that led from her apartment block to follow her and her classmates as they walked the few hundred metres to the school gate. Every day she wondered whether she was going to have to start her day wiping their spit off her face.

'Every day Na'ama would be crying and screaming that she was scared, that she didn't want to go to school. She had anxiety attacks and nightmares,' said Hadassa. Then somebody used their mobile phone to film the men tormenting the children and uploaded it onto

YouTube. Israel's secular and orthodox community went nuts and the state woke up. 'The police didn't do a thing until it was seen on YouTube,' Hadassa told me.

As the Haredi communities grow they spill over into areas previously inhabited by Orthodox and secular Jews. Once the ultra-Orthodox community expands into a new neighbourhood anywhere in the country it then insists that because it is now also present in this public space its religious sensitivities should be respected. Its men start putting up signs telling local women from all communities exactly how they are expected to dress. The ultra-Orthodox begin to barricade the roads at the beginning of the Sabbath as darkness falls on Friday to stop people driving their cars. Buses that travel through their areas at any times carrying advertisements showing even fully clothed females may be attacked and burned.[21] In other buses women, whether they are ultra-Orthodox or not, are yelled at and abused if they do not segregate themselves from the men and travel in the back of the bus. Stones are thrown at women who ride bicycles in Haredi-populated areas.

At the heart of the controversy in Beit Shemesh was a turf war. The local Haredi community wanted the newly opened school for themselves. They believed the school had been put there to mark a boundary beyond which the ultra-Orthodox would not be allowed to expand.

Na'ama's story got nationwide attention when it broke in December 2011. It focused the attention of the nation on the tensions in society as no other had for many years. It had such resonance with the wider population that Na'ama's picture was even used by one of the political parties, without her parents' permission, as part of its 2013 election campaign.

The family's plight garnered huge support, though not from everyone. Hadassa told me:

> I had a good friend, an ex-good friend, who called me up and who was just absolutely yelling at me hysterically that I caused such a huge desecration of God because it made the Jewish people look

bad, for having internal fights. And I said I didn't cause any dese-
cration, these men did. They interpret the Torah in a perverted way
that doesn't exist. They make up their own rules and they are brain-
washed from birth to believe this is the right way. I think that
they're crazy and the fact that the country accepts it is just mind-
boggling. These men, I think they sit all day and think about 'How
can we not think about women' and therefore they think about
women all day and all night. That's all they think about.

In response to the uproar by the rest of society against the abuse of the
children, a small group of ultra-Orthodox protesters among a protest
of several hundred others dressed themselves in a version of the striped
prison uniforms and Star of David patches forced on Jews in the Nazi
death camps. They were implying they were being persecuted in a
similar fashion by the state of Israel. As it was meant to, it caused
further outrage. The then Israeli Religious Affairs minister Yakov
Margi, who was also director general of Shas, warned that the deepening tensions between ultra-Orthodox extremists and less religious
Jews could 'tear Israeli society apart'.[22]

When I drove through the ultra-Orthodox community of Beit
Shemesh after the 2013 elections there were still signs hanging from
their houses saying in Hebrew things like 'We are Jews not Zionists.
We will not take part in their sacrilegious election.' The abuse of the
children had stopped, but none of the men had been prosecuted by
the police. One might wonder whether their wider community agreed
with the absurd notion that a fully dressed eight-year-old could in any
way be immodest. The answer to that question could be found in the
Yellow Pages. Or rather it could be found in the listing catalogue that
was being put through the letter boxes of the Beit Shemesh Haredi
community the day I was there.

Israel was then a few weeks away from the Jewish festival of Purim.
This marks the escape by the Jews from persecution in the ancient
Persian empire. It is celebrated by dressing up in costumes, though no
one knows exactly why. Everyone gets involved, including the

Haredim, which is why the centre spread of the listing catalogue had costumes for hire. There were small boys in cowboy outfits and firemen's uniform and spacesuits. There were small girls dressed as bees and Minnie Mouse and butterflies. The boys looked out of the pages smiling. For modesty reasons the faces of the girls, who were no older than five or six, had been blurred out. A few weeks earlier one conservative rabbi had issued modesty rules for girls from the age of three.[23]

I asked Hadassa how Na'ama was getting on. 'She's fine now,' she said,

> though she gets nervous when we go out somewhere. She asks me if she is dressed OK. I took her to the dentist's one day and there was a sign that said you should be dressed modestly and she got very nervous and I said: 'Don't worry, you are fine.' She's still scared if she sees an ultra-Orthodox because she doesn't know if they will spit at her or not, or yell at her, because they look the same most of them, so although a lot of them are very good people, she can't differentiate.

Many ultra-Orthodox people would not condone spitting at eight-year-olds. They would argue that the men in Beit Shemesh did not represent their broader community. But incidents like this have added to the social tensions that had already been inflamed by economic strife. Just like anywhere else in the world, when the economy turns downwards hard-working people start looking around for someone to take blame for their lot. So even the ultra-Orthodox who just want to get on with their lives as law-abiding people end up being demonised in Israeli society in the way benefit cheats and illegal immigrants are in the UK or the US. Most Israelis simply think Israel cannot afford to let the Haredim continue with the same lifestyle any more.

This came to a head while the Middle East's attention was on the revolutions in the Arab world. That summer of 2011 saw a revolt in Israel too, and this one was also led by the middle classes. Hundreds of thousands of people took to the streets to protest at the downturn in the quality of their lives. They were drawn from the normally quiet, law-abiding, hard-working majority who did their national service, paid their taxes but still couldn't make ends meet. The cost of housing became the catalyst for much of the anger, and tents were put up in city centres to illustrate their inability to afford a decent home. These people blamed the government but they also blamed those they thought were getting a free ride at their expense, the ultra-Orthodox. Perhaps the most enduring manifestation of the protest movement was the creation, by the former television journalist Yair Lapid, of the centrist party 'Yesh Atid' in 2012 and its surge of support in the following year's polls. Dealing with the entitlements of the ultra-Orthodox was a key plank of his campaign, because it was what mattered most to the previously silent mainstream of Israeli society.

'The majority of Israelis are not like the ultra-Orthodox, they are people like me, the Jews who go to work, pay our taxes, serve in the army and then in the reserves and go to college so we can get a good job,' said Nimrod Dotan. He is in his early thirties and works for an organisation in Tel Aviv that searches for gifted children living in the country's poorer communities and provides them with a tailored education to develop their abilities. We arranged to meet in a coffee shop in central Tel Aviv after he'd finished a meeting at the Internet giant Google. This is a man who spends his life looking for the potential in others, so the waste of human capital he sees in the Haredi community infuriates him. He joined Lapid's party as soon as it was launched because he thinks the country's demographics mean time is running out before things will be broken beyond repair. 'The future of Israel is going to be decided in the next five to ten years,' he told me:

> and what worries me is that if we don't solve the problem, society is going to be split between the ultra-Orthodox and us Zionists, and it's going to descend into violence because we can't live like this. I have friends who have foreign passports who are keeping them so they can go and live abroad because in ten years, who is going to pay the taxes? If the Haredi won't serve in the army they

lose their ticket into society, if they won't learn maths and English then they can't work, so where is the money going to come from? And look around us, with everything going on in Lebanon and Syria and Egypt and everything unstable. Who is going to serve in our army? We have been avoiding this issue for too long. This is an important moment for Israel and we have to deal with it now.

The ultra-Orthodox make up only 10 per cent of the population, but that number will have more than doubled by the late 2030s.[24] 'Jerusalem today is Israel tomorrow,' a UN diplomat told me, and he said the demographics in Jerusalem were already 'incredible', with just a small percentage of children there being educated in secular state schools. The social and physical divide within the society and the country was reflected by the voting patterns in its two most important cities: increasingly conservative Jerusalem and increasingly cosmopolitan Tel Aviv.

In Jerusalem the Haredi Ashkenazi United Torah Judaism led in the polls. In Tel Aviv it was the polar opposition, the very secular Yair Lapid's party, that swept the board, having done poorly in Jerusalem. The Haredi parties barely registered in Tel Aviv. But if the diplomat is right and Jerusalem points the way, then it is the men in beards, not the clean-cut TV personality, who will be the future faces of Israeli politics.

The demographics show an explosion in the ultra-Orthodox population because of the size of their families. Their families tend to be large because the Torah commands them to 'be fruitful and multiply',[25] and because the use of contraceptives is not allowed for men, who are forbidden to indulge in sexual acts unless it is to procreate. The increase in birth rate was also encouraged by the state, which for a while made it financially rewarding for the Haredim to have many children. In the 1990s, when they began to gain greater political influence in the Knesset, child allowances went up and so did their fertility rates. When these benefits were cut in the early 2000s, as part of the government's economic recovery programme, the numbers went down again.[26] Twenty-seven per cent of the first-grade (six-year-old) students in Israel today are ultra-Orthodox Jews, but as a group they are among the poorest in society.[27] The population of Israel as a whole is expanding by 1.8 per cent a year. The Haredim are growing at 5 per cent.[28]

Most people send their children to school to prepare them for life in the modern world. The education given to the children in the religious schools run by the Haredim deliberately doesn't do that, because their communities don't want their children to be able to operate in the modern world. At least that is the shorthand version, but things are actually more complex.

Family is at the core of the Haredim's religious beliefs. That means that putting bread on the table is as important as scripture. The reality is the Haredim are not preparing their *sons* for life in the modern world. The men don't work, so they can't support their families, and so that burden falls largely on to the state or on their community's charity. And the state no longer pays anywhere near enough. So by default, providing for the family, now that families have grown so large, has fallen to women. They *do* need to be prepared for, not protected from, life in the modern world so that they can provide for their families. So Haredi girls, who are taught separately from boys, get a broader education. The Haredi community is changing, but it is changing quietly. The Haredi men make all the noise about rejecting modernity while the women literally get on with the job. Throughout history empowering and educating women fundamentally changes societies. There is no reason to think it won't happen here too. It has already begun in the Arab communities in Israel, where rising education levels in women have produced a slow drift downwards in birth rates.

Nilli Davidovitz runs 'Realcommerce', a very successful software company in the heart of very modern and very secular Tel Aviv. She has made it successful by tapping into one of Israel's hidden pools of talent: Haredi women. Nilli looks nothing like most of the women who work for her. She was in her late forties, and when we met at a conference she was wearing a smart business suit, aquamarine eyeliner and had long wavy auburn hair. We shook hands and looked for a table among the delegates so she could tell me about her attempt to pull down the barriers that have built up between religious and secular Jews in Israel. I asked her what she got out of employing Haredi women, because it means having to create segregated work areas and separate canteens, as well as abiding by their rigid working hours so that they can also look after their children. The women will only move out of the segregated areas of their offices in pairs, and the same system has to operate for business trips or meeting clients.

> They are very reliable and they are very loyal. Having work is important to them but they are not looking for a career, so they don't jump from job to job. They are very honest. They will not talk during work, they don't go off smoking, they don't take breaks. They ask you for permission to make a private phone call and they work the extra time without pay to make up for the duration of the call. Eight hours of work means eight hours of work. And they believe they are stealing if they do not give you the time that you have paid them for, and stealing is a sin.

I asked her if she thought the skills and experience these women were getting would impact on the communities they return home to each day.

'It is changing them,' she said:

> It's rippling through their societies. These are women who when they were in school, they would address their women teachers using the Hebrew third person to show respect. Now when they are dealing with clients they are talking to a non-religious man as an equal. It's a very big change and they are not used to it. We are giving them a lot of self-confidence, and that is leading to them becoming more equal at home too. And now more girls are learning what they should do at school so they can get good jobs, not just all be

kindergarten teachers like their mothers. They get mathematics, English, geography, biology, whatever everybody else in the country learns. Whereas the boys, after fourteen they only get Jewish studies, and before that the level of maths and English teaching for the boys is very, very low.

When you live within secular communities in Israel you absorb the prejudices of the people around you. You don't realise it until the moment it slaps you in the face. My slap was delivered by the words: 'It's not my hair.'

Nilli's company only employs women, so I asked her how the non-religious women in her company had reacted.

'After a year we were accepted, they realised not all religious people are the same, they are not all called Sarah or Rivka, but they have faces and names and personalities. They understood about our boundaries, that you don't ask a religious woman about her personal life. You can talk about her work, but not why she looks tired or sad.'

At which point I blurted out: 'Nilli, are you Haredi?'

'Yes,' she said.

Without thinking I said: 'But you don't dress like a Haredi woman, you don't cover your hair.'

She smiled at me and said: 'Yes I do. It's not my hair. Why do my clothes not look like someone who is Haredi?'

Suddenly it was obvious. Nilli was a very successful business-woman. She could afford a wig that did not look like a wig. She could afford clothes that met the standards of her community's sense of modesty but that weren't black and shapeless and didn't fit the stereo-type. I apologised for shaking her hand.

'It's OK,' she said. 'I lived for some time in a Haredi community in New York and we had a very wise rabbi and he said: "If a man offers you his hand and he means no disrespect then you don't need to insult him by refusing it."'

I didn't make the same mistake with Libi Affen. She too runs a major software company. 'One of my clients he holds his hand out to

me every time and says: "I'm still hoping one day you're going to take
it" and I say to him: "I'm still hoping one day you're going to stop
sticking out your hand,"' she said with a laugh. She believes her
community can change, but it requires change from the secular Jews
too. She thinks Israelis dealing with the world outside will also help
them get along with their next-door neighbours. She told me:

> Globalisation is making a big difference, because we are working
> with the Chinese and Indians and Arabs. And people are learning
> that you have to understand different cultures. Understanding the
> Haredi world is no different from understanding the Indians or the
> Chinese. You don't want to change the Chinese, you just want to
> understand their culture and work with them. And that's how you
> have to work with the Haredi.

Libi is a little more socially conservative than Nilli. Her husband is a
prominent and highly respected rabbi. Libi feels very strongly that the
main reason it is important for Haredi women to be successful in
work is so that as many of their menfolk as possible can focus on their
studies of the Torah rather than join the workforce.

The Haredi men are seen as spongers by the secular Jews because
they spend their days exclusively devoted to this study. Their education is subsidised by the state. That subsidy is lost if they also work.
The ultra-Orthodox believe that understanding and interpreting
Jewish law to keep it alive and relevant makes a huge contribution to
the Jewish way of life and the Jewish people. They argue that it is God
who will keep the Jews safe from harm, and he'll only do that if they
merit his protection.

Libi told me:

> We need the men to sit and study because that's our army. We feel
> the reason we've been able to survive is because of these thousands
> of men sitting and studying daily from morning to night like my
> husband. Every man who gets up from his bench and goes to work

feels like someone just left the army. We're talking about a spiritual army versus a physical army [but] how do I explain to people who are not from a religious background that my husband sitting and studying is equal to your husband fighting in Gaza? But we saw it in the Six Day War. It was so obvious that there were miracles. We didn't do it because we had a great army. Even today we need a lot of miracles, but it is hard for the secular community to see that, and so the Haredim not being in the army has caused a lot of ill will within the community.

Libi was born in America. She only came to Israel in 1980. The Haredi community she left behind in the States deals with these issues differently. Only in Israel do nearly *all* the ultra-Orthodox men spend their days doing nothing but study Jewish law. In the US and the UK the percentage of Haredi men in the workforce is the same as in the rest of the population.[29] The Haredim in the West don't feel any less pious for working, and neither are they considered to be any less pious by the wider community. In fact many of Judaism's most revered rabbis, people held in high esteem by the ultra-Orthodox community in Israel, during their lifetimes also had jobs.

Becoming a rabbi means studying well into your thirties. It requires dedication, and if you are among the few who make the grade then you have a useful and hugely respected role in the wider society. But of course not everyone can become a rabbi. So the vast majority of those men who fail reach middle age with absolutely no skills to do anything else. Unlike the women, their secular education ended after primary level, so they are totally unemployable. Each year Israel produces tens of thousands of middle-aged men who are not only a waste to the labour market but a drain on the economy. And as the demographics rise, so too does the loss to the state.

But Nilli, who does believe more Haredi men should also work, says the prejudice against the Haredim in Israel makes the job of working in the secular society harder than it is abroad.

When we moved into our first apartment as a young couple the upstairs neighbour came down and shouted: 'You are stealing my money. Your food is my income tax.' That was our welcome! One time in a company I worked for, a guy came for an interview and when the manager saw the tzitzit while the guy was sitting in the waiting room, that was it. 'I don't want a religious Jew in my company' he said.

'But you were in his company,' I said to her.

'Yes, but I'm a woman. He didn't want a man because he thought this guy hadn't served in the army. He didn't even ask him, he just assumed he hadn't served in the army.'

The people of Israel recognise the value of preserving their faith. The concern of the majority secular community is that they think too many people are doing it and not all of them should be. They will accept a select group of gifted individuals being supported by the state while they learn the tenets of the faith inside out. But they think too many ultra-Orthodox men are simply learning the Torah so that they need not do anything else. The essence of this clash has changed over the last few years into a huge debate in the country about the exemption, or rather constant deferment, of ultra-Orthodox men doing their national service in the IDF. In 2012 14 per cent of Israeli young men were given an exemption from their national service because they were ultra-Orthodox studying in a religious school, a yeshiva. That figure was likely to be 20 per cent by the end of the decade if changes to the law weren't made.

At the creation of the state of Israel Ben-Gurion was asked by religious leaders to give an exemption from military service for 400 ultra-Orthodox men so that they could study the Torah. He was persuaded by the fact that as the Ashkenazi ultra-Orthodox communities were decimated by the Nazis in the Holocaust, there was value in allowing them to carry out their studies uninterrupted because it was good for the Jewish state, and the number he was asked to exempt was not huge. He agreed and the exemption stood. By 2012 that number had gone up to around 37,000 exempted from serving.[30]

The special exemption was formalised for five years in 2002 by what became known as the 'Tal Law'. It was passed by the Israeli parliament and it allowed full-time religious students to indefinitely defer military service. The 'Tal Law' was extended again in 2007. By the time it came up for a further extension in 2012 the mood of the country had radically changed. The High Court ruled that the law was unconstitutional. Haredi youths are now technically subjected to the draft, though it has still not been fully enforced. However the mood of the country means that over time it probably will be.

The politicians have pointed towards the demographics and the need to be able to secure the nation by having enough fighters. They picked the security issue because nothing focuses minds in Israel like being told there is a lurking threat. The army agrees it is important, but more for society than security.

'It's not very important from a military perspective. Some more battalions of fighters is useful but it's not the main issue,' one of Israel's top soldiers told me at his military HQ in Tel Aviv. 'From the wider national perspective, to bring solidarity in Israeli society, to create the symbol of an army of all the people, that is very important. From an economic point of view it's important that they are not left separated [from society] in these ghettos where they don't get the same education as everyone else.'

He was articulating exactly what the Haredi leadership *say* are the motivating forces behind the push to draft their young men into the IDF: dragging them into the mainstream. That is why the rabbis are fighting against the draft.

I asked this commander whether it was a good idea for the Israeli army to have lots of soldiers in it who don't believe in the state they are supposed to be willing to die to defend.

'It won't come to that,' he said.

We won't have a situation where those who don't want to serve will be serving in the military. You hear the rabbis saying: 'We will all refuse to serve,' but that doesn't reflect the reality on the ground.

There is transition going on among the Haredim. They still have their black and white suits and hats, but they are much more like Israelis than it may seem. It's been changing and it will take years, maybe a few decades, but it has started to happen. They don't have a choice and if we are patient and clever it will be a positive process, though there will be the occasional crisis.

The crisis that led to the nation's soul-searching over the issue started with a song. In September 2011 nine Haredi officer-course cadets who formed part of the small number of special IDF brigades that take only religious soldiers walked out of an official concert to mark the 2008 war in Gaza. They did so because one of their fellow soldiers began to sing a solo. It was not that the singing was bad, it was that the voice belonged to a woman. They considered listening to her to be a contravention of religious law, and so they left. Half of the cadets were dismissed for disobeying orders to stay where they were. Their actions caused uproar in the secular society, where women share the burden equally with men when it comes to military service. One rabbi said he and other religious leaders would order their young men to continue to leave these events, 'even if they are faced by a firing squad for doing so'.[31]

The controversy shifted into a broader row about the role of the ultra-Orthodox, which in the end led to the shape of the new coalition that was formed in 2013. Things might have turned out very different if the IDF had marked the Gaza war with a disco instead, because like everything else in the country the issue of women singing is complicated.

Yoel Weber explained: 'There is a phrase in the Talmud [a compilation of Jewish law] which says "the singing of a woman ignites passion".' That was why the men felt compelled to walk out. But, as Weber explained, the influence of modern technology has even made it difficult to interpret ancient Jewish laws.

There is a religious discussion about whether we are allowed to hear women singing on a tape, because we don't know what the women look like. The original [Jewish law] is related to the women being present, so if we are just hearing a tape and we don't know the women then that's a whole new question, because then there is nothing to relate that urge to. But there is the issue of what if it's a popular singer like Madonna. We know how she looks, we know how she moves. [At this point he did a brief jiggle in his chair which suggested he did indeed know her moves.] So we can relate to her, so when we hear her singing we might have in our minds the fantasy. So that's a big discussion.

While the Haredim busy themselves trying to work out how to manage and hold back the secular culture that permeates into theirs, the secular world is trying to force them into submission. The numbers in the Haredi community are growing fast, but so is the determination by the secular world to sort the issue out before the ultra-Orthodox become too big and politically powerful a group to stop them.

Yoel Weber says his community is constantly under attack from what he calls 'radical secularism'. And they are having trouble defending themselves because the modern world's most dangerous, most potent weapon sneaks past the Haredi barricades down a broadband line.

'The Internet is a very dangerous thing. There's a big fight going on against the Internet,' Weber said. Because he is a writer, he needs access to the Internet, but he does his best to avoid its insidious threat to his way of life. 'The reason I have my computer right in the middle of the house is so it can't control me too. If it's in the middle of the house I can't do whatever I feel like doing. I have a big problem. I try not to open those sites . . . the Internet is very very dangerous.'

While the Haredim do not pretend to be immune to the temptations of the modern world, they believe it is their religious duty to struggle inwardly and outwardly against these influences so that they can follow God's true path. But even within the conservative Haredi mainstream the religious spectrum is broad. Nilli, Libi and Yoel are highly respected members of their communities, and their views reflect that broad spectrum. Nilli and Libi are leading a transformation in their own communities without, they believe, damaging their fabric. They are going out into the secular world to confront its preconceptions. By contrast, in Yoel's community it is frowned upon if a woman even drives a car unless it is absolutely necessary.

'I don't think that even though my wife cannot drive that I respect her even one single per cent less than anyone else whose wife drives,' Yoel told me.

'Does your wife want to drive?' I asked.

'No, she doesn't want to drive.'

'So this is not being imposed on her?'

'Nothing is being imposed!' he said in a slightly exasperated tone.

There are those who are outcasts, who are rebels in the [Haredi] community, and when they got married nobody knew they were rebels. And then she says to her husband: 'I want to drive' and he says: 'What do you mean you want to drive!' and the husband says: 'No, you can't do it.' But my wife was brought up [to understand] her position in the family and with the values that she has, and she doesn't do that.

I suggested to him that perhaps paradoxically his community seemed to have more in common with the social values of very conservative Muslim societies in the region like Saudi Arabia than with the secular Jews just down the road.

I don't take that as an insult. I have no problem with that because to my way of thinking conservative social values are the right way because it was that way in the past. The only problem is when you take your social values and shoot people and blow up buses. I have no problem with the social values of the Muslims if they are law-abiding, quiet people. If people decide they want to live religiously, to live with Sharia and the Koran or the Torah, who are you to tell them not to?

'If you are asking me,' said the Hebrew University's Professor Alexander Yakobson, 'if the ultra-Orthodox are on their way to making Israel some kind of Jewish variant of the Islamic Republic of Iran, then my answer is the state of Israel is on its way to make the ultra-Orthodox part of modern society, at least most of them.'

And the state of Israel also has plans to integrate the other marginalised section of society, the country's Arabs, who have as much trouble as the Haredim working out their relationship with a state they too wish had not come into existence. There are attempts to force them as well to do some kind of national service, though this would not be military.

Perhaps the only comfort the ultra-Orthodox can take when it comes to their place in the social pecking order is that they are not at the bottom. That place is reserved for the Palestinians living inside the internationally recognised boundaries of Israel. These are often families that have lived on this land continuously for a lot longer than the vast majority of Jewish families living in Israel today. They are drawn from Arab communities that lived in Palestine before the creation of the state of Israel and who did not flee or were not driven from their homes during the brutally violent birth of the new nation.

Choosing to be unproductive is the key factor among the Haredi men. Discrimination seems to be a key factor in the unproductiveness of the Arab community. A report by the International Monetary Fund in 2012 said: 'For every education attainment level, Arab workers earn much less than Jewish workers, and earnings gaps are particularly high for those with university degrees. This suggests that some non-economic factors exist, including distrust and discrimination towards Arab people.'[32] In fact Arab workers earn around a third less than the country's average salary.[33] Even the brightest Arab employees in Israel believe they will eventually hit a glass ceiling.

But it is not just discrimination, it is a self-chosen exclusion from a key life experience of the Jewish majority that plays a part. The UK has the 'old boy network', the US has its fraternities, Arab countries have '*wasta*'. Israeli '*wasta*', connections, comes from the national service years. That experience is a melting pot where bonds are formed for life that stretch between social classes. The Haredim and the Arabs in Israel are outside that because they refuse to serve in the country's military, though for very different reasons. In the case of the Arabs it is because they do not want to be part of an army that is occupying and regularly in conflict with Palestinians in the territories.

The Arab community in Israel has the most complicated unresolved identity of any group of people in the Middle East. They are *not* just like the Palestinians in the West Bank and Gaza, because their history over the last sixty-odd years has been totally different. The Arabs in Israel have a unique identity. That makes the dream of some right-wing Israelis – in a final peace deal with the Palestinians, to swap those living in communities on the Israeli side of the Green Line for Jewish settler communities on the other side of it – totally unworkable. The important word among the various labels of Arab Israelis, Palestinian citizens of Israel, etc. is the word 'Israel'. These people are Israeli. They have a very complicated relationship with the state, but it is their home, and most of them given the choice would choose to live inside it, not to jump ship to a Palestinian state in the increasingly unlikely event that one were to be formed. Surveys have shown that around half of the country's Arabs have a sense of ownership towards the state of Israel.[34] What concerns almost all Arabs though is that they believe the state of Israel does not have a sense of ownership towards its Arab citizens.

'We accept the definition of the state of Israel as Jewish and democratic. But no one in the Arab community accepts the definition of the state of Israel as a Jewish state, period,' Mohammad Darawshe told me. Mohammad runs the Abraham Fund Initiatives, an organisation that promotes equality among Jewish and Arab citizens of Israel. There are eight million people living in Israel. Six million are Jewish. One point six million are Arabs. The rest are largely non-Arab Christians.[35] 'In the past the state defined itself equally as Jewish and democratic, and it was getting more democratic and that created more space for the non-Jewish members of society. The trend in the last five years is to make it more Jewish, to even triumph over the democratic identity, which is reducing the space for the non-Jews to feel some sort of belonging.' That trend is recognised by non-Arabs too. The Israeli Democracy Index's report for 2012 found that 'within the Jewish public, the balance between "Jewish" and "democratic" in the definition of the State continues to tilt toward the "Jewish" component.'

'It makes you feel that you are some sort of temporary guest and that the option of getting rid of you is possible,' said Mohammad. But that's not the only reason Israel's Arab communities feel literally unloved.

The country's Supreme Court in January 2012 upheld a ruling that says Israeli citizens may live in Israel with their spouses unless their spouses are Palestinians from the West Bank. So if you are an Arab citizen of Israel or a Jewish citizen of Israel you can bring your wife from anywhere else in the world, but you can't bring her the half an hour down the road from the West Bank. It was this ruling that *Ha'aretz* described with the headline 'Supreme Court thrusts Israel down the slope of apartheid', adding that this was a 'demographic ruling that protects Jews while harming Arab citizens'.

For a long time it was not only the Israelis who made this country's Palestinian citizens feel lonely, it was the rest of the Arabs too. Nobody wanted to speak for them because they were everyone's poor relation.

For a period before the Second Intifada, while the peace movement in Israel could still draw breath, the Arab voters were courted by the political left. But the right wing managed to turn their presence in the left camp into a taint by claiming that governments which relied on Arab members of the Knesset were illegitimate. The phrase 'Jewish majority' was bandied about to imply that a government could not be trusted unless it had a majority without Arab support.

This sent Arab political participation in the electoral process into a slow tailspin from the elections in 1999. It had gone from 75 to

53 per cent by 2009.[36] And then suddenly in the 2013 election it pulled up again to 56 per cent. When I asked Mohammad Darawshe why, he told me:

> It was a response to the encouragement by the Arab League which for the first time called for the Arab citizens to participate, which you could call 'Halal', stamping Arab citizenship in Israel. Until now being Israeli citizens as Arabs was something to hide in front of the Arab world and sometimes to even be ashamed of. The Arab League gesture towards Arab citizens seems to accept that unique nature of Israeli citizenship for this group of Arabs. It's saying it's OK, we even need you in the Arab world.

But as far as a growing number of Israelis are concerned, that is where the Palestinian Arab community in Israel should be, shoved into the Arab world.

'No, it's not bad and it's not good. It's like third gear in a car, sometimes you use it and sometimes you don't.' David was an ordinary enough-looking man. He was short and stocky with a neatly trimmed light brown beard on a broad face. He wore a casual sweater and jeans. We were sitting on a couple of rocks on a blustery hilltop where he was building himself a new home.

The only thing extraordinary about David was that the 'it' we were discussing was killing children. David did not think it was always a bad thing. He was a religious ultra-nationalist Jewish settler, and he told me he was at war with the Arabs. All Arabs.

His single-floor wooden bungalow stood on stilts on the side of a hill alongside a few others in the middle of a barren piece of land deep inside the West Bank. It was part of what the settlers call an outpost, which conjures up for them their sense of a pioneering spirit. David considered its construction to be a declaration of his war. The state of Israel says his settlement is illegal because it is built on private Palestinian land. David believed God wanted him to live here. He believed it was his duty to live here, and if that meant killing Arab children to stay, then no man could tell him that wasn't right.

'Obviously it is wrong by [your] Christian humanist rules,' he told me as he waded through a long convoluted justification for his statement. I interrupted his flow. 'Where do you draw the line? Is a nine-month-old baby a threat to you?'

'It is not a matter of threat, it is a matter of war. In the Christian understanding of the Bible, which is based on a mistranslation of the Ten Commandments, the Christians reckon it says: "Thou shalt not kill." It does not say that in Hebrew, it says: "Thou shalt not murder." Killing is fine.'

David spoke to me candidly on the basis that I would not identify him, so I have not. David is not his real name. He has served time in jail for violent gun crimes against members of the West Bank Palestinian community. But David is not just some brutish idiot. He is articulate and he works in one of Israel's hi-tech industries. He has a clear and, in his own mind, very rational argument to justify his presence here.

Men like him build outposts on the Palestinian hilltops. Then when they have created a line of dots of occupied land, more people come to fill in the gaps between the dots. As their numbers grow, and while the legal case to throw them out slowly winds its way through the Israeli courts, the IDF moves in to protect these isolated outposts from possible attacks. Once the army is there, more families feel secure enough to move in too, so the outpost eventually becomes a bigger settlement. The wooden bungalows are replaced by bricks and mortar, and as the homes become permanent, so does the determination of the less hard-line settlers to stay.

To remove all these people and their homes, the Israeli government has to send in those bulldozers Netanyahu talked about. They also have to contend with the images of Israeli families being literally dragged kicking and screaming from their homes. And those images do not play well with right-wing or even mainstream Israel. The present political leadership therefore often does everything it can to drag its feet on implementing court orders with appeals and delaying tactics until hopefully they can find a way to keep the settlers, who are also right-wing voters, where they are, or at worst in another nearby settlement with bigger and better homes.

'I'm fighting a war, I choose to be here. I'm saying, by being here, this is my land and no one else's,' said David. 'The world, the UN or international courts may or may not agree. I don't care. I'm just not interested, I believe in my rules and my rules say this land is mine. And that is why I choose to live specifically here, in a place which some people would say shouldn't be mine. And in that sense it makes this the front line of the war.'

'And where do those rules come from?' I asked him.

'The Bible,' he said. David told me he considered there to be two main forces at work within the Jewish people. Those who strongly identified themselves as Jewish – and in that group he placed the ultra-Orthodox and religious ultra-nationalists like himself. And those who wanted to merge their Jewish identity with other cultures. That is where he placed the majority of the secular community and the state of Israel.

'I'm here because I am Jewish. There is nothing else that gives me the right to claim this land. I wasn't born here. I didn't buy it from anyone. No government or law gave it to me. In fact they told me to leave, but I'm still here.'

David's vision of a Greater Israel starts with the West Bank but ultimately includes areas which are now Syria, Lebanon, Jordan, the Sinai, and slivers of Iraq. I asked him how representative he thought his views were of the wider population. 'I'm in the minority without a doubt. It used to be one per cent or less. I would guess now in some things it's ten per cent, in others it's getting to be a majority, in other aspects it's less than one per cent still, but it's growing all the time.'

'Most people would see you as a bit of an extremist nutcase wouldn't they?' I asked him.

'Yes. But throughout the history of the Jewish people, it has always been individuals or very small groups going against the will of the majority that led the way forward. I'd like to believe I'm one of those people who is paving the way for everyone else to follow later.'

He would no doubt have found proof of that statement in the success of the Jewish Home Party in the 2013 polls. Naftali Bennett, is – within the hard-line settler community anyway – a more moderate voice. Among his new MPs there are people like him and there are people like Orit Struk. She comes from the very hard-line settler community in the West Bank town of Hebron. While she was entering parliament her thirty-year-old son was serving a thirty-month jail sentence for kidnapping and assaulting a fifteen-year-old Palestinian boy who he later dumped naked by the side of the road.[37]

The West Bank settlements have the highest number of conscripts who choose to serve in IDF combat units during their national service. That figure was nearly double that of those living in the Tel Aviv area.[38] That helped add to a sharp rise in the number of IDF infantry officers who are religious Zionists from 2.5 per cent in 1990 to 31 per cent in 2007.[39] As the country has drifted to the right so has the army. That has raised concerns that there would be rebellion within the ranks if the politicians ever told them to carry out the evacuation of settlements in the West Bank as Sharon instructed the IDF over Gaza.

'An increasing number of the young people in the IDF are the children of Russians and settlers, the hardest-core people against a division of the land. This presents a staggering problem . . . It's a different Israel. Sixteen per cent of Israelis speak Russian.'[40] Those were the words of US President Bill Clinton in 2010. He was identifying the two most right-wing forces in Israel today: the settlement movement and the Jews who emigrated from the former Soviet Union.

'Russian Jews', as they are called in Israel regardless of where in the former Soviet Union they came from, have been blamed for fundamentally altering the nature of Israeli society. They are accused of making it less tolerant, less democratic, and of collectively being the greatest obstacle to peace. They are the arch-rivals of both the ultra-Orthodox and the Arabs in Israel when it comes to issues of the state. They are stridently secular and nationalist.

Around 1 million people emigrated from the former Soviet Union in the 1990s as it began to crumble. In January 2013 the Jewish population of Israel passed 6 million, so it's easy to see how their number back then would have had a profound impact on society. The Russian-speaking Jews have often been at the sharp end of proclamations by rabbis over who qualifies as a proper Jew. The embodiment of what Bill Clinton sees as the negative influence of Russian Jews on modern Israel is the former foreign minister Avigdor Lieberman and his party Yisrael Beiteinu, which formed a joint ticket with Netanyahu's Likud Party in the 2013 poll, serving neither one of them well.

The Moldovan-born Mr Lieberman is a man about whom people are not ambivalent. The *New York Times* calls him 'thuggish'.[41] The normally mild-mannered Palestinian leader Hanan Ashrawi told me she thought he was a 'racist SOB'. He has also been called a racist by Jewish politicians. When he was in the government one of his more right-wing cabinet colleagues confessed to me: 'I don't like his style. I don't think he's an extremist . . . [but he] does us some harm when dealing with the West.' The then Israeli defence minister Ehud Barak said of the country's foreign minister in September 2012: 'Lieberman's comments about the Palestinian Authority and its president do not represent Israeli policy, and harm Israeli interests.'[42]

Mr Lieberman's stint at the Israeli Foreign Ministry was catastrophic, spanning as it did the Arab revolts, because even before the first stone had been cast Lieberman's Foreign Ministry destroyed Israel's key strategic partnership with Turkey. In January 2010 Israel's deputy foreign minister Danny Ayalon, who was a member of Lieberman's Yisrael Beiteinu, invited the Israeli press to a meeting he was holding with the Turkish ambassador Ahmet Oguz Celikkol. He was calling the meeting to complain about a spy drama made in Turkey which often had the Israelis as the bad guys. Ambassador Celikkol did not know the press would be there and he did not know that Mr Ayalon was saying to them in Hebrew: 'Pay attention that he is sitting in a lower chair . . . that there is only an Israeli flag on the table and that we are not smiling.'

The Turkish government was furious. A few months later the anger was compounded by the botched raid on the Turkish activists' boat the *Mavi Marmara*, which was trying to break the blockade on Gaza. The timing of the nosedive in relations with Turkey, which led to the withdrawal of ambassadors, could not have been worse, coming as it did just months before the Arab revolts that would replace Mubarak with the Brotherhood. It took almost three years, and the confluence of the absence of Lieberman – who was by then facing criminal charges of fraud and breach of trust – and a presidential visit from Barack Obama to resolve the damaging diplomatic row between the two nations. The fact though that Netanyahu made the call to his opposite number, Recep Tayyip Erdogan, from a trailer at the airport while Air Force One was sitting on the runway ready to leave suggests that Obama had to put pressure on him to make the call and thus give the US president something to take away from his state visit in 2013.

When it came to running foreign policy during Obama's first term Netanyahu kept the American brief largely to himself, but the rest of the diplomatic toolkit he left with Lieberman. For four years the only instrument the Foreign Ministry seemed to know how to use was a sledgehammer. The sidelining of the foreign minister from foreign affairs burst out into another row when he became the first man in his job to sever ties with his country's own intelligence service, Mossad.[43] Mr Lieberman complained that Mossad was going behind his back to deal with countries outside their remit. And so they were.

Many times during Lieberman's period as foreign minister I was told privately by government officials that comments he was making did not represent the views of Israel. As foreign minister he took Henry Kissinger's comment that 'Israel has no foreign policy, only a domestic political system' to its absolute extreme. Lieberman played only to his domestic political gallery. His every utterance was made with them in mind. The impact on Israel's foreign policy seemed a distant second concern. Yisrael Beiteinu had fought the previous election in 2009 on the slogan 'No citizenship without loyalty', which was an attack on Israeli Arabs but also came to be seen in the campaign as directed towards the ultra-Orthodox.

But the social and political differences between Jews from the former Soviet Union and the communities they joined are generational. The children of the new immigrants see themselves as Israeli, not Russian. Hebrew is their first language. Russia might be part of their heritage but Israeli is their identity. Israeli political parties have a habit of coming and going. Yisrael Beiteinu might have a short shelf life. There is barely any difference any more in terms of education, income, religious observance or political opinions between the children of native-born Israelis and the children of those born in the former Soviet Union.[44] Yisrael Beiteinu means 'Israel our Home'. That notion is blindingly obvious to the generation born here. If the party continues to define itself by its past it will simply cease to exist in the future.

The issues raging within Israeli society are widely debated within the country but, as Hadassa Margolis found out from her ex-friend, there is a general reluctance among many to air their nation's divisions in public. The Israel Democracy Institute's 2012 survey showed that a majority of the country's Jewish population think people should 'be prohibited from publicly voicing harsh criticism of the state'. Many Israelis think the country is much maligned and misunderstood by the rest of the world, and so there is often a very prickly reaction to any criticism of the state of Israel from outside too. Right-wing Israelis often equate Israel with Judaism and consider an attack on the former to be a veiled attack on the latter. Many in the Jewish diaspora do not see Israel in that way, and they sometimes find themselves subject to the slur 'self-loathing Jew'.

There is a 'commonly held belief that Israel has a "hasbara problem", especially when it comes to the Palestinian–Israeli conflict,' said a report published by the Israeli think tank Molad. 'Hasbara' is Hebrew for public diplomacy. People in Israel and parts of the Jewish diaspora think the Israeli government just isn't good enough and doesn't try

hard enough to make the country's case to the outside world. Not
that individuals don't try. A diplomat's wife told me over lunch one
day in Jerusalem how minutes before she was wheeled into the operating theatre for a Caesarean section at a local hospital her surgeon
asked her why her country's policies were so negative towards Israel.

In fact the Molad report concludes that 'the "hasbara problem" is a
myth that diverts focus from Israel's real problems which are the
results of problematic policy, not flawed hasbara of appropriate
policy.'[45] Many Israelis I've met though would disagree with that
conclusion, because they perceive widespread but subtle anti-Semitism
in the outside world.

At the root of this is a fear about the survival of the Jewish nation.
David and Yoel believe this fear is because the Zionist majority have
put their faith in men, not God, to protect them. Either way that fear
is very real. It is hidden behind what many outsiders, even Jews who
have made aliyah, find to be an often belligerent and aggressive society to live in.

In my first month here, while I was getting my accreditation from
the Government Press Office I got an unprompted diatribe from an
Israeli official who had recently moved from England. He waxed lyri-
cal about his love of Zionism and how he would take up arms against
the UK if necessary because he felt like this was really his home. Then
he asked me how I was finding it. I almost finished saying something
polite before he jumped in with: 'But doesn't the driving send you
mad? And the pushing in?' And then he launched into another even
longer diatribe about all the things about Israel that offended his very
English sensibilities.

But he knew why he was here. It wasn't just his politics. Despite the
neighbourhood, the Jews who live in Israel generally feel safe. Their fear
is very real, because it is founded on the world's worst atrocity. It has
seeped into their bones. They feel safe in Israel because after generations
of persecution their continued existence as a people is no longer
entrusted to the goodness of others. They are responsible for their own
security and their own survival. It is not a polite society, but people

believe that when the chips are down the stranger born in another land who just barged past them in the bread queue would, in a war, protect them and their state with his life. I once asked one of my Israeli colleagues to explain to me the significance of a particular Jewish festival. 'It's basically like all the others,' he said. 'They tried to kill us, they failed, let's eat!'

The world has tended not to understand modern Israel because it has looked at it through the prism of the conflict with the Palestinians. The Israelis do not see their society in that way any more. The last election was fought on issues about Israel's relationship with itself, not with the Palestinians. Like the rest of the New Middle East, God and the role of religion in society and politics is at the heart of the debate in Israel too. Israel is becoming more religious and more nationalist, and those two things put it at risk of becoming less democratic. When it comes to the issue the outside world cares about, the peace process, Israel has swung sharply to the right, and it is not going to swing back again.

The areligious European Zionists were needed to create the state of Israel, but they no longer define it. They were an aberration. Israel is a Middle Eastern country. It is not a little piece of Europe that has somehow found itself in the wrong place. One day the prime minister of Israel may look and think more like Mr Klausner than Mr Netanyahu. The coming years will see internal struggles in Israel which, while not as violent as those with the Palestinians, will be equally passionate. Israel has radically changed, is still radically changing, and the world has not caught up with that fact yet. When it does it can start dealing with Israel as it is and not as it used to be. The nation that must face up to the fact first, as it struggles with all the other profound changes in the Middle East, is America.

5

America's Pillars of Sand

My ears were working perfectly so I could hear him screaming: 'Made in the US, look! Made in the US.' It was my eyes that were having trouble focusing on the metal tube he was holding in his hand. I simply don't understand why tear-gas canisters have their country of origin proudly emblazoned upon them. It's like saying: 'This vomit-inducing moment was brought to you by Uncle Sam. Now you have a nice day!' During the Egyptian revolution the experience was courtesy of Combined Tactical Systems from Jamestown, Pennsylvania. The state motto is 'Virtue, Liberty and Independence', though their export wasn't fostering any of those things on 28 January 2011, the 'Day of Rage'. Instead the 6230 'pyrotechnic grenade' had been 'discharging smoke and irritant agents through multiple emission ports'. As it was doing so, on TV the chief American diplomat, Hillary Clinton, was saying: 'We are deeply concerned about the use of violence by Egyptian police and security forces against protestors'.[1] These solemn words were being spoken as I joined others spluttering in the backstreets of Cairo from American-made tear gas, paid for by American military aid, which was playing a big role in the use of that violence by Egyptian police and security forces against protesters.

When you live in the Middle East it is not hard to understand why people here often find the things America says at odds with the things America does. And in 'the timeless city of Cairo' in particular, the United States just couldn't get its message right. It was here that a US president sent his secretary of state to apologise to the Arab world for the past actions of almost every American administration since the Second World War. Then the current American president came personally to issue another apology, this time for the administration that had delivered the last one.

On the day the Egyptian people began their revolution, Secretary of State Clinton announced: 'our assessment is that the Egyptian Government is stable and is looking for ways to respond to the legitimate needs and interests of the Egyptian people.'² She could be forgiven for the beginning of that statement, because not even the protesters believed then that they would bring the regime down. But there was absolutely nothing in the three decades of Mubarak's rule to suggest that he might have any intention whatsoever of responding to the cry for freedom with anything other than another volley of American-made tear gas. It was disingenuous to suggest otherwise. Or perhaps it was the moment America's old and decrepit foreign policy in the Middle East found itself caught in the headlights, just before the juggernaut driven by a generation of young Arab youths turned it into roadkill. The US has not yet found a replacement.

'We don't have a new foreign policy for the new Middle East,' Anne-Marie Slaughter told me. She was the Obama administration's director of Policy Planning at the State Department from January 2009 until February 2011. 'We have a set of principles that are guiding us . . . but I do not think we have taken the full measure of the historical turn and developed a coherent policy across the region, and that may just be impossible.' It may be impossible because the next foreign policy will never again be able to assume the luxury of the 'perverse simplicity' of dealing with dictators.

'It was a mistake to assume it wasn't complex before,' Ambassador Daniel Kurtzer told me. After he retired from the State Department in 2006 he wrote speeches for the then Senator Barack Obama and advised him on the Middle East as he ran for the White House, and was one of the architects of Obama's policy of engagement and persuasion with hostile foreign powers.

It may have looked like one size fits all before, but in effect you had a policy in the Middle East totally dominated by three partners, Saudi Arabia, Egypt and Israel. And everybody else kind of fit in or didn't fit in. In some respects I think Obama, whether he has articulated it or not, is looking to maintain that as things change. So it's a moving sidewalk and you can't just remain stationary but it's hard in all three places.

It is hard because all three of America's partners in the region, which have for decades been the three pillars of US foreign policy here, have been, are being or will be radically changed by the forces unleashed by the uprisings. In the coming years each time that Secretary of State John Kerry gets back to Washington after a trip to the Middle East he will often find the place he has just left has changed again while he was still in mid-air.

Decades of pent-up energy burst out into the open in 2011. It is going to take years for things to calm down. Versions of the sudden sense of shock that the US administration had in those early days will be felt again and again. Just propping up the three pillars of its policy – Israel, Egypt, Saudi Arabia – and dealing with the occasional young pretender may mean it will take some time before it can build anything new on top.

'The Obama administration was presented with a historic watershed of the like you see only every two to three decades,' said Anne-Marie Slaughter.

At least in 1989 you had a year's warning. In Egypt you had two weeks. It required overturning thirty years of a deep relationship pretty much overnight. If you had said when Obama came into office or even at Christmas 2010: 'Hey look, in two months you're going to be abandoning Hosni Mubarak! . . .' I think actually they reacted very fast, they corrected course remarkably quickly, and then in Libya they made the right decision. In Bahrain it was much more complicated and the Saudis were much more involved and it was much less clear to us what we could do.

The answer to that question was nothing. While much had changed in the Middle East, America's allies in the Gulf were determined that some things would not.

If American foreign policy was caught in the headlights, foreign policy in the Gulf went into a blind panic in the first few months of the revolts. The Saudis in particular don't take kindly to movements built around people power. Public protest in the country is illegal.[3] The speed with which the first two dictators were deposed horrified them and prompted their intervention in Bahrain when the House of Saud started catching the draught from the region's winds of change. '[The Saudis] led a counter-revolution against the Arab Spring uprisings domestically and in their own close sphere of influence like Bahrain, and to some extent also in Abu Dhabi and the UAE, where you have also a Muslim Brotherhood-like movement in the northern Emirates,' says Princeton's Professor Bernard Haykel.

The protests in Bahrain centred on the Pearl Roundabout in the capital Manama. The demonstrators camped out there for a month until the Sunni King Hamad bin Isa al-Khalifa's security services, backed by Saudi troops, used what the UN called a 'shocking' level of force to clear them out.[4] Most controversially, it even jailed doctors who had treated the injured protesters at the country's main public hospital, though they were later cleared on appeal.[5] This wasn't the end of the wider protests though, which continued on and off for years afterwards. Nor was it the end of the state clamping down on the demonstrators who came largely from the majority Shia population.

In that speech at the State Department on 19 May 2011 when President Obama gave his initial considered assessment of the events in the Middle East and North Africa, he said: 'a new generation has emerged. And their voices tell us that change cannot be denied.' He reeled off where these cries for freedom could be heard – 'In

Cairo . . . In Sanaa . . . In Benghazi . . . In Damascus' – and went on to take a swipe at Iran. He also talked about the rights of women and religious minorities. He spoke about the Israeli–Palestinian peace process and the regional economy. And he offered a rebuke against the events at Pearl Roundabout, saying: 'we have insisted both publicly and privately that mass arrests and brute force are at odds with the universal rights of Bahrain's citizens . . . you can't have a real dialogue when parts of the peaceful opposition are in jail.'[6]

In fact he addressed all of the key issues and nations of the region, bar one. Two words were missing from his speech. They were 'Saudi Arabia'. Professor Haykel told me:

The Saudis were against the toppling of Mubarak and were taken aback by it. They were particularly upset by the fact that President Obama abandoned Mubarak because they conceive of politics in terms of personal relationships and loyalty and they saw Obama as being disloyal to Mubarak. I think Obama realised fairly quickly that Bahrain was a red line and it was off limits to an independent American policy.

President Obama wasn't breaking new ground with his lack of action, as a report written for members of the US Congress pointed out: 'U.S. comments and action with regard to Bahrain may be regarded by Saudi officials as indicators of U.S. commitment to maintaining relationships that have long prioritized government-to-government cooperation over people-to-people ties and human rights and democracy.'[7] However Obama *was* breaking with his own previously held position.

In the months running up to the invasion of Iraq, then Illinois State Senator Obama spoke out against this clash between American values and American foreign policy. He asked the man he would eventually replace: 'You want a fight, President Bush? Let's fight to make sure our so-called allies in the Middle East, the Saudis and the Egyptians, stop oppressing their own people, and suppressing dissent, and tolerating corruption and inequality.'[8] Those words rang hollow by the time the now President Obama had a chance to do just that. In 2011 nothing was done to stop his 'so-called allies in the Middle East, the Saudis' helping to suppress dissent in Bahrain. Bahrain is the home of the US Navy's 5th Fleet, America's key deterrent against Iranian ambitions to influence affairs in the oil-rich Gulf region.

To be fair, the White House didn't try to hide these policy contradictions either. 'We don't make decisions about questions like intervention based on consistency or precedent,' said a spokesman when he was quizzed over the variance between the Obama administration's actions in Libya, Syria and Bahrain after the uprisings. 'We make them based on how we can best advance our interests in the region.'[9]

While the Obama administration worked out what those interests now were, as the New Middle East formed, the Gulf states took the chance to catch their breath. They had been petrified by the pace of change in Tunisia and Egypt and they feared that the wave of revolts was unstoppable. Libya reassured them, because Gaddafi proved that not all authoritarian regimes just collapsed overnight. Then the Saudis were actively encouraged by the US to take the public lead in the transition in Yemen. Through the Gulf Cooperation Council, the GCC, they ended both the 33-year rule of President Ali Abdullah Saleh, and the year-long, often bloody revolt against him. Yemen avoided a civil war, though the chaos allowed al-Qaeda to strengthen its hold on the south of the country, the young protesters did not get their political reform, and Saleh continued to interfere from the sidelines. However, their own nerves now steadied, the Saudis paused and surveyed the new political landscape. They rather liked what they saw. To take advantage of it they first exploited the absent influence of some of the dictators they'd been at first so loath to lose.

Within weeks of Mubarak's overthrow the institution that had symbolised much of what was wrong with the Arab world during his rule was suddenly in danger of losing its hard-won reputation for being utterly useless in a crisis. The Arab League was making decisions. What wasn't immediately obvious was how much the revolutions had changed the power balance in the grouping, shifting it towards the GCC. This is a political and economic alliance made up of Sunni-led nations: Saudi Arabia, Qatar, Bahrain, Kuwait, Oman and the United Arab Emirates. The first two of these countries dominate the rest. Their mutual antagonism is driven by their competition for influence within the GCC and the wider region. The biggest problem they all face is their restless Shia populations. There are 2 million Shia in the GCC states. They are a majority in Bahrain and range from between 10 and 30 per cent in the other five states.[10]

When the Libyans rose up and Gaddafi began his violent crackdown there was a push from the British and the French for a no-fly zone. President Obama didn't think that went far enough and told his colleagues: 'I want to call everyone's bluff up in New York . . . we're not going to support this resolution for a no-fly zone, we're going to redo it and authorise the use of "all necessary measures to protect civilians".'[11] It upped the ante considerably, but Russia and China didn't block the resolution, partly because the move had the unprecedented backing of the Arab League.[12]

As Gaddafi had already turned his back on the Arab world it was perhaps not surprising to them that the League turned its back on him. Russia and China realised too late that the real cause was a shift in power within the grouping away from the previously dominant members who were busy dealing with the Arab revolts and towards the Gulf. Ambassador Barbara Bodine told me:

The traditional powers in the Arab League were suddenly out of the game, and what we saw was the GCC states kind of do an invasion of the body snatchers. They have taken over the Arab League because there was a power vacuum. The Qataris had been playing in political issues for quite some time and for a while everyone giggled – 'Little Qatar running around trying to solve Sudan and Lebanon and everything else, isn't that funny?' But they kept at it and what we didn't notice was that they were actually quite serious about it, there was a learning curve. With the Arab Spring a lot of that crystallised.

In November 2009 Qatar's enthusiasm in the realm of foreign policy ambitions was being derided in the US State Department: 'Over the next 36 months . . . Qatar will also continue to pursue its classic vulnerable small-state policies aimed either at pleasing as many players as possible or – where competing demands make this impossible – at containing and counter-balancing irritation caused by these policies.'[13] It proved quite a busy thirty-six months for the Qataris, who saw the Arab Spring as their chance to step up to the big league. By the end of 2012 money from Doha had bankrolled the Libyan revolution and was co-funding the Syrian one. And the government had loaned billions of dollars to the new Islamist governments in Egypt and Tunisia.

In the past, Qatari foreign policy had seemed to be about keeping itself out of trouble with the rest of the region. Its willingness to curry favour with anyone and everyone led the then Senator John Kerry to remark in April 2009 that 'Qatar . . . can't continue to be an American ally on Monday that sends money to Hamas on Tuesday.'[14] The same year a secret State Department cable said that when it came to cooperating with the US over terrorist financing Qatar was 'the worst in the region . . . they have been hesitant to act against known terrorists out of concern for appearing to be aligned with the U.S. and provoking reprisals.'[15] The rise of Islamists to power in Tunisia and Egypt, and the potential for that to happen also in Libya and Syria, seems to have spurred Qatar into thinking they could now reshape the Middle East. Saudi Arabia saw the revolts as a threat. Qatar saw them as an opportunity, because with its native population enjoying a per capita income of around US$400,000 a year it wasn't expecting any blowback at home.[16] Instead the Qatari leadership's hope was that once the episode played out, they would have long-term grateful friends in some of the most important Arab states. But they started to get carried away with themselves. They infuriated many of their Arab

League colleagues by stifling debate and forcing through policies during closed-door sessions.[17]

The US Senate Committee on Foreign Relations stated in June 2012, when it was still chaired by John Kerry: 'There is a new equilibrium in the Middle East, as the Arab Awakening, immense oil and gas reserves, and the war in Iraq have shifted the center of gravity towards the Gulf states.'[18] In fact the war in Iraq caused a drift of influence *away* from the Gulf states and towards their enemies in Tehran. The Saudis, in particular, have used the Arab revolts to correct that slide. This wasn't immediately apparent to the Obama administration in the wake of the uprisings.

The Gulf states and the Western powers may have been on the same side, but their instincts were poles apart. The United States saw much of the early stages of the Arab Spring through the prism of its impact on Israel and oil. It didn't have a plan for the New Middle East so it defaulted back to the ideas it used to manage the old one. The US sought stability in the region. But the Gulf states, once they were sure they had sorted out stability at home, set about shaking things up everywhere else. They were much quicker to recognise that stability for the sake of stability was pointless at this stage. The region was in flux. Instead of trying to contain it they decided to steer it in the direction they wanted.

So began another round in the decades-long proxy war between the most conservative Shia power and the most conservative Sunni power. Saudi Arabia saw in all the turmoil an opportunity to dramatically weaken Iran's influence in the region. To do that they needed to reinforce to America, in the years that followed the Arab uprisings, that Tehran was the root of all evil in the region. Sometimes it was, but sometimes it was not.

In the spring of 2011 President Obama offered what seemed like partial mitigation of Bahrain's actions by saying in the aftermath: 'We recognize that Iran has tried to take advantage of the turmoil there.'[19]

In fact the kingdom's own independent report, published six months later, said: 'The evidence presented to the Commission in relation to the involvement of the Islamic Republic of Iran in the internal affairs of Bahrain does not establish a discernible link between specific incidents that occurred in Bahrain during February/March 2011 and the Islamic Republic of Iran.'[20] The Sunni leadership in the Gulf wrongly present their Shia populations as an Iranian fifth column. Iran may want to use Shia protests in Bahrain and Saudi Arabia to further its aims but that doesn't mean they own the protestors. But the longer the West continues to turn a deaf ear to the call for human rights and democracy, the easier it will become for Iran to present itself to the demonstrators as their only friend.

America has to contend with the fact that the Arab Spring has dragged it into another battle between Islamic states over the will of God. That struggle will permeate every conflict and affect every decision America must make in the coming years. It involves the 1,300-year-old conflict between Sunni and Shia, but also the decades-long animosity between the Brotherhood and the Saudis. The US now faces its greatest set of challenges in the Middle East since it began to seriously exert its influence there in the 1950s. But this is a much more complicated clash than the Cold War struggle that defined America's old foreign policy in the region.

The United States entered the Middle East on a wave of good will largely because it was not one of the old imperialists. Events in 1956 would prove conclusively that America was replacing the Europeans as the dominant Western power, but even before the Suez Crisis many could see the writing on the wall.

'For many years we have had a little American lamb bleating in Cairo, not helping and if anything hindering in most things. Well, he has got his way . . . We are losing our will to rule . . . it is a sorry day for Britain.'[21] Those were the bleatings of Captain Charles Waterhouse, one of the Tory 'Suez rebels', to his prime minister Winston Churchill on 28 July 1954, following the announcement that British forces would be 'withdrawn from the Canal Zone'.

The Americans had been trying to get Nasser to compromise with the US's key ally Britain because they feared the rise of Soviet influence. Nasser's response was that the Soviets 'have never occupied our territory . . . but the British have been here for seventy years . . . How can I go to my people and tell them I am disregarding a killer with a pistol sixty miles from me at the Suez Canal to worry about somebody who is holding a knife a thousand miles away? They would tell me "first things first." '[22]

The British could not get over their sense of humiliation, and then they compounded it with the invasion of the Suez Canal two years later. The years of being able to sail around the world doing pretty much as they pleased were over, but the United Kingdom hadn't grasped that yet.

On Monday 29 October 1956 the State Department's William Rountree was handed a press ticker tape that read: 'FLASH-FLASH-FLASH, MAJOR ISRAELI FORCES HAVE INVADED EGYPT AND HEAVY FIGHTING IS UNDERWAY.'[23] Six years earlier the US, Britain and France had signed a Tripartite Declaration pledging to oppose any state aggression in the Middle East. Now, with the first serious test of that declaration upon them, the White House issued a statement saying: 'the President recalled that the United States . . . has pledged itself to assist the victim of any aggression in the Middle East. We shall honor our pledge.'[24] But it soon became apparent that his two European allies were in fact in league with the country Eisenhower saw as the aggressor, Israel. The president told his people: 'We believe these actions to have been taken in error . . . There can be no peace without law. And there can be no law if we work to invoke one code of international conduct for those who oppose, and another for our friends.'[25] This is exactly what the US has been regularly accused of doing in the decades since by the Arab states with regard to Israel and the issue of Palestine.

If Eisenhower was seen to be publicly upset by the Suez fiasco, he was privately furious. After he learned of Israel's attack on Egypt he told his secretary of state, John Foster Dulles: 'You tell 'em,

God-damn-it, that we are going to apply sanctions, we're going to the United Nations, we're going to do everything that there is so we can stop this thing.'[26] Of Britain and France he said: 'I've just never seen great powers make such a complete *mess* and *botch* of things!'[27]

The Eisenhower administration's actions during the Suez Crisis were driven largely by Cold War concerns, and it did not want to fall out with its closest European ally. But there was also a core sense that what London and Paris had connived at was simply wrong. Eisenhower believed America had a role as an honest broker in the region. It was a role almost every president up to and including Barack Obama thought at one time or another that the US could and should play in the Middle East.

It was clear from the Suez Crisis that both European countries were losing their Great Power status and that America had replaced Britain as the key Western player in the Middle East. The consequences of Suez, and the spectre that the Soviet Union would fill the vacuum left behind by the colonial powers, led the US president, the following January, to articulate what became known as the 'Eisenhower Doctrine'. This reshaped American policy in the Middle East and created the rulebook for the Cold War period and beyond. The first issue Eisenhower spoke about during his address to the joint Congress was oil, and oil was the first thing every subsequent administration cared about. The heavy tilt towards Israel in the following years was checked only by the 1973 oil 'supply shock'. As Egypt under Nasser slid towards the communists, Israel and all future US administrations became inseparable. Never again would the US publicly side against Israel in a conflict.

The collapse of the Soviet Union changed the problem but not the solution. By that time the preoccupation with the Russians was being run a close second for public enemy number one by Islamists, in the wake of the Iranian revolution in 1979. The fact that the Shia Islamists in Iran were a totally different kettle of fish from the Sunni Islamists who murdered Anwar Sadat was not a key factor. In both cases they related back to the other two core issues of oil and Israel.

There were the odd hiccups over the years, but nothing too dramatic. The principles of the system Eisenhower established for the Arab world, oil and stability, seemed to work fine.

Two events changed that. The first took place in 1986 when a man who was trying to jog off a hangover after his fortieth birthday party decided to embrace the power of faith to stop a slow slide into alcoholism and thus transformed himself from a drunk into the most powerful man on earth.[28] The second came on a bright September morning nine months after that man had moved into the White House.

'For most of the Cold War, America's priority in the Middle East was stability,' wrote President George W. Bush when he had retired to his beloved ranch to write his memoirs. 'Then nineteen terrorists born in the Middle East turned up on planes in the United States. After 9/11, I decided that the stability we had been promoting was a mirage. The focus of the freedom agenda would be the Middle East.'[29]

It took a few years for the title of the 'Freedom Agenda' to coalesce around the various schemes to promote democracy of the Forty-Third President of the United States, but it would become what he described as the 'fourth prong' of his 'Bush Doctrine'.[30] After the 9/11 suicide attacks by al-Qaeda that crashed civilian airliners into the twin towers of the World Trade Center in New York and the Pentagon in Washington, and were narrowly averted by passengers from doing the same to the White House, George W. Bush decided he needed a new strategy to protect America from this new form of warfare. The 'Bush Doctrine' began life as the much more folksy 'War on Terror'. President Bush described it as:

> First, make no distinction between the terrorists and the nations that harbor them – and hold both to account. Second take the fight to the enemy overseas before they can attack us again here at home. Third, confront threats before they fully materialize. And fourth, advance liberty and hope as an alternative to the enemy's ideology of repression and fear.[31]

If the 9/11 attacks had defined the problem for the new president, its causes had been revealed to him in what would turn out to be a highly influential UN study by a group of scholars from the Arab world called the *Arab Human Development Report*, which was published in July 2002. It was the 'single most impactful document' on the president's thinking on the issue, Condoleezza Rice wrote later.[32] The report concluded that 'three critical deficits face all Arab countries: freedom; women's empowerment; . . . and knowledge'.[33] George W. Bush decided that the 'most important' of those was 'a deficit in freedom'.[34] The report was ignored by the Egyptian government, which was just down the road in Cairo from where it was launched, and by every other leader in the region. But it gave George W. Bush some big ideas.

It had not been given its name yet, but the physical embodiment of President Bush's 'Freedom Agenda' landed on 19 March 2003. I was there for its arrival. It was a noisy affair.

It began with the dogs. They knew what was coming just under a minute before we did. The packs of strays roaming the streets of Baghdad would all suddenly howl and bark at the silent night sky. And then there was the boom. It echoed through my body. The ground and walls shook and lurched. As I absorbed the sound, the images had already raced through my brain. A shock of white light, then an orange flash consuming the buildings before me, wrapping itself into a shawl of smoke that sloped across the skyline. Then another flash, and another.

The targets of the cruise missiles launched by the US from beyond the horizon were the symbols of power of Saddam Hussein's Iraqi regime, which were built to tower above the city and remind everyone who was in charge. Anti-aircraft tracer stuttered its way across the black canvas upon which 'shock and awe' made its debut in the world. The noise was like a blow to the head. The scene, as I gripped the balcony of my room in the Palestine Hotel, was awful, but awe-inspiring in its scale. It went on night after night until the capital began to fall.

I was one of a small number of journalists who had stayed on in Baghdad, after many others left, to watch America launch what the next president would call 'the biggest foreign policy disaster in our generation'.[35] I had already witnessed Prongs One and Two of the Bush Doctrine being played out in Afghanistan and Pakistan, but those were actions in reaction to unprovoked acts of war. I was now watching Prongs Three and Four: 'Confronting threats before they fully materialize' and the need to 'advance liberty'. This was ideology in action. It was based on the belief – for there was no real evidence – that the Iraqi regime had weapons of mass destruction. At its core was total faith in America as a force for good. George W. Bush quickly regretted using the word 'crusade' to describe the 'War on Terror', but it was an accurate description of the fervour of its proponents for the invasion of Iraq. The Bush administration had reached an 'unquestioned belief in [its] inherent morality' that inclined it 'to ignore the ethical or moral consequences of their decisions', wrote the American political scientist Karen J. Alter a few months before the war began.[36]

The chief justification for the war in Iraq began to break down when it was soon discovered that Prong Three of the Bush doctrine was missing: the Iraqi president Saddam Hussein no longer had the nuclear, chemical and biological weapons over which the US had largely made its case for the invasion. From that moment on the Bush administration had only 'Prong Four' to lean all its weight on. The 'Freedom Agenda' became the justification for everything that followed.

Its reach though was not confined to the Middle East. It was to be a global initiative. George W. Bush decided he would 'advance freedom by supporting fledgling democratic governments in places like the Palestinian Territories, Lebanon, Georgia and Ukraine' and supporting 'democratic reformers' in 'Iran, Syria, North Korea and Venezuela'.[37] He took credit for the 'Cedar Revolution' in Lebanon that forced out the Syrian army after it was accused of being behind the assassination of the hugely popular former billionaire prime minister Rafik Hariri. It 'marked', he wrote, 'one of the most important successes of the freedom agenda'.[38] But a spurt of people power in Lebanon was not going to transform the region.

Fifteen of those nineteen hijackers who inspired President Bush's grand plan were originally from the kingdom of Saudi Arabia, but just like the man who would succeed him, President Bush wasn't going to try to force policy on the men who pumped out the oil. So after a wobbly start in Iraq he looked to Egypt and elsewhere for the agenda's redemption.

These were heady days for those people, described as neo-conservatives, who believed that America had to democratise the world for its own good. In January 2005, as he began his second term, George W. Bush presided over Iraq's transitional National Assembly elections which drew up the country's new constitution. It was the Arab world's first serious attempt at a free and fair poll. The neo-cons thought their dream had been realised. One of their leading thinkers, Charles Krauthammer, announced, six years too early, that: 'The Arab Spring of 2005 will be noted by history as a turning point for the Arab world.' And he added:

> we went into Iraq to liberate Iraqis, with no motives of oil or hegemony or revenge. The president said that this was a way to begin the liberation, to change and transform the dictatorial and intolerant culture of the Middle East . . . Democracy is on the march, and if we continue with the boldness and courage that we have shown during the past few years, we could see that revolution through.[39]

But it was downhill all the way from there. They did persuade the Egyptian regime to hold elections, and the more polls that were held the more farcical they became, and of course Mubarak got 'voted' back in. The 'Cedar Revolution' morphed into a war between Israel and the Iranian-backed militant group Hezbollah in 2006. Still believing that the Freedom Agenda could prevail, Condoleezza Rice tried to explain away that conflict by saying: 'What we're seeing here, in a sense, is the growing – the birth pangs of a new Middle East.'[40]

Her words provoked fury and a particularly disgusting cartoon of her in the Palestinian newspaper *Al-Quds*, wearing a blue dress and pregnant with an armed monkey. The caption said: 'Rice talks about the birth of a new Middle East' as blood dripped from her teeth. 'So, I dropped the reference,' she wrote later, 'and started talking about a "different Middle East." Words mattered a lot in a region that loved to say one thing and do another,' she added.[41]

So did pictures. By now satellite TV channels like Al Jazeera were broadcasting into homes throughout the region, in all its vivid gory detail, the collapse of much of Iraq into a brutal sectarian civil war. Then the equally shocking images of the torture and humiliation of Iraqis at the Abu Ghraib prison did catastrophic harm to the US's moral standing in the Muslim world. Equally damaging was the CIA rendition programme that plucked suspected terrorists from their homes in one country and dumped them into a torture cell in a friendly dictatorship to extract information for the 'war on terror'. There was a simple formula according to the former CIA agent Bob Baer: 'If you want a serious interrogation, you send a prisoner to Jordan. If you want them to be tortured, you send them to Syria. If you want someone to disappear – never to see them again – you send them to Egypt.'[42]

'Why can't we send them to be tortured?' President Bush was quoted saying about al-Qaeda suspects in the immediate aftermath of 9/11. 'Stick something up their ass! . . . Look, I just can't afford to see any more people in America die.'[43] Unsurprisingly the actions that flowed from these sentiments just didn't square with the idea that America was promoting liberty in the region. Then the 'Algerian Problem' reared its head once again, but this time in the occupied Palestinian territories when Hamas beat Fatah.

The Freedom Agenda was now on the retreat.

By early 2007 the influence of the neo-conservatives, who had added intellectual substance to George W. Bush's gut-driven decision-making, was on the wane.[44] Many of them had left the administration altogether. Their ideas had been discredited by events in Iraq. In the end the neo-cons did not have the 'boldness and courage' of their convictions because what mattered to them more than giving people the vote was what the result of that vote was. But as the Arab Spring circa 2011 began toppling Middle Eastern dictators, some neo-cons were ready to declare: 'The Freedom Agenda gets Vindicated'. The 'prescient' George W. Bush, they opined, 'deserves substantial credit for envisioning and perhaps even helping instigate the Arab Spring as a whole'.[45]

'The neo-conservatives are basically trying to rewrite the historical narrative so that their foreign policy looks much less disastrous than it in fact was, so they've changed what the Bush administration was trying to do,' said Warwick University's Dr Osman Hassan, who is a specialist on the impact of the Freedom Agenda on US foreign policy. 'If your policy was to promote democracy slowly, in the same way that Morocco is being seen to reform at the minute, then the Arab Spring and the instability it has created has fundamentally contradicted many of the premises that the Freedom Agenda was trying to promote.'

George W. Bush's administration reined in its crusading tendencies so much in its final years that there were bigger foreign policy changes between the first and second terms of the Bush government than there were when President Obama took over. That is because it became clear by the beginning of the second Bush administration that his big ideas had run into the sand. He spent his last term trying to repair some of the damage caused in the Middle East by the first. American foreign policy had already begun its U-turn before Obama took office. The new president didn't have to change course much, though he did strike a fundamental change in tone, particularly when it came to dealing with adversaries like Syria and Iran. But Obama had practically run on being everything Bush was not, and so he rejected all of his rhetoric, even in the small area where their ideas about freedom and human rights might have overlapped. Promoting democracy in the Middle East slipped down the list of priorities for the new administration. Then the youngsters of the Arab world pushed it all the way back up again.

President Obama came to Cairo in June 2009 to make his famous speech promising the Muslim world in general and the Arab region in particular 'A New Beginning'. That is what the Arab world got, though it was a new start of its own making and had nothing to do with the crafted eulogy he gave on that day to the common values and aspirations of humanity. American foreign policy did not change the Arab world because it didn't really want change in the Arab world.

Obama's team spent four months crafting his Cairo speech.[46] That is an extraordinarily long time, and they still got it wrong. Many of those in the Arab world who heard it felt let down by it later because he failed to make progress on the Palestinian issue and did little to force change on the Middle Eastern dictatorships.

But perhaps its biggest immediate impact was in Israel, where it infuriated many in the leadership. It marked the start of Obama's rocky relationship with the Netanyahu government. That was a well-trodden path for Democrat presidents.

'Who the fuck does he think he is? Who's the fucking super-power here?'[47] The personalities thrown up by life in the Middle East have often been a little difficult to get along with. The Forty-Second President of the United States, William J. Clinton, found that out during his first meeting with the prime minister of Israel, Binyamin Netanyahu, in 1996 during the Israeli PM's first incarnation in that role. The Forty-Fourth President found dealing with the second Netanyahu administration even harder, and that was partly due to how politics in Israel had changed between the presidencies of the two men.

When President Bill Clinton was dealing with Netanyahu he was dealing with an Israeli hawk. Since then the political spectrum around him has surged so far to the right that by Obama's first term Netanyahu had become a moderate in his own cabinet just by standing still. Israeli leaderships nowadays are always going to feel more at home politically with a Republican president. Candidate Obama recognised this. He was reported as saying when he ran for president: 'I think there is a strain within the pro-Israel community that says unless you adopt an unwavering pro-Likud approach to Israel that you're anti-Israel.'[48] But the Netanyahu government during Obama's first term considered the disconnect to be about a fundamental re-evaluation by the president of that relationship.

'Former President [Ronald Reagan] divided the world into Good and Evil. And we were on the good side. And if you divide the world into victims and victimisers, in the Palestinian case he [Obama] considers us as victimisers. It's a formidable challenge for us,' a senior member of the Israeli cabinet told me during Obama's first term. The minister said that early on Obama relied too heavily on advisers like Rahm Emanuel, who thought they understood Israel but did not. Throughout the acrimony of the first term, during the many conversations I had with senior Israeli ministers and military commanders they all seemed to agree on the moment Israel decided Obama just didn't get it. 'I was shocked by the Cairo speech,' said the cabinet minister, 'that President Obama drew a direct line between the Palestinians as victims and American slaves as victims, as blacks in South Africa in the apartheid era as victims, as Jews in the Holocaust as victims. I felt like he doesn't understand . . . how can you compare?'

He shouldn't have been that shocked. President Obama had sent the message from day one that he considered a peace deal between Israel and the Palestinians a priority. In Cairo he promised 'to personally pursue this outcome with all the patience and dedication that the task requires'. And he indicated where he intended to show his mettle: 'The United States does not accept the legitimacy of continued Israeli settlements . . . It is time for these settlements to stop.'[49]

The plan was that a total settlement freeze would pave the way for a new round of talks, but the settlement building did not stop, and there was never any real chance that it would. A total freeze could never fly in a coalition government where the man then in charge of negotiating with the outside world, Foreign Minister Avigdor Lieberman, himself lived on a settlement. The best Obama's peace envoy George Mitchell could get from Netanyahu was a partial freeze from

December 2009 for ten months, but only of the construction of new buildings in the West Bank. Settlements in occupied East Jerusalem were not included. Three thousand homes already under way were allowed to continue.

The Obama administration tried to make the best of it but it was never going to be enough for the Palestinians. They had listened to Obama say settlements had to 'stop', and that is what they held out for. President Mahmoud Abbas's chief of staff, Mohammad Shtayyeh, told me that the Palestinians had been 'hopeful that this administration had all the good intentions to really take us somewhere'. He said Obama had made all the right noises about 'the linkage of the peace process and settlements' and so 'Obama took himself up a high tree and we went with him'. He then likened President Obama to an old man he once knew who spent his days watching pretty girls pass by. 'Obama,' he said, 'he has the desire but he doesn't have the capacity.'

Picking a public fight over Israeli settlements was a huge tactical blunder by the Obama administration. It thoroughly miscalculated the size of the challenge it had taken on. Obama quickly used most of his political capital to push through domestic policy; he had very little left to stand firm against Israel's supporters in the Congress too. But if President Obama did not intend to win the battle by whatever means it took, then he should never have fought it. It left him in Israeli eyes looking weak. Netanyahu's government easily swatted away the Cairo demand for settlements to 'stop'. Two years on he was so confident that he had the measure of Obama that he felt able to publicly rebuke the president during a visit to the White House on 20 May 2011. The previous day, during his set-piece response to the Arab Spring, President Obama had said: 'We believe the borders of Israel and Palestine should be based on the 1967 lines with mutually agreed swaps.'[50] Twenty-four hours later in the Oval Office, with Obama by his side and in front of the world's media, Netanyahu said: 'Peace based on illusions will crash eventually on the rocks of Middle Eastern reality, and . . . the only peace that will endure is one that is based on reality, on unshakeable facts.' 'Israel,' he added, 'cannot go back to the 1967 lines.'[51]

It was a deliberate slap in the face from Israel in return for their sense of being slighted. 'We felt like it was an ambush,' the senior Israeli cabinet minister told me soon afterwards. 'We don't want to embarrass the administration and we expected the administration not to surprise us. Giving the statement about the 67 [borders], it was a surprise, we were promised this issue wasn't going to be delivered.' 'There is a gap [between the White House and Israel], you can't ignore it,' he told me.

A few days later Netanyahu addressed the US Congress and received rapturous applause. By the *New York Times*'s droll account: 'Mr. Netanyahu received so many standing ovations that at times it appeared that the lawmakers were listening to his speech standing.'[52] American commentators described Netanyahu's language during his visit as 'unusually blunt for a visiting head of state'.[53]

I asked someone who was an official in the Obama administration at the time about Israel's claims that the administration had mismanaged the peace process right from the start. 'Well we brought back in [US Envoy] Dennis Ross and we didn't get any further. If that were true then round two should have gone a lot better and round two wasn't any better than round one.' But the Israeli minister complained: 'We realised, not for the first time, those we speak with like [envoys] Dennis Ross and [George] Mitchell and so forth are not in the inner circle. The inner circle is very different, different agenda with different understandings. The gaps are so wide, not just between us and the president but between the president and his staff.' This was because the formation, not just the core ideas, of US foreign policy, particularly when it came to the Middle East, was firmly in the grip of the White House.

'This is the most dysfunctional relationship between an Israeli prime minister and an American president that I have observed. I've worked for half a dozen secretaries of state and I've watched and studied this relationship even before I got into government,' Aaron David Miller told me. He worked at the State Department for more than two decades and is now a distinguished scholar at the Woodrow Wilson International Center in Washington DC.

The new Israeli government [because it is] broader will ease some
of that dysfunction, but it's a relationship that's made much more
complex by different personalities and different policy approaches.
In the past, with Begin and Carter, and with Bush 41 and Shamir,
they were very tense at times, but in both of those cases circumstances emerged that ameliorated the relationship and created a
joint basis on which the two in each case could cooperate. What's
anomalous about this relationship is that four years in there isn't a
common enterprise. Even while the US–Israeli relationship
becomes much closer, at the top there are serious problems.

The shape of the coalition that emerged after the 2013 Israeli elections has and will continue to temper Netanyahu's proven
willingness to stage big public rows with Obama, though it may
not end them all. During Obama's first term there was eventually a
casual assumption by the Israeli government, and Netanyahu in
particular, that if he wanted to he could defy the president and
speak over the heads of the administration to the people and the
Congress to successfully make Israel's case. This attitude reached its
peak during the 2012 presidential election when Netanyahu was
considered to have openly supported Obama's Republican challenger Mitt Romney.[54] By then though, Obama's personal thoughts
on the Israeli PM were very public. In November 2011 at the G20
summit French president Nicolas Sarkozy's private remarks with
Obama were caught on an open microphone. 'I can't stand him any
more, he's a liar,' Sarkozy said in French of Prime Minister Netanyahu. 'You may be sick of him, but me, I have to deal with him
every day,' Obama replied.[55]

'Israelis are damaged, lonely, neurotic people who face genuine
threats to their existence, so they need love badly,' said the staunchly
pro-Israel writer Jeffrey Goldberg on the eve of President Obama's
state visit in 2013.[56] And during that visit Obama went out of his way
to woo. It was a measure of how much they truly dislike each other
that he and Netanyahu tried so hard to pretend they were the best of

friends. Or rather that Obama and 'Bibi' were best friends. The US president went through press conferences throwing out Netanyahu's nickname so many times that the bonhomie looked thoroughly forced. The interaction between the two men was 'cringe-worthy' said an Israeli commentator.[57]

Obama had come to make friends with the Israeli people, because he knew that he wasn't going win over most of the politicians. For that reason he chose to speak before a convention centre in Jerusalem packed with university students, many of them already sympathetic to his message, instead of to the Knesset just down the road. It was clear from the excitement of the youngsters sitting around me that he was going to be warmly received, and sure enough when he walked on to the empty stage with no build-up or fanfare he still got a rock-star reception.

The speech, like his Cairo one four years earlier, was careful to press all the right buttons, but for a very different audience. It had bursts of Hebrew and lots of praise and empathy with the Jewish people in their suffering, and their struggle for a homeland. It was a fine speech, probably one of his best. During it he took the opportunity to do what Netanyahu had done to him back in Washington. He talked over the prime minister's head to appeal for a more imaginative approach to the conflict with the Palestinians, telling the youngsters before him: 'I can promise you this, political leaders will never take risks if the people do not push them to take some risks.' But then he told Israel that two years after the Arab Spring revolts it was time to accept the reality of its new neighbourhood and deal with it.

> Israel needs to reverse an undertow of isolation . . . I understand that with the uncertainty in the region, people in the streets, changes in leadership, the rise of non-secular parties in politics, it's tempting to turn inward because the situation outside of Israel seems so chaotic. But this is precisely the time to respond to the wave of revolution with a resolve and commitment for peace.

Because as more governments respond to popular will, the days when Israel could seek peace simply with a handful of autocratic leaders, those days are over.

His audience spent almost as much time on their feet as Congress did for Netanyahu, but the mood outside was more sceptical. America does not have to live within the boundaries it is trying to form. Israelis are not going to do a deal unless they feel secure, and the nature and history of Israeli society suggest that making them feel secure in this neighbourhood is probably impossible. As far as many Israelis are concerned, they tried pulling out of the Palestinian territory in Gaza and it left the south of the country exposed to regular incoming rockets fired by Islamist militants. Pulling out of the West Bank, in the minds of many people here, means potentially having those rockets fired into their biggest population centre, Tel Aviv, from just a few kilometres away. 'We left Gaza completely. There were 22 settlements, 8000 or 9000 settlers. We left it without pre-conditions, on our own initiative. It was very difficult for us.' The Israeli President Shimon Peres told me, 'To bring back the settlers from there we had to mobilise 75,000 policeman. To build new houses we had to spend close to US$3 billion but we did it. We handed it over. So tell me why are they shooting at us? What is the reason? What is the purpose? Explain it to me I don't understand. If it had gone differently it would have been much easier to then negotiate over the West Bank.'

The Arab Spring, regardless of Obama's encouraging words, has only made Israel's sense of insecurity worse. For the last forty years their two quietest borders were with their two biggest neighbours, Egypt and Syria. Dictators ran these places and, as Obama pointed out, the Israeli military had reached an accommodation with them both. Now across the northern border there is civil war in Syria with a growing jihadi presence. To the south in the Sinai Egypt's army is struggling to deal with a hotbed of Islamic militancy. 'Look at the map,' said one of Israel's top soldiers to me when we met shortly before President Obama arrived for his trip. 'We are a small fragile place that everybody likes to hate and wants to do something about.'

Having Yair Lapid's more centrist party in the new Israeli government coalition is not going to lead to a breakthrough in the peace process because alongside it is the pro-settler Jewish Home Party, which doesn't believe in a Palestinian state at all. The issue of settlements, which were the root cause of the first bust-up, is going to be tougher to tackle with the new coalition line-up. For that reason, four years after telling the Israelis that settlements must 'stop' Obama told the Palestinians they weren't going to. Standing next to Mahmoud Abbas during a brief trip to Ramallah, he said: 'I will say with respect to Israel, that the politics there are complex and I recognize that that's not an issue that's going to be solved immediately . . . I will share with the Palestinian people that if the expectation is that we can only have direct negotiations when everything is settled ahead of time, then there's no point for negotiations.'[58]

Obama said on the eve of his state visit: 'My goal on this trip is to listen.'[59] But it was clear before he climbed on the plane that none of the people he had come to meet had changed their point of view from the day he took office, so his administration clearly hadn't been paying attention the first time around. He delivered one of those candyfloss speeches that seem huge and briefly excite but contain very little to bite into. The message, four years on from his first set-piece address from the Middle East, can be summed up as: 'I do not intend to *personally pursue* this, because I've lost patience with the lot of you, so say hello to John.'

Secretary of State Kerry began with the tried-and-tested route of shuttle diplomacy to restart the process with all the enthusiasm of someone who had never experienced the huge disappointment of trying to get something substantial out of dealing with the two sides. He didn't have to wait long to be bloodied in the ways of the politics of the peace process. Kerry began his pitch in April 2013, with a plan to boost the West Bank economy.[60] That was immediately undermined by the resignation a week later of the Palestinian Prime

Minister, Salam Fayyad, who would have been the man expected to see it through.

Fayyad was the only man the West truly trusted to spend their money wisely to build the economy and infrastructure of the West Bank. But Fayyad had no political support base of his own. Both Fatah and Hamas disliked him and saw him as an obstacle to their potential reconciliation. While the economy was strong he was safe. When it took a serious downturn after 2011 he was constantly sniped at by Fatah and fell out with Abbas. He offered to resign several times over the following years. That April he tried again and this time, despite objections from Washington, Abbas accepted it. So John Kerry began his stint of peace making facing a divided Israeli cabinet, a feud between the two biggest Palestinian factions, Fatah and Hamas, and acrimony in the leadership of the Palestinian Authority. Though Fayyad agreed to stay on until his replacement was found, the West had lost the one person in the PA it really believed in. The dispute left Abbas looking increasingly imperious. Hamas cheered Fayyad's loss. Kerry suddenly saw why his boss had all but given up on the project in his first term. Kerry then made his job harder by telling Congress, 'The window for the two-state solution is shutting . . . I think we have some period of time, a year and a half or two years, or it's over.'[61] That's what you say to create a sense of urgency when all sides want a deal. They don't.

The Israeli Housing Minister Uri Ariel had said the day before, 'In another year and a half, apartments will be built in E1.'[62] E1 is the area between Jerusalem and the existing settlement of Ma'aleh Adumim. This was always one of the most controversial settlement programmes. Its opponents say building on the E1 area would almost completely cut Jerusalem off from the West Bank, and prevent the creation of a viable, contiguous Palestinian state. The UN Secretary General Ban Ki-moon had warned, 'It would represent an almost fatal blow to remaining chances of securing a two-state solution.'[63]

If President Obama does decide to brace himself and personally plunge back into the peace process, he is unlikely to do it at the beginning of his new presidential term, during the two years Kerry thinks are make or break. Perhaps as his presidency winds down he will try again. However he will not be willing to put his credibility on the line again unless Kerry tells him there's something serious to work with. He won't go out on a limb unless the Israeli and Palestinian leaders are sitting there already. But if he does try again, if the latest cumbersome Israeli coalition holds together that long and Netanyahu remains Prime Minister, it'll need to be a very different, publically tougher President than the one who sat through a telling off in his own front room.

If President Obama does decide to push things, then he now has someone in John Kerry who will be more willing than Secretary of State Clinton was to fight those battles for him. During her term in office Hillary Clinton implemented rather than shaped policy. She was never given the chance to be a great secretary of state because the White House made all the big decisions and quite a lot of the medium-sized ones too. The advice President Obama listened to most came from his own team of political advisers, not those in the State Department.

'Clinton wanted to lead from the front, not from behind,' said former State Department adviser Vali R. Nasr about her tenure as she stood down.[64] Perhaps, though, that wasn't always the case. While Secretary of State Clinton was frustrated about her inability to drive action on issues she felt strongly about, like arming the opposition in Syria, when it came to Israel and the Palestinians the back seat was where she was comfortable. That is why the peace process, in the first term, was largely delegated to envoys. 'Hillary was and is sceptical about taking on issues that look like they are likely to fail,' says William B. Quandt, who is professor of Politics at the University of Virginia and served in the Middle East office of the National Security Council under Presidents Nixon and Carter.

She is very attuned to domestic politics. So the two issues that are just poison in terms of American politics are dealing with Iran and

putting pressure on Israel, and if you are going to get an Israeli–
Palestinian agreement, at some point you are going to have to put
some pressure on both sides, including Israel. Of course she saw her
husband go through this. [Bill] Clinton tried to charm the Israelis
into peace with the Palestinians and he tried to charm Arafat, but
it didn't work at the end of the day and she I think learned something from that. He invested a lot of time and energy and
failed . . . so she focused on other issues and I think those were
deliberate choices.

John Kerry is closer to Obama's thinking than Hillary Clinton was,
though he has already felt the frustration of the White House's firm
grip on foreign policy. He is more likely to be listened to on those
occasions when his views differ from the president's. If he is called
upon to step into the fray Secretary of State Kerry may not find dealing with the Israeli prime minister any less bruising than his boss did.
'I think Netanyahu has a visceral dislike, distrust and almost a condescending attitude towards the United States,' says Ambassador
Kurtzer. 'It's nothing to do with Barack Obama, he's just the latest of
his targets. He had the problem with Clinton and he had the problem
with George H. W. Bush and James Baker, a Republican administration. I think there is a systemic internal problem with Netanyahu
relative to this country.'

The Israeli people are still not in love with the American president,
but they are still smitten with and grateful to America. Adjusting for
inflation, the US has provided Israel with $233.7 billion in aid since
the state was formed.[65] Both the Israeli public and Netanyahu know
that the US is their best friend and always will be. That is why the
Israeli electorate slapped Netanyahu on the wrist and told him to 'go
play nice'. They know the first term of the Obama administration was
very badly handled by the Israeli prime minister, though getting him
to accept that is not easy.

Binyamin Netanyahu doesn't talk to the foreign media based in the
Middle East very often. His staff are much happier to agree to

interviews on his foreign trips with journalists based abroad who are not normally steeped in the politics of the region. However once a year by tradition he speaks to the foreign media, based in Israel, and accepts a handful of questions with no follow-ups, the first of which is given to the elected chairman of the Middle East Foreign Press Association, who in 2012–13 was me. So I asked Prime Minister Netanyahu what his personal regrets were about the way he handled his relationship with President Obama in the first term and what he would change about that approach in the second. He dodged the question with a monologue:

> I very much appreciate President Obama's support for Israel during our operation in Gaza. I appreciate the fact that before that he supported Iron Dome and continues to support it with further assistance. I appreciate that he stood up against the unilateral resolution at the UN. I have had four conversations with the president in recent weeks and I will continue those conversations, I think it's important for Israel, I think it's important for Israel–American relations.

So I tried again.

'And your regrets?' By this stage the head of the Government Press Office was waving his hands at me to stop.

'Who doesn't have regrets, do you not have regrets?' Netanyahu replied.

'I'm not a prime minister, that's why I am asking you,' I said. The GPO head now looked like he was going to have a heart attack.

'You could work at it, the doors are open,' the prime minister told me, and then I had to give way to CNN. Their correspondent asked him how he accounted for the huge showing of support for him in a recent election campaign poll. He had no problem answering that one.

But even though the two leaders do not like each other on a personal level, they are going to have to deal with each other in the coming years, because the other issue that dogged their relationship is a lot less easier to kick into the long grass than the peace process is. That issue is Iran.

The Iranian regime, and its nuclear ambitions, is the only thing in the post-Arab Spring era that seriously worries all three of America's pillars of policy in the region. It was also the first thing that put all four major players in the Middle East back on the same page.

Iran wasn't originally in the 'Axis of Evil'. The 'Axis of Evil', which began life as an 'Axis of Hatred', hinged on Iraq. It was supposed to hold the unproven link, in the January 2002 State of the Union address, between Saddam Hussein's regime and 9/11. But George W. Bush's then National Security adviser Condoleezza Rice thought focusing just on Iraq might sound like war was imminent, so she suggested adding other countries. North Korea and Iran were selected.[66] 'I find it hard to believe that's a thought-through policy' was the immediate response to the speech by the European Union commissioner in charge of international relations, Chris Patten.[67]

It was a surprise too to the Iranians, who thought relations had improved after some initial cooperation with the US in Afghanistan. After 9/11, rather than weaken Iran the Bush administration's actions in the wider region, and particularly the ousting of Saddam, strengthened it. And having got the weapons assessment so badly wrong in Iraq, it had very little credibility when it made similar noises about Iran.

Obama put himself at the heart of the attempt to re-engage with Iran, though he stopped well short of an earlier campaign pledge to meet with its leaders. After two months in the White House he extended greetings for the Persian New Year, Nowruz. Then during his Cairo speech he spoke of Iran again:

In the middle of the Cold War, the United States played a role in the overthrow of a democratically elected Iranian government [of Prime Minister Mohammad Mossadegh in August 1953]. Since the Islamic Revolution, Iran has played a role in acts of hostage-taking and violence against U.S. troops and civilians. This history is well known. Rather than remain trapped in the past, I've made it clear to Iran's leaders and people that my country is prepared to move forward.[68]

And so he invited them to a party.

At the end of May 2009 US embassies around the world were told by the State Department 'they may invite representatives from the government of Iran' to their 4th July Independence Day celebrations.[69] The United States has not had relations with Iran since its embassy in Tehran was seized in 1979 and its staff were held hostage for over a year. It was an event that largely cost Jimmy Carter his presidency. Iranian diplomats had been personae non gratae from then on. It was Carter in his 1980 State of the Union address who first declared the Persian Gulf to be a region of 'vital interests' to the United States of America which would be defended 'by any means necessary, including military force'.[70]

By 2009 Obama had a lot of fences to mend, but before the 4th July bunting was even up, the Iranian leadership had pooped the party. On 12 June the Iranians held presidential elections. The interior ministry declared the following day that the incumbent Mahmoud Ahmadinejad had won with 62 per cent of the votes. Nobody believed them. Hundreds of thousands took to the streets to protest in what became known as the 'Green Movement'. It was a forerunner of the Arab revolts eighteen months later, and it too relied on social media to galvanise support.

Iran, like the Arab world, has a young population. Fifty per cent of the voters were under thirty. And like the people of Arab countries, they too were thoroughly misunderstood by the outside world. If you want to really understand this society you only need to watch the queue for the bathroom as your plane nears Iranian airspace on an inbound flight to Tehran. As soon as the pilot announces: 'We will be landing shortly' a parade of pretty young women in tight tops, heavy make-up and blue jeans forms a long line halfway down the aircraft. At this moment the small restroom takes on the transformational properties of Superman's phone box. Each woman goes in looking like she just walked out of a disco and each one comes out looking like she is ready to step into a mosque. The next time you see images of young Iranians as they march past the camera promising to martyr themselves for the Palestinian cause, remind yourself that some of them probably have a push-up bra and a 'Hello Kitty' T-shirt on underneath.

The protests of 2009 after Iran's disputed presidential elections revealed the disillusionment of the youth with the establishment. But these modern young things also have contempt for what they see as the cynical hypocrisy of the West. That is because most of the things that their government tells them about decades of conspiracies against the country are well documented and true. The Iranian nation has a whole host of genuine reasons for mistrust.

President Obama grasped that, and in that context his administration clearly didn't know what to say as the protests gathered momentum and the government's crackdown began. So he said very little. When he did speak he didn't side with the young protesters. He parked his administration on the fence. On 15 June he said he was 'deeply troubled' by the violence but that: 'My understanding is that the Iranian government says that they are going to look into irregularities that have taken place.'[71] The protests were the largest since the 1979 revolution that deposed the Shah. More than a hundred demonstrators were killed, many by the paramilitary force, the Basiji.[72]

It was the death of a 26-year-old woman called Neda Agha-Soltan, who was shot dead in Tehran, that finally produced an angry condemnation from Obama. Her dying moments were captured on a mobile phone and instantly went viral on the Internet. But it seemed even after the brutal suppression of the Green Movement that President Obama still believed there was room for engagement with the Iranians: 'I think it is not too late for the Iranian government to recognize that there is a peaceful path that will lead to stability and legitimacy and prosperity for the Iranian people.' He was clearly frustrated by the repeated call from reporters to say what action he was willing to take. 'We don't know yet how this thing is going to play out. I know everybody here is on a 24-hour news cycle. I'm not.'[73]

It played out with the Green Movement being smashed.

President Obama's attempt to engage with Iran during his first term failed, but that engagement was not launched to encourage democracy. It was part of an attempt to discourage the Iranians from building a nuclear weapon. Dealing with Iran was the only thing Israel and Saudi Arabia could both agree on. They had been clear for some time about the best way to deal with the problem: some very big bombs needed to be dropped.

'Cut off the head of the snake' was the 'frequent exhortation' of King Abdullah of Saudi Arabia to the Bush administration.[74] There was a more regular and public cry for action too from the entire Israeli administration once Netanyahu took office again in March 2009. In his speech to supporters at his 2013 election night rally, Netanyahu said of his new tenure: 'The first challenge was and remains preventing Iran from obtaining nuclear weapons.'

The rhetoric now though will have to be a little more muted, because his coalition is a little less convinced of the urgency. There will probably be less of the grandstanding that marked the first term too. The highlight of that was Netanyahu standing at the podium of the United Nations General Assembly in September 2012 with a large 'Loony Tunes'-style cartoon of a bomb, over the top of which he then drew a 'red line' in case the world's leaders sitting before him were a little too stupid to get the message. It was even more memorable than his speech earlier in the year when he said of the Iranian nuclear programme: 'If it looks like a duck, walks like a duck, and quacks like a duck, then what is it? That's right, it's a duck – but this duck is a nuclear duck.'[75]

The collective wisdom of many political commentators after both the cartoon bomb and the nuclear duck was that he had made a fool of himself. He certainly excited enough spoofs. And yet Netanyahu is no fool. If his political instincts let him down on these days it was because there is within him a genuinely stronger instinct, which is 'that a nuclear Iran is an existential threat to the state of Israel'.

'He sees his place in history to defend Israel and the Jewish people from Iran,' a Western diplomat who has had regular contact with Netanyahu told me after the cartoon episode. 'Iran is this generation's Hitler, and if he has been put in the job for a purpose that's it. The Palestinian issue is an issue he has to deal with because the Americans and the Europeans are on his back about it, but he doesn't have any sense of historical destiny for himself as the man who made peace with the Palestinians.'

Netanyahu's obsession with Iran, and European fears that he might go it alone, were used by the Obama administration in the first term to push the EU towards tougher and tougher sanctions. In fact the Israeli prime minister didn't want to go it alone, because Israel could not do the job all by itself. The best it could do, a senior member of the Israeli government told me, was 'delay it by five years' by destroying what he described as the 'pinch points' in the nuclear programme. Not being able to finish the job is why they wanted the Americans on board, because only the US has bombs big enough to destroy places like the heavily fortified uranium enrichment site of Fordo, near the holy city of Qom, no matter how deep down it is buried.

The Americans would not give those bombs to Israel. The US did not believe the threat was imminent, and Netanyahu had for years been in danger of being seen to cry wolf. He said as far back as 1992, when he was just a parliamentarian, that Iran was three to five years away from making a bomb and that the threat must be 'uprooted by an international front headed by the US'.[76]

A nuclear Iran is a key concern for the Americans, and there is a sense in the State Department that one way or another Obama's second term will be the period when the issue is conclusively dealt with. Aside from the threat to Israel, a nuclear Iran would kick-start a nuclear arms race throughout the region. But the clocks counting down to the decisive moment when action needs to be taken have always been out of sync between Washington and Jerusalem. They have also been out of sync between Jerusalem and Tel Aviv, the city where the Israeli military has its headquarters.

'Where does Israel's security stand now in the New Middle East?' I asked one of Israel's most senior men in uniform.

'May fourteenth 1948 was much tougher,' he said.

My father fought in '48 and he told me once that my generation can't even think about the sense of the crisis they felt at the prospect of losing even a battle. Nowadays if you lose a battle, OK the IDF will send two more battalions or two more F16s in order to help you. When they fought in '48 they knew if they lost the battle they might lose the state. So we are not in that situation anymore. June fifth 1967 was two or three armies, October 1973 was much tougher. So from that perspective we are in quite good times right now. Of course there is the Iranian nuclear issue, which is a little bit different.

'So you are not facing an existential threat from anybody at the moment?' I asked.

'No, except the Iranian issue, but we should keep it in proportion,' he replied.

In the same building but at another time a senior Israeli intelligence official told me sanctions 'can do the work'. And sanctions have crippled the Iranian economy.

In fact all the senior Israelis in both the military and intelligence services that I have spoken to believe that sanctions and the regular mysterious deaths of Iranian nuclear scientists are more effective than Israel going it alone on a bombing run.

There has been a ban on US officials engaging or conspiring in political assassinations since the mid-1970s. There is no such ban in Israel. Its officials don't publicly admit that it is behind the regular killings of the scientists, but privately they are willing to drop hints. 'There is a clandestine war, there is an operational war,' a senior defence official told me. 'I don't want to go into details but you can read about it in the papers, you don't need me to explain, and if you do I can't tell you.' Then he added: 'About Iran, I prefer the Syrian model. Allegedly, according to foreign sources, we destroyed the

Syrian nuclear project with North Korea in five minutes. That's it! We never proved we did and do you know why? Because if we had it would have dragged Syria into a retaliation because it's a matter of Arab honour.' He was referring to the attack in 2007, whose target has never been publicly acknowledged by either side, on Syria's nuclear weapons programme at the al-Kibar plant.

And when it came to dealing with Iran, Israel and America had also developed something much more sophisticated than using speeding motorbikes to stick bombs on car doors in Tehran. It was codenamed 'Olympic Games', but when it broke out into the public domain it was dubbed Stuxnet.

The cyber worm was designed to attack the centrifuges at Iran's Natanz nuclear enrichment plant before the scientists even knew what was going on. It was partly designed and tested by the Americans using centrifuges turned over by Colonel Gaddafi after he gave up his own nuclear weapons programme in 2003, which were similar to those being used by the Iranians.[77] The Israelis were brought into the plan because of their own technical expertise and their capacity to gather and use intelligence in ways America could not. By the time it was discovered, Stuxnet was estimated to have put back the Iranian nuclear programme somewhere between one and three years. What it didn't slow was the spat with the Netanyahu administration over when it was time to bomb.

But if Obama was fed up with listening to Netanyahu and his then defence minister Ehud Barak going on about Iran, so too were some of the military leadership in Israel. Time and again after the two men made public professions of doom they were undermined by leaks which said that their military officials did not share their urgency.

In the end they started to deal with their internal troublemakers, but that just ended up embarrassing the government even more. In May 2011 Meir Dagan, the recently retired head of the Israeli foreign espionage agency Mossad, described carrying out an attack on Iran as 'the stupidest thing I have ever heard'.[78] In April 2012 it was the turn of Yuval Diskin, the recently retired head of Shin Bet, the domestic intelligence agency. He said: 'I don't believe in the prime minister or the defense minister. I really don't believe in a leadership that makes decisions out of messianic feelings.'[79] Then he chose the final few weeks of the 2013 Israeli election campaign to damn them again on the issue: 'Unfortunately, my feeling, and many others in the defense establishment share it, is that in the case of Netanyahu and Barak, the personal, opportunistic interests came first.'[80] The PM's office said in response that he was just bitter about not being appointed head of Mossad.

President Obama has now told the Israeli people to their face that he will not allow Iran to get a nuclear weapon. 'This is not a danger that can be contained,' he said. 'And as president, I've said all options are on the table for achieving our objectives.' What remained ambiguous was how close to a nuclear weapon America would allow Iran to get. Could the Iranians remain immune from attack if they had all the parts for a bomb but stopped short of screwing them together?

As one of Netanyahu's aides pointed out to me over lunch, 2012 was frustrating for Netanyahu because from his point of view it was a great year to have attacked Iran. Hamas had shifted sponsors and so would not necessarily fire what rockets it had left into Israel in response. Hezbollah might not have wanted to use up its precious arsenal, because with the civil war raging next door arms might prove difficult to replace. The Arab public were contemptuous of Iran and were unlikely to rally around after Tehran had tried to climb on their revolutionary bandwagon with all the hypocrisy it could muster. There was inevitably also going to be pressure from the US to see how the events surrounding the 2013 Iranian presidential elections changed the dynamic. And now Netanyahu has lost his co-cheerleader over the issue, Ehud Barak, who has left politics. He's been replaced as defence minister by Moshe 'Boogie' Ya'alon. He is a hardliner on the Palestinian issue but much less of a hawk over Iran. Netanyahu had to row back during his own spring 2013 deadline for action against Iran, saying: 'If Iran decides to go for a nuclear weapon, that is, to actually manufacture the weapon, then . . . it would take them about a year.'[81]

The US will want to test out the new political leadership that emerges in Iran before it bombs them. Obama made that clear in his second inaugural address when he returned to the theme announced at the beginning of his first term: engagement with friend and foe alike. 'Enduring security and lasting peace do not require perpetual war . . . We are also heirs to those who won the peace and not just the war; who turned sworn enemies into the surest of friends – and we must carry those lessons into this time as well.'[82]

In principle most Iranians support their nation's right to nuclear power, though they may not believe it is worth the suffering currently being inflicted upon them by sanctions. But what the liberal middle classes in Tehran want more is a way out from under the oppressive rule of the mullahs, because, in the long run, the way Iran is governed means that the outcome of Iranian elections is often more about style than substance. Ahmadinejad did try though to take control, and for a period it looked as if he really might manage it, but he ended his period in office beaten and humiliated by Supreme Leader Sayyid Ali Khamenei. He sank so low he was at one stage even being accused by al-Qaeda of spreading 'ridiculous conspiracy theories'.[83]

Khamenei is still Iran's most powerful figure, and it is he, not the elected leadership, that will call the shots. The supreme leader appoints the heads of the judiciary, the military, the state broadcasters and six of the twelve members of the powerful Guardian Council that supervises all elections and decides who is suitable to even stand. Ayatollah Khamenei has stated that 'we are not seeking nuclear weapons because the Islamic Republic of Iran considers possession of nuclear weapons a sin . . . and believes that holding such weapons is useless, harmful and dangerous'.[84] The governments in the West and parts of the Middle East say he is lying. But their accusations are weakened by the fact that they were wrong on the same issue in neighbouring Iraq. The regime there did not have weapons of mass destruction, despite elaborate Western claims to the contrary.

Are the Iranians using the Western intelligence failures in Iraq as a smokescreen to cover their own ambitions? There is the real possibility that Ayatollah Khamenei may be saying he doesn't want a nuclear weapon when he really does. He could always say after the fact that he was mistranslated. His government has already shown some skill in the art of sophistry. And its position after the Arab Spring revolts is certainly more vulnerable.

The Arab uprisings left Shia Iran in a bit of a bind. They hated the old Arab dictators like Mubarak because they were tied to the West. However, the way these men were turfed out was a little too close to home. And their Sunni Islamist replacements were not much friendlier either.

In August 2012 it was Iran's turn to host the Non-Aligned Movement, NAM, one of the final relics of the Cold War era. The last three chairmen of NAM had been Egyptian, because Egypt had held the chair since the last summit meeting in Cairo in 2009, and since then it had had three heads of state: Mubarak, Tantawi and then Morsi. The chair was being passed to Tehran, but the new Egyptian president at his first grand event on the world stage clearly meant his country's tenure to end with a flourish. Iran and Egypt have not had full diplomatic ties since Sadat signed his peace deal with Israel. This was the first visit by an Egyptian leader since the 1979 Iranian revolution. In terms of drama it was worth the wait. By going to Iran despite US attempts to diplomatically isolate the country, Morsi was showing an independent streak. But he soon wiped the smiles off the Iranians' faces. With their leader Mahmoud Ahmadinejad sitting at his side, Mohamed Morsi tore into the host nation's closest ally, Syria: 'We should all express our full support for the struggle of those who are demanding freedom and justice in Syria and translate our sympathies into a clear political vision that supports peaceful transfer [of power] to a democratic system.' The world, he said, had a 'moral duty' to support the opposition 'against an oppressive regime that has lost its legitimacy'.[85]

The Syrian delegation walked out. The Iranian delegation couldn't walk out because it was their conference, so they had to sit and listen.

Iranian TV had a problem. It was the opening speech of the summit, they couldn't just ignore it in their reports. So they mistranslated it instead and changed the word 'Syria' to 'Bahrain'.[86]

Morsi's speech in Tehran went down swimmingly with the Americans, the Israelis and the Saudis. It was not a harbinger of things to come though, and Ahmadinejad was invited and received a warm welcome, from the Egyptian government anyway, on a state visit the following February. But during his August trip to Tehran Morsi did show America that the Muslim Brotherhood, while being firmly Islamist, was not blindly Islamist.

The reality of the Muslim Brotherhood running Egypt required some adjustment in Washington. Their period in the Egyptian presidency, at the time, left US allies incredulous.

'For the time being [Morsi] is clever enough to understand that in order to deal with the country's economic difficulties he needs the United States,' a senior defence official in Israel had told me.

> The Muslim Brothers were established in 1928. Most people at the age of eighty-four are retiring; they are in a renaissance. This is a golden era in front of them. The Muslim Brothers will never change their ideology but they have flexibility. They are waiting for some crisis [to exert their power]. They want to grip the opportunity. Until now they have surprised everybody, including the Egyptian army and intelligences and all the states in the West. They are doing it with a speed that is unbelievable. With us they will be very cautious, because of the US, because of the West. But we are living in a strategic early warning period ahead of dramatic changes in the Middle East around Turkey, Saudi Arabia and the Muslim Brotherhood in Egypt. Ask the Saudis [about the Brotherhood]. They hate their guts.

That is true, and it was a legacy of the Nasser years. He'd done his best to destabilise the kingdom during his time because it was on the other side of the Cold War divide. Nasser's regional power play still remains the closest the House of Saud has come to losing control. When the Arab uprisings began to sweep the region in 2011 the Saudis looked back at the Nasser era and concluded that this new leaderless phenomenon was much more manageable. Because the Saudis saw Nasser as their enemy they offered comfort and shelter during that period to his enemy, the Muslim Brotherhood. 'The Saudis rightly feel that they gave asylum to the Muslim Brotherhood from the 1950s onwards and protected the Muslim Brotherhood,' Professor Haykel said.

Then when a moment of decision came as to the loyalty of the Muslim Brotherhood in August 1990 when Iraq invaded Kuwait, the Muslim Brotherhood both internationally and very often in its different regional and domestic offices decided to choose Saddam with his Ba'athist Arab nationalistic credentials over Kuwait and Saudi Arabia. The Saudis and the Kuwaitis saw this as a betrayal and have never forgiven the Muslim Brotherhood. The other thing that the Saudis feel about the Muslim Brotherhood, is that the Brotherhood came to Saudi Arabia and indoctrinated one if not two generations of Saudis in a political ideology that ultimately came to challenge the Saudi royal family and its role. So they were traitors both domestically and internationally.

'We've been trying to reassure our brothers in the Gulf states that we are not after exporting the revolution,' the Muslim Brotherhood's Amr Darrag, who chaired the Freedom and Justice Party's Foreign Relations Committee, told me while the Ikhwan were still in power.

We believe security in the Gulf is in our national interests. We have a lot of Egyptians working in this area, so we are keen on their wellbeing. And we'd like to attract investment from the Gulf. So there is no reason whatsoever for us to do anything to destabilise the Gulf area at all, and we are trying to convince them of that, but it seems that they are still not convinced. Hopefully with time they will change their position.

But perhaps not any time soon, because as we were speaking the United Arab Emirates were preparing to put ninety-four people on trial, who they said were linked to the Egyptian Muslim Brotherhood and had been plotting to overthrow the UAE government.[87] I asked Amr Darrag whether the new Egypt felt it had a role to be more assertive in the region. 'We tried that before, during Nasser's time, but it didn't work.'

As it tries to manage the likely squabbling among its regional allies, the US will also have to deal with others competing for those countries' attention. After the first revolution in Egypt in 1952 the US had to deal with the Soviets; after the Egyptian revolution in 2011 it will have to deal with the Chinese. Beijing was the first non-Arab capital that the newly sworn-in President Morsi visited. Beijing now sees an opportunity to exploit America's predisposition towards Israel. 'China has worked equally on its relations between Israel and the Arab countries. That is the difference between China and America,' Zhu Weili, the director of Middle East Studies at Shanghai International University, told me. Mr Zhu is one of China's leading Middle East specialists and has strong links to the ruling Communist Party. 'Under President Obama America's basic Middle East policy has changed very little. Many of the Middle East countries, especially the Islamic countries, have many doubts about the United States. Whether America can continue to keep its dominance and impact in the Middle East will be decided by how it changes its policies.'

It was clear to me from the period I lived in Beijing that the Chinese Communist Party officials, like the Saudis, set great store by personal relationships. At first glance it might seem like an old-fashioned way to run foreign policy, until you remember that that is exactly the way America ran its foreign policy in the Arab world. It dealt on very personal terms with the ruling family elite. Some of those key relationships have gone. As Mr Zhu points out, for the first time parts of the Arab world are a level playing field for China: 'Now that many of the Arab countries have had a government reorganisation, there is an opportunity to reinforce mutual exchanges. There are new leaders and new officials, so personal relations need to be remade along with new mutual understandings.'

What the Chinese realised, after breaking with Gaddafi far too late, is that their diplomacy is not yet very agile. Its constant vetos in the UN over Syria aren't endearing them to the revolutionaries there either. But what China does have is something the US does not. Like the newly energetic Qatar it has huge amounts of cash that it can spend without needing the approval of either a Congress or an electorate. China will also be able to buy its friends in the Middle East, which fits quite snugly with a foreign policy, outside the Far East, based almost entirely around shopping. China just wants to purchase what it needs to keep things working at home. No questions asked. They don't seek to interfere. There is no tiresome small print on the bill of sale about human rights. History suggests that China isn't likely to consider nurturing the region's young democracies as a key plank of their policies. As America looks for a new foreign policy China is quite happy to adopt the old one, which was about stability and oil, not democracy promotion.

And China isn't just building bridges in the Arab world. There is some mutual wooing going on with Israel, which has laid out the red carpet and the helicopter rides to induce China's business elite to invest in its hi-tech industries. The contrast between how Israel has dealt with small spats with China and huge rows with America is striking. Israel knows China doesn't need it at all, and so it is much more willing to bend to Beijing's sensitivities. When a few minor members of the Knesset touched a Chinese nerve by signing a relatively unimportant petition over claims that Beijing allowed the harvesting of internal organs from death row prisoners, the government intervened to get the men to back down.[88] Yet when senior Israeli politicians have run amok attacking the president of Israel's closest ally there has been a deafening silence from the government, which rarely made an attempt to rein them in.

The next few years are going to be difficult in the Middle East, and America must keep its nerve. It must do better than it did in the aftermath of the murder of its ambassador to Libya, Christopher Stevens, at the US consulate in Benghazi on 11 September 2012. It was a terrible blow for the nation, but it was chiefly due to badly run security in a still dangerous place. It was not the start of the collapse of the region into the arms of Islamist terrorists. That may be hard to believe after the boost that the chaotic post-Arab Spring era has given to Islamist extremists in North Africa, as events in Mali have shown. But it is completely unrealistic not to expect there to be pockets of murderous resistance to the democratic promise of the New Middle East from those who stand to lose the most from it.

'The violent demonstrations . . . have convinced many in the United States and Europe that the Arab revolutions . . . are now over and that the democratic project has failed. Bitterness and a sense of impending catastrophe are replacing the enthusiasm that followed the toppling of dictators in Tunisia and Egypt,' said the Tunisian president Moncef Marzouki. He was writing at the time of Muslim protests against the film *Innocence of Muslims* in a slightly irritated op-ed piece in the *New York Times*. 'Now there is ominous talk of an "Islamist Fall" and "Salafi Winter" after a supposedly failed Arab Spring,' he added. 'The Arab revolutions have not turned anti-Western. Nor are they pro-Western. They are simply not about the West.'[89] What he forgot to say is that they may not be over.

The Gulf states have been largely buying their way out of trouble since 2011. Where that doesn't work the US turns a blind eye while they sort it out with brute force instead. Neither of those may be the case in the not too distant future. If hydraulic fracturing, 'fracking', does lead to greater or full energy independence for North America it will transform the US relationship with the Gulf in general and with Saudi Arabia in particular.

Analysts working for the financial institution Citibank were excited enough about it in 2012 to produce a study called *North America, the New Middle East?* Not far into the document the question mark at the end of its title disappeared. The economists said that the trend 'points to North America effectively becoming the new Middle East by the next decade'. They concluded their report with the words:

It is unclear what the political consequences of this might be in terms of American attitudes to continuing to play the various roles adopted since World War II – guarantor of supply lanes globally, protector of main producer countries in the Middle East and elsewhere . . . But with such a turnaround in its energy dependence, it is questionable how arduously the US government might want to play those traditional roles.

But if it happens it won't be President Obama who breaks the union. Even if the extraction of shale gas and tight oil reaches the heady heights of its proponents' claims, there will have to be a radical overhaul of transport and infrastructure to exploit the new resource. Cars will have to move from normal oil to electricity generated by shale gas. Ways will have to be found to adapt the aviation industry and industry nationwide to this new energy resource. Engineers will often want to drill under people's homes to get to the gas and oil underneath, and that will spark public opposition. But with China, Argentina, Mexico, South Africa, Australia, Canada, Libya, Algeria, Brazil, Poland and France all thought to have large shale-gas resources, the impact on the Gulf is likely to be profound.

The first Gulf state this will impact on will be Qatar. It derives most of its income from gas, and that commodity's global price will drop long before oil's. The money Qatar gets from its gas fields has already started going down and may steeply decline within a decade. It is probably not a coincidence that there has been a rush in recent years by Qatar, as gas 'fracking' proved successful, to exploit the faltering European economies and snap up good investments at cheap prices. Qatar, which has a local population of only 300,000, is estimated to have invested more than $30 billion overseas in 2012 alone. Its spending spree over recent years has included everything from European football clubs to airports and the luxury jeweller Tiffany. It has also used the post-Arab Spring era to make big investments in the Middle East. The Qataris are preparing themselves for a world where they have to earn their living rather than let some foreigner pump it out of the ground for them. The number of the expats who presently make up more than 70 per cent of the population will gradually reduce as Qataris absorb the skills needed to run their portfolios. The expats who remain will just be the ones doing the jobs that still require people to get their hands dirty.

Things will not be so easy for Saudi Arabia. The Saudis have been the most important oil-producing nation because, unlike the rest, they do not need to pump at their full capacity. Because they can turn the flow up or down they can influence the price more than anyone else. Contrary to popular perception, America does not buy most of its oil directly from the Saudis, but as this is a globally valued commodity, in a global market, it has a global price that impacts directly on what Americans pay at the pump at home.

Oil had its first surge in price after the supply shock of 1973. It doubled in price, but was still below $10 a barrel in 1974. It had a huge surge after the Iranian revolution in 1979, then drifted down through the 1980s and stayed largely stable until 2001. After the 9/11 attacks and the uncertainty of the years that followed, the price went crazy, climbing in July 2008 to its record peak of over $145 a barrel. Even if the figures are adjusted for inflation, in 1998 the price was still under $20 a barrel. The Gulf states in ten years got a staggering windfall. That meant when the Arab revolts broke out King Abdullah of Saudi Arabia could dip into the state's bulging piggy bank and drop $130 billion on the table to create jobs, cheap housing and incentives for Saudi-based companies to employ members of the woefully underskilled young people in its workforce, a quarter of whom were unemployed.[90]

Saudi Arabia has a local population of 20 million people. Keeping them happy is a lot more expensive than buying off the tiny Qatari population.[91] If other energy sources in other parts of the world prove successful it will produce a slump in the present price. The bottom won't fall out of the market, because Saudi oil will still be needed by countries without alternatives. The developing world is still developing and the engine of that growth will still need oil. But China, North

America and parts of South America and Europe may all have new energy sources as alternatives to those offered by the Gulf. And that, says Dr Aviezer Tucker from the University of Texas Energy Institute, will force change on the Gulf nations.

> There was a period when the oil price was ten dollars a barrel and these regimes did survive ten dollars a barrel. If it goes down to twenty dollars a barrel they may survive that as well, but the problem is the population is already used to the standard of living that comes with getting a hundred dollars a barrel. Will they be able to adjust back? I don't know.

Saudi Arabia's spending threatens to outgrow its income. Its present break-even price is $100 a barrel, and that break-even price keeps rising.[92] If the Saudis have less cash to throw around they will have to cut back on the funding they pump into Salafist groups around the Middle East that sometimes turn into Global Jihadists. It has been one of the great contradictions of US foreign policy that it has formed one of its closest alliances with a country with whose value system it has absolutely nothing in common. The only thing they have shared is the love of oil, but for different reasons. For the Americans oil means they can keep their society energised, creative and innovative. For the Saudi elite it means they don't have to work for a living and can hold on to cultural traditions that have more in common with the Taliban's in Afghanistan than the people walking the streets below the swank penthouse suites they own in major Western capitals. If America can sate itself at home, it will not need to hang out with the gauche Saudi princes.

The restrictions imposed by the self-appointed custodians of Saudi culture are an anachronism in the New Middle East. The US was quick to demand that the Muslim Brotherhood in Egypt showed a 'commitment to religious tolerance' while its Saudi ally strictly prohibits the public practice of faith by all non-muslims. The Saudi leadership is not only busy suppressing protests by its disenfranchised

minority Shia communities in the Eastern Province; it also has to deal
with widespread resentment and frustration from large sections of its
young population who want to see change. They talk about it incessantly online, which is the only public forum they have. By 2013
more of its population were using Twitter than in any other country
in the world.[94] They express the same frustrations as the young people
who rose up in 2011, though with all the subsidies floating around,
'bread' is missing from the list. What they want most of all is for their
voices to be heard and listened to.

All of the ordinary people I met in the Arab world during the uprisings believed that the US does not understand them and does not try
hard enough to understand them. Conversely, many of them would
have jumped at the chance to live the American way of life, and that's
because American soft power has done much of the heavy lifting in
the Middle East while the hard power was busy going around breaking things. America has entered the post-Arab Spring era in better
shape than any other foreign player in the region, but it does need to
quickly recalibrate.

Israel is happy to see the Arab nations preoccupied with their own
internal tribulations, as long as American power can help to keep
them contained. The Arab world has long considered Israel to be
America's spoilt child, but during Barack Obama's first term Israel's
leadership savaged the hand that feeds it. Obama would 'only be
human if he felt that returning to the fight he had with Netanyahu
was an opportunity to get a bit of his own back', a Western diplomat
told me. Perhaps, but either way America cannot afford to make the
same mistakes as Israel. If it wants to remain a force throughout the
region it needs a comprehensive strategy that, in the post-Arab Spring
era, needs to be seen to be built on more than just childcare. It needs
to be a tailored individualistic approach towards all the key countries
of the New Middle East.

But American inaction throughout the Arab Spring may have been
a signal that it is ready to retreat from areas and issues it no longer

feels are part of its core interests in the region. That might mean that America goes first from three to two pillars of policy.

It would arm Israel so that it can maintain military superiority over its neighbours, but otherwise disengage from even pretending to try to sort out the Israeli–Palestinian Peace process, unless the Israelis try to have their cake and eat it by seeking to absorb all the Palestinian land without making full citizens of the Palestinian people.

And the US would stay firm friends with the Saudis in return for a stable oil supply.

Everything in between and around may largely be allowed to work itself out. America will seek to support the transitions in these B-team Middle Eastern nations, which would include Egypt, with aid and via international institutions like the World Bank and the International Monetary Fund. The gamble will be that as long as these countries build up their economies and create a wide middle class there is no reason for them to breed radicalism and threaten America. 'I think at least it will be easier to deal with the Obama administration than the Republicans,' Amr Darrag had told me hopefully. 'Once we have a stable state the US will see that we just care about the interests of our country and we are practising democratic values. When they see we are not turning the country into another Afghanistan or Iran or whatever model the West does not like, I think something similar to what's happening with Turkey will take place.' Though long before they were ousted President Obama made it clear he didn't trust the Ikhwan-led Egypt: 'I don't think that we would consider them an ally, but we don't consider them an enemy. They're a new government that is trying to find its way . . . So I think it's still a work in progress.'[95]

Two years after the young revolutionaries were spluttering in the gutters from the American-made tear gas sold to the Mubarak regime, the US sold the new Muslim Brotherhood-led government another 140,000 canisters. But that did not mean the US has failed to adapt to the post-Mubarak era. The sale was allowed to go ahead on the condition that all information about the canister's country of origin was removed.[96] The youth of Egypt were still going to get tear-gassed, but their fury would be directed only at the people firing the canisters, not the people who shipped them over. That, perhaps, was the embodiment of the use of 'smart power', which had been promised from the State Department at the start of the first four years of the Obama era.[97]

Whatever new policy emerges for the Arab world from the second Obama administration, other than in the Gulf it is likely to be one with a light touch.

Over time that may grow lighter still. The new sources of energy being found in shale rock formations should dramatically ease US dependency on the Gulf states. It is a potential game changer in terms of the loss of political influence that the oil-producing nations would have over the Western world. But that prospect, if it were to be realised, is a decade or so away. It won't fundamentally change the priorities of the Obama administration, nor the immediate ones that come afterwards. In the future perhaps only Israel will remain in the A team.

In the meantime the Obama administration may have just reached the point where it simply thinks the returns are no longer worth the risks of making big investments in much of the Middle East. The president damaged his own reputation trying to re-engage with old enemies and chivvying along old friends. He got nothing in return. Stepping back from the Middle East is a policy that would be understandable, though it is also one that risks rebounding at some stage if America is too hands-off.

Whatever the foreign policy, or probably foreign policies, are for the Middle East, they will not be simple and linear. In her last meeting with reporters before she stepped down from her post as secretary of state, Hillary Clinton articulated this point more broadly, but it was particularly relevant for the New Middle East. On 31 January 2013 she said:

> I've come to think of it like this: [President] Truman and [Secretary of State] Acheson were building the Parthenon with classical geometry and clear lines. The pillars were a handful of big institutions

and alliances dominated by major powers. And that structure delivered unprecedented peace and prosperity. But time takes its toll, even on the greatest edifice. And we do need a new architecture for this new world; more Frank Gehry than formal Greek. Think of it. Now, some of his work at first might appear haphazard, but in fact, it's highly intentional and sophisticated. Where once a few strong columns could hold up the weight of the world, today we need a dynamic mix of materials and structures.[98]

But building something new is hard work and costly; it requires both commitment and a sense that all that effort is going to be worth it.

'I think we are in a period when there is a kind of fatigue with spending all our time and energy on a part of the world that doesn't seem to be very responsive to us,' said Professor Quandt of the University of Virginia.

So you are going to see more attention paid to Asia inevitably and less to the Middle East, and I think Syria is an example of that. The disinclination to get involved in what is a geostrategically important but very complicated place is a sign of a different attitude. You may see John McCain and a few others going around optimistically wanting to go in and do something in Syria, but if you look at the detail of what they say, even they don't want to do an Iraq all over again. The lessons from Iraq are being learned day by day as we reflect on what did we get out of that trillion-dollar effort, and if anybody wants to replicate that in Syria, then as Bob Gates said as he left the Pentagon they should 'have their head examined'. And that is the dominant mood, it's certainly going to be [Secretary of Defense Chuck] Hagel's view, it's going to be Kerry's view, that unless there is a very, very strong compelling American national interest to get involved militarily in the Middle East, we are not going to do it. We may do covert things, we may do economic aid, we may do drones and God knows what, but what we are not going to do is 'boots on the ground'.

6

Iraq: SNAFU

It started for me mid-morning on a quiet street, much like any other, in 2003 in central Baghdad. Two things about it were unusual. It was deserted and there was a large American tank parked by the side of the road with its barrel pointing straight at me. All I had was a dirty white tablecloth I had snatched a few minutes earlier from a restaurant in the Hotel Palestine. I think I may have overdone the waving as I walked gingerly towards the enormous beast that loomed before me. And then the spell was broken.

'How ya doing?' the young Marine said to me. 'Fine,' I replied, and that was it: I had been 'liberated'. The American occupation of Iraq had begun. It was 9 April 2003. The American army was driving into the heart of Baghdad and was moments away from dragging down the soon-to-be-famous statue of Saddam Hussein. His was the first of the old Arab regimes to be overthrown.

Saddam was a dictator's dictator. He had everything in spades. The brutal clarity, the utter ruthlessness, territorial ambitions, personal cruelty, and a couple of sons as bad as he was. He had his friends murdered, his sons-in-law killed, and he used poison gas on his own people. He launched one of the twentieth century's longest, bloodiest and most pointless wars, against Iran, that left more than a million people dead. It was an immense war that pitted the region's leading Sunni strongman against his Shia equivalent.

Saddam Hussein was a centre of gravity in the Middle East. When he was removed it changed the orbit of everything else. It produced what the Sunni King Abdullah of Jordan said was a new 'crescent' of Shiite movements arching through the region.[1] The removal of Saddam Hussein tipped the regional power balance towards his old arch-enemy, Shia Iran. The entire region began to feel the impact of the regime's collapse and Iraq became the battleground for a sectarian war between Shia and Sunni Islam. The Shia won.

The day before the American-led invasion, Iraq was in the Sunni sphere of influence. By the time the Americans left it was on the Shia side. Iraq under Saddam was a threat to the Gulf states because he coveted their resources. He was loathed by the Saudis, but they did not consider his government to be a blasphemy in the way they did the Shia theocracy in Iran. Iraq was the buffer between Iran and Saudi Arabia. The Gulf states saw Saddam as a pitbull which, while dangerous, if pointed in the right direction contained their pre-eminent enemy. But the battle in Iraq between Sunni and Shia forces saw the rise of the country's Shia, and thus a new and powerful ally for Iran. When the Arab revolts began eight years later Saudi Arabia and Qatar were ready to sacrifice the people of Syria to bleed Iran and win the rematch. The Gulf states wanted to counter what they saw as Iran's new friend in Baghdad by helping to oust its old friend in Damascus. America's painful experience in Iraq was the defining force behind how it reacted to the two civil wars that broke out during the Arab Spring.

The invasion of Iraq was a military success. The occupation of Iraq was a disaster.

The young men fell on his image like a pack of wolves. They had known nothing but the iron grip of Saddam Hussein's regime and so were venting a lifetime of rage. They swarmed over his statue stamping, spitting and smashing the iron figure that lay on the ground in front of an American armoured personnel carrier. Within minutes it was decapitated. A group of men began to drag their prize onto the street. The head of the man who was omnipresent in their lives bounced down the steps under the weight of kicks and hammer blows. Finally, it was dragged unceremoniously through the city he dominated by the people he had oppressed for so many years. The scene was being watched by hundreds of millions of people across the world. It became the iconic image of the end of Saddam's rule in Iraq, and the start of America's.

Saddam Hussein had looked down on his subjects from almost every corner, street and government building. Everywhere I went in the country during the last year of his rule his image was a constant and deliberate reminder of who was in control. Those tearing his image from the concrete pedestal in Firdos Square were the men who Saddam Hussein had promised would defend him with their blood.

Things would go so badly wrong in Iraq because his regime was not toppled by these young Arabs, as would happen elsewhere in the region a decade later, but by young Americans. The US troops, perched on their tanks, chewed gum and watched the spectacle before them. Neither they nor the people that led them knew very much about the population or the country they had just invaded. 'People have been pretty nice, they know we are here to stop terrorists,' one of them told me as he stood on his Humvee. 'They seem happy to have us here. It's sure better than being shot at.'

Neither of those two things would last.

'I wish we could have waited and done our Iraqi spring with the others,' said Shirouk Abayachi as we drank coffee in her home in a Baghdad suburb exactly nine years later in 2012. By now the American troops had all gone home. Shirouk had no love for the old regime. She had been driven into exile by it, but returned as soon as it fell to help rebuild the country. She now works as an adviser to the water ministry and runs a human rights group. 'Saddam would have been the first and it would have been done with our own hands,' she said. 'It would have been better than what the US did to us.'

'It is incredible that the Americans could walk out and not leave the lights on. That seems to me to be reprehensible,' said a Western diplomat as we sat in his fortified embassy in the Green Zone.

The partnership behind the 2003 operation does have a lot to be ashamed of. The Americans came in with great plans for improving infrastructure, but there has been a failure to put the country back together again. And electricity is by far the most obvious example of that. There were plans to build power stations and re-establish power lines, but then they fell foul of the two thousand and six, seven and eight insurgency. Everybody just panicked and it all became too difficult.

The same was true of other core needs like clean water, sanitation and health care. All fouled up is the new normal in Iraq.

'I have never seen anything that looked as set for failure from almost the beginning as Iraq,' said Ambassador Barbara Bodine. The first act of the Bush administration when it took control was to divide post-invasion Iraq into three sectors. There was a northern and a southern sector, which were to be administered by two retired US army generals. The central sector, including Baghdad, was to be run by Ambassador Bodine. Her boss was another retired army man, Jay Garner.

> The idea, and I heard this from Jay Garner directly and personally, was that we were going to go in the middle of April with 120 civilians, that we would get the ministries up and running, which presumed that the ministries were there. Convene a constitutional convention, write a constitution, get a constitution ratified, have parliamentary elections, establish a cabinet and have a fully functioning government by August. You know that's insane!

The Americans invaded in March with the expectation that their troops would be going home by September. No one at the US Department of Defense made any plans for an occupation. So what happened instead was described by a US government report, published on the tenth anniversary of the invasion, as 'nation (re)building by adhocracy'. The Bush administration embarked on America's most politically ambitious project for a generation, regime change in the Middle East, by military invasion, and found themselves making it up as they went along.[2]

Iraq was where everything in the region began to change, but it is also where America may have to eventually concede that it toppled one military strong man only to see him replaced by another. 'What you have in Iraq in Prime Minister Nouri al-Maliki is a new Saddam emerging using the forces of the Defence Ministry and the Interior Ministry to create a new praetorian guard around him,' says Professor Bernard Haykel. 'What they are trying to do is to reconstitute the power of the centralised Iraqi state with a very strong central army which, again with the population the Iraqis have, could pose a very formidable challenge to the Sunni Gulf Arab states.'

When George W. Bush gave a speech at the National Endowment for Democracy in 2003, in which he first articulated his 'forward strategy of freedom in the Middle East', he praised that body for its work in Iraq 'promoting women's rights, and training Iraqi journalists, and teaching the skills of political participation'.[3] Adnan Hussein, editor-in-chief of the *Al Mada* newspaper, was the kind of man George W. Bush would have been proud of. He was among the dwindling number of Iraqi journalists still brave enough to weather death threats and intimidation from all sides to shine a light on the workings of the country's opaque and corrupt institutions. Less comfortable for the former president was the fact that these dysfunctional institutions had been allowed to form in this way because of the US occupation. Mr Hussein was not impressed by the Iraq he had been bequeathed. 'There is no democracy here,' he told me. 'Technically, we have freedom because we have no law to limit freedom. But, practically, we have no freedom. Every month or so a journalist is killed; every week a journalist is tortured.'

I failed to find anyone in Baghdad after the US troops had left who thought the democratic gains had been worth the bloodshed. But then even the architect-in-chief of the plan seems to accept that Iraq is at least a generation away from stability. 'If,' wrote George W. Bush,

'Iraq is a functioning democracy fifty years from now, those four hard years [of the insurgency] might look a lot different.'⁴ And they might not. That 'If' cost the lives of at least 116,903 Iraqi civilians and 4,409 US soldiers. Modern medicine kept the US death toll relatively low, but 31,000 had to live with their injuries.⁵ In financial terms it cost the American taxpayer almost one trillion dollars. But President Bush may be right that until the invasion, the occupation and sectarian brutality it provoked recedes from living memory, Iraq will remain a broken nation, if it remains a nation at all.

The 19th of March 2003 was the day the people of Baghdad started getting used to huddling in their homes trying to protect their children as the windows blew in. That is because it was the day President George W. Bush told his country:

> My fellow citizens, at this hour, American and coalition forces are in the early stages of military operations to disarm Iraq, to free its people and to defend the world from grave danger . . . To all the men and women of the United States Armed Forces now in the Middle East . . . the people you liberate will witness the honorable and decent spirit of the American military . . . We have no ambition in Iraq, except to remove a threat and restore control of that country to its own people.⁶

The people of Iraq had heard that word 'liberate' before. Things had ended up in a similar fashion. There was a long and violent occupation.

The 19th of March 1917 was the day the inhabitants of Baghdad were told: 'our armies do not come into your cities and lands as conquerors or enemies, but as liberators.'⁷ At that time the promise, known as 'The Proclamation of Baghdad', was being made by Britain's Lieutenant General Sir Stanley Maude shortly after his forces occupied the city. His address turned out to be just as accurate as the one given by George W. Bush eighty-six years later to the day.

Four years after Maude made his promise there was still no sign of self-rule, and so the British were confronted with an insurgency that is known in Iraq as the 'Revolution of 1920'.[8] It began with peaceful protests, which were brutally put down, and so the uprising turned violent. The occupying forces responded with what the British historian Derek Hopwood described as 'methods that do not bear close scrutiny'. These included indiscriminate bombing of civilians from the air and the contemplation of the use of poison gas.[9]

Having quelled the revolt, the British took formal control of the country for twelve years until they nominally handed it over to their proxies in the Hashemite Sunni monarchy which they had earlier established in 1921. The monarchy was then overthrown in 1958. It was Nasser who was the inspiration for Iraq's anti-imperialist revolution, though this one turned out to be a much nastier affair than the one he had instigated in Egypt.

The coup leaders in Iraq also called themselves the 'Free Officers'. Some historians argue that it was this event, not Suez, that marked the full stop on British power in the region.

'Iraq' was a British invention formed out of three thoroughly disparate provinces of the Ottoman Empire: Baghdad, Basra and Mosul. They had nothing in common apart from, eventually, a loathing of the British. The Kurds in Mosul hated being ruled by Sunnis in Baghdad as much as the Shias in Basra in the south did. Iraq is an artificial construct, which has only ever been held together by force.

During Egypt's coup, after some discussion, the king was put on the royal yacht and packed off to exile in Italy. In Baghdad there was less debate. The king and his family were shot. The bodies of their government ministers were dragged through the streets. Baghdad descended into bloodlust.[10] It set the tone for the regime that would eventually emerge and rule the nation until the Americans took over.

The coup and the new Iraq were led by Brigadier General Abdel-Karim Qassem. He was as despotic as everyone who would follow him. Though his coup was inspired by Nasser, Qassem decided, once he had taken power, that he was not willing to be subservient to the cause of Arab nationalism.[11] He refused to join Egypt and Syria in the United Arab Republic, which was a major blow for those seeking to pull together the three powers of the great Arab capitals Cairo, Damascus and Baghdad. That brought Qassem into conflict with Iraq's Ba'ath Party. In 1959 the Ba'athists hatched a plot to kill him. Among the would-be assassins was a young party member called Saddam Hussein. They failed. Saddam fled and lived in exile for three years, at first in Damascus and then for a longer period in Cairo under Nasser's protection.[12]

In 1961, after Kuwait gained independence from Britain, Qassem claimed it as part of Iraq. But before he could do anything about it, he himself was overthrown and shot in 1963 by a coup involving the Ba'athists, though they didn't end up running the country at that time. They did though eventually lead another successful coup in 1968, and they remained in charge until the Ba'ath Party was fatefully disbanded in 2003. The 1968 coup remains remarkable by the standards of Iraqi political life because it was bloodless and the man who was overthrown, Abdel-Rahman Arif, was only sent into exile and eventually lived to the ripe old age of ninety-one.

Usual service though was promptly resumed with various brutal power plays that eventually led in 1979 to Saddam Hussein seizing power within the party in a bloodbath of murder and torture that would be the signature of his rule. At this stage there were no diplomatic relations between the US and Iraq, but the trauma of the US embassy hostage crisis in Tehran put Iran in the top five least favourite states, and that led to a warming of US relations with Iraq. The US eventually began passing on military intelligence to Baghdad to help them during the Iran–Iraq war. The diplomatic overtures also led to the famous meeting in Baghdad in December 1983 between US Middle East envoy Donald Rumsfeld and Saddam Hussein. The video of that was played over and over again in the run-up to the US invasion as Mr Rumsfeld and others in the administration made the case that dealing with Saddam was pointless.

*   *   *

In the year leading up to the 2003 war, as the people of Iraq became convinced they were going to be invaded there was a growing concern about what would happen after the regime fell, as they had no doubt it would. What the Americans failed to understand was that colonial rule was still within living memory in Iraq. Even if the Americans had forgotten what it looked like, the Iraqis had not.

One of my Iraqi colleagues, Mohammed Darwish, who was a doctor of literature and whose greatest pride was that he had translated James Joyce into Arabic, expressed the prevailing sentiment of the people to me in the weeks before the war began. 'Saddam is a bastard,' Mohammed told me, 'but he is our bastard.' Mohammed was a brilliant man who had always refused to be a party man, and so his life and the opportunity it should have promised had been stunted.

In the fog of what has happened since it is easy to forget that as the American ground forces approached Baghdad, the people of Iraq had already been through thirteen years of conflict and sanctions. You could see the exhaustion on their faces. The sanctions were imposed on Saddam's regime after the invasion of Kuwait, and didn't end until Baghdad fell to the Americans. Almost everyone below the very top of the regime had, during those years, sold off possessions to buy food or watched their sick children suffer from a lack of medicine. The sanctions were imposed largely to stop Saddam's attempt to build weapons of mass destruction. In 1999 UNICEF estimated that hunger, disease and a lack of medicines due to the sanctions had led to the death of half a million Iraqi children.[13] The world didn't know it then, because Saddam didn't want to look weak in his neighbourhood, but by this time Iraq did not have a functioning nuclear, chemical and biological programme.

Mohammed had watched the sanctions impoverish his people but do nothing to hasten the collapse of the regime, which was clearly one of the sanctions' other undeclared aims. For the sanctions and the devastating impact they had on the lives of ordinary Iraqis, Mohammed blamed the West. And so did all the people I met back then, even when the government-appointed minder wasn't listening. Dr Mohammed, like millions of his countrymen, wanted the Americans to depose Saddam, help the country get back on its feet and get out. The lack of post-war planning meant that only the first and the third of those would happen.

It was clear to those of us in Baghdad in the months leading up to the invasion that the Iraqi people shared one very strong trait with ordinary Americans. Even if they wanted the end of the regime, they were still deeply proud of their culture and history. 'We are an ancient country,' the Iraqi foreign minister Naji Sabri told those of us in Baghdad after the invasion was under way. 'We were producing literature, art and architecture when Bush's grandfathers were living in caves like animals.'[14]

The US administration made a fundamental misjudgement: being anti-Saddam did not mean you were pro-America. 'We are coming,' George W. Bush told the Iraqi people, 'with a mighty force to end the reign of your oppressor. We are coming and we will not stop and we will not relent until your country is free.'[15]

'If they come, I will take up my gun and shoot them myself,' an old retired civil servant told me in Baghdad's Shorja spice market. He was dressed in a jacket and tie, his shirt collar had been repaired too many times and was a patchwork of white stitching. I asked him his name. 'I'm an Iraqi,' he said. 'That's all you need to know. I'm not a party man. I'm an independent man, but this war is against the Iraqi people and I will fight the invaders.' He then set off through the bustling crowd that choked the narrow lanes of the market stalls.

Most people in Iraq would have disagreed with the old man's words but they would have understood the sentiment. Like him they had once been among the generations of schoolchildren who were taught about the fight for freedom against foreign invaders in places like Fallujah and Najaf in the 1920 revolt.[16] They did not want to be re-colonised, but the 'Freedom Agenda' was implemented in such a cack-handed fashion that colonised was exactly how they ended up feeling. So a new generation of Iraqi children would live through, not learn about, battles against foreign armies in these historic Iraqi cities.

The son of the first American president to invade Iraq had entirely different motivations from those of his father. George Bush Senior had an international mandate after Iraq invaded Kuwait largely in a dispute over the output and the price of oil. Saddam Hussein wanted the Kuwaitis to slow the pumps down. Kuwait's overproduction caused a slump in prices from eighteen to ten dollars a barrel, which was hitting Saddam hard. He needed more money for his own oil because he was trying to rebuild the country and the army after the long, disastrous and ultimately futile war he fought against Iran from 1980 to 1988. Much of his debt was also owed to Kuwait and Saudi Arabia, and they refused to write it off.

Saddam was therefore doubly furious. He resurrected the old claim that Kuwait only existed apart from modern-day Iraq because of British imperialism after the First World War, which he said carved this creation from his territory. So he invaded to get it back. After a month of cruise missile strikes the Iraq army was routed in a land war that lasted under a hundred hours. It fled, bruised and bloodied, but with enough fight left in it to put down an insurrection by Shias in the south who were encouraged to rise up by the US and then abandoned to Saddam's retribution when they did. This perceived betrayal by the father still lives on in the minds of the country's Shia majority, and it meant that when US forces returned under the son their motives were never going to be trusted.

The British assumed that their own colonial experience and more particularly their experience of violent militancy in Northern Ireland would mean they would do a better job at managing the Shia in the south after the invasion. In fact the Iraq war was an embarrassment for the British army. It failed to quell the violence and it was perceived to have been dragged through a humiliating withdrawal from Basra by Prime Minister Tony Blair's successor Gordon Brown. 'I don't know that you could see the British withdrawal from Basra in 2007 in any light other than a defeat,' said Colonel Peter Mansoor, who was executive officer to General David Petraeus, the man George W. Bush eventually sent in to lead the US troops out of the terrible mess they had been dumped in by Rumsfeld's now discredited military strategy.[17] In 2013, ten years after he sent the British troops in, former British prime minister Tony Blair was still having to defend the war, though he said: 'I have long since given up trying to persuade people that it was the right decision.'[18]

When the whole enterprise began though there was no talk of defeat because there was no thought of a protracted war. The Forty-Third President of the United States expected all Iraqis to welcome the Western troops as heroes. He sent them in promising to light a beacon of hope for the rest of the region to follow. Hours after I saw the famous statue, which I had watched being built just the year before, topple to the ground, I saw people enjoy their first taste of their new freedom by trying to break into a vault of the Iraqi central bank with a hammer and chisel. They were just a few hundred metres from the checkpoint set up by the US soldiers around the Palestine Hotel. When I walked further down the street I saw a government building being set on fire by a group of youths. Suddenly there was a roar behind me and a US army Humvee screamed down the road. The crowd instantly scattered. The Humvee sped up to the building, and then kept on driving. I could see the surprise on the young men's faces. They had lived their entire lives under the total control of the state. Now American troops had told them there was no one in charge any more. And they made clear their priorities by the only two things they did protect: the Interior Ministry and the Oil Ministry.

Small scenes like this were happening all over the city. The message was clear: the invading troops did not see it as their job to police the streets. So by nightfall communities across the capital were barricading their roads against looters. As rumours swept the city about violence and mayhem, the first signs of sectarian division began. Having released Saddam's hold on the country's latent communalism, the American troops did nothing to police and contain it.

The Sunni Muslims in Iraq had always had the power and money under Saddam, even though they were only 20 per cent of the population. The Shia Muslims, who made up around 60 per cent of the people, were persecuted and often left in poverty. The first looting and destruction of the institutions of the state began in the Shia areas. When nobody stopped it the Sunni population grew worried that their homes might be next. They feared revenge from the men of the sprawling slums of what was then Saddam City but would soon be renamed Sadr City after a Shia cleric assassinated by the old regime and whose son, Muqtada al-Sadr, would soon play a key role in the insurgency against the occupation. It was this man and men like him on both sides of the sectarian divide who would fill the power vacuum that the US forces created. From the start, it was the chaos that created the insurgency, and not the other way around. That was a direct consequence of American inaction on day one.

'The damage done in those early days created problems that would linger for years,' wrote President Bush. 'The Iraqis were looking for someone to protect them. By failing to secure Baghdad, we missed our first chance to show that we could.'[19]

The American forces lost control right at the start and they never got it back. The reverberations of that failure rippled out from the capital. They stretched even beyond Iraq's borders. That was because while the US government made no post-war plans, everyone else in the region did. The invasion had been telegraphed for over a year. No one expected Saddam to survive, so the Shia and Sunni forces inside Iraq, along with the Sunni and Shia nations in the wider Middle East, were all getting ready for a power grab in the country when he fell. This was the beginning of the reordering of the old Middle East.

The West got it wrong in Iraq because it didn't know, or didn't want to believe, what it was really getting into. The professor of military history Geoffrey Wawro argues that every American president 'from Truman to Clinton felt certain that inserting Western Forces into the Muslim Middle East was asking for trouble', and so 'George W Bush and his neocons' were taking a 'great conceptual leap' after they 'startlingly decided that the Middle East *was* ready for U.S. military activism – and fertile ground for a "freedom agenda"'. 'What was perhaps so striking about the George W Bush administration,' Wawro wrote, 'was its willed ignorance of history.'[20]

You didn't have to look too far back in history to see how the best of American intentions in the Middle East could go badly wrong. Twenty years earlier America had put its troops within Iran's sphere of influence, and it also led to catastrophic results.

On 23 October 1983 two bombs went off in Beirut. By then US and European forces were attempting to keep the peace in the wake of the Israeli invasion of Lebanon to drive out the PLO and Syria, which had led to the massacre in the Palestinian refugee camps of Sabra and Shatila. One truck bomb was driven into the US Marine Barracks, the other aimed at the headquarters of the French paratroopers. The latter bomb was so big it literally lifted the huge building into the air and dumped it next to the bomb crater.[21] In all more than three hundred people died. Two hundred and forty-one of them were US servicemen.

Who carried out the bombings has never been discovered, but they were blamed on Islamist groups supported by Iran. President Ronald Reagan pulled his troops out of Lebanon. Westerners including academics, aid workers and journalists who were left in the city became the prey of kidnappers who were again said to be linked to Iran. Some were held for years. The CIA station chief William Buckley was kidnapped and tortured to death. A year after his kidnap four Soviets were kidnapped. One was killed within weeks.

American attempts to get their hostages back led to the Iran–Contra scandal in which senior US officials sold arms to Iran, despite an embargo, to try to get their people released. The Soviets, according to information obtained by the journalist Bob Woodward, used a different approach to get their three people freed within a month of capture.

> The KGB in Lebanon . . . seized a relative of a leader of the radical Muslim Hezbollah, had castrated him, stuffed his testicles in his mouth, shot him in the head and sent the body back to Hezbollah.

The KGB included a message that other members of the Party of God would die in a similar manner if the three Soviets were not released. Shortly afterwards the three . . . were let out a few blocks from their embassy.[22]

Every journey made by every Westerner in Lebanon in the mid-Eighties became a potential death trap. The same would happen in Iraq once the occupation began, and with the same consequences if people were caught, though instead of hanging it was beheading. These murders were done by Sunni groups linked to al-Qaeda rather than Shia groups linked to Iran. Either way, it made covering the war in Iraq from all sides virtually impossible for Western journalists and incredibly dangerous for their Iraqi colleagues.

The Bush administration may have been wilfully 'ignorant of history' but its ignorance of Iraqi society, if not wilful, was equally striking. If there was one thing the Iraqi leader Saddam Hussein was good at, it was running a police state. The foreign secret services never successfully penetrated it for any length of time. Instead the administration relied on a bunch of out-of-touch self-serving exiles for their intelligence on Iraq, and because the exiles were out of touch and self-serving the 'intelligence' they gave was wrong.

Jay Garner, the man selected to lead the Office of Reconstruction and Humanitarian Assistance for Iraq, was drafted in at the last minute when the administration began to notice that it hadn't thought very hard about what to do the day after the statue came down. But Donald Rumsfeld's Department of Defense was so politicised that General Garner came to realise that doctrinally he didn't fit the bill. More importantly perhaps, neither did many of the team of experts he had begun to gather around him.[23] The impression he gathered was that commitment to the cause of creating a beacon of democracy in the Middle East was more important than the ability to carry out the task. He had just two months before the invasion to build his organisation from scratch. Garner struggled to get his team together, he struggled to get resources, then he struggled even to get into the country, and squandered crucial days in Kuwait waiting for a lift into Baghdad. Soon after he finally got there he learnt that his mission was already over.

Emerging through the blizzard of chaos to replace Garner less than a month after he had started the job was Lewis Paul 'Jerry' Bremer III, who would head the 'Coalition Provisional Authority'. Mr Bremer strode into town in a dark suit, white shirt, tie and a pair of tan Timberland boots. They had been given to him by his son with the words 'Go kick some butt, Dad.'[24] He set off a copycat fad among the thousands of American officials living in the Green Zone who started wearing similar combat boots. It was a trend followed too by Bremer's boss Donald Rumsfeld when he visited the country. The truth is that combat boots were no more needed in the Green Zone than they were in Washington or Wall Street. They were a symbol of the kind of war-tourist mentality that many of the Americans working in Iraq adopted during their tenure. Neither they nor Bremer bothered to properly consult the people they were ruling.[25]

Bremer just couldn't stop himself from making promises that nobody around him believed could possibly be kept. In August 2003 he said: 'About one year from now, for the first time in history, every Iraqi in every city, town and village will have as much electricity as he or she can use and will have it 24 hours a day, every single day.' That was always an utterly impossible thing to achieve, but he said it, and Iraqis believed him, and yet today they still spend much of their lives without electricity.[26]

'We worked really hard to mitigate some of the mistakes that he was making, but they were driven, these people were absolutely driven,' said the Baghdad-based Western diplomat. 'A lot of the problems go back to those first few days, to those first few months, certainly to 2003.'

It has become commonplace to say that no one expected Iraq to be consumed by murderous anarchy, that everyone was taken by surprise. It is not true. The fault lines were there for anyone to see if they were

willing to look. In September 2002 in the *Boston Globe* newspaper
Karen J. Alter, Professor of Political Science at Northwestern University, wrote:

> Ten years from now, will we be looking back asking how the United
> States could have thought that an unprovoked, preventive war on
> Iraq could succeed when the signs of danger were so clear and
> ominous? How an oil shock and deficit spending for war would
> plunge the United States and world economies into a major reces-
> sion? How an administration so focused on getting rid of Saddam
> failed to create a workable policy to shape a post-Saddam Iraq?[27]

The answer to all her questions would be a resounding Yes.

Ten years on from her article I asked Professor Alter why it had all
gone so badly wrong. It was classic 'groupthink', she said, referring to
the psychological shift that occurs when a group of people's desire for
harmony overrides a realistic view of the circumstances they face.

> George Bush surrounded himself with ideological purists. When I
> wrote that I could see what was happening. I could see the ideo-
> logical purity and I could see the effort to villainise and discredit
> anyone who raised an alternative perception. There was almost the
> moral belief that they knew what they were doing and that they
> were right.

From the very beginning the Bush administration seemed almost
purposely blind to what was going on. During a press conference given
at the US Department of Defense Donald Rumsfeld dismissed the
lawlessness I'd witnessed in Baghdad with the words: 'It's untidy, and
freedom's untidy, and free people are free to make mistakes and commit
crimes and do bad things. They're also free to live their lives and do
wonderful things, and that's what's going to happen here.' But it didn't.

People are not supposed to be 'free to . . . commit crimes and do
bad things'. That is not what is supposed to happen in a beacon of

democracy. 'Freedom' is regulated by laws. Freedom without laws is called anarchy. But Rumsfeld, in the same press conference, ridiculed any notion that things were spiralling out of control.

It was symptomatic of the mindset that created the invasion plan. Donald Rumsfeld's military operation for Iraq was built to test his own theory and rubbish that of his greatest opponent in the administration, Secretary of State Colin Powell. Powell was the architect of the first invasion plan for Iraq in 1991. His plan, defined as the 'Powell Doctrine', called for overwhelming force to be used in any invasion. Rumsfeld had nothing but contempt for the notion, and constantly encouraged, cajoled and bullied his staff to bring the numbers down to prove the job could be done with many fewer boots on the ground. The capture of Baghdad was proof of his plan, or so he believed. But what happened afterwards showed its folly. It was like climbing Mount Everest with just enough oxygen to reach the top. Having stood on the summit and congratulated yourself on this remarkable achievement, you now face the fact that you don't have the means to get down again.

When I first met Souad Abdullah she was quietly sobbing in the corner of her bedroom. Her sister Nadja was perched on an old wooden chair in fluffy baby-blue pyjamas picking shards of glass from what remained of her windowsill. 'If Bush thinks his soldiers will be welcomed with flowers and music, then he is thinking wrong,' she told me. 'We will treat them like robbers who are breaking into our homes.' It was March 2003, just a few days into the war. 'Why do they do this?' wept Souad. 'We love the British.' Their flat looked like a bomb had just hit it because one just had. But while her sister tidied up, Souad just watched. She was carefully turned out, with her hair brushed up into a grand bouffant. She may have been the elder sister but she was also the famous one. Years after the glory days of her singing career had ended, she was still a household name in Iraq.

When she opened the door to me in March 2010 I barely recognised her. Her hair was a mass of knots and tangles. She peered around the door like a frightened child as my Iraqi colleague reminded her of our visit seven years before. The only thing that stood out in her now gloomy and bedraggled little home was the photograph of her son Khalil in pride of place on the living-room wall. 'They kidnapped him in 2006,' she said. 'They would ring and I could hear them beating my son. We paid thousands of dollars but we never got him back.' Tears welled up in her eyes. 'We don't even know where his body is.' The family believed the local clerics hated Souad because she was a performer, which even back in the days of Saddam was considered a slightly disreputable profession for a woman. The death threats eventually drove her sister Nadja to move out and stay with a brother. I asked Souad the inevitable question. Was her life better before the Americans came or now? 'I don't want to talk about politics,' she said, 'but every day is dark . . . see how we live.'

It is possible to trace back the roots of the sectarian violence that destroyed Souad's life to three very stupid decisions.

'Early Friday morning May 16 2003 I signed Coalition Provisional Authority order No 1,' wrote Bremer in his memoirs. It decreed that Ba'ath Party members 'shall be removed from their employment . . . This includes those holding more junior ranks.' During Saddam's regime, being a member of the Ba'ath Party was often not about ideology or supporting the regime, it was about finding a decent job as a teacher or civil servant, or getting your children into a good school. It was basically about surviving. Two million people were in the Ba'ath Party. Bremer compared it to both the Nazis and the Soviet Communist Party under Stalin. In the preamble to his declaration he said the Ba'ath Party had to go because it had abused the Iraqi people and was a continuing threat to the Coalition Forces. He wrote later: 'our intelligence estimated that . . . only 20,000 people, overwhelmingly Sunni Arabs' would be affected. Like much of the American intelligence about Iraq before, during and after the invasion, it was wrong. He essentially threw the entire bureaucracy and everyone in it on the scrap heap. The country lost the wherewithal to function.

Then a week later, on 23 May, Bremer did something that even now looks startling in its scope. He issued 'Coalition Provisional Authority order No 2. Dissolution of Entities'. The annex then lists what he was abolishing with the stroke of a pen:

> The Army, Air Force, Navy, the Air Defence Force, The Ministry of Defence, The Ministry of Information, The Ministry of State for Military Affairs, The Iraqi Intelligence Service, The National Security Bureau, The Directorate of National Security, The Special Security Organization, The Republican Guard, The Special Republican Guard, The Directorate of Military Intelligence, The Al Quds Force, Saddam Fedayeen, Ba'ath Party Militia, Friends of Saddam, Saddam's Lion Cubs, The Presidential Diwan, The Presidential Secretariat, The Revolutionary Command Council, The National Assembly, The Youth Organization, Revolutionary, Special and National Security Courts.

At the end for good measure he threw in the National Olympic Committee. 'In retrospect I should have insisted on more debate on Jerry's orders, especially on what message disbanding the army would send and how many Sunnis the de-baathification would affect,' wrote President Bush in his memoirs.

> The orders had a psychological impact I did not foresee. Many Sunnis took them as a signal they would have no place in Iraq's future. This was especially dangerous in the case of the army. Thousands of armed men had just been told they were not wanted. Instead of signing up for the new military, many joined the insurgency.[28]

It was a catastrophe. It was pretty clear to me and everyone in Baghdad that the Iraqi army was not made up of die-hard Saddam supporters when I saw a podgy bald man running along the side of the Tigris river in a pair of baggy longjohns. He'd just got his first sight of the US troops. Crouching behind my hotel balcony I watched the capital's supposed defenders simply leap from their trenches and flee without firing a shot. The Americans got to Baghdad so quickly because they met very little resistance. In the final days before Baghdad fell I drove around the city looking for signs that the Iraqi army were massing or preparing for a siege. I couldn't find them.

Saddam's army was a mess. I'd seen for myself at parades that were supposed to show their strength that many of the soldiers didn't even have boots. These men had no reason to fight for Saddam, and so they didn't. But then after the war was supposed to be over Bremer gave them a cause. He took away everything they had: their pride, their jobs, their hopes of a place in the new Iraq. The only thing he left them was their guns. Then he gave them something to fear – each other.

'We talk a great deal about the fundamental error of demobilisation and deba'athification,' says Ambassador Bodine.

But there was a third major legacy from the American occupation that I think is going to continue to corrode Iraqi political progress. We sectarianised the country in a way that it had not been before. The way that the neo-conservatives viewed Iraq was: 'All Shia are good, all Sunnis are bad and all Kurds are small "d" democrats.' Yes Sunni, Shia, Kurds existed in Iraq, and there's a long-standing debate in Iraq as to whether they are an Arab state or is there a unique Iraq-ness to them. Those kind of identity issues have been going on for a very long time and we're not responsible for creating them, but what we did is that we basically took the country made up of twenty-seven ethnic and religious groups and we brought it down to three and we basically said: 'Which one of those three boxes you are in will determine whether you have political and economic power or not.' You could be the best Sunni in the whole world, but if you are not a Shia your chances of actually moving into a position of real power was very much circumscribed. We made it a determination and set off the ethnic cleansing, the near civil war, and you see that playing out in their politics even now.

'There is a history of sectarianism in Iraq,' said Shirouk Abayachi.

> Saddam used sectarianism but Bremer's policies escalated those
> tensions. I saw maps in Baghdad made by his administration based
> on the sectarian divide. This street is Sunni, this street is Shia, this
> is mixed. I have no idea how they knew, we didn't even know this,
> so how did they manage to divide us so easily? They shaped things
> like this from the very beginning. Even when they distributed posi-
> tions it was based on sectarian lines, which was very new in Iraqi
> political life. Paul Bremer on behalf of the American administra-
> tion created the sectarian divide in Iraqi society.

Bremer nominally handed over power to an interim Iraqi government
on 28 June 2004, two days ahead of schedule, in a brief ceremony
witnessed by just a couple of dozen people. He was already on the
plane on his way out before the wider world knew anything about it.
He may have gone, the occupation was technically over, but the power
stayed with the Americans. The fledgling democracy that he also left
behind was carrying the whole weight of the US military adventure
on its back. And though George W. Bush could rightly claim that his
administration had produced the first free and fair elections in the
Middle East, which took place for a National Assembly in January
2005 and again in that December, the polls just reinforced to the
Sunnis how much power they had lost.

Those sectarian strains spilled out across the region as Sunni leaders, and particularly those in the Gulf, saw another Shia-led
government emerge in an oil-rich and powerful nation, alongside
already resurgent Iran. Another manifestation of this was a renewal of
al-Qaeda, this time in Iraq. The conflict became a magnet, not only
for extremists from around the world who wanted to kill Americans,
but also for Sunni extremists who wanted to kill Shia.

Much of the coordination and transport of these Sunni extremists
was arranged by Syria. I was told by someone who lived in Damascus
at the time that busloads of Salafists would be gathered together in an

area near the Algerian embassy before heading off to the border. When the Americans left at the end of 2011 many of those men hopped back across the border to fight the same Shia regime that had sent them into Iraq in the first place.

Within a few months of President George Bush declaring on 1 May 2003 that 'major combat operations in Iraq have ended',[29] the commander of the US forces in Iraq, General John Abizaid, said his troops were facing 'what I would describe as a classical guerrilla-type campaign against us . . . It's a low-intensity conflict, in our doctrinal terms, but it's war however you describe it.'[30] His boss Donald Rumsfeld described them as 'pockets of dead-enders'.[31] President Bush said: 'There are some who feel like the conditions are such that they can attack us there. My answer is, bring 'em on.'[32] As he later admitted, his comment provoked a 'firestorm of criticism'. It underlined just how little his administration understood about the size of the insurgency it was beginning to face.[33]

The Bush administration made it clear that it neither valued nor wanted much to do with the United Nations or other international agencies, and so when the bomb attacks started most of them simply packed up and left, leaving the US to shoulder the entire load. The capture of Saddam Hussein in December 2003, found hiding in a hole in the ground near Tikrit, caused much excitement among the Americans but did not, as they'd hoped, dampen the violence. One of the guns he had with him in hiding was mounted and presented to President Bush.

By the following spring the insurgency had gathered steam and the US forces found themselves fighting Sunnis in Fallujah and other areas of Anbar province. They were also fighting the Shia followers of the cleric Muqtada al-Sadr.

He was the youngest son of Ayatollah Muhammad Sadiq al-Sadr, who had a huge following among the poorer members of the Shia community. Sadiq al-Sadr was assassinated by the Iraqi regime in February 1999 when the car carrying him and his two eldest sons was sprayed with machinegun fire.[34] Muqtada al-Sadr was not targeted afterwards because the regime did not think he was a threat. He was dismissed by his opponents as being a bit slow-witted.[35]

Because he lacked his father's charisma or religious credentials, Muqtada al-Sadr was not a major player before the invasion, but after it he successfully used his family name to create perhaps the biggest single problem the occupying forces would face. Al-Qaeda never offered an alternative to the government the Americans were trying to stitch together. They were spoilers, not players. But Muqtada al-Sadr and his Mahdi army did.

Like his father, Muqtada al-Sadr's power base was the poor working classes of the Shia community. Many of them had been made destitute by the UN sanctions for which they, like everyone else, blamed America. As the local government in Baghdad disintegrated, his followers filled the gap in Sadr City and other Shia areas in the south of Iraq with food, health care and, most importantly, security.

His Mahdi army though were seen by many middle-class Shia Iraqis as nothing more than criminal gangs, particularly after al-Sadr issued a religious ruling or fatwa which said that stolen property could be kept by thieves if they donated some of the proceeds of their loot to Sadrist imams.[36] His newspaper also printed lists of Iraqis it said were collaborating with the occupation, which was tantamount to issuing their death sentence.

Al-Sadr and his followers simply saw the American troops as one oppressive regime replacing another. Along with Sadr City, al-Sadr sought control of important religious cities like Kabala and Najaf.

I had visited the shrine of Imam Ali in Najaf in 2002 before the war. To add insult to Saddam's long list of injuries perpetrated against the majority Shia population there was a huge tiled image of Saddam praying inside the courtyard facing the worshippers as they mourned Imam Ali. It didn't last long beyond his fall. Neither did peace in the city. It was the scene for a series of battles with the Western forces in 2004 as they saw both al-Sadr's political and his military power grow. The constant fighting decimated the pilgrimage-related economy, and in the end the local traders and clerics were as happy to see the back of his forces as the Americans were.

In the December 2005 parliamentary elections al-Sadr essentially became kingmaker, supporting the candidacy of Nouri al-Maliki, from the Shia Dawa Party, as prime minister in the coalition government. He would play the same role again in the parliamentary elections five years later. One Pentagon report in 2006 declared that his Mahdi army was a bigger threat to Iraq's security than al-Qaeda.[37] But in March 2008 al-Maliki showed he was also willing and able to take on the Mahdi army in its strongholds in and around Basra, and in Baghdad's Sadr City. This encouraged many to think that he might be able to govern impartially, and some Sunni politicians agreed to join his cabinet. Muqtada al-Sadr had by then already fled to Iran, ostensibly to complete his religious training but actually to escape an arrest warrant. After his militia was crushed by al-Maliki's forces he recast them as a humanitarian group, but one that could easily be reconstituted into a serious fighting force.

Al-Sadr did not return until January 2011, but he then became a major influence on the decision by al-Maliki to refuse a US request for its troops to stay on, in a reduced form, beyond 2011. Al-Sadr warned in a statement released on the eighth anniversary of the toppling of Saddam's statue that he would remobilise his Mahdi army if the US pull-out did not meet its deadline. But by then, even though they were nervous of what might follow, many Iraqis believed they had already paid too high a price for having the Americans around.

The Iraq war was big business. At times there were more private contractors in the country than there were military personnel.[38] Nearly 10 per cent of these people were providing a security service. The country was made more dangerous by the way some of the tens of thousands of security contractors who rotated through the war dealt with the Iraqi people. Iraq was a licence to print money for some of the men working for private security firms if they were willing to strap on a weapon, puff out their chests and claim military expertise they did not have. The US Department of Defense didn't even begin to count how many there were until four years into the war, by which time they were feared to have undermined the country's counter-insurgency efforts. At their peak in June 2009 there were thought to be 15,279 private security contractors in Iraq, though even that figure may have been an underestimate.[39] There were of course many experienced and disciplined security contractors operating in the country, with long previous service in special forces and other such units. But these men, along with journalists and most importantly the Iraqis, soon realised there were also motley crews of racists lording it around the country, bullying, harassing and shooting at ordinary people with total impunity.[40] Their actions disgusted and infuriated the local population.

The country was on a slow boil, but the sectarian tensions built into the political process by Bremer's decisions were being stoked by the Sunni extremist 'Al-Qaeda in Iraq' group, led by the Jordanian Abu Musab al-Zarqawi. His aim was simple – kill lots and lots of people: 'It is the only way to prolong the duration of the fight between the infidels and us.' According to a computer disk the US said it found in Baghdad in January 2004, he wrote to senior al-Qaeda leaders: 'If we succeed in dragging them into a sectarian war, this will awaken the sleepy Sunnis who are fearful of destruction and death at the hands of the Shia.'[41]

Al-Zarqawi and his followers adhered to the teachings of Sayyid Qutb, but stretched them to their barbaric extremes. Not only did his men bomb and kill Shia, they terrorised Sunni Muslims too in the areas they operated in. They applied Qutb's ideas of Takfir to pass judgement on anyone who stood in their way, leaving decapitated corpses lying in the streets.

'It was really when the Global Jihadis came in that Takfir just climbed exponentially. The violence was unbelievable, I'd just never seen anything like it,' Doctor David Matsuda told me. He was among a small group of specialist anthropologists deployed with American troops after 2006 to develop a better understanding of how to implement an effective counter-insurgency strategy in Iraq. He worked in two of the country's most dangerous areas, Sadr City and Anbar province.

It became a battle for the heart and soul of Islam – who is a Muslim and who has the right to define that not just for themselves, but for everybody. There was a lot of animosity between Sunni and Shia before the two Gulf wars [but] the concept of Takfir just took everything to a completely different level. Even without rule of law, even when that was at its worst, Takfir increased the propensity for frontier justice and motivated the revenge factor. Global Jihad really got its voice once Iraq became a global proxy war for who among the Sunnis are the first among equals and then who among Muslims are the first among equals.

It would eventually be these excesses that would lead to a real turning point in the war, but before that happened a lot more people died. In April 2004 Bremer concluded of his chief foes: 'Zarqawi was the mirror image of Muqtada, a *Sunni* Muslim fascist. *Somebody has to stop them both before the poison spreads.*' (Bremer's italics.)[42]

Even the central al-Qaeda leadership ended up internally condemn-ing al-Zarqawi and his successors' vicious campaign of violence. But al-Zarqawi's excesses were not new to them. When he was previously involved with al-Qaeda in Afghanistan, before 9/11, he had to be moved by the organisation to Herat in the north because he started slaughtering members of the Shia Hazara community in the place he had been based in.[43] Killing Shias seemed to be his primary reason for coming to Iraq too, not killing Americans.

If al-Qaeda was the very fringe of violent Sunni fundamentalism, al-Zarqawi was the fringe of al-Qaeda. Although they had fallen out with him in Afghanistan they needed him when he turned up in Iraq to keep the al-Qaeda franchise in the public eye. But letters found in Osama bin Laden's hideout in Pakistan after bin Laden was killed by US special forces in May 2011 showed he considered the brutality of both Al-Qaeda in Iraq and the insurgency umbrella group 'Islamic State of Iraq' to be counterproductive. He eventually concluded that his Iraqi affiliates were in fact a liability. One of his media advisers, the

American Adam Yahya Gadahn, was infuriated by the constant attacks on moderate Sunnis and Christians which continued even after al-Zarqawi's death. He wrote in January 2011: 'The attack on the Catholic Church in Baghdad . . . launched by the organization of the Islamic State of Iraq that we support, which is – if we like it or not – known to people as [Al-Qaeda in Iraq] do not help to gain people's sympathy.' He added: 'I believe that sooner or later – hopefully sooner – it is necessary that al-Qa'ida publicly announces that it severs its organizational ties with the Islamic State of Iraq.'[44]

The irony was that it was the 'war on terror' that brought al-Qaeda into Iraq. The final report of the 9/11 commission published in the summer of 2004 found 'no evidence that these or the earlier contacts [between Iraqi officials and al-Qaeda] ever developed into a collaborative operational relationship. Nor have we seen evidence indicating that Iraq cooperated with al Qaeda in developing or carrying out any attacks against the United States.' They had not, as the Bush administration claimed in the run-up to the war, been involved with the Iraqi regime before.

Iraq, or at least the non-Kurdish areas, was dragged into civil war in 2006 after al-Qaeda bombed the golden-domed Shia al-Askari mosque in Samarra in February. This was despite a claim the previous summer by Vice President Dick Cheney in which he said of Iraq: 'I think they're in the last throes, if you will, of the insurgency.'[45] The blast itself at the Shia shrine did not kill anyone, but the wave of revenge attacks it incited did, and spurred still faster the ethnic cleansing that had been taking place in urban neighbourhoods.

Al-Zarqawi was killed by a US airstrike in June 2006, but by then the sectarian violence had a life of its own. That year also saw the death of Saddam Hussein, after a protracted trial that led to the inevitable death sentence. He was hanged on 30 December 2006. As he went to the gallows he was taunted by his executioners. 'I have saved you from destitution and misery and destroyed your enemies, the Persians and Americans,' he said. 'God damn you.'[46]

By now George W. Bush had been re-elected president. To change course in Iraq he had to get rid of the man seen as the greatest impediment in his administration to that change, Donald Rumsfeld. Even had the war not been a debacle, something else had happened that did enormous damage to America's reputation throughout the Arab world and beyond. It provided the enduring and perhaps most iconic images of a military campaign gone totally wrong.

Abu Ghraib prison was a place that scared the hell out of Iraqis under Saddam. It would do the same to the inmates under the authority of the new US guards. The man who investigated the abuse at Abu Ghraib, Major General Antonio Taguba, found: 'That between October and December 2003, at the Abu Ghraib Confinement Facility . . . numerous incidents of sadistic, blatant, and wanton criminal abuses were inflicted on several detainees.'[47] The report detailed among other appalling abuse 'credible' evidence of 'Sodomizing a detainee with a chemical light and perhaps a broom' and 'Beating detainees with a broom handle and a chair'.[48] But it was the images that leaked out to the media that were the most damaging, because they showed American soldiers treating Iraqis as if they were less than human.

The most haunting image, which for many people summed up the entire scandal, showed a man standing on a box with his arms outstretched, a black sandbag over his head and his body draped in a loose black cloth. Attached to his fingers, toes and penis were wires that the inmate believed were about to electrocute him. The prisoners were regularly forced into these outstretched positions, and the iconography they resembled was not lost on the woman who took many of the pictures of the abuse, the US army's Specialist Sabrina Harman. She wrote home: 'At first it was funny . . . but it went too far even I can't handle what's going on . . . I can't get it out of my head. I walk down stairs after blowing the whistle and beating on the cells with an asp [baton] to find "the taxicab driver" handcuffed backwards to his window naked with his underwear over his head and face. He looked like Jesus Christ.'[49]

But for the rest of the world, and particularly in the West, it was the picture of the hooded prisoner that most evoked the image of Christ on the crucifix to the millions of people who saw it. The photo was used on the front page of the *Economist* magazine under the headline 'Resign, Rumsfeld'.

Almost as elaborate as the cruel and inhuman treatment meted out to the inmates by the American guards were the legal arguments marshalled by the Bush administration in its efforts not to describe as torture what happened in Abu Ghraib and more generally in the treatment of detainees during the 'War on Terror'. A report by the Senate Armed Services Committee after President Bush had left office said the administration's support for what the CIA called 'aggressive interrogation techniques' 'conveyed the message that physical pressures and degradation were appropriate treatment for detainees in US military custody'.[50] The US government was immune from lawsuits but the defence contractors working with it were not. Lawyers acting on behalf of inmates began to sue them over claims they were involved in the torture of their clients. Details of the first successful case were reported in January 2013 with an out-of-court settlement of five million dollars to seventy-one former inmates.[51]

The American military's great success of the war was the surge of US forces that was announced by George Bush in January 2007. It made a hero of its architect, David Petraeus, who led the troops in Iraq through the build-up that began to curb the violence. The surge added another 30,000 troops. By the autumn almost 170,000 US troops were serving in Iraq, and all had had their tours of duty extended.

As important as the surge, or maybe more so, was a growing fury among the Sunni community with the extremists who claimed to be fighting in their name but who were butchering them too if they didn't carry out their orders. Petraeus was a firm believer in a more sophisticated approach to counter-insurgency that meant being seen to protect and work with the local communities rather than stopping

by only to kick down their doors in a night-time raid. This philosophy and the fatigue with the violence led to the 'Sons of Iraq'. It
began in Anbar province but soon spread across the Sunni areas. It
was these men, numbering around one hundred thousand, who by
policing their own communities turned the tide. Many were themselves former insurgents. David Matsuda recalled:

> One of the things we learned over time was that there were two
> al-Qaedas. There were al-Qaeda who became part of the [Sons of
> Iraq] and there were the flying jihadis. I remember talking to Iraqis,
> and you would get folks saying: 'The reason I turned against them
> was because if they wanted my car and I didn't want to give it to
> them I'd be shot. If they wanted my daughter and I didn't want to
> give her to them I'd be shot,' all the way to something as simple as:
> 'The last straw for me was when they said I couldn't smoke and
> that's when I pointed my guns the other way.'

The Iraqi insurgents turned because while it was clear that the Americans wanted to get out, the foreign Sunni extremists wanted to stay
and do just what the label said, create an 'Islamic State of Iraq'. The
'Sons of Iraq' tactics against the jihadists were as brutal as the ones
previously inflicted on them. 'They hunted al-Qaeda down with a
vengeance. They dragged al-Qaeda guys through streets behind cars . . .
they had videos of feet on the altars in mosques . . . It was pretty
much just a ruthless slaughter,' Doctor Matsuda told an army
colleague at the time.[52]

What happened to the Global Jihadists in Iraq sheds light because
it carries lessons for the sectarian conflict in Syria. Just as in Iraq, these
men have been welcomed into the fight by the locals in Syria too. Just
as in Iraq, the jihadists get their funding and arms from the Gulf.
Many of these same men are now in Syria fighting another sectarian
war against what they see as Shia proxies for Iran. But in Iraq, when
the local fighters grew sick of the violence perpetrated by the foreign
extremists they could draw on support from the Americans to force

them out. If the foreign fighters start to grow too powerful and savage in Syria, the local fighters will be striving to push them out on their own.

The Sons of Iraq also began taking part in the political process, and many got elected in the first provincial elections in 2009. Some of them probably had a sizeable campaign chest. The US spent $370 million between 2007 and 2009 on the Sons of Iraq. Great wads of dollars were just handed over to its leaders with no receipts required, and no idea how the money was being spent or who received it. No specific goals or benchmarks of success were set either. The financial controls were so weak that in December 2009 a US army captain pleaded guilty to tucking $690,000 of the money into his own back pocket.[53]

When the Iraqi government took over the programme in October 2008 it was much less willing to hand over the cash. There were constant complaints of late payments and, as the US troops began to wind down, some of the Sunni fighters complained they were being sidelined by the Shia-led government, harassed by the security forces and left at the mercy of revenge attacks by extremists on both sides. But six months after US troops had pulled out, the US ambassador-nominee to Iraq, Brett McGurk, claimed that 70,000 of them were now part of the Iraqi army and had government jobs. Another 30,000 were being paid $300 a month by the state to run checkpoints in Sunni areas.[54]

The surge was a success for the Americans because it created the environment that enabled them to leave. But it didn't solve any of the underlying problems in Iraq. There's no question that the fact that the Americans could and did leave was a good thing. Most people I talked to afterwards were pleased they were gone, because nobody saw them as anything like a solution for the problems that still remained. And those problems are huge.

When those combat troops finally left almost nine years later, the American forces were feared and hated by many ordinary Iraqis. The torture and humiliation of their men at the Abu Ghraib prison had destroyed all trust. US soldiers had been dishonourably discharged for appalling offences and the war campaign had been longer and harder than the American people could have ever imagined.

In his book *The Audacity of Hope* Barack Obama describes a thirty-six-hour trip to Iraq, which included a brief trip to the Marine base in Fallujah in the deadly Anbar province. While he waited for his outgoing helicopter one of his foreign policy advisers struck up a conversation with one of the unit's senior officers. 'I asked him what he thought we needed to do to best deal with the situation,' the staffer tells Obama. 'What did he say?' 'Leave.' It was advice that Obama intended to take.[55] He outlined how to do it in February 2009 in a speech entitled 'Responsibly Ending the War in Iraq':

> What we will not do is let the pursuit of the perfect stand in the way of achievable goals . . . The long-term success of the Iraqi nation will depend upon decisions made by Iraq's leaders and the fortitude of the Iraqi people. Every nation and every group must know – whether you wish America good or ill – that the end of the war in Iraq will enable a new era of American leadership and engagement in the Middle East. And that era has just begun.[56]

In September 2011, as the US forces were winding up their operation and the region was reeling from the Arab Spring revolts, Dr James Zogby, from the Washington-based Arab American Institute, was overseeing a major survey across Iraq, the wider Middle East and America about attitudes towards the impact of the war. The Iraqis were ambivalent. They wanted the Americans out yet they were scared about what might come next. But what both Sunni and Shia agreed on was an overwhelming sense that the invasion did not leave them better off.

I asked Dr Zogby whether he thought the US under President Obama did manage to responsibly end the war in Iraq. 'No, but I don't fault the administration, because this table was set long before they got involved. We got in badly and we ended up getting out with an unfinished mess that will haunt us and haunt in particular the Iraqi people for a long time to come.' It was, said Dr Zogby, a war that failed on every level:

America's leverage is much less than it was ten years ago. Our behaviour during this war was so abominable that it sullied our reputation not just in the Middle East but worldwide. The president said what he said for political reasons, because if you are Commander-in-Chief you don't put your head between your legs and say: 'My God we lost, what a disaster, this was an horrific mistake.' But the reality is that it was.

Iraq was a problem Obama couldn't wait to be rid of. Two of his team had supported the war though, Hillary Clinton and Joe Biden, so he handed it over to one of them. Obama had not been in the US Senate when their votes were cast, but if he had been it's clear that he would have voted against. By the late summer of 2009 he told his vice-president: 'You take care of it.' For the rest of the year the two men thought it was going so well that they barely discussed the political transition in Iraq, even over lunch.[57]

The March 2010 parliamentary elections in Iraq were considered the fairest and most representative in the nation's history. They may stay that way too. The polls also reached another landmark. Iraq broke the then world record for the longest period between parliamentary elections and the forming of a government. It took eight months for the government to be formed because sectarian divisions once again dragged the process into stalemate. But as I stood in line with hundreds of policemen who were waiting to cast their vote in central Baghdad, it was hard not to be impressed by their willingness to participate in a process that could quite easily have cost them their lives. Long lines of policemen are a magnet for al-Qaeda suicide bombers, so the security at the polling station in Baghdad was very tight. But the policemen lined up patiently, smiling and enjoying the day, waving their newly inked fingers to prove they had taken part. It was a scene I would witness in many other Arab states in the years that followed the 2011 uprisings, but no one suffered more than the Iraqis for their right to vote. What was questionable was whether the vote meant they had a democracy.

We all like the place to look nice when we have guests over. Few of us go to the trouble of painting the trees and grass green. But Iraq had not had much to show off in recent years, so as I stepped off the plane in March 2012 it was easy to forgive their enthusiasm as my boots began to shluck their way up through the still-sticky coat of creamy white paint that had been used to coat the gangway walls, the ceiling and the floor. The last time I had seen Baghdad look this relaxed was before the 2003 invasion. Such notions are relative, of course. There were armed soldiers and armoured personnel carriers on many corners, checkpoints snarled up the roads. Things weren't normal. But it was a measure of improvement, an Iraqi colleague told me, that now even though children were still being kidnapped it was 'only for money'. So if you paid up you got your kid back. Alive. In the old days if you paid up you often got only a body, and as Souad found with her son, sometimes not even that. And you suspected it might have been your next-door neighbour.

Iraq was putting on a show that was costing it hundreds of millions of dollars because it was about to be welcomed back into the Arab fold. It was the first time the Arab League would hold a summit in Iraq since Saddam invaded Kuwait, and the first big event the Iraqi government would run on its own since it was invaded by the American-led coalition. The centre of Baghdad was shut down. Cars were forbidden to drive. Roadblocks stopped people moving across the city. Mobile phone networks seemed to be switched off. Along with the endless power cuts almost everything that could be done to make the experience thoroughly miserable for those not invited seemed to have been thought of. And then the menu for the delegates was published and it was revealed they would be eating gold-plated dates.

The meeting, like most Arab League summits, achieved very little, but as I sat in a grand room of one of the old dictator's palaces listening to the final communiqué it was clear that the triumph for Iraq was that it took place at all. Only nine of twenty heads of state turned up, and among those only one was from the Gulf. But he was the Kuwaiti leader, which was symbolically important, because of the two nations' histories. It was a measure of what Iraq had been through that during the lunch, held in the open air in the grounds outside for the local bureaucrats and journalists, the sound of mortars landing nearby provoked no reaction whatsoever.

The summit though was proof that Iraq, while leaning towards the leadership in Iran, was also seeking to tread its own path. It wanted to recreate the leadership role it once had in the Arab world. Damascus, Cairo and Baghdad used to be the three most important Arab capitals. Iraq would like to be back up in the top tier again. It needs to be part of the Arab fold to ensure its future security. At the back of its mind is what might happen after the Syrian civil war ends. Iraq is sandwiched between two totally different positions on the Syrian crisis adopted by Iran and Turkey. The US says Iraq has been allowing Iran to use its air space to deliver arms to Syria, prompting what Secretary of State John Kerry called 'a very spirited discussion' between himself and al-Maliki.[58] If a new Sunni-led government is formed in Syria, what line will that government take towards Iraq? Will it send back and support the Sunni extremists who helped overthrow Assad to cause more trouble in Iraq? Al-Maliki thinks so: 'If the opposition is victorious, there will be a civil war in Lebanon, divisions in Jordan and a sectarian war in Iraq.'[59] Concerns about fall-out from Syria are likely to add to al-Maliki's paranoia and increase, not weaken, his attempt to centralise power around him. To mitigate the impact of the civil war in Syria he needs friends in the Arab world. He still doesn't have many.

In the meantime, as Syria plays out, Iraq faces the enormous task of rebuilding its infrastructure and re-establishing functioning and transparent institutions. That requires stabilising the political and security situation. To encourage foreign investment and diversification it has to deal with the rampant corruption, which was fuelled by the US occupation.

In March 2013, exactly ten years after the war began, the US Inspector General for Iraq Reconstruction, Stuart W. Bowen, issued his final report before closing the body down. Of the nine-year US$60 billion rebuilding programme, he said: 'Ultimately, we estimate that the Iraq program wasted at least $8 billion [due] to fraud, waste, and abuse.'

The Americans seem to have been conned at every level. His report contains a litany of mistakes, whether it was paying a subcontractor $900 for control switches valued at $7.05, or paying $40 million to half-build a prison that nobody wanted and was never used. The report said: 'in 2003 and 2004, more than $10 billion in cash was flown to Baghdad on U.S. military aircraft in the form of massive shrink-wrapped bundles of $100 bills stored on large pallets. This money was not managed particularly well.'[60] A few weeks before the war began, Secretary of Defense Donald Rumsfeld asked Jay Garner how much he thought it would cost to rebuild Iraq. 'I think it's going to cost billions of dollars,' Garner said.

'My friend,' Rumsfeld replied, 'if you think we're going to spend a billion dollars of our money over there, you are sadly mistaken.' Within five years they had spent US$50 billion trying to put Iraq back together.[61]

Iraq does though have the potential to be a hugely wealthy and powerful player in the region. The country has a population of just over 31 million people.[62] It is estimated to have the world's second-largest oil reserves.[63] The oil industry dominates the economy, producing 98 per cent of the government's foreign exchange earnings, though it provides only 1 per cent of the country's jobs, so unemployment is a big issue.[64] If it can get its oil industry back together it could be pumping out seven to eight million barrels a day. That would put it in a similar league to Saudi Arabia, but with a large standing army. According to Professor Haykel: 'The Americans have to come to the realisation that they are going to have to contain and sandwich Maliki and the central Iraqi government by maintaining troops and fire-power and influence in the south, in Kuwait, Qatar and Bahrain, and in the north with the Kurds.' Which brings American policy almost full circle, to the point just before Saddam switched from being an American ally to chief foe, when he threatened and then invaded Kuwait in 1990.

But others argue that in fact al-Maliki only looks dangerous because you just have to look dangerous to survive in Iraqi politics. 'I don't think Maliki is another Saddam, he's more like Gordon Brown. He's paranoid and thinks everybody is out to get him,' explained a Western diplomat to me in 2012 who had dealt with both men.

> He wants to keep as much control as he can. He's manoeuvring and engineering things to try to hold on to that power and actually being pretty ruthless when dealing with political enemies, but that's just being a politician, though it's nastier in Iraq. But he's not a dictator. I think the 'Oh this is a terrible dictatorship. Maliki is all-powerful' is overplayed. It's partly because the Sunnis and the Kurds are more Western-facing and articulate and are travelling off to the UK and the States, whereas the Shia don't spend as much time in the West, don't speak as good English and actually don't give a damn, they are not interested about criticism in the *New York Times*.

Al-Maliki wants central government control because he fears the abundance of oil in the areas dominated by the Kurds might allow them to one day seek an independent self-sustaining state. There are regular rows between al-Maliki's central government and the Kurdish regional government (which already has many of the institutions of state, like a parliament and a president) over the distribution of the oil wealth. The Kurds also have a militia force, the Peshmerga, of around 75,000 men. To be assured he can assert control, al-Maliki wants to run the central security forces. He has tried to keep a grip on key posts in the Defence, Interior and National Security ministries. He already has, through his Office of the Commander-in-Chief, control of the National Counterterrorism Unit and the Baghdad Brigade that runs the capital's security apparatus. And in August 2012 he created the 'Tigris Operations Command', which the Kurds considered a power play for contested areas between Kurds and Arabs.[65]

The Iraqi Kurds, who make up 20 per cent of the population, have a long relationship with the US which grew out of the safe haven set up for them in the wake of the 1991 Gulf War to stop Saddam's attacks. From that period they have been largely autonomous and they have very little interest in being part of the new Iraq, though neither do they seek military confrontation with it. In Dr Zogby's survey 60 per cent thought they were better off after the invasion. Only 4 per cent said they definitely were not. The management of the central government's relationship with the Kurds is a key test of the viability of the Iraqi state. It will be challenged further if the Kurds in Syria manage, in the post-Assad era, to form their own permanent breakaway region. Attempts by Turkey to build up energy deals directly with the Kurdish government have also soured relationships for both with Baghdad.

Al-Qaeda in Iraq has continued its bombing of government and Shia targets. These are often big and bloody attacks, but the fact that they tend to occur at the rate of around one or two a month suggests that Al-Qaeda in Iraq has nowhere near the capacity it used to have. Some of its fighters have also now moved to Syria to attack the regime there.

A Western ambassador in a Middle Eastern capital told me as Syria slid into civil war that policymaking for the post-Assad era was being driven by 'memories of Iraq' more than by anything emerging from the Arab Spring uprisings:

> We learned our lessons from Iraq. We will not have a back to year zero approach in Syria. There has to be some sort of continuation. The [Paul] Bremer approach backfired and was an absolute disaster. There will be no 'deba'athification'. We've all internalised the lessons from 'the day after' [the statue fell]. Everyone has a stabilisation team to manage this now.

The West learned from Iraq that it needed a post-war policy for Syria. What the West continued to lack though was a policy for before and during the civil war in Syria. One of the key reasons that the Assad regime proved so resilient was because the Syrian people had watched the sectarian violence orchestrated by Shia and Sunni groups in Iraq. Caught in the middle of this were minorities like the Christians, who were particularly persecuted by groups associated with al-Qaeda. It is estimated that perhaps two-thirds of up to 1.5 million Christians living in Iraq when the US troops took over have now left. The minorities in Syria looked across the border at the treatment their brethren got in Iraq and had no faith they would not meet the same fate. Christians felt safer under Saddam than they did after he fell.[66] Many minorities fear the same outcome after Syria loses its dictator, so they have not actively supported his overthrow.

The next Iraqi parliamentary elections are due in 2014. There have been attempts to pass a law prohibiting anyone from serving more than two terms as prime minister. This is aimed directly at al-Maliki. The proposal was drawn up with the support of Kurds, members of the Sunni-backed Iraqiya coalition, which includes former prime minister Iyad Allawi, and some Shia politicians once allied with al-Maliki. At the same time Muqtada al-Sadr seems to have been trying to reinvent himself as a more moderate figure, though to what end has not yet become clear.[67]

'If things had worked out the way [Bush] and Rumsfeld had imagined then Iraq would have been the beginning of a transformation in the Middle East,' says the University of Virginia's Professor William Quandt. 'It would have been Iraq and then who knows what next, maybe Syria, Iran, and so forth, and this was supposed to be a whole series of dominos which would fall in the direction of more pro-Western democratic regimes coming to power, and it failed.'

Now that he was *President* Barack Obama, as he announced the pulling out of the US troops in that February 2009 speech at a Marine base in North Carolina he could not afford to dwell on the fallacy of the war: the wounds from the conflict were too raw. He optimistically echoed the hopeful words and deeds of his many predecessors who found themselves embroiled in the trials of the Middle East by offering: 'We can serve as an honest broker in pursuit of fair and durable agreements on issues that have divided Iraq's leaders.' But when the last troops did leave, nobody in Iraq wanted to be even seen talking with the US any more. America left no friends behind in Iraq.

'If you look at the country today we have relatively little influence over the Iraq we created,' said Professor Quandt. 'It is just stunning how we spent all this money and lives and treasure and everything else to try to make a new Iraq, and we are hardly on speaking terms with them. We can't get them to do most of the things we ask of them.'

Iraq, under its Sunni strongman Saddam, was used by the West after the Iranian revolution to contain Shia influence in the region. Now it is a Shia country. The naivety of the US soldiers I met on the day they drove into Baghdad on 9 April 2003 was shared by the people who sent them to war. Those brave teenagers can be forgiven for that failing. That is not true of their masters in Washington. Not only did the Bush administration fail to think through its post-invasion plans, it did not think through the regional consequences.

The new Iraq will not simply do Iran's will, but it will cuddle up close if the Gulf states and particularly Saudi Arabia do not properly engage with it. The Arab League summit in 2012 was an important symbolic step, but it was only a small step. The summit was brimming with the tensions and mistrust between Sunni and Shia powers that the US invasion in 2003 intensified.

Saddam was toppled so that the region could be reformed. Instead it was convulsed.

The Soviet invasion of Afghanistan revealed the limits of its ability to shape regions it considered central to its interests. The Soviets reached too far, fought a war they could not win, and left humiliated, humbled and broke. The war ultimately led to the Soviet Union's collapse. Similarly the invasion of Iraq revealed the limits of America's ability to shape the Middle East, though without the catastrophic consequences that realisation brought the Soviet Union. Iraq would be 'A dumb war. A rash war. A war based not on reason but on passion, not on principle but on politics,' predicted a young state senator called Barack Obama in October 2002. Iraq was America's war of choice. It was when America overreached. It led to what a British diplomat told me felt like the sense of 'an end of empire', and he would know what that feels like.

But this is not the first time that America's decline has been predicted. It happened when they were beaten into space by the Soviets. It happened in the 1980s when Japan's economy was booming. It is happening again with the rise of China. America's failures in Iraq forced it to pause and reconsider what it wanted to do with its still-unmatched economic and military might. Empires have collapsed in the past because they did not realise they had overreached until there was no way back. Iraq may prove to be a very painful but historically important moment for America. If it had 'worked', the temptation to try to do it again elsewhere in the Middle East might have proved too tempting for the Bush neo-cons, and the long-term damage to America might have been profound. The mistake America is making when it comes to the Middle East is letting it be thought that it is losing authority. It may become less interested in the region, but it should not create an impression that it is less powerful if it wants to protect the interests it does have without having to use that power.

The war in Iraq will linger behind the making of American foreign policy until a generation comes along that is too young to remember what an absolute disaster many now believe it really was. It defined the Bush administration and it framed the way the next president ran foreign policy in the region before and after the Arab Spring. Barack Obama made it clear from the start that his administration was going to be pragmatic in the Arab world. He was going to deal with the Middle East as it was rather than try to create the one he might wish for. The war in Iraq is why America was reluctant to intervene in Syria. The White House concluded that if it couldn't stop a sectarian civil war in Iraq with tens of thousands of US soldiers on the ground what hope was there of achieving anything with a less intrusive intervention in Syria. Iraq also shaped Obama's policy in the first violent conflict of the Arab Spring, the uprising in Libya. President Obama has been accused of 'over-learning' the lessons of Iraq and so failing to take a lead role in Libya and then Syria. But he believes it is his calling to get America out of wars, not into them. In 2011, after a decade of conflict, he wanted to pull American soldiers out of harm's way. The aim under Obama was that the only people fighting and dying to control towns and cities in the Middle East would be the people who had been born in them.

7

Libya: Year Zero

If you give a boy a gun he thinks he is a man. The playground insecurities slip away. His height, his build, his age, his physical strength are all less important than the piece of metal he holds in his hands. The gawky teenager finds that suddenly he is an equal among men. The gun gives him a voice because people who hold the means of life and death must be listened to. The youngster can stop total strangers and make demands. 'You!' he may ask. 'Where are you going?' The man before him is perhaps his father's age. The stranger sees in front of him a boy. If it were his son he would slap him down. But he sees that the boy has a gun, so he swallows his pride and answers the questions. And as he does so the boy truly realises his new authority. He understands the value of his gun. He understands what he loses if his gun is taken away. The moment the cold metal touches his fingertips the boy can now feel its power.

The gun can give the boy all of this in an instant. Now that he has his gun he must be told what he is being asked to fight, kill and perhaps die for. He needs a cause to replace his conscience. In most wars an appeal is made to the soldier's patriotism, to some variant of 'King and country'. That is what happens in most wars.

The bursts of fire from the anti-aircraft gun blistered their way across the field towards the lines of government forces dug in on the other side. The deafening noise and the smell of cordite suffocated my senses. I ran down the trench, which formed the front line just outside the besieged western Libyan city of Misrata. The ground was uneven. Each step was heavy and laboured as I sprinted along, my body bent in a half-crouch, trying to keep my head below the top of the ditch over which zipped incoming machinegun fire. Occasionally there was a cry of relief as a mortar round from the government forces missed its target. When I reached 23-year-old Abu Bakr I stopped, panting heavily from the run. I was wearing a heavy flak jacket and a fragmentation-proof helmet. Abu Bakr was wearing a blue and white Argentinian football shirt and flip-flops. He had an AK-47 over his shoulder and a broad grin across his face. He offered me some couscous. Libya's was not an ordinary war.

'Right now I'm learning how to use the Kalashnikov and an RPG [rocket-propelled grenade],' he said cheerfully in his broken English. Before he spent his days shooting at the Libyan army he was at the local university studying 'Archaeology and Tourism'. He gestured around at the men with him on the front line. 'This is the normal people,' he said. 'They learn how to shoot, how to use the gun. We are in good spirits because we are right and the Gaddafi forces are wrong.' I was looking at the middle class at war. The fighters were businessmen, students, shopkeepers, farmers. They were what every man hopes he can be if his country goes to war. They fought hard and they did not run.

I don't know if Abu Bakr lived very long beyond the moment we shook hands and said goodbye, but three months later, as I stood in a refrigerated meat locker on the outskirts of his town, I did know that some of these 'normal people' had dragged the man lying before me out of a sewage pipe and beaten and sodomised him with a stick. 'This is for Misrata, you dog' were among the last words Gaddafi would hear before someone stepped forward and put a bullet into his head, ending the reign of the Arab world's longest-serving leader.

But that didn't end Libya's war with itself.

The revolution in Libya was unique among those of the Arab Spring because it was absolute. The young men fighting in towns and cities across the country were not using their weapons to fight a war *in* Libya, they were fighting a war *against* Libya, or rather they were fighting against 'The Great Socialist People's Libyan Arab Jamahiriya', which was what Colonel Muammar bin Mohammad bin Abdussalam bin Humayd bin Abu Manyar bin Humayd bin Nayil al Fuhsi Gaddafi, the 'Brother Leader', the 'King of Kings', the 'Guide of the Great Revolution', settled for on the fourth and final time he decided to rename his country. The young men knew what they were fighting against, but not what they were fighting for. And the longer the war went on, the more the loyalties of the young rebels drifted away from the already fragile idea of 'Libya' and settled instead with the men fighting alongside them and the town or city they were trying to defend.

But what happens when a young man is sent to war to destroy his own state? Once that has been achieved where does he place his loyalty? If he doesn't know what he is fighting for, how do you convince him the war is over? How does the new state persuade the young man to give up his gun? The new Libya has yet to come up with answers to the questions left over by the business of destroying the old.

During the forty-two years that Colonel Muammar Gaddafi exercised control he smothered all freedom of expression, political debate and normal civil society. The cult of Gaddafi went much deeper than that of any other Arab dictator. He had 'absolute, ultimate and unquestioned control' over Libya's state apparatus and its security forces, declared Judge Sanji Mmasenono Monageng in June 2011, when he read out the warrant for his arrest by the International Criminal Court in The Hague.

'The first thing he did was to attack the social structures, the social fabric of Libyan society,' Sami Khashkusha, professor of Politics at Tripoli University, told me after the war.

He did that by eliminating the role of the family. All allegiance was to Gaddafi and his ideology. And he did that systematically by starting with the family, then moving into the village and then reaching to the mosque and the clergy itself, depriving it of its direct influence on everyday life and people, and this way he managed to control the hearts and minds of the Libyan people.

An entire generation had, from the moment they were born, been taught that the 'Brother Leader' was infallible. He was not infallible but he was irreplaceable. The power vacuum created by his overthrow was enormous. No single person was big enough to fill his shoes.

'They are a big problem, I see them as small Gaddafis,' said Dr Abd-el Raouf of the young fighters strutting around the country after the civil war had ended. Dr Raouf worked in one of only two psychiatric hospitals in the whole country. He believes Libya will remain traumatised for many years, and that it has neither the resources nor the cultural willingness to recognise the scale of the problem. 'Most of the battles were fought by civilians, not soldiers, and they have suffered a lot. They've seen people killed in front of them. They experience sleep disorders, behavioural changes, and some have lost their minds.' The true number of post-traumatic stress cases was 'uncountable' he told me.

> I see ten to fifteen new cases each day. But because psychological problems are not recognised in this society, they are taboo, I think this is just the tip of the iceberg. The country has still not recognised the psychological impact of the war. It's a very, very huge problem. The young people who we need to build the country, they are lost. You don't need to rebuild the hospitals, or the cities, or the roads or houses. You need to rebuild the human beings, and it's difficult, it's going to take a long, long time to change their mentality, to change the way they think and to manage their problems.

Colonel Muammar Gaddafi spent his life creating a state as dysfunctional as he was. The civil war that killed him has only made that psychosis worse. The biggest problem facing Libya today is those small Gaddafis. They were a product of the forced union between disparate peoples.

The event that sparked the uprisings took place on 15 February 2011 after the arrest in the eastern city of Benghazi of a human rights lawyer, Fathi Terbil. He represented the families of prisoners massacred in 1996 by the Gaddafi regime at the Abu Salim prison in Tripoli. Inspired by the other revolts in Tunisia and Egypt, the protesters organised their own 'Day of Rage'. It took place across the country on 17 February 2011, and that is the day that Libyans see as the start of their revolution. Social media, as everywhere else, was its engine, much of it driven by Libyans in exile. People still refer to 'Feb 17th' as shorthand for their uprising and #Feb17 became its moniker on social networks throughout the civil war.

It was in Benghazi, the country's second-largest city, that the government first lost control and never got it back. It is Benghazi that was the birthplace of the 2011 uprising. But it was also the city that gave birth to Gaddafi's revolution. It was in its Military Academy, which he joined after attending secondary school in Misrata, that he met the men with whom he would later launch his coup. Benghazi was where the idea of his ascent took shape. But once he had taken control of the country he marginalised the city and the east of Libya in general, and thus sowed the seeds of his regime's collapse.

I did not know the name of the young man who was dying in the room next door, but I was watching a stream of snapshots of his life ebbing away while the door swung back and forth as the nurses rushed in and out. The doctor running the operating theatre in the small eastern Libyan desert town of Ajdabaya didn't know his name either when he came out covered in his blood to pronounce him dead.

The first law of warfare? Do not shoot yourself. During his short life the young man may have been a cherished son and a wonderful brother. As a soldier though he was an idiot. The kind of idiot who tries to clean his gun by banging it on the ground with the safety catch off, fires a bullet into his chest, and creates an exit wound in his neck from which he bleeds to death. And he was not alone. The eastern front line of the civil war was, by the spring of 2011, full of arrogant, incompetent rebel fighters roaming haplessly around with their guns slung low across their shoulders like electric guitars. And so too were the hospitals. These men were wasting their time. Some were wasting their lives.

Nobody seemed to be in command of the war effort. Diplomats joked to me at the time that the rebel leadership of the National Transitional Council or NTC, based in Benghazi, wanted the international community to overthrow Gaddafi for them. But the diplomats were missing the point. They weren't on the front line, so they couldn't see the kind of war that was being fought. The rebel fighters elsewhere in the country understood though. The east was never going to liberate the west. That simple truth revealed the tensions at the heart of Libyan society. They had existed before and during Gaddafi's rule. They were forged in the creation of the nation state, and they foreshadow many of the problems that will dog what comes in the post-war era.

In July 2011 I hitched a lift on the *Victory*, a boat taking aid across the Mediterranean from Malta and into the beleaguered city of Misrata. The rebels there first fought the Libyan army to a standstill along Tripoli Street in the heart of the city, and then slowly pushed them out. They did it largely on their own. NATO airstrikes were of little use, because it was impossible from the air to identify accurate targets in the urban centre. The people here knew they were in a fight to the death. During the stalemate of these late spring and early summer months there was speculation that the country could stay divided for years, with the Gaddafi clan holding the west and the Benghazi rebels the east. That would have left cities like Misrata, Zawiyah and the Nafusa mountain tribes firmly in the government camp.

The outcome of the whole civil war turned around Misrata. It was the only pocket of rebellion in western Libya that Gaddafi's troops failed to put down. His soldiers fought hard there because the Brother Leader would probably have settled for only having control of the west if that meant he could still survive the revolution. Without Misrata though he had nothing. It was politically and economically crucial. However there was a growing sense in the city that its survival was not at the top of the list of priorities for the new eastern bureaucrats in Benghazi.

The NTC was recognised early on in the revolution by the international community as the legitimate representative of the Libyan people. It also ran the country for the first ten months of the post-war era. After the war I met the man who became its prime minister, Mahmoud Jibril. He told me the NTC, as an organisation, was flawed from the start:

> When the NTC was composed there were no criteria, people didn't know each other, everyone came from a different city, they met for the first time at the NTC. We had different political orientations, different levels of education, different social backgrounds. They just met and agreed on one objective, 'getting rid of Gaddafi'. Other than that there was no common purpose whatsoever. Our differences came out clearly when Gaddafi was gone. We discovered we don't talk the same language. We have different perceptions of different things. Once I got angry with them at a meeting and I told them: 'You are like passengers on a bus. You met on the bus and you have nothing in common but this bus.'

Jibril fell out with his colleagues after the war. They accused him of trying to dominate the council. But the problems Jibril says became apparent only after the conflict were clearly visible at the time to those who did the fighting in Misrata. Guns were being sent from Benghazi, a local businessman who was helping to fund the war effort told me, but they came much quicker if money changed hands. The commanders in Misrata believed the Benghazi-based rebel leadership was too busy politicking to try to help liberate them too.

That deep sense of suspicion of the eastern rebels was shared elsewhere. 'We always tell the Benghazi rebels that they only fought for a week and then stopped,' a young man in Tripoli told me after the war. Some fighters did travel from Benghazi to fight in other areas, but there wasn't a flood of recruits. These deep historical regional strains had been suppressed by Gaddafi's rule, but the war to overthrow him unleashed and exacerbated them.

For most of the civil war the fighting on the eastern front oscillated up and down the road that ran along the Gulf of Sirte between and around Ras Lanuf and the equally tiny oil refinery town of Brega. They sat on either side of the southernmost tip of the Gulf, separated by 130 kilometres of desert. Just about the only place you could find easily on a map was a fork in the road, on the outskirts of Brega, where I would watch the rebels congregate each day. They would point their pickup trucks in the general direction of the town. On the back they had mounted rocket pods that had been ripped off the side of helicopters. Then they would shout 'Allahu Akbar' and fire them off. And no sooner had they done so than the Libyan army would start to pound the road junction with artillery fire. And the rebels would run away.

Once, as I followed them back, an artillery round landed just metres away from our car but then failed to explode. If it had done so all of us would have been blown to pieces. Instead we watched it bounce up and spiral away into the sand dunes to the right of us. We were all running away because, unlike the Misratans, the eastern fighters never dug in to hold ground and build for an offensive. Throughout the rest of the war the eastern rebels failed to push beyond Ras Lanuf. It only fell on 23 August. On that day I was with the fighters in the west as they overran Gaddafi's fortified Bab al-Aziziya compound in the capital Tripoli. Even at this late stage the eastern rebels didn't win Ras Lanuf, the disintegrating army gave it up. 'They just ran,' said a rebel spokesman in Benghazi.[1]

The military campaign run by the eastern leadership seemed as incompetent as it was at times comical to watch. But the fighters, too, seemed to lack not only the ability, but also the will. If the rebels in the west could capture the capital, why couldn't the eastern rebels during those five months take and hold a couple of one-horse towns in the middle of nowhere?

The fighters in the east stopped making gains exactly at the point along the coastline that had been the ancient boundary between

Cyrenaica and Tripolitania, the two biggest provinces. When I used to ask why they weren't making any movement forward the fighters would talk grandly about a 'big push' that would be launched in the next few days or weeks, which would sweep them down towards the Gaddafi clan's stronghold of Sirte. But the big push never came. Throughout the war the eastern rebels made no progress whatsoever beyond the boundaries of their old province. Their Libya had been liberated. Beyond Brega they were fighting for somebody else's turf.

The military failures of the then Benghazi-based leadership of the NTC would prove deadly in those summer months for the rebels hanging on in other parts of the country. It was something they would not forgive or forget later. It has still not been determined if this frustration was behind the mysterious assassination in July 2011 of General Abdul Fatah Younis, who had defected to the opposition and was in charge of their war effort.

During the Libyan civil war each town and city was largely left to liberate itself. That led to highly localised militias in each of those large towns or cities, which called themselves 'brigades'. The memory of that failure sustained the brigades afterwards. They were still supported by their local communities because they were drawn from the local people. They often concluded that if the centralised leadership couldn't be trusted to do the right thing during the war, why trust it to do so during the peace? And that meant the shape of that peace would often be in the hands of a bunch of armed and fractious militias. Sometimes, when they rubbed up against each other in the capital Tripoli, there were gun battles on the streets.

Libya's geography meant the war was largely fought along a fraction of its landmass, the coastline that stretches along the southern Mediterranean. The political divisions that exist in Libya post-Gaddafi are a simple consequence of the physical divisions between Libya's people. The country is huge, but most of it is desert. Even great lengths of the more fertile coastline are nothing but empty space. During the conflict it would stretch out before me for miles and then suddenly swallow the car up in a sandstorm, only to spit it out into a small patch of desert where the men were fighting and dying for a place you couldn't find on a map.

In the days of the Ottoman Empire the eastern region of what is now Libya, the province of Cyrenaica, looked further east to neighbouring Egypt. The western region of Libya called Tripolitania looked west to Tunisia. Until recent times they had little to do with each other. The remaining area of modern Libya, the province of Fezzan, which includes much of the Berber population, is part of the Sahara desert. It would become the last reluctant piece of the Libyan jigsaw.

The creation of Libya was the final act of the 'Scramble for Africa' that began in the early 1880s and three decades later had transformed the entire continent from indigenous rule to European domination. By the end of 1881, after France had grabbed Tunisia, Libya's three provinces were the only ones in North Africa not snatched by a European power.[2] At this time Libya's oil had not been discovered, so when the Italians began to wrestle the lands from the remnants of the Ottoman Empire in 1911 it must have felt to them like the best stuff had already gone to the British and the French. Libya was 'Largely desert with some limited potential for urban and sedentary life'.[3]

The Italian conquest was clumsy and brutal and was interrupted by the outbreak of the First World War. At this stage Rome, while neutral, leant towards the losing side. However in April 1915, under the secret 'Treaty of London', Article 13 promised that if the Italians agreed to break with their old German and Austro-Hungarian allies and entered the war on the opposing side, 'France and Great Britain [would] recognise to Italy . . . the right of demanding for herself certain compensations in the form of an extension of her possessions in Eritrea, Somaliland and Libya'.[4] So Italy got Libya, and the old provinces got 'Libya', a neologism the Italians created from the Greek word meaning the whole of North Africa except Egypt and which the Italians then used to describe their new possession. After 1934, by which time the three provinces were unified, 'Libya' was how the country would henceforth be internationally known.[5]

The Italians were kicked out of the country long before the oil started to flow, so they too must have wondered at times if it was worth fighting for. But fight they did, and – like colonialists everywhere – in battle they treated the local population with great cruelty, including the use of concentration camps. Italy, in the end, got little out of Libya apart from some misplaced pride about having a bit of an empire and a chunk of largely barren land on which to dump its own landless poor by the tens of thousands. Unlike other colonialists it did not co-opt, educate and train a section of the indigenous society to run things on its behalf. While this was never a noble gesture by occupiers, it did at least create a tier of locally administered bureaucracy that helped run the functions of a new state when the invaders packed up and left.

Italy did not try very hard to make any friends in Libya, and from the moment its naval contingent set foot on dry land in 1911 it was confronted with an insurgency that would take twenty years to put down. The Italians discovered what Colonel Gaddafi would find out in the century that followed: the only thing that can broadly unite Libyans, apart from their Sunni Muslim faith, is a common enemy. Ironically Gaddafi's troops would find themselves fighting against men who invoked the same symbol of resistance that inspired the guerrilla warfare against the Italians, and whose memory Gaddafi had always tried in the past to use to boost his own popularity.

Everywhere I went during the war, ninety years after the Italians began wandering these lands, I saw the image of the man who haunted them. It was carried by the early street protesters in Tripoli, on the front line in the east and in blockaded Misrata. On flags, on T-shirts and painted on the sides of their pickup trucks as fighters drove into battle was the bearded image of Omar Mukhtar. He was born in 1862 in a small village near Tobruk in Cyrenaica. He was a teacher of the Koran and belonged to the Senussi Muslim religious order that was founded in Mecca in 1837 by the Grand Senussi – Sayyid Muhammad ibn Ali as-Senussi. The Senussi order led the uprising against the Italians. They were the only institution in the three provinces organised enough to do so, but they were a firmly Cyrenaica-based order. Like the earlier teachings of Muhammad ibn Abd al-Wahhab in Saudi Arabia, the Grand Senussi sought to return to a purer form of Islam, though his teachings did not go on to produce in Libya today the kind of widespread, uncompromising Salafist groups that Wahhabism has in the rest of the modern Middle East. The Grand Senussi's revivalist, austere form of the faith appealed to the Bedouins of Cyrenaica whose own lives had not changed for generations.

The Ottoman Empire had been fairly hands-off in its administration of the three provinces and it was at least of the same faith. The Italians were quite definitely unendearing foreigners, and it wasn't hard for the Senussis to encourage revolt. By far the greatest leader of that resistance was Omar Mukhtar. From the moment he took up arms to the moment the Italians hanged him on 16 September 1931 he fought a campaign that embarrassed and undermined the occupying forces.

Finally capturing and killing Mukhtar didn't actually do the Italians any good, because his bravery and stoicism at the gallows became legendary, turning him into a martyr and a hero. He became so much a part of the Libyans' sense of themselves that Colonel Gaddafi reportedly bankrolled a 1981 Hollywood blockbuster called *Lion of the Desert*, starring Anthony Quinn as Omar Mukhtar and Oliver Reed as the 'evil' sixth governor of Libya, General Rodolfo Graziani. The film was immediately banned in Italy and only shown publicly in 2009 during an official visit by Muammar Gaddafi, during which he was photographed with what looked like a roughly crafted handmade badge of Omar Mukhtar pinned to his chest, opposite his medals, as he shook hands with the then Italian prime minister Silvio Berlusconi. The movie was played incessantly on Libyan TV under Gaddafi and it continued to be played in the areas that broke away from him. The only time I went into coffee shops during the war and found the TV was not showing the news it was showing *Lion of the Desert*.

If one world war gave Libya to Italy, the next took it away. After a long series of battles that would make then obscure cities like Tobruk household names in the UK and leave British war graves dotted along the coastline, the European allies ousted the Italians from the country in 1942. It then remained under the administration of the British and the French until the United Nations General Assembly voted in 1949 that within three years it should become an independent sovereign nation. According to Benjamin Higgins, the economist appointed by the UN in 1951 to work out a plan to develop the new nation: 'The establishment of the United Kingdom of Libya . . . [was] one of the boldest and most significant experiments ever undertaken by the United Nations Organization, or by the League of Nations that preceded it.'[6] It is fair to say that Professor Higgins was not overly hopeful. 'Libya is a gigantic "dustbowl",' he concluded in a report for UNESCO.[7] It is a damning indictment of Italian rule that he adds: 'Few countries in the world are less advanced economically, have a higher proportion of illiteracy, or have been longer under foreign domination than Libya.' 'The economy,' he said, 'offers discouragingly little with which to work.'

The man who was chosen to lead the newly created institution of a Libyan monarchy was the Amir of Cyrenaica, Sayyid Idris al-Senussi. The new King Idris, who was the grandson of the Grand Senussi, declared his country's independence on 24 December 1951. It was he that Gaddafi would depose. King Idris was the first Libyan ruler to inherit its oil wealth, and like the man who ousted him he didn't use it to build much of a state. One of his first acts as king just two months after declaring the nation's birth was to strangle its still nascent democracy. He cancelled the first and, until Gaddafi was overthrown, only multiparty elections the country had ever had.[8] For good measure he banned political parties too.

The new kingdom had two capitals, one in Tripoli and one in Benghazi. King Idris spent most of his time in the east. Not surprisingly he was unable to build a sense of nationalism around the institution of the monarchy. What he did preside over was a widespread theft of the nation's wealth. There is an argument among historians about how heavily involved King Idris was in the corruption that swirled through his court once the oil money flowed in.

There is much less debate over its scale. It was endemic. After the death in a car crash of a senior member of the family running the royal household, there was panic among the expat oil executives. One American oilman recalled that the accident 'created real uncertainty about who to bribe'.[9]

Gaddafi arrived on the international stage on 1 September 1969 at the head of a bloodless coup mounted against King Idris by a group of young army officers. Gaddafi certainly looked the part then. He was handsome: square-jawed with a wide smile revealing lots of shiny white teeth. He was the epitome of the dashing young officer, so much so that the British painter Francis Bacon declared that if he had the chance to sleep with anyone in the world, 'I'd like to get into bed with Colonel Gaddafi.'[10]

Colonel Gaddafi wanted to get into bed with the rest of the Arab world, and following Nasser's death, a year after Gaddafi came to power, he tried many times over several years to refashion Arab nationalism in his own image through abortive attempts at mergers or federations with, variously, Egypt, Syria, Sudan and Tunisia. But despite his best efforts he and his country were never really treated as equals by the leading countries in the Arab world. Geography is often a defining factor in the power plays in the Middle East. The closer the country is to the religious and political fault lines that fracture their way through the region, the more influence that nation often has. Libya is physically, and so always has been politically, on the margins. Gaddafi may have considered himself a natural replacement for his hero Nasser, but nobody else in the Arab world did. He became so frustrated by their lack of respect that he turned inward to realise his ambitions and developed a cult of personality at home like no other in the Arab world.

At first Gaddafi and his 'Free Officers Movement' were largely welcomed by the Libyan people. For the first few years there wasn't very much that was radical about their domestic agenda. The old guard left over from the monarchy was slowly replaced, but they weren't all put up against a wall and shot. The country's new governing body, the

Revolutionary Command Council (RCC), of which Gaddafi was the chairman, all came from middle-class or poor backgrounds. None of them had had any experience running a bureaucracy. They tinkered around creating a more open environment for business, and significantly they began to invest the country's oil wealth in education and health, areas long neglected by all the country's previous rulers. But when it came to relations with the outside world they were more ambitious. One of the RCC's first acts was to serve notice on the foreign soldiers still on Libyan soil. King Idris had agreed to allow Britain and the US to establish military bases in return for substantial rent during the Cold War era. Unlike the king, Gaddafi did not want their money, their friendship or their people anywhere near him. He threw them all out. And as he tore up the old agreements with the Western powers he began to rewrite the rule book for their oil men.

Because Libya came late to the oil game it learned from the mistakes made by other producers in the region. Its 1955 Petroleum Law gave most of the concessions to small independents rather than the majors. 'I did not want Libya to begin as Iraq or as Saudi Arabia or as Kuwait,' explained the then Libyan oil minister. 'I didn't want my country to be in the hands of one oil company.'[11] That decision would prove to be incredibly influential in the coming years. Apart from an historical perspective, Libya's oil managers also had two other key things going for them. Their oil was on the Mediterranean coast, so it didn't need long pipelines or to travel through the Suez Canal on its way to the market. It was also of a very high quality and there was lots of it. By bullying the smaller companies who often had most of their eggs in the Libyan basket the country undercut the bigger players. During the monarchy, oil was exploited only for its economic benefits. Gaddafi identified its political value.

To force the oil companies in Libya to push up their prices and thus increase Libya's revenue, the Colonel threatened in 1970 to stop production, declaring: 'People who have lived without oil for 5,000 years can live without it again for a few years in order to attain their legitimate rights.'[12] Daniel Yergin in his masterful history of the oil industry, *The Prize*, described how the negotiations were led on the Libyan side by the deputy prime minister, Abdel Salaam Ahmed Jalloud, who 'charged into a room full of oil executives with a submachine gun slung over his shoulder'. During another meeting he 'unbuckled his belt and set down his .45 revolver' on the table directly in front of his Western counterpart.[13]

Colonel Gaddafi may have been crazy but he was not a fool. He had all sorts of crackpot ideas and wrecked almost every institution of state, but he was smart enough to leave this one alone. The oil industry he inherited was brilliantly structured to maximise the country's control over its greatest asset. Under Gaddafi the way Libya played the international market would revolutionise the whole oil industry and put more and more power into the hands of the Middle Eastern producers.

Back then the Suez Canal was still closed, as an aftermath of the 1967 war, and the European capitals were getting 30 per cent of their oil from the Colonel's wells.[14] Gaddafi's hand was further strengthened because the appetite for oil in the West by the start of the Seventies was huge. When Prime Minister Mossadegh of Iran nationalised the Anglo-Iranian Oil Company in 1951 the West could absorb the blow and then engineer a coup to depose him. But oil consumption in the West had quadrupled by 1970. Tripoli used its position in the market to change the relationship between the industry and the oil-producing nations for ever. The oil companies were 'whipsawed by Libya', wrote Walter J. Levy, a leading petroleum specialist.[15] 'The oil industry as we had known it would not exist much longer,' reflected another American oilman. George Williamson of Occidental turned to a colleague as he prepared to put his signature to an agreement and said: 'Everybody who drives a tractor, truck or car in the Western world will be affected by this.'[16] He was right. There was a rush of demand for renegotiating deals from the other members of OPEC, the Organisation of the Petroleum Exporting Countries. By the time the Arab–Israeli war of 1973 was under way, the oil producers, thanks to Gaddafi, had their new weapon to wield against the West and reshape the political order.

*   *   *

Oil can be a financial blessing for a nation but too much of it can be a curse. While nobody likes to pay taxes, they do create an element of accountability between the people and their rulers. But look across the oil-producing nations of the Middle East, and it is clear that where money just gushes from the ground, leaders are likely to conclude they can spend it as they like. Gaddafi used his oil money to sate his desire to be taken seriously. He began diverting his windfall from the October 1973 oil 'supply shock' into sustaining and developing the political experiment he had unveiled to his supporters earlier that year. It was, Gaddafi would opine modestly later, 'the way to direct democracy based on the magnificent and practical system: the Third Universal Theory' about which 'no two reasonable adults can possibly disagree'.[17]

In April 1973 he had declared his own 'cultural revolution', using 'popular' committees in schools, universities and the workplace to 'govern' locally. These groups became the regime's eyes and ears on the ground, and until his rule was ended they helped root out and suppress democrats, Islamists or anyone else who didn't like the way the country was being run. Like China's Chairman Mao, Gaddafi would, over the next few years, collect his pearls of wisdom to guide the nation in a little book, though the Colonel's was green, not red. The colour green would soon be everywhere.

If there was any doubt in anyone's mind before he published the contents of the Green Book that Gaddafi was unorthodox in his approach to politics, they were in no doubt afterwards. It was all there in black and white: everything from menstruation to monetary policy. It was full of his homespun logic couched in convoluted, confusing prose which posed as the language of academia but which was often just very odd.

'Women, like men, are human beings. This is an incontestable truth,' Gaddafi informed the world. 'Women are female and men are male. According to gynecologists women, unlike men, menstruate each month.' 'Like men,' we learn, women also 'live and die'.[18]

Under the heading 'Parliaments', Gaddafi states that parliament 'is a misrepresentation of the people'. Much of his book was self-indulgent drivel – 'Freedom of expression is the right of every natural person, even if a person chooses to behave irrationally to express his or her insanity.'[19] But each piece of airy rhetoric changed people's lives. Gaddafi declared that people must be 'Masters in their own homes'.[20] The consequence of this was that anyone living in a rented property suddenly became the property's owner, causing a flurry of rows after the revolution when people tried to reclaim their houses. Paying someone a wage was 'virtually the same as enslaving a human being'.[21] Almost overnight Gaddafi wiped out private enterprise, the lifeblood of modern economies. It was economic suicide, but Gaddafi didn't need an economy, he had oil.

The Colonel's brave new world finally took form on 2 March 1977, when his General People's Congress adopted the 'Declaration of the Establishment of the People's Authority'. This was the moment from which Gaddafi would forever state that he stopped ruling the nation and had handed authority to the people. He would always contend that from this day he was no longer running Libya, the members of the GPC were. He castigated world leaders during the civil war who called for him to step down because, he said, he had nothing to step down from.

The last time the GPC would ever meet was exactly thirty-four years later, on 2 March 2011. It held this gathering in a plush conference centre because its own building had been burnt down during the first wave of protests in the capital Tripoli. This gathering would also prove to be the last time Muammar Gaddafi felt safe enough in his own country to turn up for a scheduled event, because, as it turned out, the start of the NATO air campaign against him was just two weeks away.

Waiting patiently among the two thousand other delegates I found Mariam Ibrahim Gurgi. She was one of the people's representatives for Tripoli. Sitting resplendent in a sparkling green scarf, she told me why everyone in the hall was so excited: 'Most or all of the people and their children love Muammar Gaddafi from their hearts, from the bottom of their hearts, really. We have no problems. We have our freedoms already. Thanks to God we are living in heaven. Everything is very good.'

Then to Mariam's and apparently everyone else's delight, Gaddafi arrived. To my bemusement he arrived driving a brand-new golf buggy, the front seat draped with a white sheepskin rug. He parked up and then struggled his way through a swarm of photographers, his hands pumping the air triumphantly. He climbed onto the podium to a rock-star reception. His burly security team linked arms to hold back the media and some large and persistent female supporters began barrelling into the crowd, pushing and shoving with all their might, trampling through a carefully arranged floral decoration set out on the floor in front of him. Other equally enthusiastic women climbed on their seats and their ululations punctuated his speech. Occasionally he paused to allow a few minutes of chants and cheers, and then he would tap his microphone when he was ready for them to shut up. And, shut up they promptly did. All except one woman who indulged in something my officially provided translator described as 'freestyle poetry' in praise of her leader. He'd clearly had enough, because someone turned off her microphone and led her back to her seat so he could continue his unscripted monologue.

Gaddafi talked for nearly three hours. And then he stopped, got up and left, surrounded once again by a scrum of media and security. The people he left behind in the conference centre were supposed to be the real rulers of the country. They were the closest thing the nation had to parliamentarians, but they were a long way from being lawmakers. Their real value to the state became apparent only when I was bussed around by the government to various parts of the capital to attend allegedly spontaneous demonstrations in support of the regime. The delegates of the General People's Congress were the Colonel's rent-a-mob. Time and again I saw the same 'locals', in particular the ululating ladies, whenever a pro-government rally was held. They were kissing newly printed posters of the 'Brother Leader' and chanting 'Allah, Muammar, Libya, wa bass,' which translates as: 'All we need is God, Gaddafi and Libya.' Everyone present knew it was theatre. But though the system of political representation introduced by Gaddafi may have been a masquerade, the consequences of not playing along with it were deadly serious.

'Held in this section was the martyr Muhammad Muftah Anis Abu-Ras, an aviation engineer at the Libyan airline company, one of its most competent engineers,' said the writing in Arabic on the prison wall.

> He was arrested in 1989 at four a.m. when he was going to morning prayers at the mosque. He was brought home after forty days in bad shape during a search order. We haven't seen him since that day. He is one of the best people of [the district of] Maslana. He was one of those people who memorised God's book [the Koran]. He left his daughter when she was nine months and his son was three years. They had grown up dreaming that one day they might see him. But God had chosen him to be with the martyrs. We pray for them and may God give them his mercy.

These words were scribbled on 29 June 2012 on the wall of the exercise yard of a wing of Abu Salim prison on the outskirts of Tripoli. It was the first opportunity Muhammad's family would have had to publicly commemorate his death exactly sixteen years earlier. The sun was shining down through the grille that covered the long narrow rectangular exercise area where I was reading the tribute. There were three high walls in front of me. The fourth led back to the cells. There was nothing in the courtyard but a large floor-level basin tucked away in the corner where the men would have been able to wash before they prayed.

Many of the hundreds of men who were all to die alongside Muhammad would no doubt have been doing just that, thanking God for the small victory they thought they had won the previous day to improve their conditions in what was Libya's most notorious detention centre. As they looked up to the heavens seeking His blessing before they prepared to prostrate themselves, they would have noticed that on this day 29 June 1996 there were more guards standing on top of the walls than normal. This may not have surprised them because the day before there had been protests in the jail in which two guards were captured, one of whom was killed. The guards in return had killed six inmates. The following morning though, Muhammad would have been told by his fellow inmates that the crisis had been resolved because the country's intelligence chief, Abdullah al-Senussi, who was also Gaddafi's brother-in-law, had agreed to their demands. Then as Muhammad stood in the yard the large steel door through which I had entered was clanged shut. The inmates, who were suddenly penned in, would have heard the weapons now turned towards them from above being cocked. They would have known that at this moment they would need God's mercy more than at any other time in their lives. Many would have begun to say the Shahadah, the basic statement of Islamic faith. And as they did so the guards opened fire.

In total more than twelve hundred men were massacred over those two days.[22] It made al-Senussi one of the most hated and feared men in the country. He was indicted in June 2011 along with Gaddafi for crimes against humanity. If he had been caught during the war he would have been killed like Gaddafi. Instead he fled and was later extradited back to Libya from Mauritania to stand trial for his crimes.

Many of the men who were killed at Abu Salim were rounded up because they were suspected of being members of the Muslim Brotherhood, a group Gaddafi saw rightly as a potential challenge to his rule. That didn't mean the inmates *were* associated with the Brotherhood. They may have just been openly religious, or they may have been privately religious and been snitched on by the country's army of informers. Perhaps they were secular and unlucky. Gaddafi and his security chief were not inclined to take chances. If there was doubt they would kill just to be on the safe side. That meant very few real Brotherhood activists slipped through the net. The Brotherhood was devastated during the Gaddafi era. That was part of the reason why Libya bucked the regional trend during its first post-revolution elections. Unlike in Egypt and Tunisia, the Islamists had no base at all to build on, and their candidates did badly.

Gaddafi did not just go after the Islamists; his regime routinely jailed, tortured, 'disappeared' or had executed anyone who opposed it. And his reach extended well beyond his borders. In the 1980s he sent execution squads abroad to hunt down his opponents, or what he called 'stray dogs', and murder them in their European homes. He said in October 1982 of those who had fled from his regime: 'They should be killed not because they constitute any danger, but because of their high treason. It is the Libyan people's responsibility to liquidate such scum who are distorting Libya's image.'[23]

But Gaddafi went after the religious groups because they did constitute a danger, though he eventually realised that his fear and loathing of them finally gave him something in common with the nations that had denounced him for decades. 'Libya has been a strong partner in the war against terrorism and cooperation in liaison channels is excellent,' a secret US embassy diplomatic cable said in 2008.[24] This partnership would produce some red faces in Western capitals after he was overthrown, because it also involved doing some of these governments' dirty work. That led to the torture of people who were the subject of illegal rendition. The details started spilling out after the war once the rebels found all the paperwork in his abandoned intelligence centres. The first government forced into offering up compensation was the UK, which paid out £2.2 million in December 2012 to settle a claim by a Libyan dissident who said Britain's intelligence service, MI6, was involved in the kidnapping and transportation of him, his wife and four children to Libya, where he was tortured by the regime.[25]

Even though Gaddafi's brutality was suddenly useful to Western governments towards the end of his rule, his absolution was not an overnight process, because of all the Arab leaders he had the most to atone for.

Some of Gaddafi's worst crimes took place on the continent he turned to when he grew frustrated by the lack of respect he won from his Arab compatriots. In 1995 he had even expelled 30,000 Palestinians in protest over the Oslo accords. Three years later, with his ambitions in the Arab world completely foiled and his revolution back home tarnished, Gaddafi looked south. 'I had been crying slogans of Arab Unity and brandishing the standard of Arab nationalism for 40 years, but it was not realised. That means that I was talking in the desert,' he said. 'I have no more time to lose talking with Arabs . . . I now talk about Pan-Africanism and African Unity . . . the Arab world is finished.'[26]

Gaddafi's new project wasn't starting from scratch though. He'd been throwing money around the continent to win friends for decades. He found buying influence in dirt-poor Africa much easier than earning it in the much richer Middle East. For years Gaddafi had been presenting himself as the supporter of worthy struggles for liberation in places like the then Rhodesia and apartheid South Africa. Some of those he had championed went on to become the leaders of their new nations, most notably Nelson Mandela. So grateful was Mr Mandela that even when the leader of the anti-apartheid struggle became the darling of the West he refused to turn his back on his old ally and rebuked President Bill Clinton, declaring: 'No country can claim to be the policeman of the world and no state can dictate to another what it should do. Those that yesterday were friends of our enemies have the gall today to tell me not to visit my brother Gaddafi. They are advising us to be ungrateful and forget our friends of the past.'[27] When Gaddafi's regime began to crumble in 2011 it was only the African Union that even bothered to push a half-hearted compromise solution that would have kept him in power.

But the Colonel's influence in Africa had always been far from benign. For years 'Big Man' politics dominated Africa, and it bred leaders like Idi Amin and Mobutu Sese Seko, who were so ruthless and demented they rivalled Gaddafi. What they couldn't match was the oil wealth that he used to bankroll his foreign adventures. These included undermining his nearest African neighbours, but it was through his 'World Revolutionary Headquarters' in Benghazi that

Gaddafi did most of his damage in the continent and beyond. It was what the historian Stephen Ellis described as 'the Harvard and Yale of a whole generation of African revolutionaries'.[28] Some of these men would go on to carry out some of the worst atrocities the African continent has ever known. In West Africa Gaddafi's Libya helped fuel and fund the civil war in Sierra Leone. The country's rebel Revolutionary United Front leader, Foday Sankoh, whose men butchered their way through the country, met his partner in crime Charles Taylor, from neighbouring Liberia, while they were both in Libya. Gaddafi's regime directly provided the funds for Foday Sankoh to buy weapons. I saw for myself the consequences of that when I reported from the country in the final years of the civil war. The refugee camps in the Sierra Leonean capital Freetown were full of men, women, children and even babies who had had arms and legs hacked off by Sankoh's soldiers.

Alongside groups from Africa and Asia, Gaddafi funded and trained gunmen from the likes of the Irish Republican Army, Germany's Baader-Meinhof gang, Italy's Red Brigades and the Spanish Basque separatist group ETA.[29] In fact there was barely an armed militant group anywhere in the world during the Seventies and Eighties that Gaddafi wasn't willing to back. If you were an enemy of Western interests you were a friend of his, and his money flowed instantly towards your cause. It was the bloody trail he left in the Western world that brought him his international infamy and the attention he so craved.

Gaddafi began to consolidate Libya's rogue-nation status in April 1984 with the murder of a young British policewoman, Yvonne Fletcher. She was shot dead by a gun fired from the Libyan embassy in London at an anti-Gaddafi rally being held outside. Two years later US President Ronald Reagan bombed his Bab al-Aziziya compound after accusing his regime of being behind a bomb attack on US soldiers in a nightclub in Berlin. It was at this time he earned Reagan's 'Mad Dog of the Middle East' label. But it was the bombing of Pan Am flight 103 over the Scottish town of Lockerbie as it carried its largely American passengers home for Christmas in 1988 that put

Gaddafi at the top of the Western world's most wanted list. It was a spot he would hang on to until Osama bin Laden made his entrance on the world stage.

Two hundred and seventy people died when the Boeing 747 exploded in mid-air and crashed onto the small town below. It was the worst atrocity against US civilians in the nation's history, and was only superseded by the attacks on 9/11. Two Libyans were indicted by the US and Scottish authorities, and the international sanctions that followed, until the men were handed over, began to cripple the regime. Gaddafi's government, however, never admitted being behind the bombing. The closest it came was in a letter in August 2003 to the United Nations Security Council in which its envoy Ahmed Own wrote: 'Libya as a sovereign state has facilitated the bringing to justice of the two suspects charged with the bombing of Pan Am 103, and accepts responsibility for the actions of its officials.'[30] The Libyan government also renounced terrorism and promised to pay US$2.7 billion in compensation to the victims.[31]

In the end only one of the two men indicted, Abdelbaset al-Megrahi, was found guilty. He was freed from a Scottish jail in 2009 on compassionate grounds because he was expected to die, within weeks, of cancer. In the end he outlived Gaddafi and his regime and died in Tripoli in May 2012. Many assumed that the prospect of finding out the whole truth of what happened over Lockerbie probably died then too. In his last interview al-Megrahi said: 'I am an innocent man. I am about to die and I ask now to be left in peace with my family.'[32]

The Syrians were among those first blamed for the bombing. After the Libyan indictments President George Bush said in 1991: 'A lot of people thought it was Syrians [but] the Syrians took a bum rap on this.'[33] Some family members of the victims of the Pan Am bombing remained unconvinced of Syria's innocence. The fall of the Assad regime, like the fall of Gaddafi's, may throw up new evidence.

Though Gaddafi's was, pointedly, only a partial admission of guilt over the bombing it was a watershed moment for his regime, because it was enough to begin his rehabilitation. The overthrow of Saddam

Hussein had focused the Colonel's mind. Months later he abandoned his own programme to develop weapons of mass destruction. This eventually brought Gaddafi back in from the cold and earned him visits to his tent from a host of world leaders, including famously Britain's Tony Blair.

The person he 'desperately' wanted to meet though was his 'African Princess'. Gaddafi 'had a slightly eerie fascination with me personally', wrote Condoleezza Rice after she became the first US secretary of state to visit the country since 1953. It was, she acknowledged, 'a major milestone on the country's path to international acceptability'. Rice though 'declined' to meet him in his tent. After dinner she had what she described as an 'Uh oh' moment when Gaddafi announced he had made a videotape of her. 'It was a quite innocent collection of photos of me with world leaders . . . set to the music of a song called "Black Flower in the White House," written for me by a Libyan composer. It was weird, but at least it wasn't raunchy.'[34]

Gaddafi was past his prime. His charms were now incapable of seducing anyone. But with the sense that time was running out on the elder Gaddafi's era, the Western world did start courting his second son, Saif al-Islam.

Saif looked the part. He was urbane, had a doctorate from the London School of Economics and, compared with his father, was articulate. He said the right things about economic liberalisation and took steps to improve the country's human rights record. Even those in the capital Tripoli who opposed his father had begun to put their hope in Saif. As it turned out, Saif's attempt to present himself as a champion of reform was as dodgy as the means by which he obtained his Ph.D. An inquiry later found he got his staff to do a lot of the research for him.[35]

Before the uprising many Libyans wanted to believe in Saif largely because he wasn't his brother Mutassim. Mutassim, who would eventually be captured and killed in Sirte along with his father, was considered to be a chip off the old block.

Gaddafi had five other sons and a daughter. Mohammed, the eldest son, headed the Libyan Olympic Committee, and the post and telecommunications network. Then there was Saif al-Islam, followed by Saadi Gaddafi. Saadi became famous for being rumoured to be the only player in history to have paid his team to allow him to play professional football rather than the other way around. He had brief and undistinguished stints at various clubs in the Italian football league and captained the Libyan national side regardless of his form. Mutassim was the fourth son, then came Hannibal, who was the reason his father petitioned the United Nations for the abolition of Switzerland. This followed the arrest of Hannibal and his pregnant wife, a former lingerie model, in Geneva 2008 for beating up two of their servants. Though they were soon released and the charges dropped, the Colonel took his son's detention very personally. He withdrew millions of dollars he had stashed away in Swiss bank accounts, halted oil exports to them and for good measure held two hapless Swiss nationals hostage. His onslaught continued until he had the 'Swiss literally bending over backwards to assuage Libyan demands'.[36]

Saif al-Arab, the sixth son, had the lowest profile and was said to have found religion. He died in a NATO airstrike in April 2011. The youngest son was Khamis, who had a reputation for brutality and was in charge of the elite 32 Brigade stationed close to the capital. He was hated by the opposition, which triumphantly announced his death on four different occasions during the war.

Gaddafi's only daughter, Aisha, was a lawyer, and part of the team that unsuccessfully defended Saddam Hussein after he was tried in Iraq following his overthrow. She was ironically a United Nations Goodwill Ambassador.

When I was in Tripoli in October 2010 it was rife with rumour and gossip about which of his sons was being groomed to replace him. The locals examined the size and positioning of the boys' faces on government posters to work out who was most likely to come next. Exactly one year later the capital had its answer. None of them. His sons were dead, on the run, or in jail. The government officials who had swaggered around their offices that winter offering me tea with one hand and throwing brickbats with the other had fled. When I left Tripoli at the end of October 2010 I had no idea that I would be back just a few months later to witness the final chapter of the longest-running, most murderous Middle Eastern soap opera of modern times. I also had no idea that my return would start with an audience with its star.

Gaddafi was one of the hardest people to meet in the world, so I expected to be taken to a secret location, or perhaps a grand pavilion in the desert. Instead our rendezvous was a seaside restaurant in downtown Tripoli. I was watching the sun starting to slip over the horizon on a spring evening in 2011 when I realised all the traffic had disappeared. Suddenly there was a row of cars, lights flashing as they hurtled along the road. One pulled up and from it emerged Muammar Gaddafi, his eyes hidden behind a pair of gold Cartier sunglasses. He was strident and grand. His brown flowing robes gave off the light scent of sandalwood. He took his seat and spoke for more than an hour.

'I don't like money,' he said. 'I have a tent.' One look at his black leather cowboy boots and you could have been fooled into believing he was telling the truth. The soles were cracked and pitted. The heels were worn. The millions he had squirrelled away were clearly not being spent on his shoes. His long rambling speeches on Libyan state TV have made many people question his sanity, but throughout the meeting he was confident, lucid and robust. I did not think he was crazy. But he was clearly out of touch.

The interview had been given to Marie Colvin of the *Sunday Times*, but the regime wanted TV cameras there too, as part of their media offensive. Marie suggested the BBC and America's ABC. She and I then sat in the Rixos Hotel with Muhammad Abdullah al-Senussi, the son of the intelligence chief, to negotiate the details. Muhammad had a bushy black beard that covered most of his fleshy young face. His nose was broad and flat like his father's. Whenever we met he was wearing green army fatigues, and over his tight curly hair he wore a beret of the revolutionary freedom fighter style. He looked like he'd ordered his outfit from central casting, but for a man born into one of the most murderous regimes in modern history he was surprisingly engaging. At this stage he had refused to tell me his full name. Sometimes he was 'Abdullah', sometimes 'Muhammad'. Only a few days later, when he got angry over media reports that his father might have defected, did he reveal what I already knew. 'Why are you all reporting that my father has defected?' he shouted at me. 'He is in his office now, I just spoke to him.' Muhammad was later reported to have died in a NATO airstrike alongside Gaddafi's youngest son Khamis, though neither one's body was identified.

When the interview took place Colonel Gaddafi had already lost the eastern side of the country. But he knew who was to blame, he said: 'It's al-Qaeda. It's not my people. They came from outside.' His détente with Western governments had come from the post-9/11 era when being against al-Qaeda covered a multitude of sins. It was a card he still hoped he could play. The same claim would be made, a year later, by the Syrian president Bashar al-Assad to explain his plight, though Gaddafi made it sound less convincing. He had already told Libyan state television that the protesters had become the unwitting pawns of terrorists who had provoked them into rebellion by putting 'hallucinatory pills in their drinks, their milk, coffee, their Nescafe'.

They did come from outside, but it wasn't al-Qaeda, it was Qatar. It gave US$400 million to arm and train the rebels and, said a US Senate Foreign Relations Committee report, 'provided Special Forces to lead the rebels in their August 2011 assault on Tripoli . . . one U.S. military official described Qatar's overall political and military contribution to the Libya effort as "nothing short of decisive." '[37] But it did not stop there. 'The Qataris kept sending very sophisticated weapons to some groups even after Gaddafi's death,' a senior Arab diplomat told me. 'It wasn't just for the sake of the Libyans and their freedoms. They have another agenda.'

But as the Qataris were gearing up for their latest regional power play, Gaddafi seemed to me to be blind to the possibility he might lose. During the interview the Brother Leader's body language made it obvious that he was a man who was not used to being challenged. His feet rocked and tapped in apparent agitation as he listened to the questions and only calmed down when he got his chance to respond. At his most angry he switched from Arabic into English. Halfway through the interview the sunglasses came off. But when he left he took the time to shake all our hands and posed for a few photographs. He even briefly began to put his arm around my shoulders. 'They love me. All my people are with me, they love me all. They will die to protect me, my people,' he had told us. 'No one is against me, no demonstrations at all in the streets.' I'm sure he believed every word he was saying. But at the time you only had to drive twenty kilometres from where he was sitting to find people willing to say openly that they wanted him and his family strung up.

'I came back to Libya from Wales where I was living and working on February 20, 2011,' Nizar Mahni told me in the capital Tripoli the year after the uprising.

> At that stage we were still in a phase where peaceful demonstrations seemed to be the way forward. We were taking our inspiration from Egypt and Tunisia. But when you see people being gunned down in the street, when you see injuries that you can't even comprehend, people with holes in their bodies, it begins to become apparent that standing in the street waving banners and flags is just not going to cut it.

Nizar witnessed these scenes on the same day I was covering another opposition demonstration in Tripoli where, because of the presence of the international media, the security forces limited themselves to rubber bullets and tear gas. During the war the vast majority of Gaddafi's intelligence and security apparatus was concentrated around the capital. Nizar, who had been training as a dentist, and his friends were driven underground by the regime's violence. They started a dangerous campaign of covert disobedience to raise the morale of the capital's population and helped run guns while they waited for the tide to turn and for the city to rise up, as it did on 20 August 2011. They styled themselves the 'Free Generation Movement'.

> It was an attempt to show that opposition existed in Tripoli. So we were rigging up speakers in and around Tripoli blasting out the [old] national anthem, which was punishable by life imprisonment even before the war. We bought speakers and fitted timers to them and recorded the national anthem on a loop. And we timed the speakers to set off ten minutes after we had placed them in strategic locations having hidden them in rubbish bags.

They placed cameras in tissue boxes and left them in abandoned cars so they could film the swarm of armed security men who arrived to rummage through the trash trying to stop the noise. They also systematically burned the huge images of Gaddafi dotted around the city, flew the independence flag and dropped leaflets. It was very dangerous, and if they had been caught they would have ended up either in one of Gaddafi's prisons or dead.

Gaddafi had already made it clear he would brook no dissent. He promised that during a typically long rambling speech on 22 February in which he warned: 'I and the millions will march in order to cleanse Libya, inch by inch, house by house, home by home, alleyway by alleyway, individual by individual, so that the country is purified from the unclean.' The 'alleyway by alleyway' reference, or 'zenga zenga' in Arabic, fast became the spoof catchphrase of the war. It was even remixed by an Israeli DJ into a dance track that was watched by millions of people in the region on YouTube.

According to a source who witnessed events first-hand, Gaddafi gathered his family around him in the Bab al-Aziziya compound for regular consultations once the uprising was under way. In the run-up to this he had barely been on speaking terms with Saif al-Islam, but as the family rallied he asked Saif to deal with what one family member described as 'the mob and the media'. By that he meant the opposition and the first waves of international media, including myself, who were invited into Tripoli.

A witness inside the compound at the time described how the hardliners on one side and Saif on the other each lobbied Gaddafi over the action he should take. Gaddafi at first believed the uprisings in Benghazi would fizzle out once people had burnt a few cars and made some noise. He did not expect the revolution to take hold. The atmosphere inside the compound became increasingly tense as the family realised its grip on the country was slipping away. To stem that, according to the source who witnessed the conversation, Saif al-Islam was told directly by his father to deliver the rant on state TV in which he famously wagged his finger at the nation promising 'rivers of blood' and that the regime 'will keep fighting until the last man standing'. When Saif was finally caught, that finger was missing. The story goes that the rebels who found him cut it off before they handed the rest of him over alive and intact. Saif, like his father's henchman, Abdullah al-Senussi, was also to be tried and punished in Libya.

Saif al-Islam's TV appearance on 20 February, three days after the uprising began, was an important moment for the opposition too. That bellicose a speech from the moderate face of the regime shocked those who had placed any faith in him. It prompted the creation of the organisation that would lead the opposition through the civil war and into the post-Gaddafi era.

Watching Saif wag his finger was Mahmoud Jibril, who was at the time in Oman. Until the uprising Jibril had been the head of Libya's National Economic Development Board, which was created by Saif al-Islam and was part of his reform programme. 'After the speech by Saif al-Islam when he started threatening a civil war will take place and mass immigration would be flooding Europe and the oil will be cut, I believed that this speech might touch a certain nerve in European countries and the West in general, and so we needed to put down those fears,' he told me after the war.

I decided that there should be a body talking to the world, a head for this revolution, and especially when you looked at the Egyptian and Tunisian cases. They had floods of people in the streets but they had no leadership. That's why their revolution was stolen so early. So I consulted with some of [the Libyan] ambassadors and I wrote the proposals for the National Transitional Council [NTC].

Jibril went on to become the opposition's prime minister and its chief negotiator with the outside world. In response Saif al-Islam declared that Jibril had betrayed him 'big time'.[38]

Unfortunately for Gaddafi, it wasn't only the opposition that was listening to the rhetoric coming out of Tripoli. After years of wanting to be centre stage he now really did have the world's attention. His threats led to a vote in the United Nations Security Council on 17 March 2011 on UN Resolution 1973, which authorised members 'to establish a ban on all flights in the airspace of the Libyan Arab Jamahiriya in order to help protect civilians' and to 'protect civilians and civilian populated areas under threat of attack in the Libyan Arab Jamahiriya, including Benghazi'.

Despite their reservations, both Russia and China decided to abstain rather than veto it, partly because the Arab League supported it and they still hadn't realised it was now being run by the GCC. The mandate from UN Resolution 1973, which authorised member states 'to take all necessary measures . . . to protect civilian and civilian populated areas', was eventually stretched so tight by the Western powers that you could get a tune out of it.

Russia and China both felt completely suckered. 'The international community unfortunately did take sides in Libya,' said the Russian foreign minister Sergei Lavrov afterwards, 'and we would never allow the Security Council to authorise anything similar to what happened in Libya.'[39] So the following year, when the West tried for a resolution to start taking action against Syria, the Russians and Chinese were having none of it. They both vetoed the resolution. Saving lives in Libya ended up costing thousands more in Syria.

The first airstrikes on Gaddafi's forces by NATO took place within forty-eight hours. If Benghazi had fallen at the start of the uprising then the country's revolt would have been over and the streets would have run with blood. A few weeks later, as I drove out of the city towards the eastern front lines, the burned carcasses of tanks and armoured personnel carriers still littered the roads. The NATO intervention was unquestionably the deciding factor in Libya's civil war. The conflict cost almost ten thousand lives; without foreign intervention it would have cost many more. But for the revolution to be complete, one life in particular had to be taken.

Muammar Gaddafi lay before me on a dirty brown mattress, his body partially covered by a blue and white woollen blanket. A patch of blood had trickled from the bullet wound in his temple. Grainy mobile phone footage shot by his captors had shown his final moments in Sirte where he was slapped and dragged around by the baying mob as he told them: 'God forbids this, what are you doing?'

His now silent face was turned towards me as I entered the shipping container. Outside, waiting for me to leave, was a long queue of men and teenage boys eager for their turn to see the greatest of war trophies. Held tightly in their hands were cameras and mobile phones. As they emerged they would chant 'Allahu Akbar', then pause to look down at their camera to make sure they had the shot. Without fail they looked up and smiled, holding in their hands proof for friends and family alike that their forty-two-year nightmare was over. The man who thought his countrymen would die for him was now slowly rotting before a parade of people he had tormented and abused. There could not be a more ignoble end to a regime that had terrified a nation for generations.

Gaddafi had fled from his compound but he didn't run far. And he didn't head for the border or the desert, as much of the world assumed he would. He ran for his home town. It was suicide because it put his back to the coast and his face to the swarming hordes of rebel fighters. The Colonel said he would live or die in Libya and he was true to his word. According to one of his security officials, Mansour Dhao, Gaddafi spent his final days scavenging for food and largely cut off from the world around him. 'We first stayed in the city center, in apartment buildings, but then the mortars started to reach there and we were forced to leave the apartment blocks and enter smaller neighborhoods in different parts of the city,' he told the group Human Rights Watch after his capture by rebels.[40]

> We didn't have a reliable food supply anymore. There was no medicine. We had difficulty getting water. Living was very hard. We just ate pasta and rice, we didn't even have bread. [Muammar Gaddafi] spent most of his time reading the Koran and praying. We moved places every four or five days, depending on the circumstances. [As time went on] Muammar Gaddafi changed into becoming more and more angry. Mostly he was angry about the lack of electricity, communications, and television, his inability to communicate to the outside world. We would go see him and sit with him for an hour or so to speak with him, and he would ask, 'Why is there no electricity? Why is there no water?'[41]

Despite his frustration it was a testament to Gaddafi's sense of invulnerability that his will was written only three days before he died. On 20 October Gaddafi's son Mutassim decided they needed to make a break for it, but their fifty-car convoy was hit by two 500-pound bombs dropped by NATO fighter jets.

'[After the strike] people tried to take shelter in two neighboring buildings,' said Younis Abu Bakr Younis, one of the sons of Gaddafi's defence minister. 'We saw Mutassim injured there, he had been at the front of the convoy when it was hit. At the entry of the villa compound, there was a guard-house, and we found Muammar there, wearing a helmet and a bullet-proof vest. He had a handgun in his pocket and was carrying an automatic weapon.'[42] As they tried to escape they were attacked by rebel fighters from Misrata, said Younis. '[Gaddafi's] guards threw grenades up towards the road, but the third grenade hit the concrete wall and bounced back. Muammar Gaddafi was . . . injured by the grenade, on the left side of his head.'[43] Moments later the rebels would realise who they had cornered. Muammar Gaddafi was moments away from a brutal and humiliating death.

The parading of the bodies of Muammar Gaddafi, his son and his henchmen was ghoulish, but it removed the possibility of a myth growing that he might still be alive. There was now no one left for his loyalists to be loyal to. That gave the Libyan people a chance at a normal life and stable future. The best hope of that being achieved will come via the generation he didn't live long enough to damage.

The girls started arriving first. The youngest children were in twos, holding hands. Their black school coats were buttoned up to the neck to keep out the cold winter wind blowing in off the sea. Their heads were covered in long white scarfs. The youngsters had them tucked into their coats. The older girls left them flowing or thrown fashionably across their shoulders. The playground separated natu-rally with the girls on one side chatting and laughing. The boys sloped in but hung around the main gate, shouting and swinging their bags at each other.

Things had been very different at the Taqadom school in Tripoli under the previous headmistress, because she had been a believer. Her loyalty to the regime was absolute and she ran the school as an exten-sion of the ruthless state she so admired. The morning assembly used to begin with children of various ages being given tracts from the Green Book to read out to their hushed classmates. Disobedience was met with violence, of course. 'It's changed a lot from the Green Book and pro-Gaddafi to February seventeenth,' said twelve-year-old Lateefa Shagan. 'I had to learn a lot of stuff about Gaddafi, his history and about him, specifically about him.'

'Did it make sense?' I asked her.

'Not at all, [but] our principal, she really cared. She used to make us say pro-Gaddafi stuff, but we didn't really want to and whoever didn't want to she'd bring the soldiers to their house. It was really scary.'

I asked her what kinds of things she used to have to say. 'Things that I'm not allowed to say now,' she replied. But then she stopped short in mid-sentence. The first few bars of the resurrected national anthem from the king's era boomed into life over the speakers, and the pupils as one stopped what they were doing and all sang at the top of their voices: 'Libya, Libya, Libya'. All apart from a five-year-old who was struggling to yank the new flag of the old king to the top of the pole.

The man given the task of stripping out Gaddafi's insidious influence on the nation's young minds was Abdulnabi Abughania, the director of the country's Curriculum and Educational Research Center. After the war schools across the country had to throw out at least half their textbooks. Even the maths books involved counting things like Gaddafi's green flag. But while Mr Abughania worked on shaping the future he knew that the mindset of the country's present generation would hold it back.

'Why was it,' I asked him as we sat in his small office in Tripoli, 'that people tell me there were no jobs for them under Gaddafi and yet the country employed around a million migrant workers?'

'Frankly this is the thinking of the society in Libya,' he told me.

They don't want to be an electrician or plumber. Everybody wants to be an engineer or a doctor. The educational system was to blame. Vocational training was a disaster. Vocational training needs to be more than just a certificate, you have to work for it. [Things might have been different] if people had been trained to use their hands instead of just learning to memorise things.

He was echoing the thoughts of another specialist on the development of education in Libya, Professor Roger Le Tourneau from Algiers University. 'Libyan education is, on the whole, too academic, which is not at all what the country requires, handicrafts are very little developed, and specialised training is practically non-existent.'[44] These two academics were united in identifying a fundamental problem in

Libya's education system. What divides them is more than sixty years, because Professor Le Tourneau was writing in 1952, the year the nation was born.

The drive I took around the capital the day after I met Professor Abughania illustrated their point.

'Why is the rubbish piling up?' I asked my driver, Farid Ali.

'Because all the African people have run away,' he said.

'But if Libyan people don't clean up the rubbish, who else is going to do it?' I asked.

'They are lazy, they are waiting for someone to come and clean.'

'But that has to change doesn't it?'

'Yes,' he said seriously, 'they are bringing Filipinos. But they are lazy. I saw they brought some Filipinos in Tajoura for cleaning but they are too slow, very slow, the people get angry [with them] there. And they have very small bodies. Not like Africans, Africans are very strong.'

'No,' I said. 'I mean, it has to change, Libyans have to do those jobs don't they? Do you think Libyans will do those jobs?'

'I don't think so. We always say we are much better [off] than Dubai or the Emirates. Our life should be much better than them. People say: "We are only five million, we have oil, we don't need to work hard."'

On cue the cars on the road snarled to a stop. It was half past one in the afternoon and I was stuck in the rush-hour traffic. Most people start work at 8 a.m. and finish by 1 or 2 p.m., their working day over. Farid was speaking as a man who had done manual labour jobs himself, but in Copenhagen, not Libya. He worked in a Turkish restaurant there for ten years, starting as a dishwasher and moving up to be a cook before moving back to Libya two years before the revolution started.

'Now some of my friends have moved from Tripoli to Copenhagen, and they phoned me and I said: "Ah now you are there you will wash dishes you bastard! You can do it there but you can't do that in your own country."' He was laughing, but during the war the inability of the Libyan people to carry out the basic industrial tasks created a food crisis in Benghazi and Tripoli.

'Always the Tunisian and Egyptian people made the bread, and when they ran away really we had a big problem,' said Farid, laughing out loud. 'At that time there's flour, there's everything, but nobody can make the bread.' He was right and it was something that World Food Programme officials in Benghazi privately fumed about during the war.

During Gaddafi's rule the biggest 'employer' was the government. The Brother Leader's edicts in the Green Book closed the private sector to most Libyans. The only people who were allowed to make money were his family, their friends and some of his most ardent supporters. Employment in the bloated government sector often meant jobs that didn't even require people to turn up for work. 'We had one and a quarter million people employed by the government and perhaps six hundred thousand of them were actually doing the job,' a former government official told me. 'The rest didn't work at all.'

'Civil society in Libya is in its infancy,' said Professor Khashkusha from Tripoli University. 'There is no clear definition of its role yet. It needs a lot of tutoring. It needs a lot of management. Civil society still thinks the state should supply them a place to have an office, salaries, a budget. Civil society [should be] totally the adversary of the state. It exists outside the state [structures], and to reach to that position we'll need years.'

The collapse of employment by the state, the lack of a private sector and the end of the war left thousands of unemployed armed young men roaming the streets with nothing to do. I asked Professor Khashkusha what the best way was to get the militias back into society. He laughed out loud. 'You tell us how and we'll make a shrine for you. We'll make a big square and we'll build a statue for you!'

The best hope for the new Libya is the next generation. The challenge for the present one is to wean them off their guns and give them a future. Libya has already lost two generations. It can't afford to lose another. The new government almost immediately gained access to the tens of billions of dollars the Gaddafi regime squirrelled away in foreign bank accounts. It used some of the money to pay off the gunmen, doubling the cost of public sector salaries compared to that under Gaddafi.[45] That is a short-term necessity that needs to be replaced with a long-term plan. Unemployment is a huge problem. Libya needs to create new industries that provide real jobs.

At an open-air market in the remains of Gaddafi's Tripoli compound I met Ibrahim Rabou. He was a high school teacher of Arabic language and Islamic studies. 'My youth was wasted under Gaddafi. Forty years of my life was during that time. Our hope is for the coming generation because for us you know . . .' His voice trailed off. 'We just hope everything will be all right,' he said quietly.

What gave Ibrahim hope was what was going to happen the following day. 'In my life, I never participated in any election. It is the first time that as a Libyan, a free Libyan, I can go and elect the people that I want, so of course everybody is happy because this is a very historic moment for all Libya.'

Sadaq Abdullah Baunny was unusual for a Libyan in that 7 July 2012 wasn't the first time he was getting the chance to vote in a multiparty election. He had voted in the first one held by King Idris in 1952 and now, sixty years later, he was going to get a chance to do it again. He was at the gates of the Mohamed Mahmoud bin Otman school in Tripoli two hours before the polls opened. The enthusiasm in the capital that day meant he still didn't get the coveted first place in the queue. That went to a young man who had fought on the rebel side and once occupied the school with his fighters during the battle for the capital. But unlike the young man, who was wearing just a yellow T-shirt, Sadaq, who was in his eighties, had dressed for the occasion. He wore a crisply pressed traditional white Arab robe and a white taqiyah, the short round cap worn by observant Muslim men. His white beard was neatly trimmed. Wrapped around his left arm was the old flag of independence. Sadaq said he had resolutely refused to work for any government during his sixty-five years in the clothing industry. He had twenty children, and as we stood in the shade waiting for the poll to open he reeled off their professions on his thick fingers. Most of them, like anyone with ambition in Libya under Gaddafi, had tried to get out of the country. Some lived in Canada, one was in Germany and another lived in Switzerland.

'Allahu Akbar,' the election monitor murmured quietly as the first vote was placed into the box. Then it was Sadaq's turn. His left hand shook slightly as he placed his folded paper into the large plastic tub, but this was age, not nervousness. I asked him how he felt. 'My feelings are I am nearly flying from happiness and I don't feel the earth beneath my feet at all.' Women and men voted in separate sections of the school. Sadaq's wife was in a wheelchair, and now that he had voted he was going home to collect her so that she could do the same. 'I voted for Jibril,' he told me. 'He's an excellent man, the country was in deep trouble but he met with the Western leaders and he got us help.'

However the man he was talking about, Mahmoud Jibril, wasn't personally standing in the July elections for the new General National Congress. The laws of the poll banned members of the NTC from running for parliament. Jibril though was the face of his party's, the National Forces Alliance's, campaign. He emerged from the vote as the country's dominant political player and was immediately touted as a possible president.

Men and women of all ages streamed through the capital's polling stations on that day. It was a trouble-free affair, with just one lone old man turned away because he forgot to bring his ID. 'But you know me!' he said to the election official. For Libya's mostly young population, this was an exciting day. You could see it in their wide grins and the proud wave of their ink-stained fingers.

There was a complacent conclusion from those who had not spent much time in the country during the war that Libya's elections would follow those of the other post-revolutionary states by voting in Islamists. It was not a feeling I shared, because I found very little sense of an Islamist insurgence on the various Libyan front lines I reported from during the war. And there is nothing like the prospect of imminent death to push you deeper into your religion, so if it was going to resurge it was likely to show up there first.

The Libyan people are religious. I haven't met a single person in the country who was not. It is a fundamental part of their personal lives, but it does not define them politically. And so the Brotherhood's candidates held very little appeal. They got just seventeen of the eighty seats allocated for parties. A voter described the failure of the Muslim Brotherhood in the post-Gaddafi elections like this: 'We don't need anyone to lead us to Islam, we already have Islam, and ours is middle [moderate] Islam, even if we pray five times a day. All these other countries like Egypt, they have Christians and Jews and Muslims so they need a party for Islam.'

'If you [the West] want to insist on labelling us as "liberals", "conservatives" or "Islamists", "non-Islamists", it's up to you, you can say whatever you like,' the Libyan economist Ahmed A. al-Atrash told me. 'But there is simplicity to the Libyan social fabric. We are all Muslims, we all practise Islam, to some extent and freely. Some of us pray one hundred per cent, others eighty per cent, others don't practise at all but respect that there is a red line.'

The Brotherhood saw their failure as the direct legacy of their vilification and suppression during the Gaddafi years. Al-Amin Belhaj was among the leadership of the newly created 'Justice and Construction Party', which was the Libyan Muslim Brotherhood's new political wing. 'The Brotherhood in Egypt started a long time ago,' he told me. 'They had years in politics. In Tunisia, Ennahda started in 1988. They had about thirty years of political experience. In Libya we had just three months. That's the most importance difference between what happened in Libya and what happened in Egypt and Tunisia. We are just starting in politics.'

During the election, to dilute voter suspicion, Belhaj's party even tried to claim it wasn't the Brotherhood at all, but a collection of like-minded individuals. 'Libyans are moderate Muslims. Ninety per cent are moderate, that is one of the reasons why we did not create a "Brotherhood" party. But when you interview a Brotherhood member you will find a normal Libyan, you will find that their beliefs are almost the same. If you go through the party you can find some are from the Brotherhood and others are not, you cannot differentiate at all.' It was a tough sell, particularly as he wanted to rush our interview because he told me afterwards he was off to catch a plane to Egypt to meet members of the Ikhwan there.

The murder of the US ambassador, Chris Stevens, gave rise to a chorus of alarm that Libya was at risk of eventually being overrun by Islamist extremists. It is not. There are Salafists in Libya, and some of them are very hard-line, but they reflect a fringe of society, in a society that now knows how to fight back. Libya's revolution was unique among the Arab Spring uprisings for its totality. Its elections were unique for their outcome. The same can also be said for the country's prospects. Unlike Syria it is a largely homogeneous population of Sunni Muslims. Unlike Egypt its population is tiny and literate. Unlike Tunisia it has huge oil reserves. Unlike Iraq its oil industry survived the civil war largely intact and was back to work within weeks of the war's end. Crucially it has no inherent strategic value to the wider world, and so it should be spared the buffeting winds of geopolitical gamesmanship. The Qataris tried to buy influence by funding the campaign of some rebel militia leaders and they got a drubbing in the polls. One Libyan official said privately: 'In funding the Islamists, they are upsetting the balance of politics and making it difficult for us to move forward. They need to stop their meddling.'[46] Libyans want to determine their own destiny.

Now that Gaddafi is gone, for the first time the Libyan people have access to their own money. By the end of 2012 the country's oil export revenues were back up to pre-war levels of US$44 billion.[47] The new Libya doesn't need to go cap in hand to Western donors to rebuild the state. It will probably stumble its way through the next few years, but any mistakes it makes will be largely its own. It will not have to manage the social tensions created by an interfering foreign hand. It has miles and miles of incredible Mediterranean coastline and spectacular ancient ruins that could attract millions of tourists from around the world.

Libya may just work. In other parts of the region and in other parts of the world, after the shine of previous revolutions has worn off some have hankered for the old days. But life under Gaddafi was absurd. Any future nostalgia can be quickly cured by flicking through the increasingly rare copies of his Green Book. There will be periods in the coming months and years when that optimism looks wildly misplaced, but Libya has a clean slate on which to build a new nation and the income to do it. Year Zero is probably the best place for it to start.

8

Syria: The Arab World's Broken Heart

The village sat nestled among cornfields and green pastures where sheep grazed in the crushing midday sun under the watchful eye of local shepherds. A dusty little road wound its way up through the surrounding fields to the small grey-brick homes sitting on a rocky outpost overlooking the countryside. As I entered the house from the dazzling light outside, it was difficult at first to understand why my boots were sticking to the ground in the dark little room. As my eyes adjusted to the gloom I saw scattered shoes and fallen cups lying on the floor. The room was silent but for the flies, which had found the evidence of the massacre before I did. Their soft drone led to the corner of the room where a small squeegee mop was propped against the wall, the kind often used to scrape soapsuds off a window. It was not up to the task it had last been used for, so it stood abandoned in a thick pool of dark red blood.

A man pushed into the room beside me and lifted from the floor a blue and white-chequered tablecloth. Each square had a little posy of flowers printed on it. What he wanted me to see though was the clump of skin and flesh stuck to the top. As I instinctively stepped back he thrust it forward into my face and a small piece of someone's brain fell from within it and landed on the floor.

I went outside to catch my breath, and as I squinted in the shimmering light, shapes that had before blurred and merged into the barren landscape came into focus. The white horse lying dead in the shade of the stables, the two dusty-coloured sheep shot by the chicken coop. The carcasses left to rot where they fell.

To understand what had happened in the Syrian village of Qubair it was necessary to walk to the house next door and submit your senses to the stench of burnt flesh. You had to make yourself understand that the piece of meat you had just stepped over once belonged inside a person who had lived, worked or played in the fields outside. You had to acknowledge that men had walked into this village with the intention of killing every living thing in it. People who could look into the face of a child, perhaps one just like their own, listen to his or her cries for mercy and then butcher it.

'I can't tell you who I am, I fear for my safety,' said a young man with a red and white scarf wrapped tightly around his face to reveal only his black eyes:

> The army surrounded the area and then the militia from the neigh-
> bouring villages came in and killed the people and then burnt them
> so no traces of the bodies would remain. They have killed everyone
> in the village, only three people are left. They did it because they
> wanted to take the land. They were protected by the army. They
> killed everyone, they destroyed everything. They even killed the
> children, they slaughtered them with knives.

The revolt was well into its second year, and these tales of atrocities no longer surprised anyone, because by now the Assad regime had dropped the charade.

At the beginning of 2011 so little was known about the reality of Syria in the wider world that Bashar al-Assad and his family were the subject of perhaps the most ill-timed puff piece in the history of magazine publishing. As the country began its slow slide towards civil war the March edition of *Vogue* magazine printed a fawning profile of Assad's 'glamorous, young and very chic wife' Asma. She was, purred its headline, 'A Rose in the Desert', the first lady of 'the safest country in the Middle East'. Her husband was a man who 'takes photographs and talks lovingly about his first computer'. He had been 'elected' in 2000 after his father's death with what the magazine described as 'a startling 97 per cent of the vote' because 'in Syria, power is heredi-tary'.[1] The piece didn't mention that the national assembly had to change article 83 of the country's constitution before he could be 'elected' by referendum because at the time Bashar was six years younger than the minimum age of forty required to ascend to the presidency.

In person Bashar al-Assad was an unlikely dictator. We had met a few months earlier at his Presidential Palace in Damascus, his slightly limp handshake and quiet lisping voice much more suited to the mild-mannered ophthalmologist he had once trained to be, than to the tyrant he had become. But for a long time he had managed to persuade the world that he was different from the other dictators, with speeches that kept promising reform. Even Hillary Clinton thought it worthwhile to say in the same month the *Vogue* article appeared that: 'There's a different leader in Syria now.' She added that: 'Many of the members of Congress of both parties who have gone to Syria in recent months have said they believe he is a reformer.' A few days later she distanced herself from her own remarks, saying she had 'referenced the opinions of others'.[2]

Assad was not like his father's generation of dictators. He is not a brutish self-made man who fought off challenges to take control of a state using violence and guile. He does not strike fear or awe into those who meet him. Even now, though he holds what is left of his father's throne, he is still a prince, not a king. He did not look, did not talk, he does not even shake hands like a dictator. But he has proved to all those who had high hopes for the reformer that he knows how to act like a dictator.

After *Vogue*'s remarkable profile, which it has now deleted from the Internet, that 'tall, long-necked, blue-eyed' man began to perpetrate sickening violence against his own people. His secret police sent back children's bodies smashed and beaten, with their genitals cut off.[3] His military massacred whole communities. Anyone caught using their computer to tell the outside world what was going on disappeared into a torture chamber. The Syrian state had been abusing and murdering its people for years, but eventually even the fashion world could not ignore something that was now being done on an industrial scale.

The conflict between the Syrian people will not end with the death of Assad or the removal of his regime. Nor if the guns are put away and a new government is formed. It can only end when the atrocities of the war are lost from living memory, because they will not be forgiven. Syria's struggle within must wait for its end because of the way it started. People make rules of war to slow the inevitable descent of their societies into savage violence. Assad's regime broke the rules on day one.

In March 2011 fifteen schoolchildren were arrested and tortured for writing on a wall the words that were echoing across the Arab world: 'The people want the overthrow of the regime'. The boys were all from the southern city of Dera'a, and on 18 March the people of that city gathered after Friday prayers to express their revulsion for this act of cruelty. The security forces opened fire and killed four people. They did the same thing at the victims' funerals the following day and another person died. The city rose up. The army's Fourth Armoured Division, commanded by the president's brother Maher, attempted to crush the revolt with tanks and troops. They failed in that but they did provoke a furious reaction to their brutality across the country in Homs, Hama and the suburbs of Damascus. In the capital small demonstrations against the regime had started on the 15th. Those countrywide uprisings against the regime never stopped.

'The government compensated for a lack of smartness with an excess of force,' a Syrian government official told me privately. 'Without that mistake in Dera'a it would have stayed quiet for six months and by that time people would have seen what was happening in Egypt and would have thought five times before doing anything.' He was right about the former, wrong about the latter. The Syrian people were as sick of their lives under dictatorship as everyone else in the region. They knew it was not going to be easy.

'I remember my father when we used to talk in the house, *in the house* he used to whisper,' Zubaida told me.[4] 'He knew people were listening because even the air was controlled. This is what kept us safe boys and girls.' Zubaida is an Alawite who lived in Damascus, where we were talking on a cool summer's evening after the crisis had moved into its second year. She comes from the same sect as the Assad regime but is not among its supporters. That truth may not make any difference in the Syria that emerges from the conflict. Stating that fact may not protect people like her. Too much blood has been shed for words to matter any more, even though it was words in the mouths of babes that brought the conflict to life.

In the old Syria, in the old Middle East, no one really knew what the truth was in the society that existed before the civil war. How will they be able to judge it afterwards? Right from the start Assad said that the truth was that his regime was fighting an opposition riddled with al-Qaeda-linked violent jihadists. His regime then set about nurturing an environment that would bring that truth to life. And as it did it, so it also systematically created an equal to the opposite.

'I've been following this from the beginning because I am Alawite,' Zubaida told me:

When [the uprising] began the Alawites said: 'Yes, I want to be part of this because I am part of society.' And then the army did something very smart. They would go to an Alawite village and they would put a red X on the doors of the houses and the Alawites got a little scared. It took them five or six months to really make them scared, because in the beginning they were not nervous. They said: 'This is a revolution for us also, like in Egypt,' but they started sending them some very smart messages to say: 'No, this is a Sunni revolution against all Alawites.' They would go into a very poor village and they would say these Sunnis are coming to kill you and they gave them some weapons. They would pick a village and send back some of their children cut into little pieces and say those people [in the neighbouring village] killed your son. So you'll find so many young men are ready to come and join [the government militia, the Shabiha]. I'm not saying they are not good people, it's that they are more vulnerable in the villages because they are not in daily contact with the other sects. They don't really understand other communities so it's easier to play with their heads. Every two hundred years there is a slaughter [of Alawites], so they have inside them this fear and it's easy to bring it out again.

Town by town, village by village Assad's men picked away at the scab that barely covered the wounds of his minority sect. 'The Assad regime is holding its own community hostage,' Professor Bernard Haykel told me. He was born and grew up in neighbouring Lebanon, so he has seen first-hand how sectarianism corrodes societies. 'Like the Jews they have this history of persecution, and they see history coming back to haunt them. The opposition, whether it's the Free Syrian Army or the opposition in exile, has just not done enough to counteract that impression, so the Alawis are terrified.'

It was always hard to say what being Syrian actually meant. The civil war made it harder. Like many European creations that would eventually crumble into violent disorder, the country felt more like a concept, created from a few stray thoughts left over from some big colonial ideas. Modern Syria had the Alawites, a branch of Shia Islam, at the top of the social order. They are the largest religious minority in Syria and make up around 12 per cent of the 23 million people in the country. The vast majority of the population are Sunni Muslims who comprise around 75 per cent of the nation's people. Around 10 per cent of the Sunnis are Kurds. The rest of the population's patchwork is mainly Christians, with smaller numbers of other splinter Shia faiths like Ismailis and Druze. There are also half a million Palestinian refugees.

The reason the Syrian revolution took so long to play out was that the quarter of the country who are in the non-Sunni minorities were not sure if they would be any safer under a new government. They had looked across the border at Iraq and seen how minority groups suffered waves of bomb attacks or were driven out of their homes by ethnic cleansing. They wondered whether a post-revolution Syria would hold the same fate for them. Some, mainly the younger generation, joined the revolution but many others held back because they feared for their prospects under whatever rule emerged from the conflict.

'A friend of mine who is a Franciscan monk went to a friend of his who is a very moderate sheik and he asked him whether he could guarantee his people would not take revenge on other sects,' said Ahmed, a Syrian journalist I met in Damascus.[5] 'The sheik said: "Yes, I do guarantee that, but not in the first one hundred days." No one can guarantee the streets in the first three or four months. People will be crazy and there will be deaths and there will be revenge.'

I asked him whether Syria's social fabric could be saved. 'No. It will need a decade or two to repair the damage. Rebuilding the infrastructure is easier than rebuilding the society, and the damage to the social fabric has already been done.'

The little Sunni Muslim village of Qubair was surrounded by equally tiny villages populated by Alawites. These villagers had stopped the United Nations ceasefire monitors from getting to the site of the massacre for twenty-four hours. They had surrounded their cars and blocked the roads. Shots had been fired. It was a long enough delay for the evidence to be dragged away or destroyed by the Syrian army and the local Shabiha.

There was no justice for the families killed on 6 June 2012. But that doesn't mean there was no retribution. The last words somebody must have heard before a bullet went into their head or a knife slashed through their body were 'This is for Qubair,' because by this time the world had to acknowledge Assad's truth. There were now violent Islamist fighters in Syria. These men had been encouraged and funded by two of Washington's closest allies in the Arab world: Saudi Arabia and Qatar.

I was told by UN officials in Damascus that at times, as the US called for peace and reconciliation, these two states were deliberately sabotaging local ceasefires negotiated by the monitors. The Salafists were mainly getting their funding from Saudi Arabia. Qatar funded fighters linked to the Syrian Muslim Brotherhood. But it was clear that the Qataris were not fussy who they dealt with if it produced the desired result. 'I am very much against excluding anyone at this stage, or bracketing them as terrorists, or bracketing them as al-Qaeda,' said the Qatari minister of foreign affairs, Khalid bin Mohammad al-Attiyah. 'We should bring them all together, we should treat them all equally, and we should work on them to change their ideology, i.e. put more effort altogether to change their thinking. If we exclude anything from the Syrian elements today, we are only doing worse to Syria. Then we are opening the door again for intervention to chase the monster.'⁶ Their differing objectives meant that Saudi Arabia and Qatar were, behind the scenes, at each other throats over Syria. The US tried, and failed, to get them to cooperate.

The Israelis were contemptuous of the mismanagement of the mess on their doorstep by the US and its allies in the Gulf. 'Nobody is running the opposition in Syria. That's the problem,' a senior Israeli defence official told me.

> There is an Arabic phrase which translates as 'You peel the onion and you keep finding more heads'. [In the opposition] you have many leaders, I could give you all the names, but if you ask me: 'Who is *the* leader? Who are the elders that Qatar and Saudi Arabia are supplying with dangerous weapons?', my answer is there is no one. Which means there is a vacuum, and that vacuum means al-Qaeda for the first time in history is in Syria. We think Bashar al-Assad is a terrible guy because he had unprecedented cooperation with Iran. He's a murderer, but the Golan Heights was the quietest area in the Middle East. Now what is the address of the person the Qataris and Saudis are cooperating with? Who is this leader? Who is responsible for making sure tomorrow they don't use these SA-14s [Russian shoulder-held missiles] to shoot down a British Airways plane?

That last bit was clearly said for my benefit, because Israel's security concerns are focused solely at home.

That is why on 30 January 2013, for the first time since they attacked the Syrian nuclear plant in 2007, twelve Israeli air force jets struck in Syria again. Their target was a convoy carrying the more advanced SA-17 anti-aircraft missile launchers. The Israeli press quoted anonymous, which were probably military sources, to assert that the attack happened to stop 'game-changing' arms being sent to Hezbollah, which in return had sent in fighters to help the regime. I was told by a senior figure in the UN that by late 2012 the bodies of Hezbollah men were regularly being brought back across the border for a quiet burial in Lebanon. By then though there was already some division within Hezbollah about its involvement in the war. So its leadership framed the group's military action to its men as protecting Shia communities and shrines in Syria from the Sunni Salafists rather than fighting for Assad, even though they were fighting alongside his forces.

In the months that followed the January strike Israel regularly had to respond to incoming fire from across the Golan Heights. Tensions steadily increased on the once quiet border. Israel knew nothing would have pleased the Assad regime, and Hezbollah, more than dragging it into the conflict so Syria could then try to rally wider Arab support around it. Tensions in Lebanon were growing as Hezbollah's increasingly public involvement in the war and the influx of Syrian refugees disturbed the country's religious equilibrium. Then in the summer of 2013 Israel again carried out air strikes in Syria on arms shipments that were destined for Hezbollah, adding to fears that the conflict was spreading. But while Israel did not want to play into Assad's hands the airstrikes were making it clear that the generals in Tel Aviv did not have to ask for international blessing to intervene to serve their interests over the strife in Syria. The United Nations did.

'Any proxy war is destructive, but particularly this one,' a United Nations official at its headquarters in New York told me. 'But even though there is a proxy war it isn't coordinated. All the parties are supporting their own proxy war. The Turks are supporting theirs, the Qataris are supporting theirs, the Saudis are supporting theirs. It's very destructive.'

I asked whether they had a common goal. 'Absolutely not.'

The Syrian opposition had been constantly criticised for failing to get its act together and present a united front. This is partly a consequence of the nature of the uprising. Syria's, like those in the rest of the region, was leaderless too. When the United Nations got involved its first act was to try to shepherd the opposition groups together under one umbrella. But as it did so it found 'we had all these parallel and competing agendas at the same time' tempting them back out again.

It wasn't only the political leadership of the opposition that could not present a united front – neither could the forces behind them. In a parallel with the early stages of the war in Afghanistan against the Soviets in the 1980s, the funding for the opposition in Syria first came from wealthy individuals in the Gulf. Money and arms were handed over to the head of each Syrian opposition group. But then two relatives leading an opposition group found that if they split into two groups they could both get funding. The decentralised funding model encouraged division within the opposition just as the United Nations was trying to encourage the opposite. 'It wasn't intentional,' the UN official told me, 'but it was very reckless.'

The United Nations secretary general Ban Ki Moon summed up the mood of the organisation during a visit to the memorial for the victims of the Srebrenica massacre in the former Yugoslavia: 'I do not want to see any of my successors, after twenty years, visiting Syria, apologising for what we could have done now to protect the civilians in Syria – which we are not doing now.'7

It was this legacy of failed UN missions, General Robert Mood told me the following year, that drove his decision to end his mission when it became clear that neither side in the Syrian civil war was ready to stop fighting:

I remember vividly we had many discussions about 'remember Rwanda, remember Srebrenica', remember how the UN has on several occasions become a silent witness, almost protecting the status quo, being accused of becoming very close to complicit. We made the choice . . . it better serves the integrity of the UN to scale down the presence to a minimum, rather than to continue the mission.

When I asked an official in the State Department in late 2012 where the resistance to America taking the lead was coming from, the answer was unequivocal: 'The President.' The contrast between the lofty words in Cairo and his inaction over Syria was a symptom of the 'innate ambivalence of this President'. Obama's unwillingness to act even after it was clear that Syria was going to descend into chaos confounded and frustrated people in the State Department under Hillary Clinton. Those who have left, like Anne-Marie Slaughter, who is now the president of the US think tank New America Foundation, told me publicly what I had heard others still serving say privately: 'This is just insane! I just find it stunning that a president who came to power wanting to forge a new relationship with the Muslim world is squandering a clear opportunity, but also risking a whole other generation of people who are going to come into power believing that we say one thing and do another. Or worse, that we absolutely betrayed them.'

There is no risk of that. It has already happened.

All four major outside anti-Assad players in the Syrian conflict – America, Turkey, Saudi Arabia and Qatar – misjudged the staying power of the regime. They assumed that Assad would last months, not years, even though the diplomats on the ground were telling them he was still in control. That is because they underestimated how much his regime would sectarianise the fighting. The Turks, encouraged by the Americans, spent the early months of the conflict giving the impression that they were going to play an active role trying to solve the crisis. When it dawned on them both that it was not going to be quick or easy, and that neither Ankara nor Washington could control the outcome, their enthusiasm waned. The Turkish public also soon grew jaded over the trouble on their doorstep and did not want to get drawn into it any further.[8]

From late July 2012 the Syrian airforce had began 'deliberately or indiscriminately' killing civilians.[9] Senator John McCain, Obama's old rival on the stump, had called that spring, when the death toll was around 7,500, for the US to 'lead an international effort to protect key population centers in Syria . . . through airstrikes on Assad's forces'. Airstrikes then might have made a difference, but by the following spring the death toll was already ten times higher. By then it had become difficult to know which among the fractured opposition fighters to root for, and whether the country they were fighting over would last.[10]

'Everybody missed the train on this crisis,' a diplomat in Damascus told me. 'The UN did not show up, the Europeans and Americans did not show up. They left it all in the hands of the Arab League. Then the Arab League started messing it up from day one. They are the ones who radicalised it.'

Before the uprising began the Syrian regime had had high hopes for the year 2013. It was also looking forward to lots of international attention. There was going to be a kind of coming-out party. Even Mickey Mouse was invited: a 22-million-dollar new home was to be built for him in 'Disney Syria'. The tourism ministry had plans for a big promotional push in 2013 to put Syria on the map. 'Every place tells a story' was its catchphrase.[11] If Mickey had moved in he would have had a lot to write home about, because he was due to live in Homs. The story of Homs changed the conflict. Homs was where the wider world first learned of the savage brutality of the Assad regime and then realised it didn't care enough to do much about it. Homs was where the world began its betrayal of the Syrian people.

In February 2012, and for the first time in the Syrian revolution, it was possible to watch the regime bombard civilians live on air. It happened in the Baba Amr district of Homs, and watch was all the world did. 'Yesterday the Syrian government murdered hundreds of Syrian citizens, including women and children, in Homs through shelling and other indiscriminate violence . . .' said President Obama on 3 February. 'Assad must halt his campaign of killing and crimes against his own people now. He must step aside and allow a democratic transition to proceed immediately.'[12] The previous August he'd said exactly the same thing, insisting: 'For the sake of the Syrian people, time has come for President Assad to step aside.'[13] None of these statements, nor any that followed, made any difference, because none of them included an 'or else' if Assad didn't stop the slaughter. Even those who broadly supported Obama have judged that his passive response will haunt the region. 'I do think the question that is going to nag at the world after the Arab uprisings is the lack of response on Syria,' Ambassador Barbara Bodine told me.

The self-styled Baba Amr Brigade had not run away when they had the chance. They had stood and held their ground with a few light weapons. A small group of activists decided that they would set up video cameras to broadcast the conflict. They were trying to recreate the 'Benghazi moment', a point at which the international community would be forced to act to stop a massacre taking place in a large city by well-armed troops attacking almost defenceless civilians. But this time the United Nations did not leap into action. As President Obama observed, the massacre was allowed to take place.

'We thought that when we started the live stream and the rockets began falling down that there would be a "no-fly zone" or that they would come immediately and stop this.' As he said these words Omar Shakir began to chuckle. He was suddenly amused at his own naivety. Before the uprisings Omar, at the age of twenty, thought he had his life all mapped out. He was going to study medicine. He had started to learn German because he had a place in a university there. He ended up crammed inside a room with twenty people hoping that a shell wouldn't come through the roof.

If you heard a voice in English on TV or radio from Homs during the fighting then it would have been Omar's. Along with a small group of activists he created what they called a 'media centre' to get the story of their city to a world outside that he thought would care.

I feel disappointed because we heard rumours that they will attack us and that they will use every possible gun. So we brought a good camera, a MacBook, all the equipment to make a live stream [of images]. I came out after twenty-one days. And as I came out of the [escape] tunnel I thought Bashar al-Assad is going to stay until 2014, because he was shelling us with rockets, tanks, field artillery, mortars, he carried out crimes, he raped the women, and I thought with this live-stream camera something big will happen . . . I don't know what more he has to do. After Baba Amr he did the whole city. So three months of shelling the city and they [the international community] were still talking about what they want to do.

One of Omar's group had studied management, so he organised the eclectic mix of youngsters into teams, each with a different task. Most were students like Omar. One sold cigarettes, another was an IT graduate. One youngster called Jedi sold vegetables. Jedi filmed the most dramatic images because he was willing to take the greatest risks. They started with mobile-phone images and then used their savings to buy cheap cameras and then borrowed money from their relatives to get better ones.

At this stage those images were much more dangerous to the regime than anything the fledgling Free Syrian Army (FSA) could muster. The regime finally stopped Omar and his friends on the nineteenth day of the bombardment when a round hit the media centre, killing among others the journalist Marie Colvin from *The Times*.

'At the beginning of the revolution, if you carried a weapon it's OK, maybe they will arrest you for one or two months and then they will release you,' said Omar. 'But we had a friend from the beginning of the revolution, they arrested him in May 2011. Over the following year they broke his arms and his fingers and every time it healed they broke them again. Even now he is in prison. Anyone filming and sending to the outside, those people were the most wanted.'

After Homs many of the young revolutionaries began to put down their video cameras and take up guns. When the rebel fighters finally fled Baba Amr, after four weeks of bombardment, most of Omar's group also made it out alive. By this time though three had been killed. Jedi escaped to Aleppo. It was there, while the city was still under the control of the government, that he was arrested. The young man considered by his friends to be the bravest of them all was tortured until he gave up the names of dozens of other activists.

Homs was where the Arab Spring woke up to the reality of the New Middle East it had created. As Syria began its civil war it became clear that the narrative had changed from the uprisings of the previous year. When it began, the protests in Syria were about the same causes that had brought about change in Tunisia, Egypt and Libya: democracy, equality, and a chance to shrug off the dictatorial regime of Bashar al-Assad. By the time the uprising had entered its second year the dynamics around it had changed. The protesters wanted the same things, but the Gulf states, and in particular Saudi Arabia, sensed an opportunity. They sought to exploit the turmoil in Syria to diminish the influence of Iran. By its third year the Syrian civil war had gone beyond anyone's control. It wasn't even clear what kind of Syria there would be when the fighting ended. 'Something has been broken in Syria, and it's not going to be put back together perfectly, immediately, anytime soon – even after Assad leaves,' said President Obama.[14]

The patchwork of religions and sects in Syria reflected the broader fragmentation of the region along sectarian lines. The Pandora's box of Sunni–Shia sectarianism had been opened by the American mismanagement of post-invasion Iraq. It had allowed the Iranians far more influence in their neighbour's affairs than they could ever have dreamed of. Saudi Arabia wanted to turn the clock back. The head of the US military's Central Command, General James Mattis, told a Senate hearing that 'the collapse of the Assad regime would be the biggest strategic setback for Iran in 25 years.'[15]

The first attempt to unify the opposition had focused on Syrian exiles. In December 2011 Hillary Clinton met with, and thus anointed, a group of exiles calling themselves the Syrian National Council, SNC. After their discussions in Geneva the State Department declared: 'The United States considers the Syrian National Council to be a leading and legitimate representative of Syrians.'[16] Then together with the EU, the Arab League and other largely like-minded countries and institutions they all met under the banner of the 'Friends of Syria' in Tunis the following February. It was a pointless meeting because the Syrian exiles were made up of largely irrelevant people with no influence whatsoever over the fighters inside the country. To illustrate its worthlessness the Saudis walked out, complaining that too little was being done to support the Syrian rebels on the ground.

The Saudi foreign minister Prince Saud al-Faisal, while sitting in a meeting with the American secretary of state Hillary Clinton, responded to a question from the media about arming the Syrian opposition with the words: 'I think it's an excellent idea.' So they did. A few days later Hillary Clinton, in a mild rebuke to the Saudi statement, said:

> We have a very dangerous set of actors in the region; al-Qaeda, Hamas and those who are on our terrorist list to be sure, claiming to support the opposition. You have many Syrians more worried about what could come next . . . but I want to make clear for anyone watching the horrible massacre that is going on to ask your-self 'OK what do you do?' If you bring in automatic weapons which you can maybe smuggle across the border, OK what do they do against tanks and heavy artillery?[17]

However it emerged the following year in public testimony to Congress that by the summer of 2012 Hillary Clinton, the defence secretary Leon Panetta and the then director of the CIA David Petraeus had all supported arming the rebels. They presented a plan to the president. He rejected it.[18] The White House was furious its internal divisions had been laid bare at the Congressional hearing.[19]

So in 2012 the US administration's policy was to wait and hope that economic sanctions imposed by the West and the Arab League would provoke either the regime's collapse or an internal coup. 'There is no plan B,' a Western diplomat I met in neighbouring Lebanon told me that summer. Throughout the year food and fuel prices did shoot up, factories closed and jobs were lost, but the regime still managed to cling on by digging deep into its foreign currency reserves. Those Syrians who could started to send their families and their money over the border into Lebanon. Iraqis who had earlier fled to Syria during the civil war there started drifting back home. Iraq was far from stable and still suffered from regular massive suicide bomb attacks, but the level of violence in Syria far outstripped that of its neighbour even during Iraq's most wretched days.[20]

Those losing the most in the economic crisis were on the same side of the sectarian divide as those trying to bring the regime down. Much of the business class was drawn from the Sunni Muslim community. They had worked within the system and profited from it. They were thought to be an influential force in the country, and the Western governments hoped that as sanctions bit they would be able to place pressure on the regime from within to resolve the crisis by adopting the so-called 'Yemeni model'. This was supposed to play out with Assad stepping aside, as Yemen's President Saleh had done, and then perhaps going into exile with some of his ill-gotten gains.

'Saddam Hussein lived under sanctions for ten years. What was the result?' said Wa'el as we sat in his still air-conditioned office in Damascus during the war. 'The sanctions on the country are affecting the poor people, not the rich. It's not affecting the regime.' Wa'el was one of those Sunni businessmen who had managed to make money under the regime. This didn't mean he was some kind of collaborator, though he was far from a revolutionary. Everyone had to work within the system if they wanted to stay out of jail, get their kids into school and provide for their families. Everyone in Syria recognised that. No one believed before 2011 that anything was ever going to change. The Assad regime had a hold on everyone because it knew all their secrets. Corruption was not a by-product of the regime, it was integral to it, because it was a tool of suppression and it touched every aspect of a Syrian's life.

'It's an unbelievable system,' Wa'el told me. 'You have to do it even when you give birth to a child, starting from the moment you take your wife into hospital. The nurse does not work unless you give her extra, the cleaning lady in the hospital does not clean the room unless you give her extra. So you start living with the system from the day you are born without knowing it.' He gave a big belly laugh. 'Somebody did it on your behalf!'

And like most of the other dictatorial Arab regimes, corruption in Syria evolved into a system of state-sponsored entrapment. 'There is always a sword hanging over you and they can at any point use it, and legally. The system has been built in such a way that you cannot apply the rules and regulations. You have to operate illegally in anything you do. Today if they come to my office and only take the papers on my desk and nothing else' – he waved his arms over the neatly stacked piles of documents in front of him – 'I'll be in jail for the next five years, because their rules do not allow me to act in the regular proper way.'

When I started working I had the fax machine in the drawer and I made a hole in the side for the wire because it was a crime to have a fax machine until 1995. How can you operate a business if you do not have a fax machine? Companies would laugh if you don't have a fax machine, but we used to tell our suppliers the fax time is from three to four p.m. We would send them a telex (through the government post office) saying: 'We have turned on the fax machine, send the faxes!' And the [Syrian officials] knew everyone had a fax machine because they were the ones involved in smuggling it to begin with from across the border.

So you have the fax machine and so you become a threat to national security because of your fax machine. The whole system is built for you to do something wrong so that they can cut your head off any time they want to. Corruption is everywhere. Dubai, Saudi, are full of corruption but they did build their countries. The difference here is we have been in a standstill for the last thirty to forty years.

From his base in Damascus Wa'el was funding humanitarian supplies for the opposition. The following year, in early 2013, Wa'el was kidnapped by a group of local Shabiha masquerading as a violent

Salafist group. They demanded a ransom. He was eventually released after some of his contacts in the regime's security apparatus intervened on his behalf.

'Can a body live without a heart?' Bashar al-Assad had demanded as he tore into the Arab League in January 2012 for what he saw as its betrayal of his nation and his leadership after Syria was suspended from the group. 'Who said that Syria is the throbbing heart of Arabism? It wasn't a Syrian, it was President Abdel Nasser, and this is still true . . . without Syria the Arab League is no longer Arab,' he declared.[21] By the time he was saying these words the heart of Arabism was already broken. Throughout his address, after his regime had finally lost legitimacy in the eyes of an institution it had once championed, Assad evoked the call of Pan-Arabism. Most of the rest of the region had buried the idea with Nasser, but decades later Assad still called it the 'symbol of our identity'. That was because of all the countries that once embraced the idea, Syria needed it most. Of all the people looking for an identity the Syrians were the most lost. Assad was standing in Damascus in one of the oldest continuously inhabited cities on earth. But as he stood raging at his podium he was lying to the world about what was happening in a country that had itself been born of deceit.

'The Sykes–Picot Agreement is a shocking document. It is not only the product of greed at its worst, that is greed allied to suspicion and so leading to stupidity; it also stands out as a startling piece of double-dealing.'[22] These are the conclusions of the historian George Antonius on the backroom deal in May 1916 that carved up the old Ottoman Empire after the First World War and led to the creation of what is now Syria. It was drawn up in secret by Sir Mark Sykes of Britain and Georges Picot of France, who coloured the map of the region into blue bits for France, red bits for Great Britain, and a brown bit, Palestine, where would 'be established an international administration'. Sykes ended up playing his role in this enterprise by what he called 'extraordinary luck' and what others deemed a large amount of guile. He had given the impression to the British prime minister of the day that he was not only an expert on Middle Eastern affairs but that he was also fluent in both Turkish and Arabic. He could not speak either language.[23]

The Sykes–Picot Agreement was signed in secret because the British had already offered to recognise the same land as an independent Arab state led by the Sharif of Mecca, Hussein Bin Ali, in return for him leading a revolt against the Ottomans during the First World War. The present King Abdullah of Jordan is a direct descendant of Hussein Bin Ali. He would also be the first Arab ruler to call for Bashar al-Assad to step down. The European powers did not honour their commitments to King Abdullah's ancestor; instead the modern state of Syria came into being as a French mandate. When they finally withdrew in April 1946 they left behind something that could only be properly called a 'country' in geographical terms. In response to this European imperialism there emerged, in the early 1940s, the Ba'ath Party, which sought to transcend cultural differences with a form of secular Arab nationalism. Ba'ath means renaissance in Arabic.

There was nothing about Syria that united the people within its borders. They were of different religions and different ethnicities. They had different regional and class identities. So it was not surprising that the nation was completely unstable. Ba'athism sought to give its people a common secular Arab identity. After Syria's independence there was coup upon coup upon coup, until the Ba'ath Party itself came to power by means of a coup in 1963, and it stayed. When it seized power it introduced a state of emergency, which lasted until it was lifted as a gesture by Bashar al-Assad in April 2011, by which time the country really was in a state of emergency.

As in neighbouring Iraq, under the Ba'ath Party most government jobs and all key posts went to its members. Because it was secular it offered no impediment to progress for the Alawites. It was functional but it wasn't inspiring. The inspiration to realise the Pan-Arab dream came from Nasser. The last putsch in Syria took place in 1970 and brought Hafez al-Assad to power. He had risen through the ranks of the air force and the Ba'ath Party. He was feared, not loved. Along with Ba'ath Party membership, membership of his Alawite sect also became increasingly important for government jobs and patronage. That concentration of power mainly in the hands of Alawites only increased under Bashar. The son was bequeathed what the father had spent his life creating.

The name Alawite means 'follower of Ali', the son-in-law and cousin of the Prophet Muhammad. It is a relatively new term, dating back only to the French mandate. Many of their practices are carried out in secret. They follow the Shia custom of Taqiyya, which allows people to hide or even deny their faith to protect them from persecution. Because very little is known about the Alawite customs their religion has been censured as heretical by many Muslims, because they see in it the deification of Ali. The sect itself, like the Druze and the Ismailis, derives from the wave of Shia Islam that swept through the region a thousand years ago. Since then they have been regularly persecuted by all comers, including the Crusaders, the Sunni Mamluks and the Sunni Muslim Ottomans.[24]

The French, like other European colonialists, wanted to use the downtrodden minorities as their tools to manage the majority. In Syria this meant the Alawites. Most importantly it led to the disproportionate recruitment of Alawites into the French-run military force. This cemented the Alawites into a military tradition that extended beyond the departure of the French and created the dominant officer class of the Syrian army that emerged. It remains that way today. The historian Daniel Pipes wrote that: 'An Alawi ruling Syria is like an untouchable becoming maharajah in India or a Jew becoming tsar in Russia – an unprecedented development shocking to the majority population which had monopolized power for so many centuries.'[25]

Hafez al-Assad rose to his position with skilful ruthlessness, and it was this trait he brought to both the domestic and the foreign arenas. His key foreign policy aim was to curb Israel's, and therefore America's, influence in the region. That meant maintaining at least arm's-length control of Lebanon, and finally in 1976 deploying his troops there and running the country as an extension of his own state.

Lebanon has one of the most complicated societies in the Middle East and the most obscure political system. Like Syria it was carved out of the Ottoman Empire and was given to the French in the European bargaining after the First World War. It got its independence in 1943, when it also got its power-sharing system, which divided up key posts based on religion. The president was always a Maronite Christian, the prime minister a Sunni Muslim, and the speaker of Parliament was Shia. The sectarian tensions bubbled along until 1975, when they exploded into a civil war that lasted fifteen years, killed or injured hundreds of thousands and laid waste to the capital Beirut. Hafez al-Assad used the war as the justification for his 1976 invasion.

The Lebanese war finally ended when a deal was reached called the Taif Agreement, named after the city in Saudi Arabia where it was signed. This agreement states that seats in the parliament will be divided equally between Muslims and Christians, and proportionately between the denominations of each sect and each district. It is the glue that holds the country together. It states as its aspiration the 'abolition of political sectarianism'.[26] Despite its fragility and failings, which enable groups like Hezbollah to wield huge political influence, the system that was worked out in Lebanon may end up as the framework for an agreement in Syria. Lebanon's deal was reached only after all sides exhausted themselves in fifteen years of civil war. 'I don't know how long it will take the Syrians before they are tired of killing each other,' a diplomat in Damascus told me in February 2013. He was clear that while either side thought it could win it would be hard to make progress with dialogue. And it was 'dialogue, not negotiations', the Syrian minister of information, Omran Ahed al-Zouabi, told me the same month. 'Negotiations,' he said, 'are held between equals.'

The uprising that broke out in Syria in 2011 was not the country's first major revolt. In February 1982 Hafez al-Assad conducted a scorched-earth policy to end a Muslim Brotherhood-led rebellion in the predominantly Sunni Muslim city of Hama. It was the culmination of a violent six-year countrywide struggle with the group that began after Hafez suggested a new constitution should mandate a secular state and that a non-Muslim could be president. In 1976 the Muslim Brotherhood began their insurrection against what they saw as the 'heretic' Alawite rulers.[27] In June 1980 Hafez was almost assassinated when Islamists attacked him as he waited for a foreign dignitary. Two hand grenades were thrown at him and he was targeted with machinegun fire. 'He kicked one grenade out of harm's way while a guard threw himself on the other and was killed instantly.'[28] The regime responded by massacring Brotherhood members already held in jail.

The conflict got nastier until its climax at Hama, when the army surrounded the city and simply pounded it into submission with tank and artillery fire. Then Assad's troops went in and carried out mass executions and rape. The assault went on for three weeks and was considered to be the single bloodiest attack by an Arab leader on his own people. At least 10,000 people were killed in Hama; some estimates put it at up to 30,000. A quarter of the city was flattened. It ended the Islamic insurgency.

Neda's father was a doctor in Hama and stayed throughout the military operation.[29] He sent his family away when a Syrian army officer searching the houses enquired whether Neda's fifteen-year-old sister was married.

> My uncle was a bank manager. They bombarded his area and destroyed his office, badly injuring his left leg and knocking him unconscious. When he woke up the soldiers had stacked him up in a pile of bodies. When they left he hid in the rubble of his office for two days. When he finally managed to get help and was taken to my father his leg was so bad it had to be cut off.

Neda recounted a whole series of stories about friends and relations who lost family members. Her family's maid had her seven sons taken from the house, never to return. An entire class of college students were killed because their teacher happened to be a member of the

Muslim Brotherhood. 'My brother's friend was killed in his house and they dragged his body around the street and then left it in the road. His mother went mad after that. She went along the whole street washing away his blood.'

The son had a hard act to follow, but follow he did. And it was clear, talking to his senior supporters in 2013, that it was still the Brotherhood – now supported by Qatar – rather than the Salafists supported by Saudi Arabia, that the regime hated the most. The Brotherhood though had been decimated by his father's regime, and while it was a heavy presence among the exiles in the opposition it did not have a significant presence among the fighters on the ground.

When his father was busy murdering people in Hama the Arab League was not up in arms and imposing sanctions. The bonds of the old world that Bashar al-Assad inherited were broken during the 2011 uprisings because the League had had its own small revolution. But when he had railed at the League, Bashar al-Assad had been right to say Syria was at the heart of the Arab world. The old Middle East's political fault lines all converged in Assad's Syria. So while the regime was loved by no one it was vital to everyone. It won quiet applause from the Americans because it kept the border with Israel nice and quiet. The Iranians were happy because the Assad family let them run guns to their proxies, Hezbollah, in Lebanon. Its credentials in respect of the Palestinian cause were second to none, and it housed and so protected key Palestinian militant groups in the capital Damascus, the most important of which was Hamas.

Like the other dictatorships, the Assad regimes always had ample amounts of something that successive American presidents did not have. Time. When they came across a political leader they couldn't deal with, the Assads just watched the clock. Despite supposedly being a pariah state and a founding member of the US's list of 'State Sponsors of Terrorism', they could always find bits of the world that would deal with them. The European Union, for example, was Syria's biggest trading partner. The Assads knew that Western and particularly European policy took regular big swings from left to right and back again. 'We as Westerners consider that when something is happening it will have an end, so we look for a logical timeline to that end,' a Western diplomat in the region told me.

> [The Syrians] tend to believe that: 'One day you are with us the next you are against.' You don't have to go back very far, just to 2005–7. Rice was saying after the assassination of [Lebanese prime minister] Hariri: 'We are in an era of regime change.' Then after the election of Sarkozy it was back to business: 'This is a regime that can be modernised, can be amended.' And the way they think is that this is temporary and they just have to wait it out.

That's what the West intended to try this time. It hoped sanctions would bite so hard that after a while the regime would just fall apart. It didn't work, and neither did the opposition group that Secretary Clinton had championed.

The SNC, which was dominated by the Syrian Muslim Brotherhood, proved itself to be a disastrous mix of self-serving, disorganised individuals who expended all their energies fighting with each other – at one stage quite literally, when a gathering in Cairo descended into a brawl.[30] Syria ground on into civil war and people died in their thousands. The Obama administration was concentrating on getting re-elected rather than doing anything serious about it. So in the absence of an alternative plan the Gulf states did what they always do when confronted with a complex political dilemma. They opened their wallets and threw money at it.

The secular groups like Omar's friends had no sponsors. They lost influence, as well as new recruits, to the groups that were getting the Gulf's arms and cash, smuggled in across the northern border. 'You could see a lot of convergence between the Turks and the Qataris [around] the Muslim Brotherhood,' a UN official in New York told me. 'The Qataris are pushing towards, in the context of Syria, to have another Islamic state run by the Muslim Brotherhood, which is a different situation altogether with Saudis and the Salafists. The Saudi government are more concerned about Iran, that's their biggest monster in the equation. What happens afterwards when it comes to Syria is almost immaterial.'

At first Israel advised America that it did not want Assad to go. Then when it was clear that his days were numbered they wanted it over with fast. They got neither outcome. According to a senior Israeli defence official, what worries Israel now is not just the geographical setting of a new jihad, but a change of focus that it says it detects since Ayman al-Zawahiri took over al-Qaeda following the killing of bin Laden: 'The al-Zawahiri al-Qaeda from our point of view is worse than the Bin Laden al-Qaeda, because Bin Laden believed in a Global Jihad. He said: "Let's destroy Washington and then we'll deal with Israel." Zawahiri says the opposite. He says: "Let's destroy Israel, it does not stop us destroying the United States, but let's focus on the Middle East."'

The Arab Spring was at first an ideological catastrophe for al-Qaeda. It fundamentally undermined one of the key planks of the Global Jihad philosophy, which was that the West will not allow peaceful change, so it must first be dealt a mortal blow before work can begin on the model Islamic society. The peaceful overthrow of the American-backed dictator in Egypt by the people in al-Zawahiri's own home town destroyed that argument. The chaos in Syria gave groups like al-Qaeda another chance.

After the US had spent more than a decade at war with al-Qaeda in the region, the conflict in Syria led to the unedifying spectacle of America and Osama bin Laden's followers being on the same side, albeit with starkly different visions for the post-conflict era. As that fact became more public and embarrassing Washington tried to distance itself from the nastier consequences of its failure to take a lead on the crisis. In December 2012 it formally declared that one of the more effective elements of the armed Syrian opposition groups, the hard-line jihadist Nusra Front, was an alias of Al-Qaeda in Iraq, and thus a terrorist organisation. The announcement was made with little fanfare. That was because to have left the way open for al-Qaeda to reconstitute itself on the border of America's most important Middle East ally, Israel, was a massive failure of US foreign policy. That money would start flowing from the Gulf states to back jihadist groups fighting in Syria was entirely predictable. It was also easy to move them there. They were just a car ride away in neighbouring Iraq. And they knew the route because it was through Syria, and with the help of the Assad regime, that they had got into Iraq in the first place.

The Nusra Front, also known as the Jabhat al-Nusra, first declared its presence in the conflict in January 2012.[31] The group has claimed to be behind most of the large bomb attacks that have taken place in the country, which unsurprisingly have mirrored those in Iraq. By the beginning of 2013 it was thought to number several thousand. However an arms smuggler in Lebanon's northern Bekaa valley on the Syria border told me that the Nusra Front was 'a kind of trademark that a lot of people are using to scare their enemies. A lot of people who claim to be Jabhat al-Nusra are not, but they think it's a better brand name than being the "First Brigade" of somewhere or other.'

The Nusra Front have seen their support grow because they are better, more experienced, more disciplined fighters than those that loosely form the FSA. While many Syrians felt intense disillusion with the West over its failure to act in their country the way it acted in Libya, by contrast the Nusra Front do not want to see Western intervention, because their aim, like Al-Qaeda in Iraq's, is a fundamentalist Islamic state in Syria. In July 2012 the Al-Qaeda in Iraq leader Abu-Bakr al Baghdadi was saying that the Syrian state should be wiped off the map. He called for 'applying the *sharia*, uniting the *ummah* [Islamic community] by demolishing the borders implemented by the Sykes–Picot [agreement], eradicating filthy nationalism and hated patriotism, and bringing back the Islamic state, the state that does not recognize artificial boundaries and does not believe in any nationality other than Islam'.[32] The following April he claimed his group and the Nusra Front had come together as the 'Islamic State in Iraq and the Levant'.[33] Al-Qaeda in Iraq made a mess of its game plan by attacking minorities and fellow Sunni Muslims with unspeakable brutality. When you are in a fight to the death you will often take all the help you can get but even the Nusra front balked at being too closely associated with its Iraqi brethren. Syria's jihadists responded by saying they would follow al-Zawahari but distanced themselves politely from the damaged goods, even by al-Qaeda standards, of the extremists in Iraq.[34] However having to publically declare an allegiance to al-Qaeda central, just to keep the even more hard-line group in Iraq at arm's length, was an own goal for the violent jihadists. There was no ambiguity anymore about their purpose in Syria and that undermined the support they had at that stage won from the local population for their more restrained actions on the ground. It also added to the fears of the country's religious minorities. The new wing of this violent extremist franchise had been trying to get it right, second time around, in Syria. But, even without having to show their true colours, in the long run they are unlikely to succeed because just like the other Arab revolutions, Syria's was not led from the mosque.

That means that not every young fighter you saw shouting 'Allahu Akbar' to the TV cameras was an Islamic fundamentalist, though they were often clumsily portrayed that way in some of the Western media. Christian soldiers invoke the Almighty before they go into battle, so what is odd about young Muslim men doing the same? But what was clear to the young activist from Homs, Omar Shakir, was that the failure of the Western powers to get involved and offer an alternative was accelerating this radicalisation.

I'm against those people, as are all the Syrian people who support the revolution. People in Syria, some of them pray, some of them they don't. People don't ask: 'Are you Alawis, or Sunni, or Shia?' or whatever, and we never had these jihadist people. But now because in this revolution the international community is not doing anything these people enter the country and the problem is they are affecting both sides, not just the regime. They will kill you if you defy them, if you don't follow them. The problem is that there are so many people in Syria who want revenge. Revenge is controlling them. People are beginning to lose their minds. When I came out I had time to rest and to think. But that's impossible inside Syria. You can't think because of the shelling.

The prospect of Islamic extremists getting a foothold in the country finally provoked President Obama to declare under what circumstances he was ready to intervene. 'We cannot have a situation where chemical or biological weapons are falling into the hands of the wrong people,' he said in August 2012. 'We have been very clear to the Assad regime, but also to other players on the ground, that a red line for us is we start seeing a whole bunch of chemical weapons moving around or being utilized. That would change my calculus. That would change my equation.'[35] It was a stark admission of just how much else the Assad regime could get away with. His remarks were prompted after Syria's Foreign Ministry spokesman Jihad Makdissi accidentally admitted for the first time that the regime even had them when he promised they would not be used: 'Any chemical or biological weapons will never be used, I repeat, will never be used in the Syrian crisis, no matter what the internal developments in this crisis are,' he had told reporters. But by the summer of 2013 the Europeans, the Israelis and finally the Americans all said there was some evidence that small amounts of chemical weapons had been used in the conflict. There were new calls from the US Senate for action to be taken. The question then became how thick Obama's red line was, and what standard of proof would be required for a more robust intervention in the crisis. In a clear reference to the intelligence failures ahead of the Iraq invasion the White House wrote to John McCain that while 'Our intelligence community does assess with varying degrees of confidence that the Syrian regime has used chemical weapons on a small scale in Syria, specifically the chemical agent sarin ... Given the stakes involved, and what we have learned from our own recent experience, intelligence assessments alone are not sufficient – only credible and corroborated facts that provide us with some degree of certainty will guide our decision-making.'[36] Obama had boxed himself in by drawing a red line in front of a regime that didn't know when to stop. Not taking action once it was crossed would mean undermining the authenticity of the red line he had drawn for Iran's nuclear ambitions. Taking action against the country's chemical weapon stockpiles though was not easy.

One of Israel's senior military commanders told me:

> It's almost mission impossible to destroy Syria's chemical weapons. In order to destroy them you have to control them, and that's a long process. If something is dug into underground tunnels you might be able to block it in but if you hit some of it then you've put it out there [released the gas]. So it is very difficult. This doesn't mean you can't do anything, but you can't be sure of dealing with all of it.

What worried Israel and the West the most was that these weapons might find their way outside the Syrian arena. The wild card was the jihadists among the opposition fighters.

Makdissi's blunder led to criticism of him within the regime. He is a Christian and was clearly considering his position when I met him in the summer. By then his family was already in Beirut. He fled the country in December. His Damascus home was ransacked by the Shabiha and his beloved collection of Syrian art was looted. He issued a statement a few months later from an undisclosed location saying: 'I left Syria because of the violence and polarisation that left no place for moderation and diplomacy.' He added that division in the country had reached a 'destructive' level.

The longer the fighting went on the more damage was done to Syria's fragile society. The UN's General Robert Mood told me while in Damascus that the massacre in Qubair and two weeks before that the larger one in Houla were 'the beginning of the sectarian aspect of the conflict'. The UN investigated both incidents, but the clean-up of any evidence in Qubair ruled out clear conclusions. Its report published the following August said that most of the people murdered in Qubair belonged to the al-Yatim family. The team found that since the uprisings had begun there had been tensions between the Sunni Muslim villagers and their Alawi neighbours in Al-Twaime. After one of the residents of Qubair had a row with his Alawite neighbour the Sunni villagers had sought protection from a handful of local FSA fighters. When the government found out, they surrounded the village, shelled it and then sent in troops and the militia. Somewhere between forty and seventy-eight people died, including women and children. The UN report found that 'reasonable suspicion exists that unlawful killing of civilians occurred at the hands of pro-Government forces, including *Shabbiha* from neighboring villages'.[37]

In Houla, where 108 people died, most of them women and children, the UN were more certain as to who carried out the massacre. These murders were thoroughly investigated by the UN, and 'little evidence was collected suggesting that anyone other than Government forces and *Shabbiha* committed the killings'.[38] It was the first big sectarian atrocity of the conflict. There was lots of talk at the time that it might mark a turning point in the conflict by provoking international intervention or stir diplomatic solution. It did not. 'I kept thinking we've hit the bottom, then we went deeper,' said a Syrian woman I met in Damascus the following year. 'Now I'm worried where the bottom will be.' The Houla massacre was the first time the outside world could see clear evidence that the government tactic of setting sect against sect was working, but Professor Haykel says that the sectarian edge to the war showed itself earlier, in Baba Amr:

> Homs seems to have been a battle that was part of a strategy by the government to evacuate as many Sunnis from the city as possible so that they can create a zone so that Homs can link up to the Bekaa Valley. There's this idea of creating a zone where you have Shiites in Lebanon connecting to Alawites along this belt west of the Orontes River all the way up through the Alawis' heartland.

The fighters of the Free Syrian Army had been hoping to make history repeat itself by holding their positions in Homs, but greater forces were determined that it would not. 'We are paying the price for Libya here,' a diplomat who was then in Damascus told me. 'It will take a while before others in the Security Council believe us again. We have shot ourselves in the foot.' He was referring to the legacy of the 'all necessary measures' clause that President Obama had championed to save Benghazi.

> [The Russians and the Chinese] did not believe the British, the French and the Americans would have what the Israelis call the chutzpah, to do it! The Russians have been completely hurt by this, there is [real] mistrust. I have had comments from my Russian counterpart, though he is very Soviet and doesn't stray out of the [diplomatic] lines, he said: 'We were betrayed' and it's played into the hands of the Syrians. This has gone beyond a matter of [the Russians'] interests it's a matter of ego.

By contrast, Chinese diplomats rarely talk to their opposite numbers in the West. Beijing lets senior academics in government-controlled universities express their unvarnished views on events on its behalf. 'We felt we were cheated,' Zhu Weili, the director of Middle East Studies at Shanghai International University, told me:

> As an expert, I feel that we have been cheated. Regarding the establishment of the no-fly zone in Libya, China abstained from the voting and allowed the resolution to pass, but the Western countries took this opportunity to launch fierce attacks there. The Western countries hoped that what happened in Libya would happen in Syria. But they know very little about Islamic sectarian policy. Syria is not Libya at all. The situation in Syria is much more complicated.

If the opposition groups collected a dollar for every time a foreign player reminded the world that 'Syria is not Libya' their revolution would have been self-funding. But both sides of the divide in the Security Council used that excuse to justify their position. For Russia though it was complicated. Its support for Syria dates back to the Cold War era, a period in which the US was building its alliances with the Gulf states. In the first year of the conflict it sold $1 billion worth of arms to Syria.[39] In June 2012 it tried to ship refurbished Mi-25 military helicopters to Syria, causing a row with the US. Russia also has huge private investments in energy, tourism and infrastructure projects. Syria's deep warm-water port in Tartus is a strategic asset for Moscow, which has a naval facility there. Western diplomats told me Tartus was where, by 2013, the Russians were delivering regular arms supplies for the Assad regime. But for Moscow, which has fought a brutal war against its own Islamist rebels, Assad was seen 'not so much as "a bad dictator" but as a secular leader struggling with an uprising of Islamist barbarians'.[40]

So important was Syria to Russia that the Israelis tracked the movement of Russian advisers to serve as a litmus test for the regime's stability. They watched for the moment when the Russians were ready to head for the door en masse because they assumed it meant the exit of the regime was not far behind.

However, says Professor Joshua Landis, the director of the Center for Middle East Studies at the University of Oklahoma and a Syria specialist, there was no incentive for Assad's troops to think about suing for peace. 'The militaries in North Africa could turn against the presidents because they knew they'd all be hired by the next guy that came along,' he told me.

> But in Syria, when Assad gets booted out and a Sunni takes over he is going to purge the entire structure from top to bottom, like they did in Iraq. So the Alawite officers are fighting not only for their jobs, but for their lives. There is no good solution. If they put down their guns and surrender they are likely to meet a very bad fate. The rebels have said they want justice and that anybody with blood on their hands is going to pay for it. And so many of them have blood

on their hands, almost every Alawite family has some soldier who has got blood on his hands. They are not talking about five hundred people going to jail, they are talking about tens of thousands of people going to jail. And the more brutality this regime uses, the more people have compromised themselves.

Even a bomb in the heart of its security headquarters in July 2012 didn't stall the military establishment. It killed the defence minister and three other senior officials, one of whom was Bashar al-Assad's brother-in-law. Other top officials, including the intelligence chief and interior minister, were injured. Bashar al-Assad appointed a new defence minister, General Daoud Rajha, and the killing just carried on. That may have been because the real military power was concentrated in the hands of the extended Assad family, including on his mother's side the Makhloufs, not the public officials. But there was another possible explanation. The talk in the capital Damascus was that the men might have been plotting a coup, and were assassinated by the regime before they could carry out their plan.

President Obama opposed acting without international sanction, and that sanction was not forthcoming. The State Department under Hillary Clinton was ready to push harder, but President Obama made it clear that he was not. He told them America would participate but he did not want to take the lead on Syria because he could not see a happy ending. He was also conscious of a sense of American overreach with regard to Afghanistan and Iraq, and he wasn't ready to do that again in Syria. Another key factor though was that he did not want to own a problem in an election year when success would be measured by differing degrees of failure. But even when the election was over, his view that there was no good outcome in getting too involved didn't change. Syria festered, and so did the mood in the Security Council.

'It's very poisonous,' said a United Nations official to me of the atmosphere Syria had created. There was huge frustration among the UN people working on the Syrian issue, because while it was obvious

that all the Permanent members wanted to avoid the inevitable consequences of doing nothing, still they 'couldn't get their act together'.
The entire Security Council feared the nightmare scenario that Israel
was talking up, but bad blood, big egos and first the Russian and then
the US electoral cycles were all factors in not wanting to be seen to be
conceding ground.

When Kofi Annan resigned his role in August 2012 as the joint
envoy he blamed everyone involved. The Europeans and Americans
privately briefed that when Annan said everyone he really meant the
Russians. He did not. He said everyone because he meant everyone.
His most enduring achievement before, as one UN official put it, the
'Security Council members dumped him' was the agreement reached
in Geneva in June 2012. It at least established agreement within the
Security Council that a political transition should occur. Assad's
supporters in Iran said he should remain in power until presidential
polls were held in 2014.[41] Annan's replacement as joint UN–Arab
League envoy, Lakhdar Brahimi, tried to build out from the Geneva
agreement. It was an impossible task. Eight months later he was ready
to quit. 'I haven't resigned,' he said. 'Every day I wake up and think I
should resign. One day perhaps I will resign.'[42]

A few months after the uprisings began a group of army deserters
announced the formation of the Free Syrian Army. As the conflict
moved into its third year the 'Free Syrian Army' was still little more
than a label for the mass of people who were fighting against the government but who were not part of the Salafist trend. The title existed in
splendid isolation from any kind of real central command and control
structure, even though it had what was called its headquarters across
the northern border in Turkey. The US and Europeans had tried to help
the fighters coordinate better by providing among their non-lethal
assistance the same type of communication equipment I'd seen suddenly
appear in the hands of Libyan rebels during the height of the fighting
there. But two years after it was supposed to have been created the Free
Syrian Army was still more of an aspiration.

In July 2012 the Red Cross formally declared that the entire country was embroiled in a 'civil war', which meant both sides were now subject to the Geneva convention regarding war crimes.[43] That drew more attention to the actions of the rebels. Videos began to emerge of opposition fighters abusing and executing captured government soldiers, though the UN said their abuses 'did not reach the gravity, frequency and scale of those committed by Government forces and the Shabbiha'.[44] But what they did do in the eyes of opponents to the regime was something worse. They started abusing the people they were supposed to be fighting for.

By the early winter months of 2013 the war-ravaged northern city of Aleppo was largely in the hands of the opposition fighters, despite the army's use of air power and Scud missiles to try to hold on. That ancient city, which had been inhabited for millennia, was in parts reduced to rubble. Having taken control the rebels had no idea what to do with it. Inflation had gone sky-high and no one had a job. There was no electricity, water was scarce and rubbish was piling up in the streets. Families were forced to sell their possessions for food and heating oil as the bitter winter set in. People stood for hours in bread queues, leaving them vulnerable to incoming government rounds. So, faced with these challenges, some of the fighters from the Free Syrian Army decided to rob the city. They stole Aleppo's flour supplies for themselves.[45] 'Welcome to Free Syria' said a resident sarcastically to one of my colleagues, pointing at the destruction in the city.[46]

The contest for Aleppo was a disaster for the Syrian opposition. They fought a totally uncoordinated battle that did as much damage to their credibility as it did to the city. Many of the fighters came from the surrounding rural areas, not the city itself, and saw Aleppo as a prize to capture, not to protect. The chaotic failures of the FSA enhanced the reputation of the much more disciplined Islamist fighters. If Homs was where the opposition realised they were going to have to fight this war alone, then Aleppo was where they realised what fighting a war actually meant. They learned the lesson Makdissi had finally grasped, that it is hard to rule an angry people. And the citizens of Aleppo were furious with the mess the FSA had made of their city.

There was anger too across the northern provinces because of the fractious nature of the opposition. Criminal gangs flourished. The Islamist fighters became a law unto themselves. The FSA could not seem to get its act together.

In October 2012 Lakhdar Brahimi tried to organise a brief truce to mark the Muslim holiday of Eid al-Adha. The UN hoped to use that pause to send around seventeen truckloads of aid to the city of Homs. They wanted to get to three areas of the city, starting with the al-Khalidiya district. They spent fourteen hours trying to gain access, but nobody on the opposition side could guarantee the safety of the convoys. That was because there were twenty-one disparate FSA brigades inside this small quarter alone. 'You had to deal with twenty-one chiefs, and each of those twenty-one had totally different ideas and policies. And each one of them wanted to dictate the rules,' an aid worker told me. The trucks had to turn back.

Part of the issue though was that the UN personnel in Syria were bearing the brunt of the abuse from the opposition fighters, which should have been directed at the Security Council members. But those members were not present on the ground, and the UN were, and were constantly hampered by a mixture of suspicion and FSA incompetence when trying to get aid for civilians into rebel-held areas.

Meantime the opposition in the capital looked with dread at the mess in Aleppo and beyond. They believed the regime would have no qualms about smashing their own ancient city. This meant that the battle for the heart of Damascus was much more protracted and less gung-ho. The opposition tried to wear the regime down with tactical strikes to cut the city off. That did not mean there was not misery and destruction. When I drove around the suburbs of Damascus in February 2013 I saw that large areas of the city had been flattened by artillery fire. Checkpoints choked the roads, manned by members of the seventeen different internal security services operating in the capital. They also sealed off the rebellious neighbourhoods that I had been able to drive around freely the year before. There was the regular 'crump' of shells landing and puffs of smoke dotted the skyline. People queued in hundreds for bread. Electricity was sporadic and the people were exhausted. The slow capture of the outskirts of the city from the regime followed a regular pattern. The security services would fight the FSA with small arms until they began to lose ground. Then they pulled out, surrounded the area and shelled it. By this time the Shabiha had been formed into a single fighting force, which was much more hated and feared than the army.

In the capital these men ran their local fiefdoms under the banner of newly created 'Popular Committees', though they were not popular with anyone outside their membership. 'Area 86' is the Alawite suburb where many of the security personnel and Shabiha live with their families. It sprawls its way across the base of Mount Qasioun, which towers over the city. Higher up the mountain was where the army placed its artillery. It then fired across the city into the suburbs on the other side. To get to the heavy weapons the opposition would have to fight their way through the Alawite security forces who were not only protecting the state but also their own families. The regime had put its soldiers' women and children in front of their last line of defence.

The United Nations had hoped it would never reach this stage. They had been trying from the start to resolve the conflict before the civil war became 'destructive beyond the point of repair'. The problem was that they really had no idea who to talk to, because the so-called unified opposition represented by the SNC spoke only for themselves. They never had any control over the people fighting under the banner of the 'Free Syrian Army'. So by the end of 2012 the Obama administration abandoned the SNC. By then the SNC had received forty million dollars, half from Libya and the rest from the Qataris and the UAE. There was nothing to show for it.[47]

'We've made it clear that the SNC can no longer be viewed as the visible leader of the opposition,' Hillary Clinton said in October 2012. She then acknowledged, obliquely, that the international community had wasted a full year on a group of exiles who were totally divorced from the reality on the ground. She said the opposition group that came next 'must include people from inside Syria and others who have a legitimate voice that needs to be heard'.[48]

It felt as if, now the US election season was over, the Obama administration was suddenly aware as 2012 drew to a close what a terrible mess it had allowed to fester around the Syria crisis while its attention was focused elsewhere. In November it oversaw the formation of a new opposition grouping, the 'National Coalition for Syrian Revolutionary and Opposition Forces'. The leader of the coalition was Ahmed Moaz al-Khatib, a former imam of the Umayyad Mosque in Damascus and one of the few figures outside Syria who had credibility within the opposition forces who were doing the fighting. In December President Obama announced: 'We've made a decision that the Syrian Opposition Coalition is now inclusive enough, is reflective and representative enough of the Syrian population that we consider them the legitimate representative of the Syrian people in opposition to the Assad regime.' 'It's a big step,' he said.[49] It made little difference. This coalition included the old SNC as a block, so it still held huge sway. The new grouping often ended up being referred to in shorthand as the 'Syrian National Coalition' or SNC. The name barely changed, nor did its nature. The reorganisation did little to stem the infighting among the exiles. The coalition was still seen by opposition activists and fighters on the ground as a Trojan horse, backed by Qatar, for the Syrian Muslim Brotherhood's domination of the post-Assad political arena.

In March 2013 the National Coalition chose Ghassan Hitto, a Damascus-born IT specialist who had the spent the previous decades living in the US, as the prime minister to head a government in rebel-held areas. 'I've met him twice,' the US ambassador to Syria Robert Ford told the House Foreign Affairs Committee that month. 'He struck me as more Texan than Muslim Brotherhood, frankly.'[50] Neither was much of a qualification to unite a divided nation or a divided opposition. His appointment prompted more infighting and infuriated al-Khatib, who said he would resign. A few days later the

National Coalition was formally given Syria's seat at the Arab League, which had been vacant since its suspension from the group in November 2011, until new elections were held in the country. The decision was pushed through by the Qataris just days before the League's annual summit, which was being held in their capital Doha. It was hailed at the time as a hugely symbolic moment, but when you stood back it was clear the excitement just reflected how little else had been achieved. It was interpreted by Brahimi as an attempt by the Arab League to close the door on a negotiated solution with the regime.[51]

Maintaining stability within Syrian society after the civil war is not going to be easy. There is no doubt that the system under Assad was hugely skewed towards the Alawite community, but that didn't make the vast majority wealthy. In Damascus there are large Alawite slums. They did get government jobs, but these paid only a minimum wage. People in the capital complained that government institutions were often packed with the people from the Alawite community. They also dominated the army officer class and eventually the government militia, the Shabiha. But when the conflict deepened no effort was made by the opposition to make the Alawites feel they had a future in the Syria that emerged from the conflict, so many came to take it for granted that on the 'day after' they would simply lose everything.

'It shouldn't be a winner-and-loser game. We should keep the nature of the Syrian society. One in three of the Syrian population one way or another supported this regime, so we cannot throw them away.' These views, expressed by the Syrian journalist Ahmed, were increasingly rare in a society losing sight of what was worth keeping of their old lives.

> I am definitely against any kind of deba'athification or dissolving the army. The minorities are scared. We are talking about around a million and half people in the Alawite community in Damascus. The majority of them are under forty, they didn't know any president but Hafez Assad and then Bashar. They didn't know any

situation apart from the situation they are in where they have the privilege to come from the village to Damascus and to find a job and to survive. So now there is a revolution that wants justice, but justice is hard for them so they will feel scared.

In the long run Professor Landis believed that allowing Syria to fight for its future, even if that meant a long and bloody civil war, was perhaps a better way of ensuring its stability in the future, because leaders would eventually emerge with revolutionary credibility. 'Because this is a problem of nation building and identity formation the Syrians have to figure this out for themselves,' he told me.

Nobody can impose a solution. We tried to do that in Iraq and in Afghanistan, and Obama just doesn't want to get involved. The Syrians have to find their own George Washington in a sense. America can't do that. We tried to do that in Iraq with Chalabi and now with Maliki. We tried to do that with Karzai, but you can't select somebody else's leader, they [have to] emerge. You could make the argument that war is a national building process, in a horrible way, and especially in these multi-ethnic countries where it's very hard to find a formula. For America to jump into that and to try to play cop is a fool's errand.

The war slowly destroyed most of the country's businesses, but a few did start to thrive. One was ad hoc kidnapping for ransom, which was dominated by the Shabiha, though there were many such incidents in opposition-held areas too. A variant of this became a big new money-spinner for the government, which industrialised the extortion. The regime ransomed off the captured FSA fighters held in its jails. The going rate, as the conflict passed its second anniversary, for the families of opposition fighters to get their loved ones back was 500,000 Syrian pounds, which was then equivalent to around US$5,000. The government rounded up rebels, sold them back to their families and then rounded up some more. It was an endless circle of supply and demand. The cost of a bribe to get anything done in the city had also gone up tenfold from the previous summer when I had visited the city.

The people who could not buy their way out of jail were the organisers of the first peaceful protests. Releasing some of the young fighters did not scare the regime, because these men suited its narrative of the opposition as bunches of violent terrorist gangs. But it saw the peaceful disciplined activists as much more of a threat. If they were released and got together with the fighters then the government might suddenly have been faced with a credible internal political opposition combined with a more organised military wing. That prospect scared them.

The question next door in Israel and among the Western nations is whether, after the war, Syria becomes a base for Sunni extremists to destabilise the wider region. 'Syria is a new opportunity for Global Jihadists. There is a repetition of what happened in the Eighties in Afghanistan, the Nineties in Bosnia, and the conflict in Chechnya. Now we have it in Syrian society,' says Professor Olivier Roy, who is one of the world's leading scholars on modern religious movements.

> But I think the Bosnian scenario is the most likely, that once they win they will expel the Salafi jihadists, so these guys will have to go elsewhere. We'll have a problem, but with nomadic jihadists. I don't believe Syria will create a strong hub for them. We tend to have a territorial approach and we fear the creation of sanctuaries for jihadists. Actually sometimes that is not a problem, because they are an easier target when they settle somewhere. The worst jihadist is the guy who looks European, travels by plane, has a British passport and operates like that.

And it may turn out that many of the Islamist fighters will prove not to be very committed to the jihadist cause beyond the fall of the regime. The money to support the opposition fighters was coming from the Gulf, and to get that money you needed to show some Islamist credentials. Previously clean-shaven fighters started to grow beards and adopt the dress code of the Salafist movement because it won them funding and arms. 'I don't think many of them are fanatics at all,' a woman very involved in the opposition movement in Damascus told me. 'I went with ten people to meet the Nusra Front people in Damascus, and three of us were women. Me and one another woman came dressed like this' – she gestured to her uncovered hair and tight Western-style clothing – 'and these men didn't care at all. They shook my hand. They've just grown beards to get money that's all, because they are funded by Qatar.'

There were also signs that while the regime leadership and opposition leadership in exile could not work out a way to talk, on the ground at a very local level, deals could be done. When the opposition groups took over parts of Syria's small but vital oilfields they looted the offices but they looked after the wells. When they realised that they didn't know how to run them, I was told by people involved in negotiating the deals that they leased them back to the local regime representatives in return for royalties. That way the oil kept flowing, the opposition got funding for its war, and so did the regime. FSA activists working from Lebanon told me their fighters even did deals with Syrian army units to buy ammunition. They assumed that the local commanders kept the money themselves. The same kind of local arrangement was made over opposition fighters captured by the Shabiha. Often the national army would act as the intermediary between the two sides to settle the ransom demands.

By the spring of 2013, in total, more than a million people had fled to neighbouring states to escape the chaos in Syria. Over half of them were children.[52] Many of the children were traumatised, having seen family members killed. Some had been themselves subjected to torture.[53] By then UN aid workers I'd met inside the country had told me four million people had been displaced. They said the health care system in parts of Syria had collapsed and in others hospitals were carrying out major surgery without anaesthetic.

By then Jordan already had 460,000 Syrian refugees in the country. It was by far the largest number anywhere. 'How are you going to turn back women, children, and the wounded?' said King Abdullah. 'This is something that we just can't do.'[54] But he warned that by the end of the year the number would have gone much higher. Many were fleeing because the rape of men, women and children, largely by the Shabiha militias, had reached epidemic proportions.[55]

Jordan was already fragile after the Arab revolts because of a resurgence of the Muslim Brotherhood and the ever-present tensions between Jordanians and the Palestinian refugee community, two million strong, and most of whom have full Jordanian citizenship. The fate of Jordan was a major concern for the US because it was a major concern for Israel. 'God save the king,' joked one of Israel's senior generals to me as the internal pressure in Jordan built up. The US based a team of its own military officials to try to insulate Jordan from the growing turmoil along its long border after there were skirmishes between Jordanian and Syrian troops. Assad warned the Jordanians there would be consequences for supporting the process of arming the opposition. 'The fire will not stop at our border,' he said, 'and everybody knows that Jordan is exposed as Syria is.'[56]

Young Omar Shakir had thought to himself when he emerged from his tunnel after the escape from Homs that Assad would survive until 2014. Few others thought so at the time. When I went to Damascus in the summer of 2012 everyone seemed to think the regime was staggering towards its end. When I went back the following summer Omar's prediction looked a lot more likely. As darkness fell and the streets emptied, the previous year's sound of a vibrant nightlife was replaced by the regular thud of artillery fire landing a few kilometres away in the Damascus suburbs. In 2012 I had had to drive several hours from the city to find the war. The following year the war had come to me. Yet Assad's supporters in the capital still believed they could hold on to what they had got out of the regime. 'I told him recently, you are our agent for change,' one of Assad's friends told me. 'I told him we have invested so much in you. Only you have the political maturity to see the country through the transition.' His supporters believed he would be vindicated in the presidential polls promised for 2014, though how they were going to hold this election in the middle of a civil war was less clear.

Even though it was now in the third year of its fight against the Syrian people the regime still didn't think it was necessarily going to lose though it knew it couldn't win. But European patience with the status quo had begun to run out.

The jihadist fighters never had a problem getting a regular supply of arms, an Arab diplomat told me, because wealthy, mainly Saudi, individuals in the Gulf funded them. The Syrian businessmen who initially funded the FSA had, two years after the uprising, largely exhausted their reserves. However an EU diplomat told me that by the spring of 2013 Britain was helping to supply arms to the non-Islamist rebel fighters but with enough distance from the process to maintain deniability. But that supply waxed and waned depending on international diplomatic manoeuverings. A senior FSA activist also told me the British were helping to arm them by working with the Saudi government. The US had made it clear it was now not going to try to convince them otherwise.[57] The diplomat said all three countries, though predominantly the Americans, had set up a camp along the border in Jordan to train rebel fighters in tactics and arms, essentially building an FSA officer class. Broader European enthusiasm for maintaining their strict arms embargo was also on the wane.

On Syria the US wasn't 'leading from behind', it was not leading at all. On his first trip to the Gulf as secretary of state John Kerry had to stand next to the Qatari prime minister and listen to him gently chide the Obama administration over its reluctance to arm the opposition. 'There is a change in the international position and the American position in this regard. They're talking about weapons,' said Sheik Hamad bin Jassim al-Thani through a translator. 'We hope that this had happened sometime ago before, because this would have maybe lessened the death and destruction that took place in Syria . . . I'm not an expert on arms, but if there is some rocket-propelled grenades or RPGs or anything provided, this will not threaten the world order.'

In response the secretary of state could only say: 'We had a discussion about the types of weapons that are being transferred and by whom. We are aware of what people are doing . . . we did discuss the question of the ability to try to guarantee that it's going to the right people and to the moderate Syrian Opposition Coalition.'[58]

The previous day in Saudi Arabia Kerry had acknowledged that in Syria 'bad actors, regrettably, have no shortage of their ability to get weapons from Iran, from Hezbollah, from Russia,' and then he had to listen to a lecture from its foreign minister Saud al-Faisal about how 'what is happening in Syria is a slaughter . . . and we just can't bring ourselves to remain quiet in front of this carnage.'[59] Unfortunately for Secretary of State Kerry US policy towards the Gulf meant he could not point up the contradictions in all their positions. The Gulf countries couldn't remain quiet about the violence, but they all kept quiet about the aspirations behind the original revolts because what they did not support was the democracy and human rights most of the Syrians were fighting for.

The first year of the conflict saw the West trying to negotiate Assad out of the country. From the second year, once it was clear that Assad was not going to go in a matter of months and that there was no appetite among the US public for military engagement, the Obama administration sought to stop the violence spilling out elsewhere. The US has not been trying to resolve the situation in Syria, it has been trying to contain it.

In an election year you can't answer the question 'What are you going to do about these massacres?' by saying 'Nothing.' The Obama administration was criticised for having no policy towards the violence in Syria, and that criticism was unfair. It did have a policy. It was a 'We're not getting involved' policy, but it couldn't spell that out until 2013.

If the Obama administration was reluctant to play a leading role during the fighting it also hinted it might take a back seat when the regime finally collapsed. When he was asked by the Senate committee if there were plans for stabilisation operations for the end of Assad's rule General Mattis said the Arab League and the GCC states 'may be able to take this on'.[60]

Syria was one of the rogue nations Obama had tried to engage with. In 2011 he sent in the first US ambassador to Damascus for six years. The post had been withdrawn after the assassination of Rafik Hariri in neighbouring Lebanon, which Washington blamed on Syria. Obama had sought to engage with Syria before the Arab Spring because it was strategically important. It could destabilise Jordan and Lebanon. It could threaten Israel. It was a player in the Middle East peace process, and the US hoped to woo it away from Iran.

All of those issues have been overtaken by events. If the war goes on much longer the country may break down into fiefdoms. That will guarantee chaos for years to come. And while the fighting goes on, the only policy the US needs, now that the strategic value of Syria has disintegrated, is to stop the mess spreading. It is one also signed up to by Syria's neighbours.

The one way that Syria might, after all, end up being a bit like Libya is if Assad should also choose not to make his last stand in the capital but in his community's heartland. In Gaddafi's case it was the desert city of Sirte. Assad's instincts are likely to take him to the coastal mountain area that forms the Alawite homeland. Hence his men fighting so hard to keep hold of the main motorway heading out of Damascus through Homs and up towards the coastal mountain area. To retreat down this road would be to return to the statelet first granted to the Alawites by the French in 1922 around the port city of Latakia.[61] If he does that, how long he can last out there would depend on how organised and cohesive the Sunni militia are. If by then the country has descended into warlordism and the FSA brigades are busy wrangling over the spoils with the Nusra Front, his group might be able to hold on and recreate an Alawite state. Opposition activists in Lebanon told me they were resigned to the fact that the jihadists, like the Nusra Front, were likely to keep control of the north. FSA fighters were likely to hold the south. Before the war was over rebel fighters were carving out territory they intended to keep. The same could also happen with the Kurds in the north-east of the country.

A retreat to the Alawite homeland might actually prove the best-case scenario for the West too, because it would allow the war to wind down. If the Syrian leadership was all simply to be wiped out in a bomb attack, or all to get on a plane, the nature of the conflict now suggests there could be a widespread slaughter of the Alawites who remain, a fury of retribution. They would probably flee the country. But if the state falls apart they won't be the only ones running for their lives. Anyone with a family, but without the protection of a militia, will contemplate doing the same.

Turkey, like Jordan, has the capacity to build a 'safe haven' for a surge of refugees on the Syrian side of its border, and if the regime collapsed that is what it would probably do. Few Syrians will go to Iraq. That leaves Lebanon. The most fragile, most complex society in the Middle East would have to take most of the impact from a collapse of the Syrian state. It is the least equipped to do so. Many Alawites would probably end up in northern Lebanon if they found nowhere safe in Syria.

The Israeli military leadership does not believe that Assad will flee the country. They think he takes his responsibilities to his Alawite sect seriously and so will, as a last resort, try to build a new Alawite strong-hold. 'The Alawites need a place to run to or be butchered by the rebels,' is the Israeli assessment.

An Alawite state would also enjoy the full support of both the Russians and the Iranians. The Russians would get to keep their warm-water naval facility in Tartus. The Iranians could still send guns to Hezbollah if they help Assad hold the land all the way to the Leba-nese border. Militarily, defending an Alawite state is a much more viable option than trying to rule the whole country. The Alawites could probably even get the international community on board by claiming that without their own state they would be annihilated. The only people who would not be happy would be the Syrian opposition – but they are likely to be exhausted – and of course the Gulf states.

The analogy for the sectarian mess in Syria is the sectarian mess in Yugoslavia. Both countries were created out of the collapse of the Ottoman Empire. The disintegration of Syria has followed the end of the Cold War dictatorships in the Middle East, and the end of the Cold War dictatorships in Europe led to Yugoslavia's collapse too. And so complicated were events in Yugoslavia that it was impossible to label Clinton's foreign policy strategy. There was no clear 'Clinton doctrine' like there is no clear Obama doctrine. But in February 1999 President Bill Clinton outlined what *he* thought foreign policy was for:

> The true measure of our interests lies not in how small or distant these places are or in whether we have trouble pronouncing their names. The question we must ask is, what are the consequences to our security of letting conflicts fester and spread? We cannot, indeed, we should not, do everything or be everywhere. But where our values and our interests are at stake and where we can make a difference, we must be prepared to do so. And we must remember that the real challenge of foreign policy is to deal with problems before they harm our national interests.[62]

The Syrian conflict does not harm America's national interests. President Obama said in January 2013:

> As I wrestle with those decisions, I am more mindful probably than most of not only our incredible strengths and capabilities, but also our limitations. In a situation like Syria, I have to ask, can we make a difference in that situation? Would a military intervention have an impact? What would be the aftermath of our involvement on the ground? Could it trigger even worse violence or the use of chemical weapons? What offers the best prospect of a stable post-Assad regime? And how do I weigh tens of thousands who've been killed in Syria versus the tens of thousands who are currently being killed in the Congo? Those are not simple questions. And you process them as best you can. You make the decisions you think

balance all these equities, and you hope that, at the end of your presidency, you can look back and say, I made more right calls than not and that I saved lives where I could.[63]

In similar circumstances the last two Democrat presidents reached similar conclusions. Eventually Bill Clinton decided after four years of conflict that he *could* make a difference in the former Yugoslavia. Perhaps President Obama will reach the same conclusion, and by that time we may also be talking about the former Syria.

Before he even boarded the campaign bus to run for the White House, Barack Obama had thought long and hard about the use of American power overseas. His words in 2013 were an echo of those he wrote in 2006 in his book *The Audacity of Hope*, in which he criticised the framing of US foreign policy.

Instead of guiding principles, we have what appear to be a series of ad hoc decisions, with dubious results. Why invade Iraq and not North Korea or Burma. Why intervene in Bosnia and not Darfur . . . Are we committed to use force wherever there's a despotic regime that's terrorising its people – and if so, how long do we stay to ensure democracy takes root?[64]

President Obama is wrestling with those questions today. That guiding principle still seems to be eluding him. The younger version of himself suggested:

a revised foreign policy framework that matches the boldness and scope of Truman's post-World War II policies – one that addresses both the challenges and the opportunities of a new millennium, one that guides our use of force and expresses our deepest ideals and commitments . . . To begin with, we should understand that any return to isolationism – or a foreign policy approach that denies the occasional need to deploy U.S. troops – will not work.[65]

For now today's President Obama has made it clear he does not think the US can easily end the bloodshed in Syria. Iraq, in his own mind, taught him the folly of trying. It also showed him America's limits and priorities. The Arab Spring has revealed to him that America cannot manage the region any more.

As he began his fifth year in office, academics and policy wonks still could not work out what label to hang on President Obama. They too had not discovered his guiding principle. Obama's outgoing secretary of state was asked at a gathering of foreign affairs specialists: 'Is there an Obama doctrine, is there a Clinton doctrine, that somehow ties together, gives a sense of priorities, helps explain what it is we should do and not do and how we should do it in the way that other doctrines historically have played that role?'[66] They wanted to know: is Obama a realist, or an idealist, or a pragmatist? The answer to those questions is yes.

The world now knows much more about Syria than it did when *Vogue* sent its fashion photographers to take snaps of Assad playing with toy cars with his kids. The world knows exactly what is going on in his country. The nations of the world are outraged by the human suffering in Syria, but not enough to send any of their own people to suffer with them. Secretary of State Kerry had promised not to keep the opposition 'dangling in the wind', but with the conflict in its third year that is where many felt they still were.[67] That fact may come back to haunt the West. 'The sense of betrayal from the civilians, from the weak, from the victims of the violence in Syria is justifiably such that it could easily have a negative impact on the relationship between, not only the Syrians, but also the other young people in this part of the world, and the Western powers for generations to come,' believes General Robert Mood. When Assad is driven from Damascus the Western world will hope to put in train all those contingency plans it never did have ready for the day after in Iraq. The post-Assad era may therefore be less bloody and chaotic than the post-Saddam era, once the initial lust for revenge has been sated. Equally likely though is the prospect that the bloodletting may not stop, plunging the country into a prolonged sectarian conflict.

If the Arab Spring and the years that followed have been a revelation to the world, then it has been an education for the Syrians too. The most important thing they have learnt is this. While the war rages there will be no foreign cavalry coming over the horizon. Until the fighting ends the Syrian people are on their own.

Afterword

The winter sun was low in the sky and snow still lay on the ground as the small group of men busied themselves changing the face of the Middle East. They were working on a hilltop that overlooked the town of Bethlehem. Every brick they laid, every clod of earth they dug out, would have consequences that presidents and prime ministers across the globe would eventually have to wrestle with. These men were building new homes for more Israelis to move into the settlement of Gush Etzion on occupied Palestinian land. Each action they took on this and other settlements they worked on across the West Bank made the peace process harder and the prospects of a Palestinian state more remote. The men before me were the vanguard of the growth of the settler population, and they hated themselves for it. These men were all Palestinians.

Settlement building is one of the few growth industries on the West Bank. Abdel-Rahman Alami said he'd tried everything else: odd jobs, grape harvesting, driving a tractor and living through long periods of unemployment. Then one day the needs of his family became greater than his pride. 'The first time I walked onto one of these settlements I damned myself and I damned my luck, but I had no choice,' he told me. 'I would leave this settlement today if the PA would give me another job, but Abbas and his people do nothing for us.' I asked him if he thought he'd ever get the chance to build new homes for a new Palestinian state. 'No.' he said.

The Arab Spring has swept through the Middle East but it hasn't changed the life of Mr Alami. Nor is he expecting it to do so any time soon, because the rest of the Arab world has enough problems of its own to deal with. The struggle between Israelis and Palestinians defined much of the old Middle East. It will not define the new one.

At the moment there is great division between secular and religious Zionists, and ultra-Orthodox Jews in Israel. It's unclear how that will be resolved. Perhaps the next generation of the Haredim may learn to love the state and so fuel the growth of religious Zionism. That would enormously increase the number of settlers on the West Bank who believe their homes are a God-given right.

Israelis react badly to anything they think smacks of bullying from the outside world. They have not learned that lesson at home. Forcing change on the ultra-Orthodox faster than their complicated community can cope with it will push them further away from the state and society. For its own sake, Israel needs to be a better diplomat within its borders than it has been abroad.

In the past, conflicts in the region were primarily about land. In the future they will often be over the perceived will of God. Religious Zionism and political Islam are the forces shaping the New Middle East. No one can say for sure exactly how the region will evolve in the coming years. All that can be said is that people's faith will increasingly play a bigger part in their political choices, whether they are Muslims, Jews or Christians. People will want their societies to reflect their values. But their politicians will be judged by their performance, not their preaching. If they don't provide good jobs and functioning public services they will be booted out no matter how many times a day they pray. There will be no new Islamic Caliphate. The forces of political Islam may be the biggest winners of the revolutions but that process has also revealed the deep divisions within them, even at national level. The senior members of the Egyptian Muslim Brotherhood put their differences aside to confront a common foe in the shape of the Army, but once power was within their grasp they began to bicker and fight. The deep distrust between branches of the Sunni establishment across the region will undermine any attempts at unity.

The conflict between faiths will often boil over now that the dicta-tor's hand is off the lid of the pot he so carefully stirred. The sectarian wounds of civil war in Iraq have yet to heal. Christians across the region seek shelter from a hurricane of change that is randomly crashing into their fragile communities. The oppressed Shia faithful are fighting for equality within the Sunni states of the Gulf. And at the heart of the Arab world there is raging one of the most complicated and devastating civil wars the region has ever known. The UN says Syria has produced the greatest humanitarian crisis the institution has had to tackle. Its high commissioner for refugees, Antonio Guterres, warned, 'The polit-ical geography of the modern Middle East emerged from the Sykes–Picot agreement . . . The conflict in Syria might for the first time put that political geography into question.'[1] Men drew the lines that formed the old Middle East. God will shape the new one.

Now that the people of the Arab world have risen up to kick out their dictators and have held internationally acknowledged free and fair elections, does Israel still think it is the only democracy in the Middle East? 'Yes!' President Shimon Peres told me.

President Obama asked me 'Who is against democracy in the Middle East?' I answered him, 'The husbands.' They won't give equality to their wives. They won't permit women to play an equal role. If they don't do it [then these countries] won't recover. If the women are not educated, neither are the children. And half of the children are illiterate. And today without knowledge you cannot move around. Look, I don't want to smear them, why should I, draw your own conclusions. I think, for example, if you don't give equality to women you don't have a democracy.

My conclusion is that President Peres is wrong. There are now other democracies in the Middle East. The popular coup in Egypt though was a step backwards. Deeply conservative views on the role of women are widespread in the region, but they are not exclusive to the Arab world.

They can be found within walking distance of where I sat with President Peres in Jerusalem, in Israel's ultra-Orthodox community. The rights of women though are much better protected in Israel than they are anywhere else in the region. The potential for women's rights to be rolled back in these new democracies is very real, but so is the fact that women played a huge role in the revolutions. They too showed immense courage and fought for their countries' new freedoms. They will have a tougher road ahead than the men, but that doesn't mean they won't walk it.

The Gulf countries have been driving policy since the secular dictatorships began to collapse. It is hard to see how that can last. Qatar has locked itself into giving, no matter how ungrateful the recipients may become, because that's the only foreign policy tool it has. The Libyans were the first to tire of the meddling by the Qataris. The Egyptian economy has only been kept afloat because of their loans, but the Egyptian people increasingly saw Doha as just bailing out the Brotherhood for their own political ends. Similar sentiments can be found in Tunisia. Qatar stands tall now only because the countries shaken by the Arab Spring are still on their knees. Once these nations find their feet, they will send Qatar back to its gilded playground.

Things will be less cheery for Qatar's only other competitor in the Gulf, Saudi Arabia. The problems within its society are unlikely to be resolved after the passage of time ends the succession crisis of its gerontocracy. There is no guarantee that a new generation of cosseted princes will bring with it any new ideas. And even if they do, they have very little experience of managing transition, because changing Saudi society has been something they have only ever been taught how to avoid. The Gulf countries should enjoy their moment in the limelight because it is likely to be fleeting. Money has bought them time, nothing more. The only real question is how quickly will change come and how brutal will it be? The Gulf kingdoms keep saying, 'It will not happen here.' So did Mubarak and then Gaddafi and then Assad. The Arab monarchies are now scared of their people. They should be.

Over time Egypt will regain its rightful place as the most important and influential Arab nation. Egypt's problems are huge but they are not insurmountable. The Muslim Brotherhood has looked at Turkey as a model. A more realistic one is India. India has the same sectarian divide, the same disastrous infrastructure, a bloated, corrupt bureaucracy and huge tracts of poverty. Like Egypt's, India's political establishment, with a few notable exceptions, is divided, self-serving and incompetent. But, also like Egypt, India is a democracy with a huge, ambitious, educated middle class that believes its nation's manifest destiny is to be great again. India works despite its politicians. Egypt is going to have to learn to do the same. The crucial thing for Egypt's success is to make sure that its army acts like the Indian one, by being subservient to the state, rather than the one across India's border with Pakistan. All old soldiers think they know better than the civilians. A professional army doesn't try to prove it. This is where the Egyptian generals' American paymasters have a crucial role after the July coup.

The war in Syria sums up the complexity of the New Middle East. No one had foreseen the revolutions before they happened. There was an attempt afterwards to suggest that the White House had been busying itself for just such an event. The existence of a Study Directive signed by President Obama in August 2010 to look into the potential for change in the Arab world was offered as an example of prescience that really didn't exist.[2] The study got no further than initial discussions about the merits or otherwise of preemptively engaging with the forces of political Islam. The project soon descended into interagency fighting, with the State Department on one side and the CIA and the Department of Defense on the other. It never reached the stage of predicting a timescale for what would happen and what the Obama administration was going to do about it.[3] There were very few specifics and it ended up being delayed and then overtaken by events. But more than two years after the revolts, when it was now into its second term, the Obama administration had still not got its ducks in a row on some of the key challenges in the region. There were still signs of that disconnect between the State Department and the Department of Defense. On the same day at two different hearings in Congress John Kerry and Chuck Hagel gave two different assessments of the trustworthiness of the Syrian opposition and the state of the conflict.[4] With Syria now in its third year of crisis, Congress asked Hagel, if the US policy to try to bring about an end to the violence and produce a political transition to a post-Assad authority was working. 'It hasn't achieved its objective obviously,' he said 'That's why we continue to look for other options and other ways to do this.' If the US still cannot resolve its interagency differences over Syria then there's little hope of achieving unity in the more fractious UN Security Council.

Only people with no long-term vested interest in the wellbeing of the subjects of the state could have conjured up Syria and Iraq. Neither the countries nor the political power structures within them would have naturally come about without the mischievous hand of foreigners. Ba'athism was a reaction to the selfish audacity of colonial rule. Neither country necessarily has a future within its present borders. In both nations removing the Ba'athist regimes has been a thoroughly brutal exercise. Fortunately it only has to be done once, but that's no comfort for the people who have to live through it.

The battle between the Sunni and Shia forces in the Middle East will continue beyond the outcome of the war in Syria. The more the Gulf states turn the Syrian crisis into a proxy war over God, the more that sectarian poison will flow out into the region. If the Sunni and Shia are seen to be slaughtering each other in Syria that will impact on communal relations in countries not directly connected to the conflict. America and its allies may be able to contain the physical war within Syria's borders, but it's already clear they will not be able to contain its influence on the region.

George W. Bush led America into Iraq without a plan. Barack Obama kept America out of Syria without a plan. Not acting is not passive. Not acting is a decision that has consequences. The Obama administration made a mistake allowing the untried and undemocratic Gulf states to run the show at the beginning. The opportunity to stop the descent into bloodlust has been lost. There can now be only a policy of containment. The warring sides will have to exhaust themselves into a solution.

The Iranians though will not want to sacrifice Hezbollah for Assad.

The militant group has been their most successful foreign policy tool in the region and hanging on to it will be their priority. The Syrian regime long threatened to drag Lebanon down with it, but that is not in Hezbollah's interest, because whatever might emerge from another civil war in Lebanon would only leave it in a worse place than it is today. A new Sunni power in Syria though may embolden Sunni groups in both Lebanon and Iraq. In the coming years there will be tensions and violence. Lebanon will keep trying to pull itself back from the edge no matter how hard forces in Syria push. Memories of the last civil war are too raw for the Lebanese people to forgive anyone who tries to take them down that path again. The Iraqis will also hope they can weather a storm which is unlikely to respect their borders.

That young state senator from Illinois would probably have had some harsh words to say about the world sitting back and watching live on TV, day after day after day, the brutal murder of tens of thousands of people at the centre of the most volatile region on the globe. The killings in the Congo and Syria may be equally brutal. European colonialists planted the seeds of the present-day carnage in both countries, but that is where the comparison ends. The repercussions for the rest of the world of both states collapsing are nowhere near the same. Obama began his presidency promising the Muslim world 'A New Beginning'. What happened to it?

Whatever the West does now to help the rebels could have been done earlier. The Arab world won't forget that. The inaction over Syria may end up harming America's standing in the Muslim world just as much as the worst excesses of the 'War on Terror'. One wonders whether a few years from now another US administration will be looking for a venue in Cairo and crafting a speech to explain why the last guy got it wrong and offering a better deal for the future.

America believes that what it calls the 'Islamist phase of terrorism' is receding and could end by 2030.[5] That may be true with regard to the Global Jihadists, but the war in Syria has prolonged their presence in the region, though they are becoming less global and more local. That makes them much more of a problem for Israel, which has not faced a violent Salafist threat before on this scale. What the jihadists won't be though is more legitimate, because the Arab Spring has proven that their ideology is bankrupt. Real change does not come only from the barrel of a gun. The overwhelming majority of Muslims always believed that to be true. They never bought into the ideology of al-Qaeda. It frustrates them enormously that sections of the Western world even now still don't believe them when they say that.

The Arab Spring was the beginning of the reshaping of the Middle East. The process is not over yet. Now that it is under way China has been looking to fill any space the US leaves behind if it does begin a slow withdrawal. China will not champion human rights and support the region's fledgling democracies. Europe is becoming more engaged in the Middle East but it is too divided to speak with one firm voice. The temptation to leave the Arab people to sort things out for themselves may be strong for the US, which has reaped very little reward for its efforts in the region. But to bow to it would be a mistake. America's decades-long support for the dictatorships helped break the Middle East. The US should help fix it.

But in the eyes of the Arab world America has lost too much credibility; first over the peace process, then in Iraq and now in Syria, to entitle it to claim the role of 'honest broker' again. The US has an agenda just like every other player in the Middle East. It would be more honest to stop pretending otherwise.

The region has huge problems but equally great opportunities. Under the corrupt dictatorships the Arab people usually had to leave the Middle East if they wanted both a clear future and a clear conscience. Now, apart from Syria, the other countries of the Arab Spring have the chance to use their ingenuity and creativity at home and to build new states. They will need help with their economies and to resolve their differences. However the revolutionaries expect to be treated with the respect they now feel they have earned. The new societies emerging from the uprisings intend for the first time in their history to shed their client-nation status.

The people of the New Middle East now have a voice. Whether the West likes what they have to say or not, the world after the Arab Spring means it is going to have to listen to them.

Notes

INTRODUCTION

1   Megan Price, Jeff Klingner and Patrick Ball, *Preliminary Statistical Analysis of Documentation of Killings in the Syrian Arab Republic (commissioned by the United Nations Office of the High Commissioner for Human Rights)*, The Benetech Human Rights Program, January 2013.

2   BBC News, 'Kofi Annan quits UN Syria role', 2 August 2012.

3   Office of the United Nations High Commissioner for Human Rights, 'Statement by the High Commissioner for Human Rights to the Security Council', 12 February 2013.

4   Iyad el-Baghdadi, 'The Arab Tyrant's Manual', www.el-baghdadi.com/projects/the-arab-tyrants-manual.html.

5   UNESCO Regional Bureau for Education in the Arab States, *Arab Youth: Civic Engagement and Economic Participation*, September 2011.

6   Louisa Loveluck, *Education in Egypt: Key Challenges*, Chatham House, March 2012.

7   Jeffrey Goldberg, 'Obama: "Israel Doesn't Know What Its Best Interests Are"', Bloomberg, 15 January 2013.

8   'Associated Press: Israeli ultra-Orthodox projected to triple by 2059', *Guardian*, 12 December 2011.

9   Tobias Buck, 'Israeli coalition in military draft row', *Financial Times*, 4 July 2012.

10 Zvi Bar'el, 'Only the IDF can get Israel to recognize "Jewish terrorism"', *Ha'aretz*, 21 December 2011.

11 International Monetary Fund, 'Concluding Statement of the 2012 Article IV Consultation Mission to Israel', February 2012.

12 *Ha'aretz* editorial, 'Supreme Court thrusts Israel down the slope of apartheid', 13 January 2012.

13 Gil Hoffman, 'Poll Finds Huge Drop In Israelis Who See Obama As Hostile', *Jerusalem Post*, 29 March 2013.

14 Agence France-Presse, 'Obama plunges into Mideast with snap call to Palestinian leader', 21 January 2009.

15 BBC World News, June 2012.

16 BBC Religion, 'Sunni and Shi'a', bbc.co.uk/religion/islam, 19 August 2009.

17 The White House, Office of the Press Secretary, Press Conference by the President at the Nuclear Security Summit, 13 April 2010.

18 Ryan Lizza, 'The Consequentialist: How the Arab Spring remade Obama's Foreign Policy', *New Yorker*, 2 May 2011.

19 BBC News, 'Tony Blair: Life in Iraq 10 years on not as I hoped', 26 February 2013.

20 Alfred Thayer Mahan, 'The Persian Gulf and International Relations', *National Review*, September 1902, pp. 26–45.

1: THE COLLAPSE OF THE OLD MIDDLE EAST

1   Alexis Arieff, 'Political Transition in Tunisia', Congressional Research Service, 16 December 2011.

2   Tamara Cofman Wittes, 'The Promise of Arab Liberalism', *Policy Review*, no. 125, June 2004.

3   Catherine Smith, 'Egypt's Facebook Revolution', *Huffington Post*, 2 February 2011.

4   Ashraf Khalil, *Liberation Square*, St Martin's Press, New York, 2012, p. 144.

5   *Global Post*, 'Omar Suleiman, Egypt's vice president, blames violence on "foreign influences"', 3 February 2011.

6   Paul Salem, 'Qatari Foreign Policy: The Changing Dynamics of an Outsize Role', Carnegie Middle East Center, 31 December 2012.

7   Ali Hashem, 'The Arab Spring has shaken Arab TV's Credibility', *Guardian*, 3 April 2012.

8   Maggie Michael, 'Calls grow in Egypt to delay elections', Associated Press, 19 June 2011.

9   President Ronald Reagan, News Conference, 9 April 1986, The American Presidency Project.

10 *Wall Street Journal*, Interview with Syrian President Bashar al-Assad, 31 January 2011.

11 Ibid.

12 BBC News, 'Bahrain Government moves to disband Shia opposition', 14 April 2011; Dale Gavlak, 'Jordan searches for answers to Arab Spring demands', BBC News, 4 November 2011; BBC News, 'Moroccans celebrate King Mohammed's reform speech', 18 June 2011.

13 Jeffrey Goldberg, 'The Modern King in the Arab Spring', *The Atlantic*, 18 March 2013.

14 The International Center for Transitional Justice, *Algeria Background: No Redress for Victims*.

15 Joby Warrick and Michael Birnbaum, 'As Bahrain stifles protest movement, U.S.'s muted objections draw criticism', *Washington Post*, 14 April 2011.

16 See Condoleezza Rice, *No Higher Honor: A Memoir of My Years in Washington*, Kindle edition, Crown Publishers, New York, 2011, p. 327.

17 *New York Times*, 'Libya's Succession Muddled as the Al-Qadhafi Children Conduct Internecine Warfare', US Embassy, Tripoli, 9 March 2009.

18 *New York Times*, 'Qadhafi Children Scandals Spilling over into Politics', US Embassy, Tripoli, 2 February 2010.

19 President George W. Bush 2nd Inaugural Address, January 2005.

20 Ewen MacAskill, 'George Bush: "God told me to end the tyranny in Iraq"', *Guardian*, 7 October 2005.

21 WikiLeaks *07TUNIS1064, TUNISIA: PROMOTING THE PRESIDENT'S FREEDOM AGENDA*, US Embassy, Tunis, August 2007.

22 Christopher Alexander, *Tunisia: Stability and Reform in the Modern Maghreb*, Kindle edition, Routledge, London and New York, p. 3.

23 Ibid., p. 4.

24 *New York Times*, 'A Selection From the Cache of Diplomatic Dispatches, US Embassy, Tunis', August 2008.

25 'The Assad emails, The "Ming" vase', *Guardian*, 14 March 2012.

26 Associated Press, 'A Coup is Reported in Tunisia', *New York Times*, 7 November 1987.

27 David Williams, 'Wife of Tunisian president fled riot-torn country with 1.5 TONNES of gold (that should help feed the son-in-law's pet tiger)', *Daily Mail*, 17 January 2011.

28 WikiLeaks, *08TUNIS679, CORRUPTION IN TUNISIA: WHAT'S YOURS IS MINE*, US Embassy, Tunis, 23 June 2008.

29 WikiLeaks *09TUNIS516, TUNISIA: DINNER WITH SAKHER EL MATERI*, US Embassy, Tunis, July 2009.

30 International Crisis Group, *Popular Protest in North Africa and the Middle East (iv): Tunisia's Way*, Middle East/North Africa Report no. 106, 28 April 2011.

31 WikiLeaks, *08TUNIS493, TUNISIA: WHAT SUCCESSION SCENARIO?*, US Embassy, Tunis, May 2008.

32 International Crisis Group, *Popular Protest . . .*

33 Ibid.

34 WikiLeaks, *08TUNIS679, CORRUPTION IN TUNISIA: WHAT'S YOURS IS MINE*, US Embassy, Tunis, 23 June 2008.

35 Middle East and North Africa programme, 'Defining and Tackling Corruption', Chatham House, February 2012.

36 Frank Gardner, 'Tunisia one year on: Where the Arab Spring started', BBC News, 17 December 2011.

37 Eric Goldstein, 'A Middle Class revolution', *Foreign Policy*, 18 January 2011.

38 Middle East and North Africa programme, 'Defining and Tackling Corruption', Chatham House, February 2012.

39 Ibrahim Saif, 'The Arab world's looming crisis', Carnegie Middle East Center, September 2012.

40 Joshua Landis, 'The Syrian Uprising of 2011: Why the Asad Regime Is Likely to Survive to 2013', *Middle East Policy Council*, Spring 2012, vol. XIX, no. 1

41 Encyclopedia Britannica online.

42 Ibid.

43 Alexander, *Tunisia*, p. 33.

44 Clement Henry Moore, *Tunisia Since Independence: The Dynamics of One-party Government*, University of California Press, 1965, p. 55.

45 Ibid., p. 57.

46 Ibid., p. 53.

47 Ibid., p. 57.

48 Ibid.

49 Ibid., p. 41.

50 WikiLeaks *07TUNIS1068, THE TUNISIAN SECULAR STATE: A MODEL FOR THE MUSLIM*, US Embassy, Tunis, August 2007.

51 Lisa Anderson, 'Demystifying the Arab Spring', *Foreign Affairs*, May/June 2011.

52 Alexander, Tunisia, p. 58.

53 Alexander, *Tunisia,* p. 59.

54 International Crisis Group, *POPULAR PROTEST IN NORTH AFRICA AND THE MIDDLE EAST (IV): TUNISIA'S WAY* Middle East/North Africa Report no. 106, 28 April 2011.

55 Alexis Arieff, 'Political Transition in Tunisia', Congressional Research Service, 16 December 2011.

56 Ibid.

57 International Crisis Group, *Popular Protest . . .*

58 Ibid.

59 Alexander, *Tunisia,* p. 66.

2: EGYPT'S LONG WAR

I: THE BATTLE BEGINS

1   Gabe Fisher, 'Israeli MK denies getting $25,000 a month from Mubarak', *Times of Israel*, 14 March 2012.

2   Jeremy M. Sharp, 'Egypt: Background and U.S. Relations', Congressional Research Service, February 2011.

3   James Zogby, 'American Attitudes Towards Egypt and the Muslim Brotherhood', *Zogby Research Services*, March 2013.

4   Robert S. Leiken, Steven Brooke, 'The Moderate Muslim Brotherhood', *Foreign Affairs*, March/April 2007.

5   Richard P. Mitchell, *The Society of the Muslim Brothers*, Oxford University Press, New York, 1995, p. 7.

6   Encyclopedia Britannica online.

7   Author interview with Dr Brynjar Lia, Research Professor at the Norwegian Defence Research Establishment, author of *The Society of the Muslim Brothers in Egypt 1928–42.*

8   *Time* magazine, 'EGYPT: Down Goes the Brotherhood', 25 January 1954.

9   Eugene Rogan, *The Arabs: A History*, Kindle edition, Allen Lane, London, 2009, p. 271.

10 Richard P. Mitchell, *The Society of the Muslim Brothers*, Oxford University Press, New York, 1995, p. 65.

11 Ibid., p. 68.

12 Ibid., p. 70.

13 Ibid., p. 71.

14 Ibid.

15 Gamal Abdel Nasser, *Egypt's Liberation: The Philosophy of the Revolution*, Public Affairs Press, Washington, DC, 1955, pp. 87–8.

16 Mitchell, *The Society of the Muslim Brothers*, p. 100.

17 Ibid., p. 104.

18 Alison Pargeter, *The Muslim Brotherhood: The Burden of Tradition*, Kindle edition, Saqi Books, London, 2011, loc. 447.

19 Mitchell, *The Society of the Muslim Brothers*, p. 111.

20 Ibid., p. 109.

21 Rogan, *The Arabs*, p. 283.

22 Kenneth Love, 'Egypt Condemns 6 to Hang as Plotters', *New York Times*, 5 December 1954.

23 Robert C. Doty, 'Nasser Escapes Attempt on Life', *New York Times*, 26 October 1954.

24 *Economist* magazine, 'Nasser Versus the Brotherhood', 20 November 1954, p. 26.

25 *Time* magazine, 'EGYPT: The Revolutionary', 26 September 1955.

26 Mitchell, *The Society of the Muslim Brothers*, p. 149.

27 *Time* magazine, 'Egypt: Eight shots', 8 November 1954.

28 Ibid.

29 *Time* magazine, 'Egypt: Snapping the Trap', 6 December 1954.

30 Ibid.

31 Ibid.

32 Mitchell, *The Society of the Muslim Brothers*, p. 156.

33 Ibid., p. 152.

34 Love, 'Egypt Condemns 6'.

35 Ibid.

36 John Mecklin, 'EGYPT: The Counterpuncher', *Time* magazine, 27 August 1956.

37 David A. Nichols, *Eisenhower 1956: The President's Year of Crisis, Suez and the Brink of War*, Simon & Schuster, New York, 2011, p. 126.

38 Mecklin, 'EGYPT: The Counterpuncher'.

39 Nichols, *Eisenhower 1956*, p. 203.

40 Nazar Abbas, 'Gaddafi is gone, long live Libya', *The News*, August 2011, quoting Mohamed Hasnain Heikal from his book *The Road to Ramadan*.

41 *Time* magazine, 'World: Libya: The Enfant Terrible', 2 August 1971.

42 *Time* magazine, 'World: Nasser's Legacy: Hope and instability', 12 October 1970.

43 John Calvert, *Sayyid Qutb and the Origins of Radical Islamism*, Kindle edition, Columbia University Press, New York, 2010, p. 6.

44 Robert Worth, 'The Deep Intellectual Roots of Islamic Terror', *New York Times*, 13 October 2001.

45 Calvert, *Sayyid Qutb*, p. 186.

46 Ibid., p. 142.

47 Ibid., p. 279.

48 Ibid., p. 8.

49 Barbara H. E. Zollner, *The Muslim Brotherhood: Hasan al-Hudaybi and Ideology*, Routledge, New York, 2009, p. 43.

50 Sayyid Qutb, *Milestones*, SIME epublishing loc. 12754.

51 Ibid., loc. 1312.

52 Ibid., loc. 818.

53 Calvert, *Sayyid Qutb*, p. 263.

54 Ibid.

55 Laura Mansfield, *His own words: Translation and Analysis of the writings of Dr. Ayman Zawahiri*, TLG Publications, USA, p. 48.

56 Ibid., p. 51.

57 US embassy cables, 'Egyptian military's influence in decline, US told Guardian', 3 February 2011.

58 *Time* magazine, 'The World: Middle East: The Underrated Heir', 17 May 1971.

59 Kirk J. Beattie, *Egypt during the Sadat Years*, Palgrave Macmillan, 2000, p. 43

60 Ibid., p. 38.

61 *Time* magazine, 'The World: Egypt: Sadat in the Saddle', 31 May 1971.

62 *Economist* magazine, 'The Man least Likely', 22 May 1971, p. 16.

63 *Economist* magazine, 'A Lasso of Sad Garlands to Catch Nasser's Heir', 22 May 1971, p. 35.

64 Beattie, *Egypt*, p. 76.

65 Pargeter, *The Muslim Brotherhood*, loc. 533.

66 Sadat and Begin were awarded theirs in 1978. Carter was awarded his Nobel Prize in 2002 for his efforts at promoting peaceful solutions to international conflicts.

67 'Memorandum of Conversation The White House, April 1974', The Gerald Ford Presidential Library.

68 Rogan, *The Arabs*, p. 365.

69 William E. Farrell, 'SADAT ASSASSINATED AT ARMY PARADE AS MEN AMID RANKS FIRE INTO STANDS; VICE PRESIDENT AFFIRMS "ALL TREATIES"', *New York Times*, 7 October 1981.

70 John Kifner, 'Jubilation in Beirut', *New York Times*, 7 October 1981.

71 Associated Press, 'All But 3 Arab states boycott Sadat's funeral', 11 October 1981.

72 Gilles Kepel, *Muslim Extremism in Egypt: The Prophet and Pharaoh*, University of California Press, Berkeley, 1985, p. 192.

73 Mansfield, *His own words*, p. 52.

II: REVOLUTION

1   Mark Landler, 'Obama Seeks Reset in Arab World', *New York Times*, 11 May 2011.

2   Richard Stengel, Bobby Ghosh and Karl Vick, 'Transcript: *TIME*'s Interview

with Egyptian President Mohamed Morsi', *Time* magazine, 28 November 2012.

3 Condoleezza Rice, *No Higher Honor: A Memoir of My Years in Washington*, Kindle edition, Crown Publishers, New York, 2011, p. 374.

4 Ibid.

5 George W. Bush, *Decision Points*, Kindle edition, Crown Publishers, New York, 2010, p. 435.

6 Rice, *No Higher Honor*, p. 375.

7 Ibid.

8 Secretary Condoleezza Rice, 'Remarks at the American University in Cairo', US Department of State Archive, 20 June 2005.

9 Ibid.

10 Secretary Condoleezza Rice, 'Question and Answer at the American University in Cairo', US Department of State Archive', 20 June 2005.

11 *New York Times*, 'A Selection From the Cache of Diplomatic Dispatches US Embassy, Cairo', 29 November 2005.

12 BBC News, 'Egypt vote in run-off election amid fraud row', 2 December 2010

13 Secretary of State for War (Mr Antony Head), 'Statement to the British House of Commons', 31 January 1952.

14 Yolande Knell, 'Egypt's police still in crisis after revolution', BBC News, 5 March 2012.

15 Human Rights Watch, 'Egypt: Prosecute Police in Beating Death', 24 June 2010.

16 David Wolman, 'The Digital Road to Egypt's Revolution', *New York Times*, 10 February 2012.

17 Reuters, 'Egypt govt warns activists against Tuesday protest', *The Dawn* newspaper, 25 January 2011.

18 Amos Elon, 'One Foot on the Moon', *New York Review of Books*, 6 April 1995

19 BBC News, 'Egypt protests: Eyewitness accounts', 25 January 2011.

20 Human Rights Watch, 'Egypt: Documented Death toll from Protests Tops 300', 8 February 2011.

21 I have changed Nihad's name and avoided giving details that would identify her, as this was in conversation, not a formal interview. I have included her comments because of the insight they give into the thinking of the people serving in the police force.

22 BBC News, 'Deaths in Egypt's Suez after Port Said football unrest', 3 February 2012.

23 *New York Times*, 'A Selection From the Cache of Diplomatic Dispatches, US Embassy, Cairo', 16 March 2008.

24 *New York Times*, 'A Selection From the Cache of Diplomatic Dispatches, US Embassy, Cairo', 23 September 2008.

25 Jane Kinninmont, '*Bread, Dignity and Social Justice': The Political Economy of Egypt's Transition*, Chatham House, April 2012, p. 16.

26 Melissa Bell, 'Amnesty International: Egypt military admits to "Virginity tests," promises to end practice', *Washington Post*, 27 June 2011.

27 Amnesty International, Annual report 2012: Egypt.

28 Eric Trager, Katie Kiraly, Cooper Klose and Eliot Calhoun, *Who's Who in Egypt's Muslim Brotherhood*, The Washington Institute, September 2012.

29 Reuters, 'Egypt's Islamists say not looking for power', 12 February 2011.

30 Mohammad Khawly, 'Nose Job Scandal Topples Egyptian Salafi MP', *Al Akhbar*, Beirut, 6 March 2012.

31 Al Arabiya, 'Egyptian Islamist MP caught in "indecent act" with teenage girl', 8 June 2012.

32 Reuters, 'Egypt won't see "Algerian civil war": El-Katatni', Ahramonline, 21 June 2012.

33 Ahramonline, 'Shafiq blames arrest warrant on "settling of scores"', 20 February 2013.

34 Stengel, Ghosh and Vick, 'Transcript: *TIME*'s Interview with Egyptian President Mohamed Morsi'.

35 BBC News, 'Egypt army chief warns of "state collapse" amid crisis', 29 January 2013.

36 Heba Saleh, 'Egypt Struggles as joblessness soars', *Financial Times*, 27 February 2013.

37 Jennifer Blanke and Thea Chiesa, *The Travel and Tourism Competitiveness Report 2013*, World Economic Forum, p. 33.

38 Borzon Daragahi, 'Egypt's Public Sector Salary Bill Soars', *Financial Times*, 18 April 2013.

3: THE PROBLEM

1   Associated Press, 'UN Report Suggests Palestinian Rocket Killed Baby in Gaza', *Guardian*, 12 March 2013.

2   Isreal Military Advocate General, 'The Examination of Alleged Misconduct During Operation "Pillar of Defence" – An Update', 11 April 2013.

3   Ashraf Khalil, 'Morsi's Gaza Challenge: How New Can the New Egypt Afford to Be?', *Time* magazine, 16 November 2012.

4   Boaz Fyler, 'Defense official: Appalling dictatorship in Egypt', Ynet, 2 November 2012.

5   Bush, *Decision Points*, p. 405.

6   Office of the Press Secretary, The White House, 'Remarks by the President on the Middle East and North Africa', 19 May 2011.

7   Herb Keinon, 'Palestine wins historic upgrade at the UN', 30 November 2012.

8   UN General Assembly, *194 (III) Palestine – Progress Report of the United Nations Mediator*, 11 December 1948.

9   Full text of Netanyahu's foreign policy speech at Bar Ilan, *Ha'aretz*, 14 June 2009

10 Gil Hoffman, 'Bennett: "Obama's Policies Could Lead To Violence"', *Jerusalem Post*, 30 March 2013.

11 Ma'an News agency, 'President says Palestinian Spring has begun', 5 July 2012

12 Oussama Kanaan, Udo Kock and Mariusz Sumlinski, 'Recent Experience and Prospects of the Economy of the West Bank and Gaza Staff Report prepared

for the meeting of the Ad Hoc Liaison Committee', International Monetary Fund, 23 September 2012.

13 *Summary Report of the Palestine Royal Commission,* League of Nations Publications, July 1937.

14 Ibid.

15 *Full Report of the Palestine Royal Commission,* League of Nations Publications, July 1937, p. 142.

16 Ibid., p. 370.

17 Rogan, *The Arabs,* p. 333.

18 Ibid.

19 US Department of State Archive, 'Telegram From the Embassy in the United Arab Republic to the Department of State', Cairo, 21 May 1967.

20 Rogan, *The Arabs,* p. 335.

21 On this Day, '1967: Egypt and Jordan unite against Israel', BBC News.

22 David S. Robarge, *CIA Analysis of the 1967 Arab–Israeli War,* Central Intelligence Agency.

23 Ibid.

24 Ibid.

25 'Address by Prime Minister Begin at the National Defense College, 8 August 1982', vol. 8:1982–1984, Israel Ministry of Foreign Affairs.

26 Rogan, *The Arabs,* p. 415.

27 *Financial Times,* 'UN Probe says Israel Must Remove Settlers', 31 January 2013.

28 Israel Ministry of Foreign Affairs, *Israel, the Conflict and Peace: Answers to Frequently Asked Questions,* 1 November 2007.

29 United Nations General Assembly, *Report of the Special Committee to Investigate Israeli Practices Affecting the Human Rights of the Population of the Occupied Territories,* 13 November 1979.

30 Associated Press, 'Bye-Bye America', *Ottawa Citizen,* 3 January 1978.

31 Rachel Brandenburg, *Iran and the Palestinians,* United States Institute of Peace.

32 BBC News, 'Intifada Toll 2000–2005', 8 February 2005.

33 Exchange of letters between PM Sharon and President Bush, www.mfa.gov.il, 14 April 2004.

34 UN News Center, 'International Court of Justice finds Israeli Barrier in Palestinian Territory Illegal', 9 July 2004.

35 Exchange of letters between PM Sharon and President Bush, www.mfa.gov.il, 14 April 2004.

36 Kofi Annan with Nader Mousavizadeh, *Interventions: A Life in War and Peace,* Kindle edition, Allen Lane, 2012, p. 288.

37 Bush, *Decision Points,* p. 404.

38 Rice, *No Higher Honor,* p. 54.

39 Ibid., p. 144.

40 Elliot Abrams, 'Testimony before Committee on Foreign Affairs, Subcommittee, United States House of Representatives, 2nd session, 112th Congress', 10 July 2012.

41 Annan, *Interventions: A Life in War and Peace*, p. 289.

42 'CASHLESS IN GAZA?', *Aftenposten*, 5 January 2011.

43 Israel's Ministry of Defence, Coordination of Government Activities in the Territories, 'Food Consumption in the Gaza Strip – Red Lines', 1 January 2008.

44 BBC News, 'Israel forced to release study on Gaza', 17 October 2012.

45 Sir Geoffrey Palmer, President Alvaro Uribe, Mr Joseph Ciechanover Itzhar and Mr Suleyman Ozdem Sanberk, *Report of the Secretary General's Panel of Inquiry on the 31 May 2010 Flotilla Incident*, September 2011.

46 Amnesty International, *ISRAEL/GAZA OPERATION 'CAST LEAD': 22 DAYS OF DEATH AND DESTRUCTION*, 2 July 2009.

47 British Prime Minister's Office, 'A transcript of a speech given by Prime Minister David Cameron in Ankara, Turkey', 27 July 2010.

48 European Commission Development and Cooperation Union – Europe Aid, Occupied Palestinian Territory Website (accessed February 2013) / Jim Zanotti, 'U.S. Foreign Aid to the Palestinians', Congressional Research Service, 1 January 2013.

49 Adiv Sterman, 'Israel to Withhold Taxes From Palestinians Until At Least March', *The Times of Israel*, 12 December 2012.

50 United Nations Office for the Coordination of Humanitarian Affairs – Occupied Palestinian Territory, *AREA C OF THE WEST BANK: KEY HUMANITARIAN CONCERNS*, January 2013.

51 Ibid.

52 Ibid.

53 Ibid.

54 Jon Donnison, 'Gaza's precious space and the cost of real estate', BBC News, 12 October 2012.

55 Reuters, 'In official visit to Gaza, Qatari emir endorses Hamas, slams Israeli settlements', *Ha'aretz*, 23 October 2012.

56 Natasha Mozgovaya, 'Palestinian Prime Minister Salam Fayyad: Hamas delivered, we have not', *Ha'aretz*, 30 November 2012.

57 'Foreign Secretary welcomes agreement to end hostilities in Gaza and southern Israel', Foreign and Commonwealth Office, 21 November 2012.

58 Gilad Sharon, 'A decisive conclusion is necessary', *Jerusalem Post*, 18 November 2012.

59 *Ha'aretz* live blog: 'Day 4 of Israel–Gaza conflict 2012, 7:55 P.M.', 17 November 2012.

60 Human Rights Watch, 'Israel/Gaza: Israeli Airstrike on Home Unlawful', 7 December 2012.

61 Israel Military Advocate Generals, 'The Examination of Alleged Misconduct During Operation "Pillar of Defence" – An Update', 11 April 2013.

62 Human Rights Watch, 'Gaza: Palestinian Rockets Unlawfully Targeted Israeli Civilians', 24 December 2012.

63 Report of the United Nations High Commissioner for Human Rights on the implementation of Human Rights Council resolutions S-9/1 and S-12/1

– Concerns related to adherence to international humanitarian law in the context of the escalation between the State of Israel, the de facto authorities in Gaza and Palestinian armed groups in Gaza that occurred from 14 to 21 November 2012, 6 March 2013.

64 Associated Press, 'Abbas Avoids Clash with Israel Over State Symbols', *Ha'aretz*, 8 January 2013.

65 Palestinian News and Info Agency, '4.29 M Total Population of Palestinian Territory Mid 2012, says Statistics', 10 July 2012.

66 Stengel, Ghosh and Vick, 'Transcript: *TIME*'s Interview with Egyptian President Mohamed Morsi'.

67 David D. Kirkpatrick, 'Morsi's Slurs Against Jews Stir Concern', *New York Times*, 14 January 2013.

4: ISRAEL: IT'S COMPLICATED

1 Philologos, 'A Nude Who Inspired Modesty', *The Jewish Daily Forward*, 1 August 2003.

2 Ilan Ben Zion, 'Culture Minister calls for self-censorship by filmmakers', *The Times of Israel*, 28 February 2013.

3 Tamar Hermann, Nir Atmor, Ella Heller and Yuval Lebel, *The Israeli Democracy Index 2012*, The Israel Democracy Institute.

4 Gili Cohen, 'Top Official: "Price Tag" Attacks are Acts of Terror Meant to Drag Israel into Religious War', *Ha'aretz*, 10 September 2012.

5 Noam Dvir, 'Vandals desecrate Latrun Monastery', ynetnews.com, 4 September 2012.

6 Kotaro Ishi, Nicoletta Batini and Jason Harris, *INTERNATIONAL MONETARY FUND: ISRAEL*, 9 March 2012, p. 6.

7 Ibid.

8 Ibid., p. 2.

9 Nachman Ben-Yehuda, *Theocratic Democracy: The Social Construction of Religious and Secular Extremism*, Oxford University Press, 2010, p. 106.

10 Yael Branovsky, 'State helpless in face of skeletons in haredi closet', ynetnews. com, 3 April 2008.

11 Yaron Doron, '"Modesty Patrol lynched me"', ynetnews.com, 29 February 2012.

12 Amir Oren, 'Israel's Haredi minority is ruining the majority's life', *Ha'aretz*, 8 January 2012.

13 M.F. Hammer et al., 'Jewish and Middle Eastern non Jewish populations share a common pool of Y chromosome biallelic haplotypes', *Proceedings of the National Academy of Sciences of the United States of America*, 97 (12), 9 May 2000.

14 Gabe Fischer, 'Israel's middle class erodes amid growing wage disparity report shows', *The Times of Israel*, 31 December 2012.

15 Itamar Rabinovich and Jehuda Reinharz, *Israel in the Middle East: Documents and Readings on Society, Politics, and Foreign Relations, Pre-1948 to the Present*, University Press of New England, Lebanon, 2008, p. 58.

16 Matthew Wagner, 'Shas accepted into World Zionist Organization', *Jerusalem Post*, 20 January 2010.

17 Rotem Starkman, 'Coalition Math: Settlers in, Ultra-Orthodox Jews Out', *Ha'aretz*, 17 March 2013.

18 Yair Ettinger, 'Ultra-Orthodox to Feel the Blow as Unprecedented Power in Israeli Government Ends', *Ha'aretz*, 11 March 2013.

19 Jeremy Sharon, 'Haredim Denounce "Hateful" and "Evil" New Gov't', *Jerusalem Post*, 15 March 2013.

20 Raanan Ben-Zur, 'Israeli Neo Nazi Leader detained', ynetnews.com, 3 January 2011.

21 Amy Teibel, Associated Press, 'Gender Segregation on rise in Israel', yahoo.com, 8 November 2011.

22 Reuters, 'Religion minister fears Jewish divides', ynet.com, 8 January 2012

23 Kobi Nahshoni, 'Rabbi issues modesty rules from age 3', ynetnews.com, 6 January 2013.

24 Ishi, Batini and Harris, *IMF: ISRAEL*, p. 7.

25 Genesis 1:28, 9:1, 7.

26 Ishi, Batini and Harris, *IMF: ISRAEL*, p. 4.

27 Ophir Bar-Zohar, 'Ultra-Orthodox Population Growing too Fast Not to Join Workforce, Panel Told', *Ha'aretz*, 6 June 2012.

28 Yedidia Z. Stern, 'The Haredim and the State of Israel', The Israel Democracy Institute, 20 September 2012.

29 Ishi, Batini and Harris, *IMF: ISRAEL*, p. 2.

30 Ibid., p. 4.

31 Kobi Nahshoni, 'Troops will die rather than listen to women', ynetnews.com, 18 November 2011.

32 Ishi, Batini and Harris, *IMF: ISRAEL*, p. 6.

33 Gabe Fischer, 'Israel's middle class erodes'.

34 Hermann, Atmor, Heller and Lebel, *The Israeli Democracy Index 2012*.

35 Gad Lior, 'Israel's Jewish Population Passes 6 Million Mark', ynetnews.com, 28 March 2013.

36 Kufr Qasem, 'What's the point?', *Economist* magazine, 12 January 2013.

37 Yesh Din: Volunteers for Human Rights, 'Supreme Court Extends Sentence of Settler for Assaulting Palestinian Youth', 13 August 2012.

38 Yaakov Katz, ' "60 percent of Israelis won't serve in IDF by 2020" ', *Jerusalem Post*, 18 November 2011.

39 Amos Harel, 'Sharp rise in number of religious IDF officers', *Ha'aretz*, 15 September 2010.

40 Josh Rogin, 'Bill Clinton: Russian immigrants and settlers obstacles to Mideast peace', *Foreign Policy*, 21 September 2010.

41 Thomas L. Friedman, 'My President Is Busy', *New York Times*, 10 November 2012.

42 'Barak: Lieberman's comments on Abbas harm Israel's interests', *Ha'aretz*, 30 September 2012.

43 Barak Ravid, 'Lieberman, Mossad chief meet in bid to end row', *Ha'aretz*, 20 November 2011.

44 Hermann, Atmor, Heller and Lebel, *The Israeli Democracy Index 2012*.
45 Avner Inbar, 'Israeli Hasbara: Myths and Facts', Molad, December 2012.

5: AMERICA'S PILLARS OF SAND

 1 US Department of State, 'Remarks with Colombian Vice President Angelino Garzon After Their Meeting', 28 January 2011.
 2 US Department of State, 'Remarks with Spanish Foreign Minister Trinidad Jiménez After Their Meeting', 25 January 2011.
 3 UK Foreign and Commonwealth Office, 'Human Rights and Democracy: The 2012 Foreign and Commonwealth Office Report', April 2013, p. 210.
 4 Stephanie Nebehay, 'U.N. rights boss urges Bahrain to rein in forces', Reuters, 17 March 2011.
 5 Associated Press, 'Bahrain: 21 Medics Cleared of Charges in 2011 Protests', *New York Times*, 28 March 2013.
 6 Office of the Press Secretary, The White House, 'Remarks by the President on the Middle East and North Africa', 19 May 2011.
 7 Christopher M. Blanchard, 'Saudi Arabia: Background and U.S. Relations', Congressional Research Service, 27 November 2012.
 8 Transcript: 'Obama's speech Against The Iraq War on October 2 2002', NPR, 20 January 2009.
 9 The White House, Office of the Press Secretary, 'Press Gaggle by Press Secretary Jay Carney and Deputy National Security Advisor Denis McDonough', 28 March 2011.
10 Zahra Babar, 'Sectarian Politics in the Gulf', *Center for International and Regional Studies – Georgetown University*, 9 October 2011.
11 James Mann, *The Obamians: The Struggle Inside the White House to Redefine American Power*, Kindle edition, Viking, England, 2012, loc. 119.
12 Permanent Mission of the People's Republic of China to the UN, 'Explanation of Vote by Ambassador Li Baodong after Adoption of Security Council Resolution on Libya', 17 March 2011.
13 The US Embassy cables, 'Qatar using al-Jazeera as bargaining tool, claims US', US Embassy, Doha, *Guardian*, 19 November 2009.
14 John Kerry, 'Restoring Leadership in the Middle East: A Regional Approach to Peace', The Brookings Institution, Washington D.C., 4 March 2009.
15 Wikileaks, *09STATE131801, TERRORIST FINANCE: ACTION REQUEST FOR SENIOR LEVEL ENGAGEMENT ON TERRORISM FINANCE*, dated 30 December 2009.
16 Blake Hounshell, 'The Qatar Bubble', *Foreign Policy*, May/June 2012.
17 Background briefing for author from senior Arab diplomat.
18 *The Gulf Security Architecture: Partnership with the Gulf Co-operation Council, a Majority Staff Report Prepared for the Use of the Committee on Foreign Relations United States Senate: One Hundred Twelfth Congress Second Session*, June 19, 2012.
19 Office of the Press Secretary, The White House, 'Remarks by the President on the Middle East and North Africa', 19 May 2011.

20 *Report of the Bahrain Independent Commission of Inquiry* presented in Manamah, Bahrain, on 23 November 2011.

21 'Foreign News: Decline of Empire', *Time* magazine, 9 August 1954.

22 Peter L. Hahn, *United States, Great Britain, And Egypt, 1945–1956: Strategy and Diplomacy in the Early Cold War*, The University of Carolina Press, 1991, p. 159.

23 Nichols, *Eisenhower 1956*, p. 200.

24 Dana Adams Schmidt, '1950 PLEDGE CITED', *New York Times*, 29 October 1956.

25 'Text of Eisenhower Broadcast on the Middle East crisis', *New York Times*, 1 November 1956.

26 Nichols, *Eisenhower 1956*, p. 203.

27 Ibid., p. 207.

28 Bush, *Decision Points*, p. 2.

29 Ibid., p. 398.

30 Ibid., p. 396.

31 Ibid.

32 Rice, *No Higher Honor*, p. 326.

33 United Nations Development Programme, Arab Fund for Economic and Social Development, *Arab Human Development Report 2002*, UNDP, 2002.

34 Bush, *Decision Points*, p. 398.

35 Associated Press, 'Dem front-runners play defense at Soldier Field', NBCnews.com, 7 August 2007.

36 Karen J. Alter, 'Is "groupthink" driving us to war?', *The Boston Globe*, 16 September 2002.

37 Bush, *Decision Points*, p. 397.

38 Ibid., p. 410.

39 Charles Krauthammer, 'An Arab Spring?', *Hoover Digest*, 30 April 2005.

40 'Secretary Rice Holds a News Conference', *Washington Post*, 21 July 2006.

41 Rice, *No Higher Honor*, p. 510.

42 Stephen Grey, 'America's Gulag', *New Statesman*, 17 May 2004.

43 Patrick Tyler, *A World of Trouble: America in the Middle East*, Portobello Books, 2009, p. 8.

44 Bob Woodward, *Bush at War*, Simon & Schuster, New York, 2002, p. 342.

45 Clifton Yin, 'The Freedom Agenda gets Vindicated', FrumForum, 23 August 2011.

46 Mann, *The Obamians*, loc. 2954.

47 Aaron David Miller, *The Much Too Promised Land: America's Elusive search for Arab–Israeli Peace*, Kindle edition, Bantam Books, New York, 2008, loc. 4279.

48 Yitzhak Benhorin, 'Obama: Not only Likudniks can be pro-Israeli', ynetnews.com, 2 February 2008.

49 Office of the Press Secretary, The White House, 'Remarks by the President on a New Beginning', Cairo University, Cairo, Egypt, 4 June 2009.

50 Office of the Press Secretary, The White House, 'Remarks by the President on the Middle East and North Africa', 19 May 2011.

51 Office of the Press Secretary, The White House, 'Remarks by President Obama

and Prime Minister Netanyahu of Israel After Bilateral Meeting, Oval Office',
20 May 2011.

52 Helene Cooper and Ethan Bronner, 'Netanyahu Gives No Ground in
Congress Speech', *New York Times*, 24 May 2011.

53 James Kitfield, 'Netanyahu's "Unvarnished Truth" Tour', *The Atlantic*, 25 May
2011.

54 Max Fisher, 'Does Obama's victory mean defeat for Netanyahu?', *Washington
Post*, 7 November 2012.

55 BBC News, 'Sarkozy called Israeli PM Netanyahu "liar"', 8 November 2011

56 Ari Shavit, 'Obama coming here to create the space to combat Israeli policy',
Ha'aretz, 20 March 2013.

57 Assaf Friedman, 'Watching the POTUS on Israeli TV: Each Sound Bite More
Cringe-Worthy than the Last', *Ha'aretz*, 21 March 2013.

58 Office of the Press Secretary, The White House, 'Remarks by President Obama
and President Abbas of the Palestinian Authority in Joint Press Conference',
21 March 2013.

59 Margaret Talev and Jonathan Ferziger, 'Obama Heads for Israel to Bridge
Gaps From Two-States to Iran', Bloomberg, 19 March 2013.

60 US Department of State, 'Solo Press Availability [with John Kerry] in Tel
Aviv, Israel', 9 April 2013.

61 Paul Richter, 'John Kerry Says Need For Action Israel-Palestinian Conflict Is
Urgent', *Los Angeles Times*, 17 April 2013.

62 Gil Hoffman, 'Livni's Party Angered by E1 Building Plans', *Jerusalem Post*,
17 April 2013.

63 BBC News, 'Israel settlements: Netanyahu defies outcry over E-1', 3 December 2012.

64 Michael R. Gordon and Mark Landler, 'Backstage Glimpses of Clinton as
Dogged Diplomat, Win or Lose', *New York Times*, 2 February 2013.

65 Ora Coren and Nadan Feldman, 'U.S. Aid to Israel Totals $233.7b Over Six
Decades', *Ha'aretz*, 20 March 2013.

66 Bob Woodward, *Plan of Attack*, Simon & Schuster, London, 2004, p. 87.

67 Jonathan Freedland, 'Patten lays into Bush's America', *Guardian*, 9 February 2002.

68 Office of the Press Secretary, The White House, 'Remarks by the President on
a New Beginning'.

69 Mark Landler, 'A New Iran Overture, With Hot Dogs', *New York Times*,
1 June 2009.

70 President Jimmy Carter, 'The State of the Union Address Delivered Before a Joint
Session of the Congress. January 23, 1980', The American Presidency Project.

71 Office of the Press Secretary, The White House, 'Remarks by President Obama
and Prime Minister Berlusconi of Italy in Press Availability', 15 June 2009.

72 *Iran – Amnesty International Report 2010*.

73 Office of the Press Secretary, The White House, 'Press Conference by the
President', 23 June 2009.

74 *New York Times*, 'A Selection From the Cache of Diplomatic Dispatches, US
Embassy, Riyadh', 20 April 2008.

75 James Reynolds, 'Why is Israel calling Iran a nuclear duck?', BBC News, 7 March 2012.

76 Scott Peterson, 'Imminent Iran nuclear threat? A timeline of warnings since 1979', *The Christian Science Monitor*, 8 November 2011.

77 David E. Sanger, *Confront and Conceal: Obama's Secret Wars and Surprising use of American Power*, Kindle edition, Crown Publishers, New York, 2012, p. 196.

78 Yossi Melman, 'Former Mossad chief: Israel air strike on Iran "stupidest thing I have ever heard"', *Ha'aretz*, 7 May 2011.

79 Yaakov Lappin, 'Former Shin Bet chief slams "messianic" PM, Barak', *Jerusalem Post*, 29 April 2012.

80 Dror Moreh, 'Diskin: Netanyahu, Barak too weak', ynetnews.com, 4 January 2013.

81 Office of the Press Secretary, The White House, 'Remarks by President Obama and Prime Minister Netanyahu of Israel in Joint Press Conference', 20 March 2013.

82 Office of the Press Secretary, The White House, 'Inaugural Address by President Barack Obama', 21 January 2013.

83 BBC News, 'Al Qaeda chides Iran over 9/11 "conspiracy theories"', 28 September 2011.

84 Associated Press, 'Iran's supreme leader denies Tehran is seeking nuclear weapons', *Guardian*, 22 February 2012.

85 Richard Spencer, 'Morsi tells Iran that Syria's Assad must go', *Daily Telegraph*, 30 August 2012.

86 Associated Press, 'Bahrain: Iran Translation Sidestepped Syria', 1 September 2012.

87 Simeon Kerr and Camilla Hall, 'UAE puts 94 on trial in crackdown', *Financial Times*, 3 March 2013.

88 Barak Ravid, 'How Israel and China got into a diplomatic row over Knesset members and organ harvesting', *Ha'aretz*, 5 November 2012.

89 Moncef Marzouki, 'The Arab Spring Still Blooms', *New York Times*, 27 September 2012.

90 International Monetary Fund, 'Saudi Arabia: Selected Issues, IMF Country report No. 12/292', September 2012 , p. 21.

91 Donna Abu-Nasr, 'Saudis Skip Arab Spring as Nation Pours Money Into Jobs', Bloomberg, 3 April 2012.

92 US National Intelligence Council, *Global Trends 2030: Alternative Words*, December 2012, p. 74.

93 US Department of State, Daily Press Briefing, 17 January 2013; UK Foreign and Commonwealth Office, 'Human Rights and Democracy: The 2012 Foreign and Commonwealth Office Report', April 2012, p. 212.

94 Globalwebindex, 'Twitter Usage is Booming in Saudi Arabia', 20 March 2013

95 Interview Transcript, 'President Barack Obama with Jose Diaz-Balart', NBC Universal, 12 September 2012.

96 *Egypt Independent*, 'Egypt imports 140,000 teargas canisters from US', 23 February 2013.

97 Hillary Rodham Clinton, 'Nomination Hearing To Be Secretary of State: Statement before the Senate Foreign Relations Committee', 13 January 2009.

98 US Department of State, 'Remarks on American Leadership at the Council on Foreign Relations', 31 January 2013.

6: IRAQ: SNAFU

1   Robin Wright, Peter Baker, 'Iraq, Jordan See Threat To Election From Iran', *Washington Post*, 8 December 2004.
2   *Learning from Iraq: A Final Report from the U.S. Special Inspector General For Iraq Reconstruction*, Stuart W. Bowen, March 2013, p. 37.
3   'Remarks by President George W. Bush at the 20th Anniversary of the National Endowment for Democracy', 6 November 2003.
4   Bush, *Decision Points*, p. 268.
5   Barry S. Levy and Victor W. Sidel, 'Adverse Health Consequences of the Iraq War', *The Lancet*, vol. 381, issue 9870, pp. 949–58, 16 March 2013.
6   Office of the Press Secretary, The White House, 'President Bush Addresses the Nation', The Oval Office 10.16 pm est, 19 March 2003.
7   Imperial War Museum Department of Documents RB/1 c. 1918.
8   Rogan, *The Arabs*, p. 173.
9   Derek Hopwood, 'Iraq: Conflict in Context, British Relations with Iraq', *BBC History*, 2 October 2003.
10 Rogan, *The Arabs*, p. 313.
11 Ibid., p. 316.
12 Andrew Cockburn and Patrick Coburn, *Out of the Ashes: The resurrection of Saddam Hussein*, Harper Perennial, 2000, p. 73.
13 'Iraq surveys show "humanitarian emergency"', Unicef.org/newsline/99pr29.htm.
14 Paul Danahar, 'Iraq sees little to cheer in seven years since war', BBC News, 24 March 2010.
15 BBC News, 'Bush promises Iraqis "freedom"', 31 March 2003.
16 Rogan, *The Arabs*, p. 173.
17 BBC News, 'Britain suffered defeat in Iraq, says US general', 29 September 2010.
18 BBC News, 'Tony Blair: Life in Iraq 10 years on not as I hoped', 26 February 2013.
19 Bush, *Decision Points*, p. 257.
20 Geoffrey Wawro, *Quicksand: America's Pursuit of Power in the Middle East*, Penguin Press, New York, 2010, p. 12.
21 Robert Fisk, *Pity The Nation: Lebanon at War*, Oxford University Press, 1991, p. 512.
22 Bob Woodward, *Veil: The Secret Wars of the CIA 1981–1987*, Simon & Schuster, New York, 1987, p. 418.
23 Thomas E. Ricks, *Fiasco: The American Military Misadventure in Iraq*, Penguin Books, New York, 2007, p. 103.
24 L. Paul Bremer III with Malcolm McDonnell, *My Year in Iraq: The Struggle to Build a Future of Hope*, ibook edition, Simon & Schuster, New York, 2006, p. 45
25 *Learning from Iraq*, p. 40.
26 Agence France-Presse, 'As Arabs demand democracy, Iraqis want electricity', 16 February 2011.

27 Alter, 'Is "groupthink" driving us to war?'

28 Bush, *Decision Points*, p. 258.

29 Office of the Press Secretary, The White House, 'President Bush Announces Major Combat Operations in Iraq Have Ended', 1 May 2003.

30 Brian Knowlton, 'Top U.S. General in Iraq Sees "Classical Guerrilla-Type" War', *International Herald Tribune*, 16 July 2003.

31 'U.S.: Leading Saddam aide caught', CNN.com/world, 19 June 2003.

32 Office of the Press Secretary, The White House, 'President Bush Names Randall Tobias to be Global AIDS Coordinator', 2 July 2003.

33 Bush, *Decision Points*, p. 261.

34 Patrick Cockburn, *Muqtada al-Sadr and the fall of Iraq*, Faber and Faber, London, 2008, p. 119.

35 International Crisis Group, *Iraq's Muqtada al-Sadr: Spoiler or Stabiliser?*, Middle East Report no. 55, 11 July 2006, p. 6.

36 Ibid., p. 8.

37 Julian E. Barnes, 'Sadr Army is called Top Threat in Iraq', *Los Angeles Times*, 19 December 2006.

38 Moshe Schwartz, *The Department of Defense's Use of Private Security Contractors in Iraq and Afghanistan: Background, Analysis, and Options for Congress*, Congressional Research Service, September 2009, p. 8.

39 Ibid., p. 9.

40 Ibid., Summary.

41 David Teather, 'US claims to uncover war plot', *Guardian*, 10 February 2004.

42 Bremer, *My Year in Iraq*, p. 464.

43 Told to me by a senior Arab diplomat who met regularly with the Taliban leadership in Afghanistan in the years before the 9/11 attacks.

44 Nelly Lahoud, Stuart Caudill, Liam Collins, Gabriel Koehler-Derrick, Don Rassler and Muhammad al-'Ubaydi, *Letters from Abbottabad: Bin Ladin Sidelined? SOCOM-2012-0000004, pp. 7–8*, Harmony Program, West Point, 3 May 2012.

45 CNN, 'Iraq Insurgency in "Last Throes", Cheney says', 20 June 2005.

46 Marc Santoro, 'On the Gallows, Curses for U.S. and "Traitors"', *New York Times*, 31 December 2006.

47 Major General Antonio M. Taguba, Deputy Commanding General Support, Coalition Forces Land Component Command, *AR-16 Investigation of the 800th Military police brigade investigating officer*, 27 May 2004, p. 31.

48 Ibid., p. 32.

49 Phillip Gourevitch and Errol Morris, 'Exposure, The woman behind the Camera at Abu Ghraib', *New Yorker*, 24 March 2008.

50 *Senate Armed Services Committee Inquiry into the Treatment of Detainees in U.S. Custody*, Thursday, 11 December 2008.

51 BBC, 'Ex-Abu Ghraib inmates get $5m settlement from US firm', 9 January 2013.

52 Mark Wilbanks and Efraim Karsh, 'How the "Sons of Iraq" stabilized Iraq', *Middle East Quarterly*, Fall 2010, pp. 57–70.

53 Office of the Special Inspector General for Iraq Reconstruction, *Sons of Iraq Program: Results are Uncertain and Financial Controls Were Weak*, SIGIR 11-010, 28 January 2011.

54 Kenneth Katzman, *Iraq: Politics, Governance and Human Rights,* Congressional Research Service report for the Congress, 13 December 2012, p. 20.

55 Barack Obama, *The Audacity of Hope: Thoughts on reclaiming the American dream*, ibook edition, Canongate, 2006, p. 350.

56 Office of the Press Secretary, The White House, 'Remarks of President Barack Obama – As prepared for Delivery, Responsibly Ending the War in Iraq', 27 February 2009.

57 Jonathan Alter, *The Promise, President Obama, Year One*, Kindle edition, Simon & Schuster, New York, 2010, p. 228.

58 US Department of State, 'Solo Press Availability in Baghdad, Iraq, John Kerry', 24 March 2013.

59 Adam Schreck and Qassim Abdul-Zahra, 'AP Interview: Iraq PM Warns Syria War Could Spread', Associated Press, 27 February 2013.

60 *Learning from Iraq*, pp. 3–9.

61 U.S. Special Inspector General For Iraq Reconstruction Stuart W. Bowen, Jr., *Hard Lessons: The Iraq Reconstruction Experience*, February 2009, p. 42.

62 Central Intelligence Agency, *The World FactBook,* 12 February 2013.

63 International Monetary Fund, 'Program Note: Iraq', 5 October 2012.

64 *Learning from Iraq*, p. 119.

65 Katzman, *Iraq*, p. 15.

66 Ibid., p. 31.

67 Eli Sugarman and Omar al-Nidawi, 'Back in Black: The Return of Muqtada al-Sadr', *Foreign Affairs*, 11 February 2013.

7: LIBYA: YEAR ZERO

1 Robert Birsel, 'Rebels take Ras Lanuf oil port, see no damage', Reuters, 23 August 2011.

 2 Dirk Vandewalle, *A History of Modern Libya,* Cambridge University Press, 2006, p. 21.

 3 Encyclopedia Britannica, 'Libya: History', Encyclopedia Britannica online.

 4 Lawrence Martin, *The Treaties of Peace 1919–1923*, vol. 1, The Lawbook Exchange Limited, New Jersey, 2007, p. 17.

 5 US Department of State, *International boundary Study No. 3 (revised), 1978 Chad–Libya Boundary*, 15 December 1978.

 6 Benjamin Higgins and Roger Le Tourneau, *Report on the Mission to Libya*, UNESCO, Paris, 1952, p. 7.

 7 Ibid., p. 11.

 8 Vandewalle, *Modern Libya*, p. 4.

 9 Daniel Yergin, *The Prize: The Epic Quest for Oil, Money and Power*, Free Press, 2008, p. 511.

10 Henry Porter, 'The west can't just dictate democracy to the Arab world', *Observer*, 13 March 2011.

11 Yergin, *The Prize*, p. 510.

12 Ibid., p. 560.

13 Ibid., p. 561.

14 Ibid.. p. 560.

15 Walter J. Levy, 'Oil Power', Foreign Affairs, July 1971.

16 Yergin, *The Prize*, p. 562.

17 Muammar Al Gathafi, *The Green Book,* The World Center for the Study and Research of the Green Book, Tripoli, 2009, p. 22.

18 Ibid., p. 74.

19 Ibid., p. 31.

20 Ibid., p. 44.

21 Ibid., p. 47.

22 Human Rights Watch, 'Libya: Abu Salim Prison Massacre Remembered', 27 June 2012.

23 US Department of State Bulletin, vol. 83, no. 2079, October 1983, p. 72.

24 *New York Times*, 'A Selection From the Cache of Diplomatic Dispatches, US Embassy, Tripoli', 29 August 2008.

25 Dominic Casciani, 'UK pays 2.2 m to settle Libyan rendition claim', BBC News, 13 December 2012.

26 Abdelaziz Barrouhi, 'Libya's Gaddafi turns attention to Black Africa', Reuters, 16 September 1998.

27 'Remembering Nelson Mandela – and Muammar Gaddafi', *Pravda*, 18 July 2011.

28 Stephen Ellis, *The Mask of Anarchy: The Destruction of Liberia and the Religious Dimension of an African Civil War*, Hurst and Company, London, 1999, p. 72.

29 Eban Kaplan, 'How Libya Got Off the List', Council for Foreign Relations, 16 October 2007.

30 Libyan UN envoy Ahmed Own, 'Libya letter: Full text', BBC News, 16 August 2003.

31 Felicity Barringer, 'Libya Admits Culpability in Crash of Pan Am Plane', *New York Times*, 16 August 2003.

32 'Lockerbie bomber Abdelbaset al-Megrahi dies in Tripoli', BBC News, 20 May 2012.

33 Donald M. Rothberg, 'Pan Am Victim's Relatives Offended at Administration Defense of Syria', Associated Press, 20 November 1991.

34 Rice, *No Higher Honor*, p. 701.

35 London School of Economics and Political Science, 'LSE response to the Woolf Inquiry', 30 November 2011. The LSE says a separate panel by the University of London 'concluded that the PhD should not be revoked [but] that it should be annotated to show where attribution or references should have been made'.

36 *New York Times*, 'A Selection From the Cache of Diplomatic Dispatches, US Embassy, Tripoli', 9 March 2009.

37 A Majority Staff Report Prepared for the Use of the Committee on Foreign Relations United States Senate One Hundred Twelfth Congress Second

Session, *The Gulf Security Architecture: Partnership with the Gulf Co-operation Council,* 19 June 2012, p. 16.

38 Vivienne Walt, 'Meet Mahmoud Jibril: The Man Who May Be Libya's First Elected Leader', *Time* magazine, 11 July 2012.

39 Emma Alberchi, 'Sergei Lavrov Interview', ABC Australia, 31 January 2012.

40 Human Rights Watch, *Death of a Dictator: Bloody Vengeance in Sirte,* HRW, 2012, USA, p. 21.

41 Ibid., p. 22.

42 Ibid., p. 26.

43 Ibid., p. 27.

44 Roger Le Tourneau, *Report on the Mission to Libya: Libyan Education and development,* UNESCO, Paris, 1952, p. 19.

45 Heba Saleh, 'Militias Drain Libya's Coffers', *Financial Times,* 10 April 2013.

46 Steven Sotloff, 'Why the Libyans Have Fallen Out of Love with Qatar', *Time* magazine, 2 January 2012.

47 Brigitte Scheffer, 'Libyan Oil Revenues Exceed $44 Billion in Year through October', Bloomberg, 21 November 2012.

8: SYRIA: THE ARAB WORLD'S BROKEN HEART

1 Joan Juliet Buck, 'A Rose in the Desert', *Vogue* magazine, March 2011, p. 529.

2 Bret Stephens, 'Remember Bashar Assad, "Reformer"?', *Wall Street Journal,* 23 July 2012.

3 Liam Stack, 'Video of Tortured Boy's Corpse Deepens Anger in Syria', *New York Times,* 30 May 2011.

4 I have changed Zubaida's real name to protect her identity.

5 I have changed Ahmed's real name to protect his identity.

6 The 8th International Institute for Strategic Studies Regional Security Summit, 'The Manama Dialogue, Second Plenary Session – Questions and Answer Session', 8 December 2012.

7 United Nations, 'Secretary-General's remarks at Memorial Centre in Srebrenica', 26 July 2012.

8 Tim Arango, 'Turkish Public Sours on Syrian Uprising', *New York Times,* 18 September 2012.

9 Ole Solvang and Anna Neistat, 'Death From the Skies', Human Rights Watch, 11 April 2013.

10 www.mccain.senate.gov/public/index, 'Remarks by Senator John McCain on the Situation in Syria on the Floor of the U.S. Senate', 5 March 2012.

11 Disney Syria, 'Disney Syria a new project that is about to be signed', welcome-tosyria.net.

12 Office of the Press Secretary, The White House, 'Statement by the President on Syria', 4 February 2012.

13 Office of the Press Secretary, The White House, 'Statement by President Obama on Syria', 18 August 2011.

14 Office of the Secretary, The White House, 'Remarks by President Obama and

His Majesty King Abdullah II of Jordan in Joint Press Conference', 22 March 2013.

15 Phil Stewart, 'US efforts on Iran not working, Syria planning underway: Mattis', Reuters, 5 March 2013.

16 Senior State Department Officials, 'Background Briefing on Syria', US Department of State, 6 December 2011.

17 US Department of State, 'Interview With Kim Ghattas of BBC', 26 February 2012.

18 Reuters, 'Obama blocked US plan to arm Syrian rebels', *Guardian*, Friday 8 February 2012.

19 Adam Entous, 'Inside Obama's Syria Debate', *Wall Street Journal*, 29 March 2013.

20 David Kenner, 'Syria Is Already More Violent Than Iraq', *Foreign Policy*, 20 March 2013.

21 SANA, 'President al-Assad: It Is No Longer Possible for the Regional and International Parties Seeking to Destabilize Syria to Forge Facts and the Events', January 2012.

22 Clare Hollingworth, *The Arabs and the West*, Methuen & Co Ltd, London, 1952, p. 6.

23 James Barr, *A Line in the Sand: The Anglo-French Struggle for the Middle East, 1914–1948*, Kindle edition, W.W. Norton & Company, p. 3.

24 Encyclopedia Britannica online.

25 Daniel Pipes, *Greater Syria: The History of an Ambition*, Oxford University Press, Oxford, 1990, p. 175.

26 Al-Bab.com, 'The Taif Accord approved on November 4 1989'.

27 Leon Goldsmith, 'Alawites for Assad', *Foreign Affairs*, 16 April 2012.

28 Patrick Seale, *Asad: The Struggle for the Middle East*, University of California Press, London, 1989, p. 328.

29 I have changed Neda's real name to protect her identity even though she was willing for me to use it. I have decided not to because at the time of writing she is still in Syria.

30 Edmund Blair and Yasmine Saleh, 'Syrian opposition rifts give world excuse not to act', Reuters, 4 July 2012.

31 Brian Fishman, 'The Evidence of Jihadist Activity in Syria', Combatting Terrorism Center at West Point, 22 May 2012.

32 Jeremy M. Sharp and Christopher M. Blanchard, *Armed Conflict in Syria: U.S. and International Response*, Congressional Research Service, 21 August 2012, p. 8.

33 Reuters, 'Iraqi al-Qaeda wing says Nusra Front is its Syria branch: SITE group', 9 April 2013.

34 Michael Peel, 'Syrian Jihadist Pledge Fealty to al-Qaeda', *Financial Times*, 10 April 2013.

35 Office of the Press Secretary, The White House, 'Remarks by the President to White House Press Corps', 20 August 2012.

36 Miguel E. Rodriguez, assistant to the President, Letter to the Honorable John McCain, 25 April 2013.

37 United Nations Human Rights Council, 'Report of the Independent International Commission of Inquiry on the Syrian Arab Republic', 15 August 2012, p. 71.

38 Ibid., p. 65.

39 Thomas Grove and Erika Solomon, 'Russia boosts arms sales to Syria despite world pressure', Reuters, 21 February 2012.

40 Ruslan Pukhov, 'Why Russia is backing Syria', *New York Times*, Opinion Pages, 6 July 2012.

41 Ian Black, 'Syrian Regime Accused Of New Massacre', Guardian, 22 April 2013.

42 Louis Charnonneau, 'Syria Mediator Brahimi Says Not Resigning Post But Considers It Daily', Reuters, 19 April 2013.

43 BBC News, 'Syria in civil war, Red Cross says', 15 July 2012.

44 BBC News, 'Syria Conflict: Aleppo shootings by rebels condemned', 1 August 2012; Stephanie Nebehay, 'Syrian government forces, rebels committing war crimes: U.N.', Reuters, 15 August 2012.

45 Paul Wood, 'Syria: Islamist Nusra Front gives BBC exclusive interview', BBC News, 17 January 2013.

46 Ian Pannell, 'Aleppo's winter of discontent', BBC News, 12 December 2012

47 Borzou Daragahi, 'Libya helps bankroll Syrian Opposition', *Financial Times*, 5 November 2012.

48 Hillary Rodham Clinton, 'Remarks with Croatian President Ivo Josipovic after their meeting', US Department of State, 31 October 2012.

49 Matt Spetalnick, 'Obama: U.S. now recognizes Syrian opposition coalition', Reuters, 12 December 2012.

50 Hearing: 'Crisis in Syria: The U.S. Response', House Committee on Foreign Affairs, 9:45 am, 20 March 2013.

51 Briefing to the Security Council by Joint Special Representative of the United Nations and the League of Arab States for Syria, 19 April 2013.

52 Save the Children, 'Half of Syria's one million refugees are Children', 6 March 2013.

53 Save the Children, 'Untold Atrocities: The Stories of Syria's Children', 25 September, 2012.

54 Office of the Press Secretary, The White House, 'Remarks by President Obama and His Majesty King Abdullah II of Jordan in Joint Press Conference', 22 March 2013.

55 Lauren Wolfe, 'Syria Has a Massive Rape Crisis', *The Atlantic*, 3 April 2013.

56 BBC News, 'Syria Crisis: Bashar al-Assad Says West Will "Pay Price"', 17 April 2013.

57 U.S. Department of State, 'Remarks With Australian Foreign Minister Bob Carr After Their Meeting', 18 March 2013.

58 U.S. Department of State, 'Remarks With Qatari Prime Minister and Foreign Minister Hamad bin Jassim bin Jaber Al Thani After Their Meeting', 5 March 2013.

59 U.S. Department of State, 'Remarks with Saudi Foreign Minister Saud al-Faisal After Their Meeting', 4 March 2013.

60 Phil Stewart, 'U.S. efforts on Iran not working, Syria planning underway: Mattis', Reuters, 5 March 2013.

61 Seale, *Asad*, p. 17.

62 William J. Clinton, 'Remarks on United States Foreign Policy in San Francisco', The American Presidency Project, 26 February 1999.

63 Franklin Foer and Chris Hughes, ' "Barack Obama is Not Pleased": The president on his enemies, the media, and the future of football', *The New Republic*, 27 January 2013.

64 Obama, *Audacity of Hope*, p. 352.

65 Ibid., p. 353.

66 Hillary Rodham Clinton, 'Remarks on American Leadership at the Council on Foreign Relations', US Department of State, 31 January 2013.

67 U.S. Department of State, 'Remarks with Foreign Secretary William Hague After their Meeting', 25 February 2013.

AFTERWORD

1 Martin Chulov, 'Half of Syrian Population "Will Need Aid By The End Of Year"', *Guardian*, 19 April 2013.

2 Mark Landler, 'Secret Report Ordered by Obama Identified Potential Uprising', *New York Times*, 16 February 2011.

3 Background briefing for author with person with detailed knowledge of the study.

4 Michael R. Gordon, 'Top Obama Officials Differ on Syrian Rebels in Testimony to Congress', *New York Times*, 17 April 2013.

5 U.S. National Intelligence Council, *Global Trends 2030: Alternative Worlds*, December 2012, p. 71.

Acknowledgements and sources

I want to thank and pay tribute to the many, many people who made time to talk to me throughout the Arab Spring revolutions and the war in Iraq, periods that were for them often the most traumatic of their lives. Huge numbers of people over this last decade risked their own safety to help journalists in the Middle East like myself. It is proof that war and conflict often also bring out the best in people.

I carried out most of the interviews in these pages exclusively for this book. The rest, and some of the reportage, are drawn from my reporting on events for the BBC while I was its Middle East Bureau Chief based in Jerusalem between 2010 and 2013 and its Baghdad Bureau Chief during the invasion of Iraq in 2003. When I conducted the interview myself, or I was present when a statement was made, I have not provided a source note to the quote so as not to overly disrupt the narrative. I have changed the names of some of the people I spoke to, particularly in Syria, for their own protection. When I have done that I have listed it in the notes.

The Arab uprisings were remarkable and I was lucky enough to work with some equally remarkable people during them. With me, sharing the incoming fire, the non-alcoholic beers, the rocks, stones and tear gas, the bitter coffee, the sand storms and the endlessly long days were: Rushdi Abu-Alouf, Jeremy Bowen, Richard Colebourn, Darren Conway, Lyse Doucet, Wyre Davies, Jon Donnison, Ian Druce, Tim Facey, Gabriel Gatehouse, Jonny Hallam, Andrew 'Sarge' Herbert, Raouf Ibrahim, Jimmy Michael, Ian Pannell, Hamada Abu Qammar, Ghadi Sary, John Simpson, Cara Swift and Paul Wood.

Along with sharing the above experiences during the revolutions a number of friends and colleagues also gave me their time and advice while I was writing this book. Lina Sinjab in Damascus was kind enough to read the section on Syria and offer wise words, as was the equally brave Rana Jawad, the BBC's correspondent in Tripoli, for the Libya section. I am hugely thankful to them both. Without Gidi Kleiman and Avi Halfon it would have been impossible to get access to the people and stories I did for the sections of the book dealing with Israel. Gidi also read several chapters for me, including the ones dealing with Israel and the conflict with the Palestinians, as did Jeannie Assad. Yolande Knell read several chapters and offered much helpful advice for which I am very grateful. Thank you to Kevin Connolly who was kind enough to read the whole book and offer me his insights. The brilliant Angy Ghannam was my invaluable guide on the ground in Cairo as I researched this book, and she fact-checked the Egypt sections for me. However, if there are any errors in this book then they are mine alone. Almost everywhere I went during the fighting and upheaval in the region I had Youssef Shomali alongside me. He is a living legend on the West Bank and a force of nature everywhere else, as is Kevin Sweeney who is, quite simply, the bravest man I know.

BBC News is packed with brilliant, creative journalists many of whom do not get any where near the credit owed to them because it is not their face or voice on the airwaves. Many of the best work for the Newsgathering operation in London and I'd like to thank them all for their help over the years. I'd particularly like to thank the following past and present colleagues for their advice and support during my time in the field: Andrew Roy, Andrew Whitehead, Anna Williams, Ben Blackmore, Caroline Howie, Chris Booth, Fran Unsworth, Joanne Cayford, Jonathan Baker, Jonathan Chapman, Jonathan Paterson, Kate Riley, Malcolm Balen, Malcolm Downing, Mark James, Mark Tyrrell, Paul Greeves, Sarah Ward-Lilley, Sarah Whitehead, Simon Marr and Tarik Kafala. I'd like to thank Jon Williams who was, until recently, my Foreign Editor, but more importantly has been a good friend stretching back to our time decades ago in local TV.

I would not have got my start in journalism via BBC local radio if it had not been for Liz Meech, Graham Henderson and Mike Cartwright. I thank you all.

I have been lucky enough to spend more than a decade living and working around the globe. Along the way I have been even luckier to have been able to share that time with the following people, all of whom are good friends and brilliant in their respective fields: Ali Faisal Zaidi, Andrew Kilrain, Annie Phrommayon, Bilal Sarwary, Daniel Lak, Dylan Nalid, Fred Scott, Karishma Vaswani, Jin Ni, Joe Phua, Nick Bryant, Sanjay Ganguly, and Zaffar Abbas.

I'd also like to thank in a similar vein: Alice Budisatrijo, Alex and Sarah Spillius, Allan Little, Andrew Harding, Anthia Wan, Barbara Plett, Bernice Poetiray, Colin Hancock, DanDan Chen, Duncan Stone, Fergal Keane, Jacky Martens, Jennifer Pak, Jo Floto, Jone Chang, Kim Ghattas, Mark Doyle, Martin Turner, Mike Wooldridge, Milton Nkosi, Moska Najib, Navdip Dhariwal, Peter Beaumont, Peter Emmerson, Ravi Lekhi, Sana Abdeljalil, Sanjoy Majumda, Shilpa Kannan, Sanjeev Srivastava, Soutik Biswas, Subodh Sen, Tony Parker and Vinod Mehta.

I want to say thank you to Christine Yu, Niraj Nirash, Mr Li, Mr Madan, Linda Miranda and Landrain Nazareth for looking after my family for the weeks, which over time added up to many months, I was away on stories.

I especially want to thank Jason Burke, who is a good mate and a fellow traveller in some of the less comfortable places in the world and who kindly shared his experience of writing books and offered advice to get me started. I'm grateful to have had my friend Rageh Omaar alongside me during some of the most amazing experiences of my working life. I'd like to thank Mark Nicholson for his support and friendship, forged over cold beers during long hot Delhi evenings.

'Bearded' Bob, David Brown, Debbie Durrant, Emily Crossland, Eric Nelson, Paul Blackler, and Richard Mills are my oldest friends whom I've known since the days when none of us had any idea where we were going.

There are a few people without whom there would have been nothing to read and so I offer them my sincere thanks. My agent Karolina Sutton is the reason I got to write this book. Without her clarity and determination it would have remained an unfulfilled ambition. I'm very grateful to her. I want to thank my Editor at Bloomsbury, Bill Swainson, for his belief in the book and for his invaluable help and guidance along the way. Anna Simpson, also at Bloomsbury, worked through my constant updates and tweaks right up to the moment it went to print. Owen Bennett-Jones is one of the finest journalists I have had the privilege to call a friend. He read through every stage of the manuscript and helped me shape it into what it eventually became.

I want to thank Nirmal and Suguna for the love and support they gave our family while we were in India and I apologise for taking their daughter and their only grandchildren off around the world and out of reach. I offer the same thanks and a similar apology to Meghna for denying her time with her only nephews.

My family in England have hardly seen me for more than a decade. I apologise to Marcy, Ella, Lois, Iza, Beau, Gene and Riley for being the perpetually absent uncle. I hope when you are older you'll read this book and understand what I was up to. I am grateful for the love of my baby sister Kathryn who did everything she could to keep me a constant presence in her children's lives, as did my sister Amanda with hers. I love and miss you both. My greatest regret is that my Poppa, Harry Bird, along with my Aunts Minnie and Dolly never saw me achieve so many of the things denied to them and their generation.

I escaped that trap because of the love and sacrifice of my parents Allan and Valerie Danahar. I thank and love you both. Again, I'm sorry for keeping two of your grandsons on a different time zone for their entire lives.

My boys, Zayn and Aden, have brought me more joy and laughter than I could ever have imagined. I want to thank them for the wonderful surprises they made for me upon my return from the many trips I made away from home. I love you Zayn. I love you Aden.

I have been blessed to have had my best friend with me as I moved around the globe. Without her, this life would not have been possible and it would not have been worth it. I began, and now end, this book dedicating everything to my wife and the great love of my life, Bhavna.

Index

A NOTE ON THE AUTHOR

Paul Danahar was the BBC's Middle East Bureau Chief (2010–13) and ran the organisation's news coverage of the Arab Spring. He was awarded an MBE in 2003 for his work as the Baghdad Bureau Chief during the American-led invasion. Prior to his present posting he was the BBC's East Asia Bureau Chief for three years, and previous to that he was the BBC's South Asia Bureau Chief, covering the rise, fall and eventual return of the Taliban. He is one of a small number of journalists to have worked in all three countries that make up the so-called 'Axis of Evil': Iraq, Iran and North Korea. In 2013 he was appointed the BBC's North America Bureau Chief, based in Washington.

Follow him at @pdanahar